Duty Free

Australian
Women
Abroad

For Marcus, Anna and Sophie

Duty·Free
Australian Women Abroad

Ros Pesman

Melbourne
OXFORD UNIVERSITY PRESS
Oxford   Auckland   New York

OXFORD UNIVERSITY PRESS AUSTRALIA

Oxford   New York
Athens   Auckland   Bangkok   Bombay
Calcutta   Cape Town   Dar es Salaam   Delhi
Florence   Hong Kong   Istanbul   Karachi
Kuala Lumpur   Madras   Madrid   Melbourne
Mexico City   Nairobi   Paris   Singapore
Taipei   Tokyo   Toronto

and associated companies in
Berlin   Ibadan

OXFORD is a trade mark of Oxford University Press

National Library of Australia
Cataloguing-in-Publication data:

Pesman, Ros
    Duty free: Australian women abroad.

    Bibliography.
    Includes index.
    ISBN 0 19 553639 8.

    1. Australians — Travel — Europe. 2. Australians
    — Travel — Great Britain. 3. Women travellers —
    Europe. 4. Women travellers — Great Britain.
    I. Title

910.82

Edited by Jo McMillan
Cover design by Cora Lansdell
Text designed by Cora Lansdell
Cover illustration © Thea Waddell
Typeset by Desktop Concepts P/L, Melbourne
Printed by OUP China
Published by Oxford University Press,
253 Normanby Road, South Melbourne, Australia

Contents

Abbreviations

ADB   *Australian Dictionary of Biography*
CUP   Cambridge University Press
ML   Mitchell Library
MUP   Melbourne University Press
NLA   National Library of Australia
OUP   Oxford University Press
SLSA   State Library of South Australia
SLV   State Library of Victoria
SMH   *Sydney Morning Herald*
SUP   Sydney University Press
UQP   University of Queensland Press

Acknowledgments

My greatest debt in writing this study is to libraries and to the librarians who gave so generously of their time and expertise. I thank the National Library of Australia; the Mitchell Library and especially Jim Andrighetti and Jennifer Broomhead; the State Library of Victoria and especially Shonar Dewar; the State Library of South Australia; the University of Sydney Archives; Rosemary Annabale, Archivist, Women's College, University of Sydney; Shirley Jones and Robin Porter of the Jessie Street Library; Deborah Edwards of the Art Gallery of New South Wales; the Art Gallery of South Australia; the Australian War Memorial and especially Brendan O'Keefe; the Karl A. Krober Library, Cornell University; and the Centre for the History of the Resistance, Como. My starting point in the search for travelling women was that very rich resource for Australian history, the *Australian Dictionary of Biography* (ADB) and the files held in the offices of the *ADB* at the Australian National University. I am very grateful to those who work on the *ADB* and especially to Martha Campbell, Suzanne Edgar, and Sheila Tilse, for their willing help and the leads that they gave me. I also express my thanks to those who gave me access to material and memories on their own travels, or on those of family members, and particularly to Heather Astles, Nancy Cato, Kerri Anne Cousins, Lilian and Juliana Edwards, Modesta Gentile, Rachel Fitzhardinge, Marie Haselhurst, Patricia Hopper, Ann Moyal, Irene Rush, Margaret Sabine, Christine Stevenson, Marjorie Whiffen and Suzanne Wynyard. Many colleagues and friends shared ideas and provided leads, in particular Ursula Bygott, Patricia Clarke, Emilio Gentile, Luigi Goglia, Bridget Griffen Foley, Joy Hooton, Beverley Kingston, Martha Sear, Stephen Scheding of Scheding Berry Fine Art, Barry Smith, Catherine Snowdon, Marion Stell, Nancy Underhill, David Walker and Richard White. Richard Bosworth, Peter Cochrane, Stephen Garton, Helen Lucas, Allan Martin and Shane White gave of their time to read early drafts of chapters, and Iain Cameron, Robin Cooper and Albert Pesman read the entire manuscript. The book's editor, Jo McMillan, saved me from numerous infelicities and errors.

The research for the book was begun in the spring of 1992 when I held a fellowship at the Humanities Research Centre, Australian National University. My own university provided financial assistance for travel. The research for the book depends in part on the Australian Research Council funded *Annotated Bibliography of Australian Overseas Travel Writing*, edited by Ros Pesman, David Walker and Richard White, compiled by Terri McCormack, which is to be published in 1996 as a Bibliography on Disk by the Australian Library Information Association, University of Canberra. The search for material was also much helped by the bibliographies of Australian women's writing: Debra Adelaide, *Australian Women Writers: A Bibliographic Guide* (Pandora, London, 1988); Debra Adelaide, *Bibliography of Australian Women's Literature 1795–1990*, (Thorpe, Melbourne, 1991); Joy Hooton, *Stories of Herself When Young: Autobiographies of Childhood by Australian Women* (OUP, Melbourne, 1990). For a guide to artists, Caroline Ambrus, *The Ladies Picture Show: Sources on a Century of Australian Women Artists* (Hale & Iremonger, Sydney, 1984) and now *Heritage: The National Women's Art Book: 500 works by 500 Australian Women Artists from Colonial Times to 1995*, Joan Kerr (ed.) (Craftsman House, Sydney, 1995), which appeared after this study was completed. While the printed sources gather together women from all parts of Australia, the search for manuscript material has been confined to libraries in Canberra, Sydney, Melbourne and Adelaide. Exploration in the libraries of other cities would, if not change the general outline, certainly yield more stories of the lives that Australian women have created abroad. My goal has been to create images of the variety and extent of trips and lives overseas, and there are countless more stories than those that have been told.

For permission to reproduce images for the illustrations, I am grateful to the following: for Grace Cossington Smith, *The Refugees*, Mrs Ann Mills; for Margaret Preston, *Self Portrait*, Permanent Trustee Co. Ltd; for Hilda Rix Nicholas, *Poster*, Estate of Hilda Rix Nicholas; for the photograph of Dora Ohlfsen, Dora Stanford; for the photograph of Doris Gentile, Modesta Gentile; and for Stella Bowen, *Self Portrait*, Mrs Suzanne Brookman.

Ros Pesman
Sydney 1995

CHAPTER 1

Travel and Travellers' Tales

We are wanderers, on the whole, especially when young.
We seek out something undefined when we race off to
foreign wars, to extended stays in other cultural meccas.
Australians tend to believe that they can and should go
anywhere, whether it is the Royal Enclosure at Ascot,
the top of Mount Everest or the best table at the current-
ly fashionable restaurant in New York.[1]

This story begins in a journey over thirty years ago when, as a young arts graduate, I stepped into a four-berth inside cabin on D deck, well down in the bowels of the *Fairsky*. Boarding this far from elegant Italian ship was the first step towards what had so long been the goal of my life, to escape to Europe. What were the conjunctures that lay behind that departure: of time — the end of the 1950s, the beginning of the 1960s; of place — an Australia that was a distant outpost of the Eurocentric world and still British and colonial; of social identity — a middle-class educated single woman; of childhood cultural formation — The Little Princesses and Milly Molly Mandy — and the later accretions of Jacob Burckhardt's myth of rebirth in Italy and contemporary images emerging from Cinecittà; of personal identity formed by the adolescent longing to escape the suffocating confines of family and neighbourhood and a profound sense of non-belonging *here* and a belief in the existence of a world out *there* in which I would belong?

There was nothing particularly interesting or distinctive in my departure. From at least the end of the last century, young Australian women appear to have been infected with a passion for overseas travel.[2] The ships that sailed from the docks in Sydney and Melbourne in the 1950s and 1960s were laden with young Australian middle-class women. Our journeys were made possible by our time — the affluence of postwar Australia, the expansion in higher education in the 1950s, and the cheap fares on the return journeys of migrant ships. *Fairsky*, *Patris* and *Neptunia* are names that reverberate in the memories not only of a generation of immigrants, but also in those of a now aging generation of Australians.

My time, education and class deemed that I should believe that everything that was important lay on the other side of the world. The beneficiaries of the new postwar affluence chafed under what they saw as the complacency, conformity and puritanism of the hand that fed them, but while the next generation was to attack and overthrow the rule of the fathers, the discontented and unassimilated of the 1950s and early 1960s simply ran away. We had no doubt that life was freer, more tolerant, and less repressive over *there* — and of course we were right, not because *there* was necessarily different, but because the constraints were not our constraints, the neighbours were not our neighbours. The erotic capital of the world is always somewhere else — for Swedes it is Italy, for Italians it is Sweden. Indeed, the overseas journeys of the young of that time involved two rites-of-passage; not only leaving Australia, but also leaving home. In the 1950s and 1960s, there were only three acceptable reasons for leaving the nest: marriage, nursing and travelling overseas. Thus, embarking on the ship was for most of us the first experience of independent life; Freud has pointed to adolescent flight as an important component in travel. [3]

When we boarded our ships we believed that we were engaging in a once-in-a-lifetime experience. The North Americans and Europeans we met on the road were always bemused by the Australian pattern of travel — from Inverness to Istanbul in three months — and by the Australian travellers' discourse of how far, how fast and for how little. Ruby Rich, who journeyed to Europe via a rapid transit of North America early in this century, later recalled: 'It was really an Australian trip, we stayed two days here and two days there'. [4] Proximity in terms of both mileage and money could place the Continent within North American or British sights every year; it was possible when home was Boston or Birmingham to linger in France if Italy was on the horizon for the next summer. Such expectations were unimaginable to us when between Australia and Europe stood not only the fare but also a sea journey of five weeks.

The trips of the 1950s and 1960s were a turning point in the story of Australian overseas travel. We were the first beneficiaries of the democratisation of travel and the last generation to understand distance as a sensory experience and to arrive in a world that had not been excessively prepackaged and predigested for us. My journey to Europe in 1961 consisted of a five-week voyage; I returned five years later on a thirty-six hour Boeing 707 flight. The arrival of the jet obliterated distance, the communications revolution overcame the information gap, and television conveyed closer and clearer images of Michelangelo's *Last Judgement* than could be obtained in the Sistine Chapel itself. The jumbo jet, the package tour, and the development of tourism as a major sector of the economy in most parts of the world transformed travel into an activity of mass culture. [5] A parallel change was the increasing attraction of Asia as place of holiday or adventure, a destination that was closer, cheaper and more exotic. These changes meant not only that overseas travel had come within the range of far more Australians, but that it was an activity to be engaged in on several occasions over a lifetime.

The beginning of mass travel signified the decline, if not the disappearance, of 'the overseas trip' as a ritual event, a rite-of-passage, a convention in Australian middle-class social and cultural life, an event that had its beginnings in the first return voyages from Sydney Cove to Plymouth. When an event ends, its history begins. Thus I became curious about the thousands of women who had accompanied and preceded me in voyaging to Europe, about what was common to our experiences and discourses and what divided us, about women like Gladys Marks who made her first trip to Europe in 1913 and who, as a lecturer in French at the University of Sydney in the 1920s and 1930s, had preceded me in an academic career.

There are both similarities and differences in our patterns of travel. She left Australia at the age of thirty, travelled with friends, was subsidised by her father's money, and was caught up in a thick web of family connections when she arrived. I was ten years younger, travelled alone on my limited savings, and came from a family that had generations ago lost its contacts with the 'old world'. Her desire to prolong her stay, to undertake further studies, was opposed by her family, mine was encouraged. But she, like me, believed that her first trip might be her only one, 'it may be the only chance of my lifetime and I'm for making the most of it'. We shared the financial inability to indulge our equal passion for concerts and clothes, and we both experienced a moment of *frisson* when we first saw paintings by Giorgione.[6] Each of us was in search of adventure, but our notions of adventure were divided by the forty years that separated our journeys. We both found life more exhilarating on the Continent than in England. I identified with her declaration that her trip to Europe was the most exciting thing that had ever happened to her, with her reluctance to return, and with her conviction that Europe offered a better life for single women. Of the two things that most separated us, one I felt was her loss, the other mine. Changing social conventions made it possible for me to travel at a much younger age and in more independent ways. But beyond language studies and shopping sprees, art galleries and concerts, Gladys Marks had attended suffragette meetings in London and Paris, and conferences of the International Council of Women in Rome and Copenhagen. The thirty-year-old 'spinster' ridiculed her English relatives, who thought that she should concentrate on getting married rather than gadding about, and who informed her that 'men don't like clever girls', a message still loudly transmitted forty years later. As a product of the 1950s, I was more conscious of transgression or even failure in pursuing a single life, I attended no women's meetings or conferences, and I had no consciousness of feminism or of sisterhood. I knew nothing about all those Australian women who half a century earlier had gone to Europe in search of independence, qualifications, careers, a more congenial world, a moment of escape and liminality. I wish that I had.

If there were conjunctures in my departure in 1961, there were also traditions and myths of travel, some that were universal and others that were more peculiar to place, time and gender. The journey is both the richest and the most banal of all tropes.[7] The narratives through which we construct our lives are those of journeys, of rites-of-passage from childhood to maturity, from innocence to experience, from birth to death. Travel is loaded with inherited meaning and associated with central myths and sacred journeys of culture — the expulsion from Eden, the journey from Paradise Lost to Paradise Regained, the wanderings of Ulysses and of Gilgamesh, the journeying of the people of Israel to the promised land — and with archetypes of eternal return — to a Golden Age, to Eden, to Ithaca, to childhood, to the womb, to the union of animus and anima. Travel is many things besides Freud's adolescent flight; it is migration, diaspora, exploration, adventure, pilgrimage, recreation, escape, quest. It is also desire.[8] The travel of European Australians shares in these universal myths as well as in more particular discourses in which other peoples also participate — of migration, of colonialism, and of the world constructed in terms of centres and peripheries.

What perhaps most distinguishes the experience of Australians is our exceptional mobility both across and beyond our own borders.[9] The history of the non-indigenous settlers begins in travel, in the journeys of wanderers, exiles, adventurers and emigrants. We now understand that for most people for most of time immigration has been neither voluntary nor intended as permanent settlement; of those who arrived at Port Jackson on the First Fleet, perhaps as many as half made the return journey.[10] And for immigrants whose travel is not circular and does not end in repatriation, the visit home is part of the migration process, an obligation to self and to the community in which they were born and nurtured.[11] Thus much of Australian travel was and is the journey home; in the past for the vast majority of colonists home was the British Isles, now it can be anywhere in the world. Accompanying emigrants on their voyages to new lands are the memories of family and place and *mentalités* constructed of the customs and culture of the first home, which may be handed down to the next generation. Thus, for a century and a half at least, European Australians claimed two homes, that of birth, family and friends, of memory and family history, and that of domicile. Despite the *cri de coeur* of the constructors and the critics of the cultural cringe, few colonists felt any conflict between their loyalty to the old land and to the new. Margaret Tripp, who emigrated to Australia as a child and visited Britain in 1872, was not alone in using 'home' indiscriminately when referring to both England and Australia.[12]

The founding journeys of white Australians belong not to some mythical and mythologised past, but to the industrial age, and thus in our origins lies the restlessness of modernity. Henry Handel Richardson recalled that 'life at my restless father's side had engendered a liking for change and movement'; painter Janet Alderson remarked that 'I've always had a theory that if you lived in the 20th century, you had to travel the world'.[13] Christina Stead, who traced her own travels to youth's natural yen to wander, characterised all Australians as Ulysses. Indeed the Greek hero is the colonial archetype, the classical persona most revered and called upon in Australian literature.[14]

At the beginning of this century writer Louise Mack voiced the consciousness of Australians that they lived on the far edge of the world.

> I wonder are we more than a little hysterical as travellers, we Australians, packed away there at the other end of the world, shut off from all that is great in art and music, but born with a passionate craving to see, and hear, and come close to these great things and their homes…
>
> Twelve thousand miles removes Australians into a realm of such ardent hero-worship as no peoples living nearer the world's centre could ever understand.[15]

Self-awareness was reinforced by the attitudes of those at the centre. Peace activist Eleanor Moore, who attended a Congress of the Women's International League for Peace and Freedom in Zurich in 1919, later wrote about the experience.

> According to Australian habit, we three delegates went to Europe with a sense of being outsiders converging to a centre. Once there, it was plain enough that the centre felt itself to be the centre, looking out on a world whose circumference was very far away, and diminishing in importance in proportion to the distance. This European-mindedness, or, to be exact, this North-West-Central-European-mindedness was to us quite understandable, for we ourselves were of that tradition.[16]

Australians were on the periphery because their world was Eurocentric and they were denizens of an empire and then a commonwealth whose centre lay on the other side of the globe. Long before the creation of empires, centres were sacred places, the sites of knowledge, power, culture, authentication, recognition, redemption.[17] The pilgrimage to the centre is a mythological topos, and Australian journeys to Europe have always had some of the qualities of pilgrimage. True pilgrimages were long, arduous hauls, and Australians have been only too ready to impress others with the extent of their journeying, whether five weeks by ship or twenty-four hours in a jumbo jet. Centres were to be approached with awe and deference, attitudes which so often inform Australian arrivals in

Europe; Florence Finn called her account of her travels to the Coronation of George V, *Pigmies Among Potentates*.[18]

Yet there is nothing particularly Australian about the craving and the 'cringe' with which we approached our sacred centres. Two thousand years ago the inhabitants of Londinium made the journey from the margins of another empire to the sacred centre in Rome. North Americans' journeys had much in common with those of Australians. Nathaniel Hawthorne called England 'our old home'.[19] Provincials have always felt the lure of the metropolis, whether living in Brisbane, Banff or Birmingham; Adelaide-born painter Stella Bowen shared a flat in London at the end of the First World War with an aspiring actor whose main ambition in life was never to go back to Birmingham.[20] And while the young Australians who flocked to London in the 1960s may in the era of decolonisation have been mistaken in their belief that London was the heart of the world, sacred places retain their attraction and arouse deference long after their power has ebbed away. Thus, the Romans made their pilgrimages to Greece, seventeenth-century British milords to Italy, nineteenth-century North Americans to Europe, and Australians to postwar London.

It is men who have embarked on the heroic journeys of myth and literature, of exploration, of naming, of adventure, of quest, of discovery of self and the world. The Grand Tour was a male rite-of-passage, a process of male acculturation and 'sowing of wild oats'. Travel was male territory and its metaphors were male-gendered; the language of travel is of conquering virgin territory, of penetrating the landscape, of knowing and possessing.[21] When women travelled, they had no metaphors of their own; on arriving in Madrid, Winifred James wrote that outside her hotel room lay 'a new city unravished yet by my eye'.[22]

Woman's archetypal role is that of Penelope, the immobile point of stability, the guardian of the hearth, the audience for the telling of the tale.

> But when the two had their fill of the joy of love, they took delight in tales, speaking each to the other. She, the fair lady, told all that she had endured in the halls ... But Zeus-born Odysseus recounted all the woes he had brought on men and all the toil that in his sorrow he had endured, and she was glad to listen, nor did sweet sleep fall upon her eyelids, till he told all the tale.[23]

It has been customary to represent women's travel as transgression. But women have always been on the move, and Mother Courage is as much a female archetype as Penelope. The convict women who came to Australia underwent one of the most terrifying voyages on earth. Women from the beginning of time have journeyed across frontiers and borders, as immigrants and refugees, as agents of their own survival and that of their families, as the victims and camp-followers of men. The *Sydney Herald* of

December 1827 reported the sad incident of the massacre of the captain and crew of the shipwrecked barque *Juno* by 'Feejee cannibals'; his wife and children had been for the moment spared in the belief that they could be ransomed. Mrs Banks was but one of the many women who accompanied their husbands to sea.[24] In the immediate postwar years some 120 000 war brides and children entered the United States in one of the greatest mass movements of young women in history, and there was a considerable Australian presence.[25]

If women have always travelled at the behest of men, they have also dreamt of independent travel and autonomy. Australian women who sought through travel more adventurous, interesting and fulfilling lives, and who reflected on their wanderings, traced the origins of their journeys back to childhood, to that time before they were subjected to the restrictions of gender. When journalist and activist Alice Henry finally went overseas for the first time in 1905, she wrote that the desire of her heart was being granted. She had grown up on the edge of the Gippsland forest, had freely read boys' adventure books, and had expected her life to be full of adventure and travel: 'no sex division, still less sex inferiority obtruded itself on my mental picture'.[26] Winifred James also traced the origins of her life of travel and expatriatism to her childhood.

> Centuries and centuries ago, in an existence when a calm and gentle pleasure lay in the chewing of pinafore strings, and ecstasies grew in jam jars, a mulberry tree in the fruit garden fell. At that moment I began to travel …
>
> On the mulberrry tree, I with one other went abroad, leaving no corner unvisited. Boarding the craft down at the root end, you made your way along the trunk to the branches where all the joy and danger lay. You hung out perilously on yardarms, over seething ocean graves … you yielded your own magnificent life a hundred times a voyage to save some inglorious enemy.[27]

But unlike Henry, at least in her later construction, James was already playing in a gendered world: 'in that incarnation we were men', men who saved women.

At the outset of any consideration of women and travel what needs to be distinguished is the type of travel. What forms of travel have been represented as transgression for women, and what forms have been permissible? In which travel discourses have women participated, and from which have they been excluded? Until very recently independence and agency, exploration, adventure, travel in pursuit of knowledge, sexual identity, and self-formation were forbidden to women. Yet exceptional women have always transgressed. There have been women soldiers, sailors, pilgrims, and strolling players.[28] Mary Wollstonecraft took off alone from London in 1791 to witness the remaking of the world in the

Paris of the Revolution, and Margaret Fuller left North America half a century later to participate in the overthrow of church and state in Rome.[29] The second half of the nineteenth century saw the appearance of the lady explorer in the 'good thick skirt', sanitised by self and audience as exceptional, but also eternally feminine. The same period saw the increasing presence of women on 'the grand tour' of Europe as the most conspicuous clients of Thomas Cook.[30]

In colonial Australia exploration and adventure, or heroic travel, was the inward journey over land, directed towards the penetration, knowing and naming of the inland frontier. This frontier was a masculine preserve, the territory of the 'lone hand'.[31] Women could not participate in the telling of this adventure; on this frontier their presence was transgression. But there was another, the one that lay behind, in the past, Europe, that could now be constructed as tame, domesticated, effete. As such it became open to women. By the last quarter of the nineteenth century, as one male commentator pointed out, there was neither adventure nor romance in voyaging to Europe.

> Now-a-days, the journey from almost any part of Australia to the old country is an undertaking so simple and easy, it calls for so little preparation on the part of the individual ... that the average colonist very readily convinces himself that an occasional trip home is one of the duties that England expects every loyal subject to undertake ...
>
> After all, the trip to the old country has lost half of its romance, and, no doubt some considerable portion of its charm, by being robbed of all the dreariness and discomforts which at one time attended a voyage ...
>
> No romance — although there may be an abundance of sentiment — attaches to a voyage in an ocean-going steamer.[32]

The frontier to Europe and beyond may have become open to women, but the circumstances and purposes of their journeys were long an area of contestation.

The story of women and travel since the mid-nineteenth century is that of their challenges to taboos, of the extension of the kinds of travel open to them, and of the opportunities available to participate beyond the exceptional few. It is the story of their successful assertion of their desire to travel in pursuit of their own agendas, when, where and how they saw fit, alone as well as chaperoned, as independent persons as well as wives, mothers and daughters. Between women and their desire to travel stood the constraints that proved negotiable for some women, insurmountable for others, up to and including the 1950s and 1960s. And as women began to journey in new and different ways, more literary models for the recounting of their tales became available.

The variety of ways in which Australian women travelled to and experienced Europe — in dependent as well as independent conditions, in obedience to the dictates of patriarchy as well as in defiance — is also part of the story. There is no woman's trip, no woman's travel experience. Australian women embarked on many different voyages, for holidays and periods of recreation, for visits to family and ancestral homes, for transformation into ladies, for status and privileged speech, for the experience of being there and ticking off the sights, for culture and self-improvement, for education, training and professional experience, for recognition and fame, for adventure, for romance. They travelled to flee, to follow and find men, to make good marriages, to escape bad ones, to participate in war and promote peace, to fulfil some aspiration to a more liberated and interesting life, to live according to their own scripts. Joan Colebrook simply 'wanted to discover the world', Winifred James travelled 'for fun', and Marie Byles 'to ramble, tramp, hike and climb mountains'.[33] The trip could be a voyage towards self-formation, discovery or invention of new selves; it was the opportunity to play new roles, don new masks. Some women went to encounter variety and difference, to learn about the world, other people, and other ways of doing things, or, like Henry James's Isobel Archer, to embark upon a search for self. But there were also women on whom other worlds scarcely impinged, and for whom the benefits of travel lay in joining privileged conversation back at home.

Women went overseas at different ages, pursued different agendas, and followed different itineraries both in the world and in their heads. They went for varying periods of time, the world in six months or forever, or for six months that turned into forever, and forever that turned into six months. Little distinction is made here between overseas trips and expatriation; the line between the two is rarely clearcut as is beautifully etched out in Jessica Anderson's narrative of the overseas life of Nora Porteous, the protagonist of *Tirra Lirra by the River*.[34] While some women, such as Jill Ker Conway, left Australia with the intention never to return and their lives conformed to intention, others bent on expatriation returned.[35] My own steps towards securing expatriation, a European marriage and a higher degree in one of the temples of European *haute bourgeois* culture, ironically brought me home. Events could also turn short trips into lifetimes abroad. Would Christina Stead have become an expatriate had she not met and married William Blake? And would Jill Ker have gained her exile had she not met and married Harvard don, John Conway? Christina Stead, so often a scapegoat for expatriatism, refused all attempts to treat her living abroad as a deep and meaningful issue.[36]

What did their journeys mean for the women? What did they make of the worlds they encountered, both interior and exterior? And what of the world they had left behind, which informed their perceptions? What we seek from travel is often an indicator of what we desire and of what we are denied at home.[37] Women shared with men the categories of time and place, but their gender framed their experience in countless ways. Even in the 1960s young women who left Australia were regaled with tales of the white-slave trade, and single women could rarely stop to gaze in Italy without themselves becoming the objects of male gaze. As objects of this attention, women become conscious of image. Two hundred years ago, Mary Wollstonecraft observed that when a woman went on a journey, among her chief preoccupations was the impression that she made upon others.[38] But if constrained abroad, women were also the more restricted gender at home, and thus escape and the promise of independence and autonomy were powerful motives fuelling women's travel. Indeed, women were travellers long before they left home and their imaginary travel created enticing and romantic worlds. And while 'home' as domestic space was women's territory, in the public world this concept could be problematic for women. They might be outsiders in a society constructed by men, 'exiles at home' in Drusilla Modjeska's telling words.[39] North American travel writer, Mary Morris, wrote that as a single woman in America in the 1970s she felt as if she lived in a foreign land.[40] If they are foreigners at home, are women doubly exiled abroad or are they better constructed to deal with the alien, the foreign, to read the cues of adaptation? As the custodians and transmitters of genteel European culture in Australia, how did women, inferior by gender and provenance, cope and respond in the temples of high culture? These questions will recur. One question that will not, however, is that of the difference between male and female experience. This narrative is of how and why women travelled and told their stories.

If the focus is on the wide range and richness of the experience of women abroad over a century, equal attention must be given to the framing of the tale. The story, after all, is of what women wrote about their travel. They responded and expressed their responses within inherited conventions and expectations, and within the discourses in circulation at the time — not only discourses of travel but also of empire, of geography, of femininity and of first-wave feminism and the new woman, of identity and nationality. The first discourse that framed their responses was that of the significance of the journey. It could hardly have been otherwise given the investment of time and money and all the associations of tradition, history and literature and the rituals that marked off and surrounded the event. A niece recalled the trip to Europe of an aunt in the early 1950s.[41] Her aunt had lived at home with her parents, and as the unmarried daughter and sister enjoyed little position or status within the family. At the age of 28 the aunt decided to make the trip to Europe. She was the first in the family to go abroad and in the weeks and days before her departure became the centre of attention. The niece remembers farewell parties and gifts, and later the excitement occasioned by the arrival of letters with foreign stamps, which were read aloud and passed among family and friends. She recalls, too, the aunt's return, and the souvenirs and gifts that were brought home. The niece's present was an Italian mosaic brooch, which she treasured and which she now connects to her own desire to travel in Italy. Following her trip, the aunt had a new authority and status within the family. This is a commonplace tale of the time, variations of which have been told to me on countless occasions. It points both to the connection between travel and status and to the rituals of the trip.

These rituals began months before departure with the choosing of a ship and the payment of the fare. The protagonist in actor Mary Marlowe's autobiographical novel, *Kangaroos in Kingsland*, described the first event in her journey to Europe on the eve of the First World War.

> Shall I ever forget the thrill of rapture that went through me when we walked into Dalgety's shipping office in Sydney, and plonked down the money for three passages on a White Star liner?
>
> I felt as if I were performing some sacred ceremony with all due ritual and solemnity.[42]

There then followed months of preparation, which were often as exciting as the trip itself. Farewell lunches were *de rigueur*, and the social pages from the end of the last century to the middle of this devoted as much space to women departing overseas as they did to that other female rite-of-passage, marriage. Gift-giving rituals accompanied travellers onto their ships, where their cabins were filled with fruit and flowers. Borders are traditionally seen as dangerous places, and departure is a metaphor for death, so the regaling of the traveller with gifts for the voyage echoes the filling of the tomb of the dead Pharaoh with objects of sustenance for the next life.

The travel experience could involve entry into a world of difference, of encounters with new places perceived in terms of their unfamiliarity, foreignness, 'otherness'. It also, for many, involved entry into dream worlds, fairylands, and a life that could be constructed as the opposite of the everyday round at home. Travel was extraordinary not ordinary life. 'How shall I ever settle down to ordinary every day life again?' one traveller asked herself in Nuremberg.[43]

Testimony to the significance attached to the trip and its separation from ordinary life is the extent of the written record. Stored away in trunks, attics and basements across Australia are the diaries and letters that women wrote while journeying. Letter-writing and the compiling of a diary were part of women's lives. One woman travelling as her husband's companion on a business trip in the 1930s related that when she asked him to write a letter home, he refused, saying that it was 'not his department'.[44] In her work on Australian volunteers working and fighting in Spain during the Civil War Amirah Inglis has observed that most of her sources were diaries and letters written by women.[45] The keeping of a journal was also a well-established and integral component of travel, and travel diaries were a conventional gift for those departing on a journey. The travel experience, because of its fixed points of departure and return, its narrative structure as a sequence of events through time and space, and its clearly marked separation and difference from ordinary life, is peculiarly adapted to diary-writing, and the travel diary was often the only diary that a woman wrote.[46] The substitute or supplement for the diary was the ritual weekly letter home, which was intended as a permanent record. Gladys Marks informed her family that she was not bothering with a diary, but admonished them to 'keep my letters, such as they are'.[47] The letters usually came back into the possession of the writers, who hoarded and cherished them — whether in 1870 or 1970.

> I now have all the letters I wrote here with me, thanks to my mother keeping them all these years. I am very proud of my letters and always will be, they covered an enormous part of my life that I will never forget. I will cherish them forever.[48]

Diaries were also treasured and passed down the generations. Juliana Edwards went to Europe in 1961, using her mother's 1930s travel diary as her guidebook.

If women were more likely to write, they were less likely to be published. Around 20 per cent of just under one thousand items in an annotated bibliography of Australian overseas travel books up to 1970 were written by women, but these published works are clearly only a small fragment of the record of women's travel.[49] Just as the travel diary was often the only piece of writing, apart from letters, that women engaged in, its publication was usually their only venture into print. Often privately published, the travel memoirs usually carried prefaces in which their writers disclaimed any pretensions to literary ability or authority, and attributed the publishing initiative to the persuasion of others.

> This Journal was posted to my Mother as opportunity offered along our trip; and now at her desire — not because of any merit of its own — appears in book form, with (at her special request) but few erasures from the original.[50]

> In response to the request of many friends, who tell me they have found pleasure in reading my simple and informally-written letters, with great diffidence I venture to send them forth, hoping they may be a small help to others contemplating such a tour.[51]

Publication attests to the significance of overseas travel in the lives of the women, as well as to the existence of an audience for travellers' tales, no matter how jejune.

Alongside the published journals and letters of women who made no claim to be writers are the journalism and books of women who did aspire to be travel writers. The expatriate sculptor Margaret Thomas appears to have been the first Australian woman to publish a travel book. *Scamper Through Spain and Tangier* was published in 1892, and was followed in 1900 by *Two Years in Palestine and Syria* and in 1902 by *Denmark Past and Present*. The first of Mary Gaunt's travel books, *Alone in West Africa*, appeared in 1912. However, even at this level of published writing, women often still dissociated themselves from high purpose. The very deployment of 'scamper' in the title of Margaret Thomas's book on Spain is suggestive of frivolity. Margaret Gilruth, in her account of her journey from Australia to Europe in the early 1930s as 'steward, purser, ship-chandler, hostess and A.B.' on a Norwegian tramp steamer, wrote:

> This book is not meant to be discursive or descriptive in the manner of the best travel books. It is merely a collection of diary-letters written home to Australia during a five-months voyage on a little Norwegian tramp ship with a personality.[52]

In the preface to her book on Jamaica, Mary Gaunt gave her views on travel writing; when she was young, travellers took themselves very seriously and seldom condescended to tell of mundane daily happenings with the result that the books were dull, 'leaving out a great many things I wanted to know'. She felt that she was being very daring in writing about trivial things, but believed that good writing based on one's own eyes 'can make the crossing of a mean and commonplace street' in London more graphic and dramatic 'than a tale of the treasures of the Inca'.[53] Catherine Robinson, in the foreword to her account of her journey down the Amazon in the 1930s, wrote that her memories of South America were not of the terrors of the jungle or of the poisoned arrows of hostile Indians or of the terrible fight against fevers, but of 'the dainty little humming-birds in their delicate and iridescent beauty, with wings awhirr in some gorgeous bell-shaped flower'.[54]

Autobiographies and oral histories provide a further source for the travel experiences of women, a source in which the experiences occupy proportionally more space in the text than they did in the life.[55] Clare Davies made her first trip overseas in 1955 when she was already in her fifties, and this trip, together with two further ones made in 1958 and 1962, account for three quarters of her memoirs.[56] The importance given to the travel experience again attests to the cultural significance of travel, to travel as extraordinary not ordinary life, and to the greater ease with which the extraordinary can be narrated.

For the most part, the travel tales of women who did not identify themselves as writers belong to the genre of 'what I did in the school holidays' and move little beyond a listing of sights seen, things done, and dollops of information from guide books. In Ada Carnegie's 1966 recollections based on her travel diaries the adjective 'beautiful' occurs thirty times, 'famous' fifteen, and 'wonderful' ten in the space of ten pages devoted to Italy and France.

> Florence, a city of the finest arts, contains beautiful statuary. Here Dante and Michelangelo were born. Florence is situated on the beautiful banks of the Arno River, and has four famous bridges. One of the bridges has shops on both sides and is very intriguing.
>
> We went to see the famous gallery of Uffizi and here we saw the portraits of Raphael and Michelangelo, and some of the works of Rubens the great portrait-painter of olden times.
>
> We went to see the famous Cathedral of Florence, with the Baptistery and Campanile. It was superb. Then to the museum with its beautiful setting of trees and flowers of every hue and the fountain of Neptune.[57]

Yet Ada Carnegie felt that she had gained much from her trip.

> Many advantages occur from a trip such as we have taken. The mind is enlarged in its scope — our sympathies are broadened — the outlook is vaster — and the pulse is quickened by the inspiration of so many noble things seen and heard.
>
> Life is enriched in many ways by reason of this trip, and if I have succeeded in imparting any of the enthusiasm I have felt, or given out any of the inspiration I have received, on this delightful trip, my diary will not have been written in vain and I myself shall feel doubly rewarded, by my journeying around the world.[58]

There seems no reason to doubt her enthusiasm or that of others. The problem was that of conveying their reactions and of a want of confidence, which were functions of their status as colonials, women and 'non-writers'. The experience of travel was supposed to enlarge understanding, improve minds, educate sensibilities. In recording their responses, many women must have felt overwhelmed by the gulf between the sites that they were contemplating — sites loaded with significance, described in countless texts, appropriated by the poets — and what they saw as the deficiency in their own descriptive powers.[59] Mary Kent Hughes explained it thus:

> I thought of E.V. Lucas, and all the talented writers who have given such marvellous word-pictures of this city, and decided it would be beyond me to do the same. All I could do would be to write about the wonders as they appeared to a very ordinary Australian, and attempt to pass on something

of the feeling of history to those of my country and others who may never have the good luck which has fallen me.[60]

It is hardly surprising that women unaccustomed to writing should resort to cliché, crib from Baedeker and Murray, embellish their texts with quotations from Byron, find so many sights 'indescribable', 'beyond description', 'too beautiful to describe', 'beyond me to describe'.

It can be argued that accounts of travel are about writing and 'textuality', rather than experience, and that the record may not tell us anything about the experience. Yet the women did travel as well as write, and if the records follow story-lines in culture, so too does the experience; we craft ourselves in the world as well as in writing, 'we live immersed in narrative'.[61] The first tale is always the one that the subject tells herself in the moment in order to make sense of experience. Thus the division between experience and record partly dissolves — but not quite. Travellers' tales are always suspect, travel is the area for tall stories. After all, who can verify or confound? And much of the point of travel is to gather tales. Indeed, the tale can be more important to the traveller than the experience. Who dares return without some adventure to recount? Florence Finn noted in 1911 that Port Said had the reputation for being 'the Wickedest place on Earth', a reputation without foundation since the arrival of the British. Nevertheless, disappointed travellers were not done out of their story:

> when they return to their hum-drum friends they are careful to emphasise the 'wickedest place on earth' and their 'Pretty hot, I can tell you' gives the stay-at-home the impression that the traveller has seen life and wickedness to the full.[62]

When Ida Haysom had a car accident in Tunbridge Wells during her 1936 trip to England, she wrote in her diary: 'I took the wrong turn and then *it* happened. Even my diary will never know the sordid details'. [63] Image of self, as well as consciousness of audience, of the expectations of others, and of reputation, both censor and embellish writing — just as they shape our construction of ourselves. Thus, while the conventions of the nineteenth century may have enjoined avoidance — or suppression — of sexual encounters, those of the 1970s just as oppressively demanded such tales — or their invention. And memory has its own life. When she came to write her book about her visit to the Soviet Union in the late 1930s, admittedly a special site, Doris Hayball mused:

> I am writing all this eighteen months after my visit and much is blurred. It would seem that I remember things which disappointed me and surprised me more than things which pleased me and which I expected to see.[64]

And few travellers are as open as Doris Gentile was when she wrote 'if I have done nothing else with my life I at least have made it something fantastique like a fairy story'.[65] But what is the fairy story, the life or the telling? Does it matter? The tale discloses much about self image and self construction, about perceptions of social expectations and of audience, about the possible and permissible range of roles within culture specific to time, place, class and gender.

The international novel is one other source for the story of Australian women travelling overseas. With action set in both the new world and the old, it had become an important genre in Australian as well as North American literature by the end of the nineteenth century. Among its exponents were Ada Cambridge, Tasma, Rosa Praed, Alice Rosman, Louise Mack and Winifred James, as well as many other relatively unknown women writers. The subject of the quests of Australian women in Europe continued to preoccupy following generations of writers, including men, and created some of the strongest female characters in Australian fiction — Christina Stead's Teresa Hawkins, Martin Boyd's Alice Langton, Patrick White's Theodora Goodman. Nor has the theme lost its appeal in the present. Cynthia Nolan, Shirley Hazzard, Patricia Rolfe, Jessica Anderson, Jill Neville, Barbara Hanrahan, Glenda Adams, Kate Grenville, Suzanne Falkiner, and Frank Moorhouse have all taken their female protagonists overseas. Women who write about the overseas quests of Australian women have themselves quested, and it is their own journeys from which the fictions are furnished.

In my exploration of the records created by the women who preceded and accompanied me in departing Australia in quest of something — (anything?) — else, I draw little distinction between letters, diaries, oral histories, life stories, and fiction, since all reveal the stock of representations of self and the world available at any given time, representations which could be evasions and subversions as well as reflections and recreations. My search is for the variety of the richness — and the dullness — of a wide range of experience, variety occasioned by education, wealth, class, time, circumstances, accident, subjectivities, desires, fantasies, constraints, fears. Since travel was the preserve of those with money and time at their disposal, this study is largely about middle- and upper-class women. Within that group, it is the experiences of women who wrote for the market whose voices inevitably prevail. As Dora Birtles observed, 'for every woman who bursts into print about what she has done, there are twenty who don't but who go on travelling just the same'.[66] And accompanying me in my investigation of the travelling and writing of others are my younger self, who fled both time and place, and my present self, who now, thirty years later, reconstructs that younger self.

Like most women who went overseas, my travel and cultural interests were Eurocentric. While the majority of women's travel until the 1970s was to and in Europe, that is by no means the whole picture, and some of the most interesting travel and travel writing by Australian women relates to the world beyond Europe. On the voyages to Europe, ships stopped in Colombo and Aden, and side trips were taken to Cairo and to the cities of the Middle East. Other routes took women to Cape Town, Panama, Manila, Hong Kong, Port Arthur and Vladivostok. North America was early on the itineraries of Australian travellers, and Australian women moved about the empire and Asia from the late nineteenth century as missionaries, teachers, nurses, governesses, actors, tourists and cultural pilgrims. While I have followed the lives of some women beyond Europe, the focus of this study, like that of my own travel, is Europe.

If this telling of the story of women's journeys and their lives abroad has its origins in the life of a young Europhile Australian woman, it is also written in sympathy with Donald Denoon's argument that the proper study of Australian history is Australians and not Australia.[67] As Nicholas Jose has written, the interplay between Australia and over there is a perennial in Australian life, an interplay that is part of the personal history of those who have lived on 'two bits of terra firma'.[68] To ignore Australians once they leave their own shores is to diminish our history, to suppress international and cosmopolitan links and strands in Australian life and the contribution that Australians have made to other histories and other societies. Recent biographies of Alice Henry, Christina Stead, Louise Hanson-Dyer and Jessie Couvreur ('Tasma') are telling exempla of the enriching perspectives that emerge from the exploration of the lives of Australian women abroad.[69] To reject Christina Stead's *For Love Alone* and Frank Moorhouse's *Grand Days* from the Australian literary canon is also to cast out from Australian history the lives of many significant Australian women and significant parts of the lives of countless others.

While abroad Australians meet other travellers and these encounters are a timely reminder that our distinctiveness can only be found in a comparative context. To place Australian experience in a wider framework is not to reject Australian nationality and culture, but to emphasise their connections with the rest of the world, their porous and permeable qualities. Identity and nationality are, like everything else, not fixed structures, but processes in the making. There is no Australian 'identity', only 'identities', and these have been forged abroad as well as at home, in contact and collision with others, as well as in isolation. As Frank Moorhouse reminds us, travel is not only about encounters with foreign ways, 'it is also an encounter with one's own nationality'.[70] Yet, as Australia moves towards a republic and the centenary of federation, and politicians and their ideologues seek to focus on the construction of one Australian identity, it might be wise to look closely at Europe, at ethnic cleansing in Bosnia and the resurrection of Nazi fascist ideologies in the heartlands, and to remember that almost all the elements that make up our identities are the ones that we share with the rest of the world's peoples.

Interlude

⨏ntecedents

Australia's best-known pioneer woman, Elizabeth Macarthur, was indeed a colonial Penelope, weaving the Australian wool industry while her husband, John Macarthur, emulated Odysseus in his travails and wanderings. In her conformity to the mythical archetype of woman as sessile, and in never leaving New South Wales, she was unusual among the women of the colonial élite. Her own eight-year-old daughter was taken to England in 1801 by her father for her education.

The wealthy emancipist entrepreneur, Mary Reibey, made the return voyage home in 1820, in the company of her two daughters.

> It is impossible to describe the sensations I felt when coming to the Top of Darwin St, my native home and amongst my Relatives and on entering my Grandmother's House where I had been brought up and to find it nearly the same as when I left nearly 29 years ago.[1]

Much of Reibey's twelve months in Britain was spent visiting relatives, the scenes of her own and her mother's childhood. But the journey home was important for the education of her daughters, whom she placed into a school in Edinburgh. While in Scotland Reibey sat for her portrait and did the tourist sights; in the Castle she saw the Crown of Scotland and the room in which King James VI had been born. In London she engaged in more sightseeing.

While Reibey's touring was confined to England and Scotland, that of the young Grace Black from the Western District of Victoria, whose European sojourn also began with family reunions, extended to the Continent. In January 1852 Black set off with her father and sister on what she described at the beginning of her diary as 'a tour of pleasure'.[2] She spent five months travelling in France, Italy and Switzerland, and then stayed one month in Rome where she took Italian lessons, participated in the Easter ceremonies of an alien church, and assiduously visited monuments and galleries. Nothing, Black believed, could be 'more beautiful, sublime and majestic' than the Colosseum by moonlight. Like many others she felt that describing the experience was beyond her, so she invoked the words of Lord Byron. The Romantic poet also accompanied Black on her inspection of the paintings in the Brera Gallery in Milan. Her act of rebellion against the 'tyrant' — *Murray's Guide* — in appreciating a disparaged painting by Guercino was legitimised when she found that

18

Lord Byron had also admired the work. Catholic though Black may have been in her taste for art, her religion was firmly Protestant. The rituals of the Catholic church offended her, as did the Continental Sunday. To travel in Switzerland from the Protestant canton of Berne to the Catholic Lucerne she found most unpleasant because the people of Lucerne 'who are Roman Catholics were dirty, their cottages the same & out of repair & the fields not nearly so rich as what we had passed through'. Despite its Catholicism and its Sabbath *en fête*, Black thought that Paris 'far surpasses poor old London in point of beauty', even though her Paris was one that had recently experienced a revolution and the coup of Louis Bonaparte. To Black, 'the people all seem as contented & happy as if no revolution had taken place', but she also observed that no-one 'seemed willing to say anything about it'. If she had designated her European journey as 'a tour of pleasure', it was in its route and cultural purposes a latter-day and female version of the Grand Tour.

When Jane Murray Smith, also from Victoria, visited the Continent in 1864 and 1865, she was equally worried about the inadequacies of her responses and equally offended by the Catholic religion — she too preferred the Protestant parts of Switzerland.

> It was a great treat to get into the Protestant part of Switzerland. People may say it was prejudice, but the people in the Protestant part were better and cleaner-looking, the houses better and more prosperous looking altogether. The awful looking creatures you see in the Valleys! Our blacks really are superior, I think.[3]

The young Victorian matron also disapproved of High Church practices within the Church of England, of the moral laxity in Britain, where 'divorce cases are spoken about as openly as possible', and of the theatre in Paris, where 'there was a dance that made me quite ashamed'.[4] Murray Smith had gone to Europe with her husband and small daughter in pursuit of his business interests and to visit family. She found the constant round of relatives wearing, and wrote home after she had been in Britain for three months that:

> I don't consider that I have seen anything yet, but I shall commence soon. We have devoted ourselves to our relations. I think we have finished them off now.[5]

But sightseeing was not always fun either. 'We have passed this morning at the British Museum. It is awful heavy, but we have done it as a duty'.

Odysseus rather than the Grand Tour provides the model for the wanderings of Sarah Wentworth. She sailed from Sydney for England in 1853 with her seven youngest children, accompanied only by a governess.[6] Her younger sons having been placed in English schools, Wentworth, who had been joined by her husband William Charles, passed the next eight years traipsing about England and the Continent. She lived in Brussels for a year and then in Paris for nine months for the education of her daughters. Much of Wentworth's time in Europe was absorbed by the health problems of her husband and children, and she became a frequent visitor to the spas of Germany. In quest of warmth, she took her consumptive daughter, Sarah Eleanor, to Corfu in December 1857. The journey was to no avail; the young Sarah died shortly after they reached the Adriatic island. Sarah Wentworth was to bury two more children in Europe. She and her husband returned to Australia in 1861, but in the following year the Wentworths moved back to Europe, where William Charles died in 1872.

Sarah Wentworth's wandering life had its source in the political agendas and restlessness of her husband. But the Wentworths were also in retreat from a colony in which their tainted convict origins and the illegitimacy of their early relationship compromised their social position and the futures of their children. Wentworth wrote of London as a 'place where women were treated better than anywhere any other place … for they are loved and cared for here'.[7] Living in two worlds meant that the family became divided between them, that marriages were made and children and grandchildren settled in both England and Australia. Thus in the last eight years of her life Wentworth criss-crossed the oceans.

If the extent of Sarah Wentworth's wandering was distinctive, her dilemma was common enough. Hannah Rouse of Rouse Hill took her son and two daughters, Emma and Lizzie, to Europe in 1868.[8] On the return voyage the following year, Emma Rouse met Lieutenant Dudley Batty and sailed back to England to marry him. In 1874 Rouse and Lizzie left Sydney for London, where Emma was expecting her first child. They remained in England for three years, visiting Australia in 1877, but leaving again in 1878. Lizzie also married in England and, apart from a further brief visit to Australia in 1888, Hannah Rouse lived the rest of her life in England near her daughters.

Mary Reibey had put her daughters into a school in Edinburgh and Sarah Wentworth's children attended European institutions. The education of children was clearly a major factor in the northern journeys of the colonial élite. Mary Stawell, whose husband William was the Chief Justice of Victoria, passed five years in Europe because he wanted their sons educated in England. The party that left Australia in 1873 consisted of William and Mary, ten children, a tutor, and a nurse. The sons were placed in English schools and Stawell spent most of her time in Paris and Switzerland supervising the education of her daughters. When her husband returned to Victoria, she remained behind.

It was indeed a trial to be left alone in a foreign land, with such grave responsibilities and such a family of young children to look after, and yet I felt it must be done. William said 'I wish our boys to be educated in England, and if you will not stay with them it cannot be done. We owe a duty to our children, and must not let our happiness interfere with it'.[9]

Mary Stawell's situation is a timely reminder that travel was also travail. When Martha Knox, wife of Edward Knox, the founder of the Colonial Sugar Refinery, made the trip in 1857 with her husband, a maid, and six children under the age of twelve, the journey must have been a three-month test of endurance.[10] Life on small sailing ships, even for cabin passengers, meant cramped space, exposure to the elements, to the freezing cold and the icebergs of the Antarctic.

> About dinner time the man on the look out shouted out 'Iceberg', and we did rush up in a hurry. It was eight miles off, such an enormous white thing like a great hill. A few minutes after another was seen on the other side about the same distance off. They saw three more that night. On Thursday afternoon it was very foggy, and we were steering right on to one, we fortunately saw it when we were two miles off. It really was a beautiful sight but it made you quake. You can form no idea what it is like, if you could imagine Station peak floating about. They are dead white, and you never see them twice in the same shape.[11]

The cold, which Jane Murray Smith, like other colonial travellers, fended off with her 'opussum rug', was followed when ships turned north by tropical heat and becalming.

> August 24th. It is oppressively hot … I have been obliged to sleep on the floor for some nights, as my bed-place is so near the deck that I can hardly breathe. The floor is uneven so it is a difficult matter to lie there. I am curled up like a kitten.[12]

Much time on board the ships was taken up in the schooling and control of fractious children, and in the effort to keep them, oneself, and one's clothes clean and seasickness at bay. Diversion was provided by the sighting of whales and flying fish, the trapping of albatrosses, endless games of chess and cards, the writing of diaries and letters, the weekly church service, the ship's concert and the occasional night of breathtaking luminosity and perfect day 'that made you wonder at the beauty of creation'.[13]

The journeys of Mary Reibey, Grace Black, Jane Murray Smith, Sarah Wentworth, Mary Stawell and Martha Knox encapsulate the travel experience of the women of the colonial élite of the mid-nineteenth century. Their journeys were undertaken in their roles as wives, mothers and daughters, and were related to family, education and culture, the spheres of women. So their lives abroad reflected their lives at home. The next generation saw enormous changes in the conditions of travel, but modernisation in the means of travel was not immediately followed by modernisation in the travelling lives of women. Family, education, culture, status and the needs of men remained the main functions of their journeys. But Sarah Wentworth's retreat to Europe to escape local pressures and prejudices does point to the possibility of travel as subversion of women's enclosure in an ascribed and defined domestic sphere, and to other future modes of women's travel.

If it is women from the ranks of the élite who predominate in the telling of the story of early return visits to Europe, travel was by no means their preserve. The sailing ships also carried second- and third-class passengers. As well as looking after her own son on her voyage to England, Caroline Le Souef nursed a woman travelling third class, who was dying of consumption and journeying in the hope of being able to deliver her small daughter into the care of her parents in Ireland. Maids, nurses and governesses also travelled in the entourages of women such as Sarah Wentworth, Jane Murray Smith, Mary Stawell and Martha Knox. Janet Mitchell, who made her first trip to Europe as a child at the beginning of this century, recalled that her nurse Kate kept a voluminous diary from which the young Janet copied for her weekly letters home.[14] That diary is not at our disposal, and all we know of Kate's responses to her travels is what her charge chose to relate. Mitchell, who became a Catholic convert, told of the Irish Catholic Kate's joy at being in Rome and attending a papal audience.[15] Molly Skinner worked her way back to Britain as nurse to a family of five children, sharing a cabin with three of the children and taking her meals with them. After the children had gone to bed, the only space she could find to read and write was the deserted dining-room. She did place her experiences on the public record, but the collaborator of D.H. Lawrence can hardly be regarded as typical of the serving class.[16] It may well be that the less well-off in the colonies had a greater chance of returning to Europe at the beginning of the nineteenth century than they did at the end of it, the more so since repatriation was so often the goal. By the late nineteenth century, when the Australian-born began to predominate in the population, when steam had replaced sail, and when the voyage to Europe was transformed from an ordeal into pleasure, wealth and leisure were the normal prerequisites for travel to Europe.

CHAPTER 2

Travel and Status

Those returning in such ships were invincible, for they had managed it and could reflect ever after on Anne Hathaway's Cottage or the Tower of London with a confidence that did not generate in Sydney.[1]

Nancy Adams, daughter of Sir Edward Mitchell, a leading Melbourne barrister, recalled her childhood in the first decades of this century: 'Looking back, it sometimes seems to me that a great part of my formative years was spent in Port Melbourne Pier welcoming ships or watching them recede'.[2] Her experience was typical of her time and class. The Australian élite was a travelling class to an extent that has not as yet been fully explored in the writing of social and cultural history. While accurate statistics are difficult to find, it seems that by the 1890s some 10 000 people were arriving in the ports of the United Kingdom each year from Australia, and while this figure includes people whose normal domicile was Britain and who were merely visitors to Australia, it no doubt also ignores some Australian travellers.[3] If only a small proportion of the total population, the number of Australians who travelled was far from inconsequential, and it may be that Australia's travelling class was larger in proportion to the total population than its North American counterpart, despite the greater distance of the voyage. The size of the Australian presence in London was sufficient by the 1880s to sustain the London weekly, the *British-Australasian*, which recorded the comings and goings of Australians and New Zealanders and the activities of the more or less settled Anglo-Australasian community, as well as promoting the careers of musicians, writers and artists who were trying to establish themselves in Europe. These events were also related in the women's pages of the Australian press in their regular 'Australians in London' or 'Australians in Europe' columns.

The coming of the steamship to the Australia run in the 1850s, and the opening of the Suez Canal in 1869, with the subsequent reduction in the duration of the voyage from three months to little over one, opened up travel to the expanding ranks of wealthy colonists. It was for their custom that the shipping companies advertised and competed to fill the new large passenger liners. There were other reasons for the growing Australian presence in Europe, and particularly in London. The newly emerging intelligentsia of writers and artists travelled to the metropolis to hone their talents and receive recognition abroad. Colonial leaders felt the need to confer with, take instruction from and report to their imperial masters, and to participate in great Empire events like jubilees, coronations, and exhibitions such as that of the Colonies and India of 1886. Her father's appointment as a Victorian commissioner for this exhibition gave Helen Mitchell, the future Nellie Melba, her first taste of overseas travel.[4] Other colonists visited London as agents and lobbyists for the various colonies; Amie Livingstone realised her dream of going to Europe when her father was appointed as Victoria's mining representative in London.[5] And with the new speed and comfort in the mode of travel, both the sea voyage and the subsequent touring had become a form of recreation.

The structure of the Australian presence in Britain was varied. For many colonists, such as Mary Reibey, the visit home was a once-only event. Others journeyed backwards and forwards, turning up in England every, or every second, April. Emily Dobson, whose wealthy husband was premier of Tasmania from 1892 to 1894, appears to have made thirty-three trips to Europe in the late nineteenth and early twentieth centuries.[6] Other rich and successful Australians, such as the Wentworths, gravitated between Europe and Australia. Some settled permanently in Britain, or less frequently on the Continent; they might be immigrants who had never intended to remain in Australia, or people, either immigrant or native-born, whose economic and political interests led to domicile in the metropolis, or who, for one reason or another, did not get around to returning, or who found life more congenial in Europe.[7]

Intention and outcome did not always correlate — some of those who stayed had not planned to, others who settled in Europe eventually returned to Australia. New South Wales squatter Edward Ogilvie retired to Florence after his marriage to the daughter of the English chaplain, but the economic crisis of the 1890s brought him back to Australia.[8] He left his eight daughters behind, all but one of whom settled permanently in Britain.[9] Mabel, the daughter who returned, was the mother of Jessie Street, that doughty reformer who was among the best-known — and most widely travelled — women of her generation. The example of the Ogilvie family is a reminder of how Australian families continued to be divided between two worlds, that Martin Boyd's Anglo-Australian families lived beyond the pages of his novels.

The migration of Edward Ogilvie's seven daughters to Britain makes less surprising a set of statistics that has puzzled some historians. In 1911, the first year for which there is a record, the Australian-born present in England and Wales numbered 24000, of whom just under 60 per cent were women.[10] Accounting for this preponderance is part of the narrative of this and succeeding chapters. The story begins in the overseas journeys of the women of the élite and in travel to the centre as the acquisition of badges that proclaimed status, refinement and culture.

The work of historians such as Leonore Davidoff on Britain and Beverley Kingston on colonial Australia has emphasised the crucial role of women in the drawing and maintaining of status boundaries and social distances.[11] In a society like that of late-nineteenth-century Australia, where origins were tainted by the convict past, where a hereditary ruling class had not established itself, and where wealth was being newly and rapidly created, the maintenance of social distinctions as a tool of control depended very much on rigid rules and elaborate forms of social organisation and ceremony, on behaviour codes and patterns, on manners and dress, on style. And these were the province of women who had the responsibility for establishing the boundaries of and assessing claims to genteel status. Their role was that of 'beautifiers, civilisers, orderers'.[12] As Beverley Kingston expressed it, a man might rise by talent, make a fortune, buy his way to power and privilege, but unless or until his wife was accepted as a lady, they were excluded from élite social circles and social life, and thus the opportunities for their children to secure better social standing and good marriages were limited.[13] This was the lesson that Sarah Wentworth had learnt. But she also knew when she took her daughters overseas for their education that real ladies were made in Europe.

Real ladies not only acted at all times with breeding, refinement and decorum, they also displayed culture. This was understood as an ability to converse in a foreign language, to draw, play the piano and sing, to appreciate art and ruins. In nineteenth-century Australia, it was women, whether equipped or not, who were responsible for the preservation and transmission of the processes of traditional European cultural refinement. Stella Bowen recalled that in prewar Adelaide, the Australian brother was usually much less civilised than his sister, who had utilised her leisure to cultivate her person, manners, and sometimes even her mind.[14] In novels it is women who represent culture and men who represent the material, physical world. Thus in Rosa Praed's *Mrs Tregaskiss,* there is mutual incomprehension between Clare Tregaskiss, a 'keenly sensitive, emotional and intellectual woman' who had been educated in England, and her embattled squatter spouse, whose temperament contained a 'dense and stifling materialism'. When she speaks of ideals and imagination, he replies:

> 'I hate hearing you talk like that. It makes me think of those long-haired South Kensington painters and the ladies in queer dresses, with out-of-the-way notions that you used to tell me you were so sick of; ...
>
> 'Ideals', he went on wrathfully: 'poetry, sentiment — the sort of stuff you read in novels. Fine words and infernal tommy-rot, as I always said to you, dear. We don't breed 'em out West.'

'No; you laughed me out of my fancy that ideals might exist in the Bush.
That's one of the vanished illusions' …
'I have made you practical, my dear.'[15]

It was above all in Europe that culture was acquired. Refinement, good
taste and culture were the virtues of Europe — not only for Australians
and other colonials but also for North Americans, for all denizens of new
settler societies that lacked the patina of time and tradition and aristocra-
cies to show the way.

The first trips of the women of the élite were often those undertaken as
young girls for education, cultural and social finish. Lady Eliza Mitchell
recalled the experience in her memoirs, *Three Quarters of a Century*.[16] The
daughter of the headmaster of Scotch College in Melbourne who had
arrived from Scotland in 1857, she and her sister were taken to Europe in
1881 in the care of their aunt. Two months were spent in a ladies educational establishment in Neuchatel. The party then sojourned in
Switzerland before making a lengthy tour through Austria, Bavaria and
Italy. After a month in Rome, the return journey to London was made via
Paris. The sisters then visited the ancestral lands in Scotland before going
to Dresden for four months, a city 'swarming with English and
Americans', where they were occupied with music, German and china-
painting lessons as well as with a surfeit of concerts. In 1906 it was the
turn of Eliza Mitchell's own daughters.

> We had long had in mind the possibility of my taking our daughters abroad
> — not to finish, but in a sense to begin their education. My own early expe-
> riences had shown me the value of impressions made by foreign travel on
> receptive young minds …[17]

The 'Australians in Europe' newspaper columns leave the impression
that late-nineteenth- and early-twentieth-century Europe was swarming
with Australian girls filling in time with lessons in music, art, French,
German and Italian. The *British-Australasian* faithfully reported their
activities: during 1908, Mrs Marmion and her daughters of Western
Australia had returned from Dresden, where the girls had been studying
music; Mrs E. Russell and Miss Unie Russell were to settle in Paris for
some time to further Miss Russell's musical education; Miss Mabel and
Miss Kate Thynne were in London studying art; and the wife of Sir Rupert
Clarke had decided to live in England 'for the education of her daughters'.[18] It was not only the daughters of the established families like the
Clarkes and Russells who were being finished in Europe. They had been
joined by the daughters of the professional and business classes in search
of social position. The 'Australians in England' column in the *Sydney
Morning Herald* of 19 November 1904 noted that the railway commis-

sioner for New South Wales, Mr David Kirkcaldie, was leaving for Europe accompanied by Mrs and Miss Kirkcaldie. Miss Kirkcaldie was to reside in Paris for a year to study French and music. In *Myself When Young*, Henry Handel Richardson wrote of her mother's decision to remove her two daughters to Europe to study music.

> Yet, again, Mother may have hoped that a year's 'finishing abroad' would help to remove the disadvantage we laboured under as the daughters of an ex-postmistress. Otherwise, there seemed little chance of our getting in with the 'right people' even though we bore a double-barrelled name, with a carefully preserved hyphen. [19]

By the outbreak of the First World War, the more informal arrangements for the private education of daughters in various cities of Europe were being replaced by the more formalised stint at the finishing school. Maie Ryan (later Casey), after schooling in England, went to Paris for a year 'where Mme Chevalier in Neuilly had the assignment of polishing some twelve girls from England, America, Canada and Australia'.[20] Margaret Allen, a member of the Sydney legal family, was dispatched to a finishing school in a village near Paris in 1914.[21] She named six Sydney friends who were there at the same time. At 'Camoposenia', she learnt fencing and Dalcroze eurhythmics, as well as French, history and literature, and was taken on regular excursions to the opera and the Comédie Française. If culture brushes off, the girls were indeed in a fortunate situation. Their next-door neighbour was the sculptor Auguste Rodin: 'we would sometimes see the old man with his long white beard when we went for a walk'.

Maie Ryan's reference to the presence of Canadian and American girls at her finishing school is a reminder that it was not only Australian women who journeyed to Europe for genteel accomplishment. North American poet Natalie Barney, who was to be a prominent figure in the expatriate literary community on the Left Bank of Paris in the 1930s, was a student at a boarding school in France for a year before embarking upon a carefully chaperoned Grand Tour, which included some months in Germany where she studied the violin, fencing and dancing.[22]

Once daughters had been turned into European ladies, the next stage for the better connected, the more ambitious, and those whose home was as much Britain as Australia, was their launching into London society via presentation at Court. Emmeline Macarthur, who curtsied to Queen Victoria in 1853, thought that she was the first Australian woman to participate in this ritual of social recognition.[23] By the end of the century, as Mrs Warden remarked in Tasma's *Not Counting the Cost*, 'it is quite the thing to take one's girl home to be presented now', and the women's pages in the Australian press displayed endless photographs of women in their Court dress. Local etiquette books contained precise instructions for behaviour at Court. Dame Mabel Brookes who was presented at the age of seventeen to Edward VII is among those who have left descriptions of the event. Her father bought her mother a tiara for the occasion and the party went to the palace accompanied by coachmen and footmen. Facing 'the procession of feathered heads', the King looked 'supremely bored and fat'.[24]

The ultimate goal behind the finishing of daughters was the making of suitable marriages. Travel and education in Europe were a form of cultural capital, a dowry that women could bring to marriage. A short story by Mrs Richard Armstrong, published in the *Centennial Magazine* in the 1880s, places two young Australian sisters in Florence. One had just entered a period of long engagement with a brilliant but poor man trying to make his way at the Bar.

> Rosie had a great idea of making herself in some degree worthy of the brilliant man she had promised to marry, and welcomed the idea of foreign travel as an aid to such a development.[25]

Thus she was learning Italian, with the intention of reading Dante in the original. Barbara Baynton, when she moved to London on the death of her second husband, was 'intoxicated' by the idea of her daughter's making a good marriage.[26] To that end the twenty-year-old Penelope was sent to Paris to study ballet, and her behaviour was under constant maternal surveillance so that great propriety always prevailed. In the event it was the mother not the daughter who acquired the titled husband.

The necessity of maintaining the reputation and good fame of young women for the marriage market was part of the reason for their close chaperoning. Travel was sexual threat for women. Culture might lie in big cities, but so did moral danger. While Nancy Mitchell was in London with her father in 1914, a maid was engaged to accompany her on her public excursions.

> This was not quite as silly as it may sound. England was the in the grip of a panic about the White Slave Traffic and, as soon we landed, one of Father's old friends warned him that I should never go about alone.[27]

Margaret Allen, staying with her English aunts in London in 1913, was not allowed out alone, not even to the local shops in South Kensington: 'This was because of something called the white slave traffic. I had no idea what this was but was warned never to speak to kindly old ladies and nuns'.[28] Perhaps Sir Edward Mitchell and the aunts had heard the sad story reported in the *British-Australasian* in the previous year of the seventeen-year-old daughter from a well-known Victorian family who had been put in a taxi by her mother to go to her music lesson and had never been heard of or sighted again.[29] Katharine Susannah Prichard, however, did travel on her own to London in 1908. Not interested in marriage, she may have been less concerned about reputation. But she later recounted in her autobiography that 'it was disconcerting to discover that a young woman travelling alone, was not considered quite respectable, in those days'.[30] Her mother's concern for her daughter's welfare had been somewhat allayed when included in her luggage was a general letter of introduction from Alfred Deakin, which in the event did not save her from a nasty encounter in her shabby lodging house near Russell Square, but did secure her an interview with George Meredith. Dulcie Deamer's mother — perhaps more worldly or confronted with a far more rebellious daughter — quickly agreed to her daughter's marriage at seventeen so that Dulcie's picaresque romp around the world would be in the company of a husband, even if their travels were periodically interrupted to bring another baby home for mother to raise.[31]

In her *Australasians Who Count in London*, published in 1913, Mrs Leonard Matters noted that 'the accident of marriage had placed many of the women of Australasia in the inner circle of London's social world', and that their capacity to fulfil their obligations proved their adaptability.[32] A few Australian girls did make it into the ranks of the aristocracy. For example the Countess of Darnley, the former Miss Florence Rose Morphy who as a governess to the family of Lady Clarke met her husband while returning from a visit to England.[33] In 1921 Barbara Baynton secured a titled husband in the bankrupt fifth Baron Headley. Margaret Chisholm was probably unique among Australian women in acquiring three titled husbands: Lord Loughborough, whom she married in Cairo in 1915 and divorced in 1926; Sir John Charles Peniston Milbanke, 11th baronet of Halnaby, Yorkshire; and after his death, Dimitri Alexandrovitch Romanoff, who gave his occupation on the marriage certificate as 'Russian prince'.[34] Usually, Australian girls had to make do with younger sons or officers in the army and navy. American heiresses captured the best marriage prizes.[35] Indeed, the marital success of American women relative to those from the colonies was the subject of an article of lament by the anonymous 'Colonial' in the *Contemporary Review* in June 1905. Between 1840 and 1900, 33 peers or eldest sons of peers had married Americans; those who had taken brides from the colonies numbered 23.[36] This trend was far from an advantage to the aristocracy. What 'Colonial' was also anxious to show was that the American women were less fecund, producing fewer children per marriage than the wives from the colonies. Anglo-American marriages were the effect of plutocratic social ambition, Anglo-Colonial of Imperial unity — the influence of the former being feminine, frivolous, and fleeting, of the latter, masculine, vigorous and wholesome.

The number of Australian women who married and subsequently settled in Britain provides part of the explanation as to why there were more Australian-born women than men listed as present in England and Wales in 1911. And, as Margaret Chisholm's union with a member of the Russian royal family indicates, Britain was not the outer perimeter of the marriage field. There were also husbands to be found in Europe, where titles were in fact more plentiful. But Molly Fink went too far when she became the bride of the raja of the southern Indian principality of Pudukkottai in 1915. Having fallen foul of Australian and local Indian society, as well as Imperial interests in Delhi and London, Molly and her raja were forced into exile. They settled in Cannes in 1922 where, first as a wife and then after 1928 as a widow, Molly moved in Paquin, Patou and Chanel originals among the smart and famous of café society.[37]

The agendas of the women who married in Europe may not have been restricted to social ambition. For those for whom the voyage to Europe was intended as escape or flight, marriage was a sanctioned means of remaining abroad. If first-hand exposure to European culture was the experience of more young women than men, then the option of an English husband may have seemed more attractive than attachment to a local boy of less refinement, as was the fate of Clare Gardyne after her marriage to Keith Tregaskiss in Rosa Praed's *Mrs Tregaskiss*. Beverley Kingston's question of the role of dissatisfaction with the availability and quality of Australian men is one that recurs in any consideration of Australian women and travel.[38] In some cases there may have been problems in marriages where wives were more travelled than husbands, but in other cases the polish may have been lightly acquired and worn. Mary Turner Shaw told of her two sisters, who were 'finished' in Paris in the first decade of this century. Both came home to marry Victorian squatters and become exemplary wives and mothers — 'and neither was ever again required to speak a word of French, attend a concert or visit a picture gallery'.[39] And they may not have cared; European 'finish' may have been no more for them than a necessary ritual of time and class.

If Australian girls could go to London to find suitable husbands, a long trip abroad could also provide the means to end unsuitable relationships or to test the depth of feelings. Thus, when seventeen-year-old Mabel Emmerton became engaged to Norman Brookes, her father took her to England to see how definitely her mind was made up,[40] and Amy Lewis's mother sent her to England 'to make sure' that she really wanted to marry her future husband: 'she thought distance would help me clarify my thoughts'.[41] Long voyages and fresh fields were also a conventional cure for broken hearts. Writer Ruth Bedford went to London in 1912 after her mother died and her engagement was broken.[42] And how many real-life counterparts were there to Rosa Praed's Christina Chard, who fled to Europe after her bogus marriage and seduction resulted in pregnancy?[43] There may well have been remittance women in Europe as well as remittance men in Australia. Travel abroad could also provide a means to escape bad marriages, either permanently or temporarily. An anonymous diary of a voyage from Melbourne to London in 1861 recorded the story of a woman who embarked with her children to escape the ill treatment of her husband. When he came on board to prevent her departure, he had to be tied up and forcibly put ashore.[44] The need to supervise the education of children and to chaperone daughters abroad may have been a necessary duty in Mary Stawell's case, but for other women it may have been a welcome relief. In 1987 Barbara Cullen recalled the trip to Europe she had made at the age of seventeen with her mother. When asked whether there was any question of her father accompanying them, she replied: 'No. No, he had his own holidays'.[45]

While mother-and-daughter travel was one form of the overseas trip, much of women's travel was as companions to and dependants of men. Not all women adjusted to their role of travelling companions, the more so when it separated them from their children. It was her husband's wish and need for a voyage of rest and recuperation that forced Ada Weigall to part from her children: 'after my husband and I had been ten years married he took a sorely-needed rest for a year, and I, with a heart torn in two, left my three children in good hands, and went with him to England'.[46] Pattie Deakin, accompanying her husband Alfred to the Imperial Conference in London in 1907, suffered from homesickness and loneliness and took little pleasure in her life in London as the consort of the Australian prime minister.

> Callers, messengers and interviewers keep coming all day. Motor waiting, off we go to luncheon, then to a reception, then a tea, home, dress for dinner, motor again to a reception and drop into bed in tears overtired and feeling it quite impossible to do the list of the next day's engagements.
>
> My nerves are quite gone — I can sit and weep at any moment so you can imagine how this pace has told on my strength. As for father... He scarcely ever says one word to me — writing or seeing men all the time we are together... I long and long for someone to befriend and love me.[47]

Thirty years later, Jessie Mitchell, travelling to look after her husband on a business trip, wrote home that 'I am looking very thin and miserable and don't feel too wonderful'. She was looking forward to a '*good holiday*' when she came home.[48]

Abroad the colonial élites could share in the lifestyle of their British counterparts, with whom they often had ties of family and business. They bought or leased grand country houses and mansions in London and made leisurely progresses around the counties as guests on the estates of their friends and relatives. The *Sydney Morning Herald* in one of its 'Australians in London' columns in 1905 noted that Mrs Pat Osborne of Victoria had taken a country house in Warwickshire, where her daughters were enjoying the hunting and the hunt balls.[49] The women's page in the *British-Australasian* gave advice on what clothing to take when invited to a country estate for the weekend — tweed skirts for rough walking with the guns, different outfits for golf, tennis, church, tea gowns 'to slip on for tea and bridge between the time of coming in from the shooting to the hour of dressing for dinner', evening gowns including a special one for Sunday. To the weekend grip should also be added the right shoes for all occasions, and gloves and handkerchiefs on which no expense should be spared — the whole effect could be ruined by the production of a handkerchief that had lost its freshness or was made of coarse linen.[50]

In London, well-connected women followed the events of the season. Ena Lilley published an account of her 1901 trip with her husband, the son of Queensland barrister Sir Charles Lilley, in the form of letters and with the title *A 'Possum Abroad,* which left no doubt as to its provenance. In the space of a couple of weeks in June, she went to the Royal Tournament and the Grand National Bazaar 'where all the wealth, beauty, rank and art of England were represented', to Ascot for two days, to a garden party hosted by Lord and Lady Jersey, to several operas at Covent Garden where the divas included Nellie Melba, to a *conversazione* held by the Royal Society of Architects at the Guildhall, to receptions at the Museum of Natural History hosted by the Royal Geographical Society and by the Society of Arts, to a matinee performance of Charles Dickens's *Tale of Two Cities*, to a supper at the Savoy, and to a Handel festival at the Crystal Palace.[51] Lord Strathcona, who had been one of Ena Lilley's hosts, was a Canadian railways millionaire; the world in which she was moving was Imperial rather than English, a London that was the heart of the Empire rather than the capital of Great Britain.

Travelling Australians followed fashionable routes on the Continent; visits to the German spas, tours of the art capitals of Italy. Christmas and New Year in Switzerland for skating and skiing was a common ritual, so much so that a heading in the *British-Australasian* in 1913 proclaimed that 'San Moritz is full of Australians this year'.

> After spending Christmas in Paris, Mr and Mrs Hugh R. Denison and their three sons went on to the winter sports at Kloster, Switzerland. At the Grand Hotel there they found quite an Australian party, consisting of Dr and Mrs W. Chisholm, and their son and daughter, Sir Edward and Lady Samuel, and their son and daughter, Miss Cropper, Miss MacCormick, and two Master MacCormicks, and Mr and Miss Foster Rutledge, all of Sydney.[52]

Barbara Baynton spent some time at the fashionable resort of Grindelwald, where her frienship with Lord and Lady Kinnaird developed.[53] And the ritual continued well into the twentieth century; in the 1920s Patrick White's family joined such friends as the T.H. Kellys in Switzerland for the Yuletide.[54]

The Mediterranean was also an Australian playground. The actor Essie Jenyns, after her marriage in 1888 to John Robert Wood, son of a wealthy brewer, and her subsequent retirement from the stage, sailed the Mediterranean and Aegean seas with her husband for five years aboard their yacht, *Imogen*. Luxurious in every way, *Imogen* carried an eighteen-member crew, as well as two cooks and four stewards to attend to the needs of the Woods and their guests.[55] Equally splendid was Mabel Brookes's life in Cannes with her tennis-champion husband, Norman Brookes. Serious tennis had been taken up by the international aristocracy and thus she socialised with the Kings of Portugal and Sweden, the Dukes of Westminster and Marlborough, the Grand Duke Michael of Russia, American millionaires, and figures from the *demi-monde*.[56] Although confident in her jewels, she was at first self-conscious about her colonial status and wardrobe, but came to enjoy being the wife of a Wimbledon champion and advising the Duchess of Westminster on dress.[57]

Not all of the Australian women who were finished and polished in Europe gained entry into English society, nor did they all want to. Among those who aspired but failed were sisters Fanny and Janey Rowe, whose richly informative letters have been recently edited by Teresa Pagliaro.[58] John Rowe, a wealthy Victorian medical practitioner turned squatter and businessman, took his wife and four unmarried children to Europe in 1873. The son and youngest daughter were placed in English Catholic schools, and his two older daughters first spent a month in Rome, where they were tutored in Italian and singing, and assiduously visited the galleries and monuments.

> Papa has given us a beautiful book, 'Hare's Walks in Rome' — We take it everywhere with us, and it teaches us much — We are trying all we know to improve ourselves — as we have wasted so much time — Papa has been very good — he has engaged the best singing master in Rome and also a lady to teach us.[59]

From Rome the girls went to London on their pilgrimage of self-improvement. Despite the fact that their maternal grandparents had been convicts, they saw themselves as belonging to the best society in Melbourne. But they made little headway in London. Their father's relatives were a disappointment — modest business people in Liverpool, not part of 'refined society'. From their perception of their own importance and from their notions of upper-class English life, derived from magazines like the *Illustrated London News*, the Rowe sisters had very romantic expectations of the lives that they would lead in London. But they were disappointed. As their mother wrote home: 'you must not imagine from this that we have made many friends here, the girls are greatly disappointed in this respect & they have never been to a Ball'.[60] Not having been welcomed into smart society, the girls were upset: 'I do not like English people a little bit, of course I have not met many as yet but I am sure they are all alike so fearfully narrow-minded'.[61] So, much as the sisters enjoyed London and found it more interesting than Victoria, they felt lonely and outcast.

> I would like to return to Australia about this time next year — I do not think I would like to live here, but it is not fair to judge as we are such perfect strangers in the land, and no one likes that feeling of perfect loneliness however delightful the country may be — I am sure for people who have friends it must be too charming — I do not know how they can bear to live in Australia, but, for us it is not such a Paradise.[62]

The Rowe sisters were critical of English ladies who did not conform to their ideas of fashion and smartness, but, as Teresa Pagliaro points out, they were unable to read English codes.[63] And they avoided acknowledging — at least aloud — that the fault might lie in themselves. In this respect, they were unusual, since the descriptions that women in England give of their travels often reflect status anxiety and consciousness that as colonials they were regarded as inferior. Particularly sensitive was the issue of 'the accent'. When Stella Bowen arrived in London she took elocution lessons, and she was but one of many Australians who over the generations attempted to eliminate their native accent so that they could move more easily among the English upper and middle classes. Their loss of voice was certainly a product of colonial structures and attitudes, but they were not alone. Until the 1970s, Britons with regional, provincial or lower-class accents usually found it necessary to discard their voices if they wished to make their way in the world.

The Australian accent was not a problem for the women who belonged to the élite, such as the Mitchell sisters and Mabel Brookes, whose father had taken her out of kindergarten because he thought she was developing a bad accent. These women had spoken southern English from birth, and when in England they took offence when told that they did not sound like Australians — all their Australian friends spoke as they did.[64] According to Ethel Kelly, the 'twang' was no more heard in polite society in Sydney than was broad Cornish or Cockney in the salons of Mayfair.[65] A generation later, Allison Howorth ridiculed the assumption that all Australians spoke with the accent.[66] At work in the attitudes of these women are issues of class as much as national identity, and of course there was and is more than one way of being Australian, more than one Australian identity. Anglo-Australians, Austral-Britons, women who spoke with 'proper' English accents, did not deny that they were Australian. Although she dined and wined with aristocracy on her frequent trips to Europe, in her novels Mabel Brookes criticised English presumptions to superiority: 'It is a great mistake to imagine that the average colonial cannot appreciate the refinements of life. That is a typical English error'.[67]

Status anxiety and resentment of British attitudes of superiority towards colonials were sufficiently widespread to provide a major theme in late-nineteenth-century novels that placed young Australian women in Britain. When she arrives, the colonial girl is expected to be coarse and unrefined, and is presumed to be inferior. Thus, for example, Lady Isherwood says of her niece Esther Haggert in Rosa Praed's *An Australian Heroine*: 'She was a perfect barbarian when she came to England, and we have gone to great expense in having her educated and in making her presentable'.[68]

The norm in the novels is to make a spirited defence of the young Australian woman and to mock and subvert British attitudes of superiority. When Kitty, the protagonist of Ada Cambridge's 1879 novel, *In Two Years' Time*, arrives from Australia via Paris, where she has been outfitted with the aid of her mother's natural taste, her English cousins are amazed:

> But she doesn't look the least colonial, uncle, that is what surprises us so much. Mamma says she cannot understand it. We thought she'd be — well, a little shy and awkward — and a little uncomfortable in society — that sort of thing.[69]

Winifred James's heroine in *Bachelor Betty* notes that the English were rather disappointed in her because she did not 'stroll down Piccadilly cracking a stockwhip and shouting "Coo-ee" light heartedly and cheerily' nor attempt to boil her billy in Hyde Park.[70] Sophie Osmond poked fun at English pretentiousness in *An Australian Wooing* when Nora Diss, confronted with a plate of small eggs that she has no idea how to eat, announces that since there are no chopsticks, which she would use to eat such delicacies at home, she will use her fingers; the other guests follow suit.[71]

In the novels the natural charm of the Australian heroines often wins them a place in London society. Ada Cambridge's Kitty became 'a star of the first magnitude' in her London season, and Rosa Praed's Christina Chard takes London by storm.[72] Some also win the affections of and marriage proposals from Englishmen, including titled nobles, as in *An Australian Wooing* and *In Two Years' Time*. But in both cases the aristocrats are rejected in favour of wholesome colonial boys.

The Australian girls are often presented as superior to their English sisters, possessing not only a natural, unaffected charm, but an independence and initiative born of an education that had not aimed at reducing them to helpless and useless idleness. Cambridge's Kitty finds her English cousins 'very silly', and Lottie Boldero, in Ethel Karr's *The Australian Guest*, remarks: 'I have heard of English girls' lives. They sit at home all day and do crochet and think of lovers'.[73] In Alice Rosman's *Miss Bryde of England*, the Australian Katherine liberates her genteel, but useless, English cousin from the tyrannical rule of her father and teaches her to make her own way. The defence of Australian women in the novels is linked to a debate about the future of the British race in a new world blessed — or cursed — with a Mediterranean climate, and about 'The Coming Man' and 'The Coming Woman', the emerging Australian national 'type'.[74]

There is obviously some dissonance between the fictional triumphs of the Australian girl and her colonial virtues in London and the real-life dispatch of the daughters of the élite to England to have the colonial tarnish removed. The much touted triumphs in fiction may themselves be compensatory for the sense of inferiority that Australian women felt or were made to feel in England.

Whatever their status in Europe, when they returned home the women enjoyed positions of superiority. Travel to Europe *per se* conferred status and social power. The very ability to engage in the trip indicated both wealth and leisure. Knowledge of distant places, of the foreign, of the exotic has always been a means to and a sign of power.[75] In the remoter past, travel was the only means to acquire such knowledge, but even in the age of cable and wireless, journalists in Australia went out in launches to meet incoming ships to interview passengers for the latest news. The local press was filled with the opinions of returning travellers, whose only claim to knowledge was having 'actually' been there. Mrs Alphen, who was interviewed by the *Sydney Morning Herald* in August 1914, had relevant knowledge. She had been in the Rhineland in the previous year.

> 'It is hard to believe that the beautiful places which we then saw are to-day in a state of war and misery', said Mrs Alphen, who, when met with, was busily clicking her needles on a sock for a soldier, as five out of every six are doing at present...
>
> We liked the people; they were very civil, though not excessively friendly. It was to their own interest to be polite to the English, for the great majority of the tourists to that part are English and American.[76]

Mrs Alphen's views are banal; they were privileged because they were first-hand.

The special knowledge that travel could give women was that on taste and fashion, what music was being played at soirées in London, what hats were being worn in Paris. Frances Maguire wrote of returning from London in 1910 and displaying the latest fashions to her astonished and admiring sisters.[77] In 1890 the *Bulletin* informed its readers that Mrs Alick Osborne of Moss Vale, who had just returned from the Continent, intended to have the floors of her residence taken up and Swiss tiles laid down; 'Swiss tiles are the latest craze "at home"'.[78] Young women finished in Europe had an authority denied to and envied by those whose world was restricted to the colonies. In Louise Mack's novel, *Girls Together*, Lennie's friend Mabel returns to Sydney after two years in Paris with a new style, a new formality, and a new accent. Lennie attributes the change to travel: 'Yes, in books, girls always come back from abroad with a cultured manner, and that's what happened to you'.[79] Evoking her early life in Adelaide in the first decade of this century, Stella Bowen wrote of the return of a friend from Europe who was possessed of a wardrobe from London and 'lots of polish', and who was willing to instruct the as yet untravelled Stella 'in the better conduct of my life'.[80] Travellers' speech was privileged speech. This point was made explicitly by Lady Doughty, the Australian wife of an English baronet, in a talk she gave to the Imperial Colonial Club in 1908. She argued that as an Australian woman who had lived abroad, she was more qualified to speak on the subject than an Australian 'who had never travelled beyond the boundaries to obtain any standard of comparison for valuable criticism'.[81]

Travellers returned with more than first-hand knowledge. Travel involves consumption, not only of sites, but also of goods. Like foreign knowledge, objects from distant places have always carried high value precisely because of their exotic origins and their role as tangible evidence of foreign experience, and hence as visible symbols of power and status. The wealthy nineteenth-century colonists went on buying sprees in Europe and weighed down first ships and then their mansions with the proof of their travels and taste — furniture, paintings, tableware, *objets d'art*, portraits of themselves.[82] When the Wentworths decided to return to Australia, Sarah made trips to Paris to order wallpaper and to Germany to buy furniture for Vaucluse House. Twenty-five cases of furniture weighing almost 40 tonnes were dispatched from Hamburg at the end of 1859.[83] On their trip to Europe in 1883, Edward and Edith Knox spent some £4000 on goods, packing, freight and insurance.[84] The *British-Australasian* in 1905 announced to potential advertisers that when Australians arrived in London , they wanted many things — 'the best of jewellery and clothes — the ladies the best of English models in costumes and of French models in millinery'.[85]

Much of the established pattern of travel by women of wealthy background and social standing, or aspirations to such, continued into the mid-twentieth century. The women's pages devoted as much space to arrivals and departures in the 1920s or the 1960s as they had done at the beginning of the century. Young Australian women continued to be sent to finishing schools in Europe until well into the 1970s, and were presented at Court until the ceremony was abolished in 1958. Margaret Allen, who had been taken to finishing school in Paris in 1913, and who settled in England in the 1940s after her marriage to an aide-de-camp to the governor of New South Wales and heir to a baronetcy, provides an example of postwar life among the travelling upper class.[86] In 1920, at the age of 25, she went on a trip to India with her brother, where their hosts included an uncle who was a judge for the Calcutta Turf Club and an old friend who was married to the military secretary to the viceroy in New Delhi. Travelling again in 1924 and 1926, Margaret Allen visited eastern Europe as a guest of cousins who were first secretaries in the British Embassies, one in Constantinople and one in Vienna, of another cousin whose husband worked with a British company in Bucharest, and of an infinite number of friends and relatives in Britain. In 1928 she travelled to Honolulu with Nellie Melba. Two years later, she was in Europe again, staying with yet more cousins who had an apartment in the centre of Florence, before making a tour of Yugoslavia and Albania, where she noticed 'that there appeared to be no "gentry" at all'. Margaret Allen also engaged in the new mode of travel when in the early 1920s she flew from Skopje to Zagreb to catch the Orient Express to Paris.

The speech of the returned travellers continued to be both privileged and authoritative. In 1922 the painter Thea Proctor, who had just returned from a seven-year sojourn in Europe, informed the readers of the *Home* that 'Australians must Develop Taste' — which included wearing their hats level with the brows, as was done in Paris and London, painting their houses Mediterranean colours, and doing something about 'the carelessness of their speech'.[87] And the returning travellers still brought back their trophies, which marked them apart — as more sophisticated, up-to-date. Radio actor Hazel Hollander made her first overseas trip just before her seventeenth birthday, which, in her later recollection, she did not enjoy.

> And we travelled around a lot and it wasn't usual and being the age I was, I wasn't considered adult enough to do the adult things and I didn't have anybody of my own age there at all and I didn't enjoy it, not a bit.[88]

But when she returned home she felt that she 'was terribly grown up, terribly sophisticated' and did not want to mix with people of her own age, whom she found 'terribly young and terribly unsophisticated'. She came back with shingled hair, when 'nobody else had a shingle here. Nobody could cut shingles then.' And her clothes were different.

> I had quite beautiful evening frocks that were made for me in Paris and they were very rich sort of colours and I think that girls were still wearing pink and blues and taffetas and things and these weren't. These might have been with lurex threads through them and brocaded sort of things and a black velvet slinky dress, they were short then, that girls of my age didn't wear at all.

The finishing education that members of the upper and middle classes bought for their daughters in Europe involved accomplishment, preparation for good marriages and life among 'the best people'; it was certainly not intended as the kind of professional education or preparation for careers that their brothers were receiving at public schools, Oxford and Cambridge, the medical school in Edinburgh, and the Inns of Court. Lady Mitchell, in discussing her own education in Europe and the trips that she made for the education of her daughters, made it clear that accomplishment was the purpose.

> I tried to give the family the same kind of education that I had had myself in Dresden, for though I wanted them to get a good enough working knowledge of German to enable them to read and understand the language, and to converse intelligibly with people they met, I did not want them to have so many lessons as to prevent their hearing good music and seeing good plays and operas.[89]

Nancy, the second of her daughters, who attended classes at the famous Julian art studio in Paris, had no doubt that she was engaged in amateur accomplishment, 'no illusions as to my capacity as an artist'.[90] Janet, the youngest Mitchell daughter, had more professional aspirations. She wanted to train seriously for a music career, but did not believe that she would be allowed to do so.

> It was so entirely at variance with the whole tradition of our home, with my father's desire for us, that any of us should have a career. In the pre-war days, before the old values were shattered, it was the usual attitude of his generation, especially in Australia.[91]

Janet Mitchell's experience was usual for her class and time. When Edward Ogilvie was told by his daughter Mabel's singing teacher in Florence that her voice was so good she should be trained as an opera singer, he stopped her lessons at once.[92] Stella Bowen was anxious to study painting with Rose McPherson (Margaret Preston) when she left school in Adelaide in the first decade of this century but her mother only agreed to the cultivation of her daughter's talent if it was in moderation and attendance at classes was confined to two days a week.[93] Future feminist activist Ruby Rich studied piano with Artur Schnabel in Berlin in the first decade of this century; she wanted to become a concert pianist, but her father thought that it was more important for her to make a good marriage, and that earning money through music was degrading and reflected on his ability to keep his daughters.[94]

In Tasma's 1892 novel, *A Knight of the White Feather*, the boundary for cultivated women is clearly drawn. The protagonist, Linda Robley, was educated in Paris, but the Paris that she brought back to Australia was not the city of 'boulevard bonnets and Worth's dresses' but that of intellectuals and artists. Her education had included the doctrines of Positivism, absorbed at the feet of Auguste Comte himself. When Linda proposes to give lectures on Positivism, her admirer Jack expostulates:

Then, I admit, for the first time, I disliked Miss Linda. I could stand her
painting, and sketching, and playing, and singing, and talking all the modern languages, but the idea of a young girl standing up before a lot of people
to teach them an atheistical belief — for, after all, Positivism's nothing else
— having the face to do it, somehow I didn't like it all.[95]

By the 1890s, Linda Robleys enough existed beyond the pages of fiction. Her creator, Jessie Couvreur, had delivered widely acclaimed public
lectures in Paris and Brussels, admittedly on Australia rather than on
Positivism, but the subjects of the articles she sent back from Paris to the
Australasian in the 1880s included not only Positivism, but Communism,
experiments in collectivist living, and the radical issues of the day.[96] Linda
Robleys had also emerged in the bosom of the Mitchell family when Janet,
after having studied music at a professional level, enrolled in 1919 at
Bedford College, University of London, to read for a degree in literature
and philosophy.

By the time Janet Mitchell undertook her professional training, Linda
Robleys had for some four decades been travelling to Europe alongside
those women whose journeys were undertaken in compliance with the
agendas of patriarchy and class. Their goals were not amateur accomplishment, but professional training and the acquisition of qualifications
and reputation as the means to a self-supporting life. Women were travelling not only as wives, mothers and daughters, but as independent single
women seeking self-fulfilment and social roles beyond those of dependent wife or degraded spinster. The areas they first chose as the means to
professional life and travel were those of traditional accomplishment and
sanctioned travel patterns — music, art, writing, teaching. These new
forms of women's travel were prefigured in the 1850s by Adelaide
Ironside, the first Australian of either gender to study art in Europe.

Interlude

Adelaide Ironside

Squatter's daughter Grace Black dabbled in art, music and the Italian language in Rome in 1852 as part of her finishing as a genteel lady whose accomplishment and refinement would attest to her future husband's status. Four years later, another young Australian woman arrived in Rome to study painting, but her agenda was very different from that of Grace Black or from that of any other colonial woman who had hitherto gone to Europe. Adelaide Ironside's goal was to establish herself as a professional and acknowledged artist.[1] What is significant in the 23-year-old Ironside's departure with her mother for Europe in June 1855 is not so much her position as the first Australian artist to study abroad, but her gender; she was a woman bent on achieving the highest professional status and winning fame. While unique as an Australian, in Rome she worked alongside a small number of exceptional North American and British women painters and sculptors — Henry James's 'white marmoreal flock' — who were claiming the right to cultivate their talents to the fullest extent.[2]

Adelaide Ironside never returned to Australia. Her declared intention when she left was to spend ten years abroad perfecting her painting and establishing her reputation, and then to place her talents at the service of her native land, for which she always demonstrated deep attachment. The intention was never put to the test — Ironside died in Rome of consumption in 1867. But there were good reasons why she might not have carried out her original intention, even if she had lived longer.

Born in Sydney in 1831, Adelaide Ironside included among her grandparents a convict woman transported for forgery and the chief gaoler of the colony. A brilliantly gifted girl of considerable scholarship, who was a poet as well as a painter, Ironside was taken up by Sydney's literati, both radical and conservative; her patrons and supporters included writer Daniel Deniehy, that republican, popery-hating parson, John Dunmore Lang, and the first chancellor of the University of Sydney, Charles Nicholson.

When Ironside decided that she must go to Europe, Rome was her goal: 'You all know that when I left Australia, my sole destination was to Rome. My soul is there and to Rome I must go!'[3] Her choice of Rome is not surprising. The facilities for art training did not exist in mid-nineteenth-century Sydney, and Rome, yet to be overtaken by Paris, was still considered the art centre of Europe. Expatriate artists from all over Europe and from North America clustered in the streets and squares of the area between the Piazza del Popolo and the Spanish Steps, a noisy *tableau vivant* of models and beggars.

Rome was well known in the colony's cultivated circles for its classical associations, for the artefacts of the Renaissance, for its role in English Romantic and early Victorian literature, and for the contemporary struggle for independence.[4] In Sydney in the radical political circles of Deniehy, Lang and the *People's Advocate*, Adelaide Ironside had thrown her lot in with the Italian patriots and the 1848 revolution, Elizabeth Barrett Browning and the *Casa Guidi Windows*, and linked the causes of Independence for both Italy and the Golden Lands of Australia.

> I had been reading that soul-larging book,
> The Casa Guidi Windows all the day-light
> And had laid down the poem with the cry of,
> O my God our Country save from Italy's
> Political pollution and her woes![5]

Before leaving Sydney, she sketched a likeness of Risorgimento hero Alessandro Gavazzi, doubly blessed in Sydney's Pope-hating circles as a patriot and a renegade priest. In London, she met Gavazzi:

> My heart is too full to tell you all that I think of the noble, generous, courtier-like and graceful Ideal of my Soul's early dreams, of everything magnanimous and heroically noble, kind, gentle, warmhearted, he is indeed worthy of being the Ideall of Italy.[6]

After spending six months in London, Ironside and her mother arrived by ship at Rome's rather seedy port of Civitavecchia in January 1856, and made the 30-kilometre journey to Rome by carriage, entering the Eternal City through the Porta del Popolo. At that time Rome was a city of less than 200 000 inhabitants, still ruled by the Pope in the wake of the failure of the 1848–49 revolutionary bid for independence. Ironside's compatriot Edward Ogilvie, who was in Rome in 1853, found the city depressed and discontented, in dread of espionage and arbitrary authority, '*triste* and gloomy'.[7] Adelaide Ironside journeying to a place of imagination was somewhat more enthusiastic on her arrival.

> Italy, my dreams, is the soul's home of the Poet, the Artist and the Seer... In my enthusiasm I kissed the dust of Italy, where in the night-time we landed; I could not believe it possible, and 'Is this indeed Italy'![8]

On arrival, the Ironsides settled into rooms in the Via delle Quattro Fontane in the expatriate quarter, and Adelaide began her 'siege and battle'. Her taste was for biblical subjects, paintings in a style that looked to the

Nazarenes and Pre-Raphaelites and back to Italian Quattrocento frescoes. In 1858 she journeyed to Perugia to study fresco painting, and in 1861 to Florence to work with the frescoes of Fra Angelico in Savonarola's convent of San Marco. Permission for her entry into San Marco had been given by the Pope when he received her in audience in 1861. Her republican and Protestant sympathies did not restrain her admiration for Pio Nono or prevent her from telling him that she regarded him 'as a romantic Pope'.[9]

In Rome, Adelaide Ironside slowly established her professional status. She received commissions for portraits, and her sitters included members of the families of the colonial élite who visited her studio. In the winter of 1859 she received a very elevated visitor when the Rome-based Welsh sculptor, John Gibson, brought the Prince of Wales to her studio. The Australian painter informed the Prince's equerry that the honour was to her country as well as to herself. The Prince reputedly paid £500 for one of her paintings.[10] International recognition came with the hanging of four of her oil paintings in the Great Exhibition in London in 1862, including the large painting, *The Marriage at Canae*, which attracted favourable attention from the British art establishment. Another painting, *Saint Catherine of Alessandria as Patroness of Philosophy*, was reputed by Amelia Pemell, who had known Ironside in Sydney, to have won a gold medal. Amelia had first seen this painting on exhibition in Rome and it was bought by her father in London in 1862. Further prestige came in the next year when Ironside was admitted to the Roman *Accademia dei Quiriti*. She was delighted, and informed Lang that the fellows of the Academy numbered 'the most distinguished of the artists, sculptors and scientific men in the world'.[11] American sculptor Harriet Hosmer had been equally proud when she had been made a member four years earlier; she saw the honour as a rebuff to 'those who laughed at the idea of a woman becoming an artist at all'.[12] In 1864, Adelaide Ironside was invited to place a work in the annual exhibition of the Academy.

Mother and daughter returned to Rome after the Great Exhibition, but Ironside was already being consumed by tuberculosis. The extent of her illness was of great concern to all who met her when she again visited England in 1865–66, including the Wentworth family with whom she stayed for a time.[13] Indeed, she returned to Rome, where she had been so happy, to die. To John Dunmore Lang she wrote in 1859:

> We have now been four years in Italy ... I am quite happy here; as regards my beautiful Italia, in this classic land I have food in the spiritually artistic; with the real Old Masters, the grand prophet-poets of the past, my soul's soul unburdens itself.[14]

This was an Italy of the imagination, and when Ironside contemplated the present, she also looked at a romanticised land. Her early enthusiasm for the Italian patriots did not wane. Describing Garibaldi's abortive approach on Rome in 1860, she wrote to Lang: 'come what may, I shall go on with my Art, and cry "Viva Garibaldi" with the Republicans'.[15] And when she came to depict the face of the bridegroom in *The Marriage at Canae*, Garibaldi was the model, although she had never seen the romantic hero — twenty miles away was as close as he came to Rome in 1860.

Rome's foreign artists had by the mid-nineteenth century developed a ritualised social life. They were to be found at the Café Greco at the foot of the Spanish Steps, at the colourful evening parade of *tout le monde* on the Pincio, at dinners and musical evenings in the salons of the wealthier expatriates such as Adelaide Sartori, sister of the actor Fanny Kemble, where the Brownings and Thackerays might be found at table.[16] These meetings of compatriots were no doubt a means to solace, comfort and help in a foreign world. Adelaide Ironside had no compatriots beyond the birds of passage, and she was in all probability the only Australian living in Rome. She had arrived there furnished with introductions from the colonial networks in London and she certainly moved on the fringes of the Anglo-American world, whose leading figures included Robert Browning, Joseph Severn, painter and British Consul in Rome, John Gibson and Harriet Hosmer. In these circles, Adelaide Ironside also had some reputation as a spiritualist and medium. It may have been while she was taking lessons with John Gibson that she met Hosmer, whose life in some ways had parallels with her own. Gibson, of whom Macaulay wrote with Victorian delicacy that 'the mightiest of all instincts seems barely to have awakened from its repose', attracted the devotion of young women.[17] Although Ironside is not mentioned in any biography of Hosmer — a neglect perhaps due as much to her Australian provenance as to her lack of importance — the little surviving correspondence suggests social contacts between the two, as well as friendly rivalry for Gibson's affection.

> My fair Foe,
> I am desired by our mutual friend to inform you that he has a very bad cold — caught I suppose while swimming up to see you — so for a few days he will be deprived of the pleasure of seeing your fair face, which is the only thing that reconciles him to his illness — but alas! he declares that as soon as he is able, he will make you a visit.[18]

Adelaide Ironside is represented in the writing of her male contemporaries as a child-woman, imaginative, excitable, enthusiastic, extravagant, passionate, somewhat unrestrained. Robert Browning wrote to Harriet Hosmer from Paris in 1856:

> Next tell me a matter: do you happen to know or to have seen a young lady with a mother to her called Ironmonger, an Australian bent on studying

painting in Rome, who made a memorable transit thro' this place at the end of last year; memorable, I mean, for her enthusiasm and wild ways? She had a letter for Mr Gibson, she said — how has it all turned out?[19]

She must have made some impression on Browning because two years later, he was again enquiring after her.[20] Her excitability is conveyed in the letters that John Ruskin wrote to her in avuncular, patronising tones while she was taking drawing lessons with him at Denmark Hill in 1865:

> I cannot separate the nonsense from the sense in you — you will gradually be able to do it for yourself, a very noble creature, if you will only take care of your health, and work quietly. You shall come if you like. I think it will be better; and if you're too fireworky I'll give you some ice-cream; but do be good and quiet — Or you'll kill yourself …[21]

The 'fireworky' recipient of the ice-cream was 34 years old. No doubt Ruskin's attitude in infantilising Ironside is linked to his own sexual tastes, but he was hardly treating her as a serious professional person. Harriet Hosmer faced similar problems and her riding cross-dressed and alone around Rome and the Campagna was also regarded as eccentric. If Ironside was a little girl to be humoured, Harriet Hosmer was represented in the guise of a young boy. But neither sexual scandal nor innuendo touched them; they were to all intents and purposes asexual, a stance that gained them respectability and hence tolerance.[22] The women's own presentation of themselves and the representations of them made by others, suggest elements of men infantilising, trivialising and asexualising the women to neutralise their positions as independent, self-sufficient professionals living their lives outside the parish in foreign places and in international worlds, and of women themselves adopting the protective clothing of the child who does not threaten and who is to be indulged. From the time of the women humanists in the Renaissance, sexuality and learning in women was a threatening combination and tolerated for the most part only in the prepubescent and postmenopausal. And the perceived eccentricity of the women may have been the product of the pressures and frustrations they encountered, of their straying from prescribed gender roles, or perhaps it simply required a degree of nonconformity and eccentricity to claim and act on the right to travel abroad in quest of the realisation and recognition of talent.

Adelaide Ironside may have had the febrile, emotional temperament of a very gifted girl brought up in a hothouse environment who was to become a consumptive. But she was also as time went on frustrated and bitter at the failure of Sydney to take her seriously. She always declared that she was honing her talents for the beautification of her native land, to adorn public buildings like the University of Sydney with huge fresco

cycles. In 1860 John Dunmore Lang tried to secure a government sub-
vention of £200 a year for three years to help finance her studies. His
motion was rejected in the Legislative Council. Ironside was bitter and
humiliated when she heard the news. To Lang she wrote that the 'time was
not far off, I trust, when they will see that I am not dependent on Australia
for my fame'.[23] When that happened, Australia must call for her; she
would never return to Australia until 'my fame is fully established in the
Old World and that will (D.V.) not be too long in coming'. Ironside, confident in her vocation and of her talent, felt that all her efforts and her reputation in Italy and England meant nothing back in the colony.

> Does it appear a small thing for a girl to have left a remote colony and to
> have battled with and won the spoils of warfare and the distinguished
> authorities of the first judges of art and artists in Europe?[24]

And it is legitimate to wonder whether, had she lived longer, she would
have remained in Europe where she was not an isolated artist and where
she was gaining some recognition, and become not only the first
Australian to study art abroad, but also Australia's first expatriate —
reluctantly expatriate — artist.

Ironside's bitter plaints about her lack of recognition may well be but a
variant on the age-old theme of prophets without honour in their own
country, which in Australia's case her expatriate intellectuals, artists, writers, musicians identified with home-grown philistinism and lack of culture.

> My country has everything gifted of Nature — wealth unbounded, climate
> and the flowing warmth of a Southern Sun. She is worthy of being the sec-
> ond Italy, all save Italy's appreciation and strong call from the heart for the
> Beautiful![25]

Given her exclusive dedication to her art and the persona she had developed, Adelaide Ironside may also have begun to feel that life was better
for her among artists in Rome than in Sydney. One of the artists in
Nathaniel Hawthorne's *Marble Faun* explains:

> Rome is not like one of our New England villages where we need the per-
> mission of each individual neighbour for every act that we do, every word
> that we utter, and every friend that we make or keep. In these particulars
> the papal despotism allows us to breathe freer than our native air.[26]

And Harriet Hosmer wrote from Rome: 'What country is mine for
women! Here every woman has a chance if she is bold enough to avail
herself of it'.[27] However, it was not so much Rome itself, but Rome as 'not
home'; the freedom was that of the outsider abroad. And if not Ironside,
then many of her successors, echoed Harriet Hosmer in her powerful
affirmation of one of the forces that lies beneath journeying — and espe-

cially that of the more confined gender at home. But there were also limits to women's freedom abroad; Harriet Hosmer's solo rides around the city came to an end when some of Rome's matrons complained.

The Australian painter was no less an independent and interesting personage than the American sculptor, but Harriet Hosmer had the advantage of a large and wealthy domestic market for her works. She had talented and famous compatriots who came to Rome and spread her fame in literary works for the same market. Adelaide Ironside, a lone colonial, was of no interest to Henry James or Nathaniel Hawthorne. She had no compatriots of her own of such reputation. It was not only her gender that relegated her to the margins, but also her place of origin. Obscure national origins were to continue to be a problem for Australian artists in Italy. Studying sculpture in Florence at the end of the 1880s, Theo Cowan felt that her provenance made life more difficult.

> Being an Australian, I was at once met with difficulties for I was without credentials. Every facility is afforded there for study but they allow no student admission without an introduction from a recognised school of art. Australia being unknown in that respect, I was expected to furnish English credentials.[28]

Adelaide Ironside was the harbinger of a new form of travel by women, but it was one that was not really to develop until almost three decades after her departure. In the year she died, the second Australian artist, again a woman, came to Italy. The 27-year-old sculptor Margaret Thomas spent almost three years in Rome, her arrival coinciding with that of her Melbourne teacher, Charles Summers, whose marble bust she was later to carve and whose life she was to write.[29] Margaret Thomas left no record of her time in Rome other than her short story, 'The Story of a Photograph', in which one of the protagonists is an Australian woman who journeys to Rome to make a name for herself and to be 'a credit to Victoria'.[30] Like Adelaide Ironside and so many of the women of her time and background, Margaret Thomas was not restricted to one vocation. She also painted and wrote poetry and guides to the appreciation of art and in her later life embarked on a career as a travel writer.

Italy, with its marble quarries and artisan traditions, was a natural place of work and study for sculptors. Thus Theodora Cowan, born in the year after Adelaide Ironside's death, was brought by her family to Florence in 1889 to study sculpture.[31] She began her apprenticeship in the studio of the American, Longworth Powers, son of Hiram, who had been working in Italy in Adelaide Ironside's day. Also linking her to her predecessor was a meeting with Harriet Hosmer and the Risorgimento associations of her sculpture model, *Carmela*, which illustrated a contemporary story of a Sicilian girl who lost her reason on her lover's death and who recovered when one of Garibaldi's officers took care of her. But Theodora Cowan differs from Ironside in that her presence in Europe as an Australian woman studying art was no longer unique. By the last decade of the century, Australian women were moving to Europe in increasing numbers to pursue Ironside's precocious goal — professional qualification and recognition. Most of the obstacles that had stood before Adelaide Ironside and the realisation of her dreams also blocked the paths of the next generation.

CHAPTER 3

Travel and Aspirations

If you've a song for singing,
If you've a deed to do
Then you must go to London,
Where all your dreams come true.[1]

The quest of an Australian woman for professional recognition overseas is
the theme of a number of novels by Australian women in the late nine-
teenth and early twentieth centuries: the protagonists are singers in Rosa
Praed's *An Australian Heroine*, Anne Wilson's *Alice Lauder* and Louise
Mack's *An Australian Girl in London*, writers in Praed's *The Ghost* and
Winifred James's *Bachelor Betty*, a painter in Margaret Thomas's short
story, 'The Story of a Photograph', and actors in Mary Marlowe's
Kangaroos in Kingsland. [2]

Fiction was mirroring life. A number of sources in the first decade of
this century spell out the message that Europe, and London in particular,
were awash with would-be musicians, singers, artists, actors and writers
from Australia — the vast majority of whom were struggling with little
hope of success. Nellie Melba wrote of the 'huge stampede' of Australian
singers to Europe, and an anonymous contributor to the *Lone Hand*
reported the comment of a musical freetrader that the principal exports
from Australia were frozen sheep and pretty-voiced girls.[3] Another
Australian singer, Amy Castles, when asked whether she came across
many Australian girls in England and Paris, replied:

> Yes, quite a lot. In fact I think that far too many Australians are going home
> to try their fortunes. Competition is very keen and, besides, there are so
> many American girls always coming over — girls with glorious contralto
> voices. The thing is overdone. There are a number of Australian girls in
> London, too, but I am afraid that it is pretty hard work for most of them.[4]

Writer Louise Mack in two letters to the *Bulletin* early in 1902 warned
that London was full of aspiring Australian musicians and actors, very few
of whom had met with any success. Only six Australians had any reputation in London and they were singers and actors; no artists or writers or
poets or musicians 'had lifted themselves above the middle rank of innu-
merable English men or women of like professions'.[5] Indeed, only one
Australian lifted herself into the international hall of fame, and that was
Nellie Melba. Ironically named by Louise Mack as not rising above the
pack was Amy Castles, 'whose recent appearances here did no little dam-

age to the Australian singing profession'. Writer Barbara Baynton also warned that what going to London generally meant for artists was starvation.[6]

It is difficult to quantify the number of Australian women in Europe at the turn of the century who were trying to hone or make a living from their talents, since eventual success is often the only means of identification. Lessons in music and painting were established as legitimate paths to Europe and there seems little doubt, as Beverley Kingston has suggested, that there were young women enough who proclaimed the desire and need to develop talents and make a career as the *raison d'être* for escaping abroad and who merely dabbled at their art.[7] But it would be a mistake to underestimate the number of women who were in genuine pursuit of professional qualifications, work and success. Failure to win fame and glory abroad — or at home — does not signify the absence of serious professional intent or of talent.

In her 1913 article of advice to Australian girls going to London in the hope of making their fame and fortune on the stage, Alice Grant Rosman named Marie Lohr, May Beatty, Alice Crawford and Carrie Haase as among those who had succeeded, and Mrs Matters, in her 1911 compilation of Australians who counted in London in the same year listed ten women who were actors.[8] From the days of the strolling players, acting has always been a profession characterised by mobility, and among the first and most widely travelled women in nineteenth-century Australia were actors; both overseas women such as Lola Montez who performed in Australia, and Australian women touring Asia, America and Britain. When a number of actors were asked by the *Australian Stage Annual* in 1904 about the advantages and drawbacks of a stage career, the opportunity for travel was commonly identified as the foremost benefit.[9] Until late in the nineteenth century, women actors were for the most part the daughters or wives of men involved in the theatre and they usually travelled as part of family troupes. Nellie Stewart, who was born in Sydney in 1858, and whose stage career embraced opera, light opera, musical comedy, drama and pantomime, was the daughter of an opera singer and an actor.[10] She made her stage debut at the age of five and when she was nineteen she toured India, England and North America with her family. Stewart returned home in the following year, but appeared from time to time on the stage in London in musical comedy and pantomime. A further tour of the United States came to a dramatic end in 1906 in the aftermath of the San Francisco earthquake.

By the end of the nineteenth century, women were departing on their own to make their way in the theatre. Mary Edgeworth David in her memoirs wrote of her great friend Una 'who was bent on a stage career'.[11] When she was left a few hundred pounds by a relative, she used her portion to take herself and her sister to England, where she studied dramatic art for a year. Her money ran out and Una joined a third-rate theatrical touring company. The tour came to a sudden end in 'an unattractive town called Macclesfield' when the manager vamoosed with the takings and there was no money to pay the landladies. Edgeworth David gave no information on the eventual success or failure of Una, other than mentioning that she worked for a brief period as Bernard Shaw's secretary. Mary Marlowe, after some experience in the theatre in Victoria, set off at the age of 26 with two friends to try her luck in England. In both her autobiography and her novel *Kangaroos in Kingsland*, she gives accounts of her days in repertory — of digs in the slums of northern England, where she lived among people who struggled for a bare existence, where the tails of her chops went into the stew pot, and where her early mornings were disturbed by the 'knocker-up', whose rumbling clackers roused the mill workers.[12]

Mrs Matters's list of important Australians in London included 35 women singers, pianists and violinists, and the names of scores of others who were performing at some public level occur in the pages of the *British-Australasian* of the period. Ada Holman wrote in London in 1912 that her patriotic pride was gratified by the frequent appearance of Australian names in the list of singers: 'Indeed so largely is Australia entering the musical world here that one could get very fair sustenance alone by following up the recitals of Australian artists in London'.[13] Not only did the Australian troupe include a Nellie Melba, but also a Miss Lalla Yarra and a Miss Ballara from Ballarat. The degree of success of the Australian performers ranged from the stupendous heights of the diva herself to those whose public appearances were confined to the odd moment on the stage with provincial musical societies, or at private soirées, or at the Austral Club, an organisation formed specifically to assist aspiring Australian performers.[14] For others it may have been enough to return home with the calling card that announced a voice trained by Marchesi — or any other teacher in Paris — or a diploma from a German music school.

Among writers, Jessie Couvreur ('Tasma'), Rosa Praed, Catherine Martin, Louise Mack, Winifred James, Barbara Baynton, Mary Gaunt, Alice Rosman, Helen Sumner Locke, Katharine Susannah Prichard, Nettie Palmer, and Helen Simpson all moved to London in the two decades before the First World War. In the same period, Miles Franklin and Alice Henry left for North America, and Mary Gilmore for William Lane's Utopian experiment in Paraguay. The majority spent long periods or the rest of their lives abroad. The writers supported themselves by journalism, reporting on the overseas scene for the Australian press, and were thus an important conduit of information. Ada Holman's travel jottings for the

Sydney *Daily Telegraph*, as well as describing the bluebells and daisies of the south of England in April and the opening of Parliament, also reported on factory conditions in Manchester and housekeeping in Paris.[15] The articles that Jessie Couvreur, who eventually became the foreign correspondent of the *Times* in Brussels, wrote for the *Australasian* have been described by her biographer as probably providing her readers with a coverage of European intellectual life of a depth and consistency unrivalled before or since.[16] Women who did not necessarily aspire to write novels were also working as journalists overseas by the end of the nineteenth century. Jessie Couvreur's youngest sister, Edith, who lived in Paris in the late 1880s, wrote art and literary criticism for the London *Spectator* and the *Universal Review*,[17] and Margaret Baxter, who went to London in 1904 to study singing, stayed on as a journalist, writing for the *Daily Telegraph*, the *Catholic Press*, and for North American and British newspapers.[18]

In an article in 1978 on Australian artists abroad, Ann Galbally identified seventeen 'significant' Australian artists who left Australia between 1880 and 1914.[19] All seventeen were men. They studied at art schools in London and at fashionable ateliers like Julian's and Colarossi's in Paris. Working alongside them were Australian women artists, ignored by Galbally. For the same period more than sixty Australian women who aspired to professional ambitions and who attended art schools in Europe, twenty before 1900, have been identified.[20] The qualification of 'significant' presents problems; it is a mobile not a fixed term, and over time the criteria can change, the significant can be marginalised, and those at the margins can be given a central importance, the invisible come into sight. 'Significant' implies not only quality, but also professionalism. Not all students at art schools in London and Paris aspired to careers and recognition. The students at Julian's in Paris included not only Tom Roberts, but also Nancy Mitchell, by her own cheerful admission bereft of talent. But while the daughters of the élite may have played with their brushes and pencils, and some young women may have seen art school as a way to relieve the boredom of their lives and to taste *la vie bohémienne* either in South Melbourne or the Latin Quarter, the women who have been identified as having professional aspirations studied in Europe for considerable periods of time, had their work hung in the Royal Academy or in the Paris Salons, and exhibited and worked for the market. If not all of them can be claimed as 'significant', they regarded themselves as serious professionals and today many of their names are indeed well known as highly significant figures in Australian art: Dorrit Black, Grace Cossington Smith, Bessie Davidson, Bessie Gibson, Hilda Rix Nicholas, Kate O'Connor, Margaret Preston, Thea Proctor, Norah Simpson, Ethel Spowers, Jessie Traill and Marie Tuck, all of whom studied in Europe before the First World War. It is now argued that the contribution to art development in their own country of this generation of Australian women far outstrips that of their European and North American counterparts, indeed, that of Australian male artists.[21]

No doubt the minimal crude criteria of exhibiting and selling would augment the number of men painting in Europe — men such as Jessie Couvreur's brother, John Huybers, who attended Julian's atelier in 1877 and exhibited at the Old Salon — but a more thorough search would reveal more women, women, for example, such as sisters Alison and Iso Rae, who moved to Etaples in France in the 1880s and studied for a time at Colarossi's Academy and exhibited at the Paris Salons. They did not appeared on lists of women painters until very recently, and become visible only because Margaret Thomas in an 1891 article on Australian artists in Paris mentioned Alison Rae as one of best students at Colarossi's and referred to her painting in the New Salon, and Grace Joel in her 1906 piece on 'Australian Artists in London' singled out Iso Rae as an artist who had often been hung on the line and sold at the Paris Salon.[22]

The number of women working abroad as artists needs to be linked back to the number studying art in Australia. In the art schools in the late nineteenth and early twentieth centuries women predominated among students: the National Gallery School had virtually twice as many female as male students enrolled, and by the end of the century women accounted for half the exhibitors at the 1898 annual exhibition of the Victorian Artists Society.[23] Because women had far fewer choices and career opportunities than men, and because art was a traditional area of cultivation, it is not surprising that so many women should turn in that direction to develop a career and the means to travel.

On their first trips to Europe, particularly if still young, the women had not necessarily developed professional aspirations. Travel and exposure to art classes and galleries in Europe could stimulate the progression from accomplishment to career. Jessie Traill, whose father was the manager of the Oriental Bank of Melbourne and owned a vanilla plantation in the Seychelles, was sent to school in Switzerland in 1892 at the age of eleven.[24] She went to Europe again with her widowed father and sister in 1900. It was on her return from this trip that she began to attend the National Gallery School in Melbourne, and on her next sojourn in Europe, 1907–09, she took classes at Colarossi's in Paris and with Frank Brangwyn in London. In 1909 her paintings were hung at the annual exhibitions of the Royal Academy in London and the Old Salon in Paris. Grace Cossington Smith, whose mother in her youth had studied music in Germany, attended classes at Dattilo Rubbo's atelier in Sydney before going with her father and sister to Europe for two years. A few art classes at the Winchester art school and a three-month stay in Stettin in Pomerania with a friend of her mother do not suggest a woman moving towards a professional career. But who knows? Her biographer, Bruce

James, suggests that Cossington Smith had grown up among educated, encouraging women, and that her mother in guiding her to Stettin may have been directing her daughter towards the career that she herself could not have.[25] It was within two years of her return from Europe that Grace Cossington Smith was to paint *The Sock Knitter*, now recognised as one of the first modernist paintings in Australia.

That the origins of independent travel lay in traditional accomplishment is also evidenced by the versatility and flexibility in talents and choice of careers. If the quest for skills in the arts provided the rationale for exodus for Australian women, the particular area does not seem at times to have been important. Winifred James claimed that she only took up writing when her diffidence made careers in singing and acting impossible; Mary Marlowe went to London as an actress and returned to Australia as a writer; Henry Handel Richardson studied music in Leipzig before beginning her career as a writer; and Alice Muskett wrote a novel and short stories as well as exhibiting as a painter. But few women could have been as versatile as Dora Ohlfsen.

The details of Dora Ohlfsen's life have been gleaned mostly from press interviews in which there are inconsistencies in detail and in which either she, the journalist, or both, constructed a romantic narrative of the life of 'the lady artist', a little outré and eccentric, including early exotic adventuring and later participation in a cosmopolitan and sophisticated art world.[26] The 'tall, willowy girl of sixteen years with a very distinguished manner', who left Australia in 1885, was the daughter of an Australian-born mother and a father described as born in Poland of Scandinavian stock and as either a civil or sewerage engineer. After two years at Sydney Girls' High School, Ohlfsen left Sydney in the mid-1880s to study piano in Berlin. According to her later accounts, just as arrangements had been finalised for her debut and a concert tour through Germany, a tour for which she was to be paid, an unprecedented circumstance for a 'debutante' and a foreigner, neuritis of the arm forced her to abandon the piano. Her illness coincided with her father's loss of his money — presumably around 1893. She then saw herself as having two alternatives, to return to Australia and find work, or to learn some other art by which she could maintain herself in Europe.

Ohlfsen turned to teaching, but soon after an opportunity arose for her to go to Russia, possibly as governess or private music teacher. In St Petersburg, she gave lessons in the theory of music and then became 'a sort of private secretary' to the American ambassador, for whose newspaper in St Louis she prepared summaries of events in Europe. She also made 'an exhaustive study of the rise and development of Russian music'. Her later accounts of her life in tsarist Russia add the drama of fear and suspicion, espionage and conspiracy, secret societies and secret police, as well as the mystique of her own dabbling in the psychic and occult. In one version of Ohlfsen's life the idea of taking art seriously took root after the tsarina bought a 'great matchbox of wood' that she had painted, in another, after her caricatures had created interest, and in yet another, after voices she believed to be those of spirits urged her to take up sculpture. Thus in 1902, Ohlfsen went in the entourage of a Russian family to Rome where, presumably following the advice of the spirits, she studied sculpture at the French Academy. She remained in Rome and during the war nursed with the Italian Red Cross and 'had some sensational experiences from areoplane attacks and shells'.

It was sculpture that eventually provided Dora Ohlfsen with a career and reputation. Specialising in relief sculptures and medallions, her works include the war memorial at Formia just out of Rome, bronze medallions of Benito Mussolini, Gabriele d'Annunzio, the Duca d'Aosta, and Garibaldi's son, General Pippo Garibaldi, as well as of Lloyd George, Herbert Asquith, General Monash and Nellie Melba, and a life-size marble bust of Nellie Stewart.[27] Ohlfsen claimed that she was the first woman to have been involved in a public building in Italy and the first foreigner to work on a war memorial.

A studio in Via San Nicola da Tolentino in Rome became Ohlfsen's home, and she presided every Monday afternoon over her respectably bohemian salon.

> Among the guests are well known singers, artists, men of letters, society leaders, both men and women. Between cups of tea and slices of plum cake discussions take place on matters of art, and every language may be heard within these walls during the too short hours of the waning afternoon before the guests must separate.[28]

There is no record of what the society leaders made of the bronze bears, possums, platypuses and bandicoots that, according to Australian writer Doris Dinham who visited Ohlfsen in 1932, filled the studio.[29] Dinham confirmed that among other guests were 'numbers of Ambassadors and Ambassadresses and Ducas with eyeglasses and without them', and one other Australian woman, Madame Groye from the Swiss Embassy, 'who used to be Miss Bass'. Bronze bears and bandicoots were not the full extent of Ohlfsen's deployment of Australian images; her murals of St Antony of Padua and St Francis of Assisi portray the Italian saints surrounded by wattle and Australian birds.

Dora Ohlfsen made a number of trips back to Australia from Rome and actively sought to exhibit her work and find patronage in her own country. In 1931 she lobbied very hard to obtain work on the War Memorial in Melbourne, and particularly for a commission to carve an equestrian monument of Sir John Monash. She was strongly critical of the cultural cringe that led to the assignment of the sculpture on the War Memorial to an Englishman, little known in his own country and without any reputation in Europe.[30] Dora Ohlfsen also ridiculed the plans for the reliefs in the Sydney War Memorial, describing the idea of seated soldiers in a row as a 'latrine parade' and asking if a 'naked woman strung up on a cross' was intended to commemorate the German brothels in Belgium, 'where women of every rank, age and class were requisitioned'. In defensive mode, and reminiscent of Adelaide Ironside, Ohlfsen outlined her achievements to Sir Robert Garran. In recognition of the war memorial she had carved for Formia, she had been given the freedom of the city, and this

> was the highest honour that any artist can ever receive in the world (and I am the only English artist who has received it) for it is not a complimentary honour but a legal one and conferred on me by the unanimous vote of the population. It is equal to the Legion d'honneur but more difficult, and yet in a way, it is more rare.[31]

The messages that Dora Ohlfsen sent home about her success abroad functioned in part as compensation for her lack of recognition in Australia, for her membership of the band of prophets without honour in their own land. Like Adelaide Ironside, she was hurt and bitter. Dora Ohlfsen passed the rest of her life in Rome, where she died in 1948.

The Australian women writers, musicians and artists studied and worked alongside similar women from other provinces and edges of the Eurocentric world. The women painting in Paris, for example, often noted — and enjoyed — the cosmopolitan nature of the world in which they moved. Hilda Rix Nicholas, recalling in the early 1920s her time in pre-war Paris, wrote of

> Neatly dressed Americans, fiery-eyed Russians, dainty or picturesque French and well-tubbed English; red-haired Scots, fair-haired Danes, plump Dutch, heavy Germans, a Jap in precise black kimono, a corn-coloured Swede, and a mellow-eyed Italian.[32]

The Australians were a tiny band when compared to the North American artists who flooded France and numbered more than one thousand in the last two decades of the nineteenth century.[33] Late-nineteenth-century Australia did not export a Gertrude Stein, a Sylvia Beach, a Romaine Brooks or a Natalie Barney. No Australian woman moved in the circles of Picasso and Matisse — nor for that matter did any Australian man. But the vast majority of Americans had more in common with the overseas experience of the Australians than they did with their superstar compatriots. Cincinnati-born painter Elizabeth Nourse lived in Paris from 1883 until her death in 1938. Her sister accompanied her to Paris, and she began working in a studio on the Left Bank in Rue de la

Grande Chaumière, where Western Australian painter Kate O'Connor lived.[34] Like many of the Australian women, Nourse studied at Julian's — and in her list of the different nationals working at the school, she includes Australians. In the summer of 1889, she went to paint in Etaples in Picardy, where the Rae sisters had made their home and where Hilda Rix Nicholas leased a studio for eight years.[35] Like the late-nineteenth-century Australian women, Nourse was in no way an avant-garde painter, and it was acceptance and recognition by the Salons that she sought. In the last resort, she was in Paris because, as one of her compatriots wrote in the *Atlantic Monthly* in 1875,

> Fame may be acquired in other pursuits than that of art as well elsewhere as in France. But fame in art can only be acquired in Paris and only then by exhibiting at the Salon.[36]

Nothing then really separates Nourse's experience and motives from those of the Australian women of the period other than, as was noted in the context of Adelaide Ironside and Harriet Hosmer, the larger market and greater opportunities that were available to the North Americans for both sales and fame.

If writing, painting, singing and acting were traditional activities that afforded women the opportunity for independent travel, teaching was another. By the late nineteenth century British governesses were to be found all over the world — including Australia — and young Australian women were following in their footsteps. After journeying to London with her family in 1899, twenty-year-old Amie Livingstone set out for Paris alone, where she taught English first at the Berlitz school, and then as a private teacher, before travelling widely as governess to a French family.[37] *New Idea* in 1903 carried an article by 'An Australian Governess in Constantinople', and Hilda Freeman published her memoirs of life as a governess in Germany in the first months of the First World War.[38]

From the early 1880s women had begun to be admitted to university education and gifted women were soon joining their male compatriots in travelling to study in overseas institutions of higher learning.[39] Melian Stawell, the youngest of the ten children Mary Stawell had taken to Europe for education, returned to England in 1889 to read classics at Girton College Cambridge, despite her mother's belief that French and German were more useful to a woman.[40] She was followed in her pursuit of classical education at Cambridge by Susannah Williams, who enrolled at Newnham College in 1897. Williams, whose career in education led her to the position of principal of Women's College at the University of Sydney, also read archaeology at London University.[41] Gertrude Roseby, who obtained her Bachelor of Arts from the University of Sydney in 1895, was another early woman who journeyed to Britain to obtain teaching diplomas and experience.[42] Again indicative of the ties between accomplishment, travel, and the new professional education were the women seeking qualifications as teachers of modern languages. Both Nettie Higgins, the future Nettie Palmer, and Margaret Bailey, the founder of Ascham School in Sydney, studied phonetics at the Tilly Institute in Berlin before the First World War.[43] It was their interest in science that took Ellen Benham and Freda Bage overseas and into education. Benham graduated in science from Adelaide University in 1892 and then travelled to Britain to obtain the Oxford Diploma in Education and some overseas experience.[44] Bage, after receiving her Master of Science from the University of Melbourne in 1907, went on to London where she worked at King's College and held a fellowship of the Linnean Society.[45] In 1914 she returned to Australia to take up her appointment as the first principal of the Women's College at the University of Queensland.

Florence Martin stepped much further across gender boundaries when in the early 1890s she became the second Australian to work in Cambridge's Cavendish Laboratory, which at that time was acquiring its fabled reputation as the centre of experimental physics.[46] Less unusual were the circumstances that brought to an end any aspirations Martin may have held for a scientific or academic career. Shortly after she returned to the University of Sydney in 1896 her professor patron departed, and at much the same time she became responsible for the care of her senile mother. However, Martin befriended a young American explorer, William Cooke Daniels, and his fiancée, and after her mother's death and their marriage, she travelled the world with them. In 1918 William Cooke Daniels died, and in the following year his wife fell victim to the influenza epidemic. Florence Martin inherited their large estate, based around a department store in Denver, USA. She subsequently settled in Denver, where she became an important patron of the arts.

Ambitions for medical careers also led women overseas from the 1880s. Emma Constance Stone went to North America in 1884 to undertake medical studies.[47] Eleven years later, Mary Booth and Agnes Bennett enrolled at the University of Edinburgh, where so many Australian men had taken their medical degrees. Nursing was another profession for which women travelled to undertake further training. Isla Blomfield trained at Royal Prince Alfred Hospital in Sydney before going to London in 1899, where she obtained her obstetrics certificate.[48] On her way back to Sydney, she toured hospitals in the United States. After a second period of nursing at Royal Prince Alfred Hospital, she travelled to China to gain experience in the treatment of infectious diseases. From China she crossed Siberia to London, where she was a delegate to the 1909 International Nurses' Congress.

Following the example of ambitious men in obtaining overseas qualifications and experience did not necessarily open up the same limitless opportunities to women. In her 1938 memoirs, Janet Mitchell portrayed a very disoriented self returning to Melbourne with her London Bachelor of Arts in 1923.

> I wanted vaguely to do something in the way of social work, something constructive. As usual my day-dreams would crash on the hard reality that there seemed to be no place for me. Did Australia really want educated women with overseas degrees? What opportunities were there? I looked about for a job. But there seemed to be nothing. Australia did not want me.[49]

Women with a greater sense of direction than Mitchell faced male opposition to full careers and often found acceptance only on the margins of professions. Principalships of Women's Colleges were the highest positions that women were to gain in the Australian academy until the 1970s. Some women, like their male counterparts, remained to make careers in Europe. Marion Phillips, who completed her Bachelor of Arts at the University of Melbourne in 1904 won an overseas scholarship. She obtained her doctorate at the London School of Economics in 1909, and went on to work with Sidney and Beatrice Webb and to become deeply involved in working-class issues, and in the Fabian and women's movements, and to sit in the House of Commons as a Labour member from 1929 to 1931. She reputedly rejected her birthplace as crude and uncivilised, preferring to participate in the intellectual, artistic and cultural life of Europe.[50]

By the beginning of the twentieth century sporting prowess was opening up another opportunity for overseas travel.[51] Women with ambitions in sport faced the same barriers as those wishing to develop their academic talents to the full. Annette Kellermann, the fastest woman swimmer in New South Wales at the beginning of this century, saw show business as the best opportunity for the exploitation of her prowess. In 1905, after touring Australia, nineteen-year-old Kellermann sailed with her father for Britain, where her two attempts to swim the English Channel — the first woman to try — brought instant fame.[52] Kellermann then toured Europe giving exhibition swims in the Seine and the Danube, as well as in a glass tank. From Europe she travelled to America where she appeared at the Chicago World's Fair, took up the study of ballet and physical culture, and achieved further fame when she was arrested for wearing a one-piece skirtless bathing suit on a Boston beach. She was to fight one of the first campaigns to free women's bodies from the restrictive clothing that curtailed their freedom of movement. In 1909 Kellermann achieved another Australian first when she played a lead role in an American film. Reputedly the best-known Australian celebrity after Nellie Melba in the first decades of this century, Kellermann spent much of her life travelling the world, first with her vaudeville acts, which included the earliest displays of underwater ballet, and then lecturing on health and fitness.

Seven years after Annette Kellermann had gone to England, Fanny Durack and Mina Wyllie won gold and silver medals at the 1912 Stockholm Olympic Games, the first games to stage swimming events for women.[53] To reach Stockholm, the young women had to overcome a number of obstacles: hostility to women's swimming events from within the International Olympic Committee, opposition in Australia to sending and financing two young women halfway around the world, and the policy of the New South Wales Ladies Amateur Swimming Association that forbade its members appearing in competitions when men were present. The Olympic success of the two swimmers led to tours of Europe and the United States and to problems with swimming officials, which were also to dog later generations of women swimmers overseas, including another gold medallist, Dawn Fraser.

When Fanny Durack returned to Sydney after the Stockholm Olympics, she had knowledge to impart; Australia was one of the few modern nations where fear of mixed bathing was still strong The views of the 23-year-old Olympic champion were not accorded the status of privileged speech. She was informed in one press article that there were things going on abroad that 'very properly' should not be allowed into Australia.[54] By the first decades of the twentieth century, the world beyond Australia was not only the site of knowledge and culture, but also of contamination and corruption.[55]

The focus in this chapter has been on women who travelled to Europe in search of new careers. But they do not by any means cover the full range of women's independent travel in the late nineteenth and early twentieth centuries in relation to purpose, place or class. The coming of the railway, the travel agent, the guided tour, and the ubiquitous Mr Cook sanitised touring, making the experience more available to women.[56] Part of Margaret Thomas's purpose in publishing her account of her journey through Spain with a female friend, *A Scamper Through Spain and Tangier*, was to show that travel was open to unaccompanied women of modest means. The two women had travelled by third-class rail, a mode that was not only cheap, but also more secure. Passengers enjoying the privacy of first-class carriages were more likely to be murdered than those in the crowded third-class cars; safety lay in numbers.[57]

With the assistance of Thomas Cook, the travel itineraries and experience for at least some Australian women quickly expanded as — usually in pairs — they engaged in more exotic 'grand tours'. In December 1902 Violet Chomley and Frances Mackinnon travelled to Europe by way of Manila, Hong Kong, Canton, Kobe and Port Arthur, then by train across Siberia to Moscow, and through Russia to the Black Sea and Constantinople.[58] Florence Finn and a friend, on their way to the coronation of George V in 1910, left their ship in Port Said and visited Jaffa, Jericho and Jerusalem before returning to Egypt to join a tour up the Nile to the temples at Luxor. Thomas Cook was at their side all the way. When their boat arrived in Jaffa, despite the total confusion on the docks, they remained placidly on deck 'until a Syrian clerk wearing "Cook's" on his collar escorted them *à la princesse* to a boat by themselves'.[59]

Mary Brennan's trip to Britain in 1916 was far from *à la princesse*, but her story indicates that it was also occasionally possible for enterprising and determined working-class women to realise their dreams to see the world. At the age of 95, Mary Brennan related the story of her life. She was born in 1889, the fifth of twelve children of an Irish-born father and Cornish-born mother, who were settler farmers in Victoria. As she grew up and the girls around her were preparing their glory-boxes, she knew that getting married was the last thing she wanted to do: 'I wanted to go places. I wanted to get around a bit and see the world'.[60] At eighteen, Brennan went into domestic service and then worked as a cook-laundress in various hotels in rural Victoria and in Western Australia, where she had joined some of her brothers. In 1916 when a friend who was a 'Pommie orphan' was recalled to England by relatives, Brennan, having 'knocked up a bit of dough' — thirty pounds — decided to join her. She had always had it in her mind to travel; geography had been her favourite subject at school and she had read about 'the various old castles and things in England'. Brennan was 27 by then, and her parents raised no serious objections, even if her father thought she was 'crazy' to go. In her recollections, she also placed her journey in the context of her family background of migration.

> I s'pose it was a bit unusual for a young woman to be travelling around but Father came out here on his own from Ireland fifty years before almost. Aunty Margaret (at Bacchus Marsh) was another one. She came out from Ireland in 1870, with two or three of her cousins.[61]

In London, Brennan rented a room in Regent's Park and went to work in a munitions factory at Willesden because 'war work was the best pay', but she left when she was transferred to the cordite room, where the powder turned the workers into 'Yellow Girls'. She moved on to waitressing in the ABC tea rooms in Oxford Street near the British Museum and then joined the Women's Land Army. Mary Brennan returned to Australia in 1919, and having seen something of the world married nine years later. Her trip to Europe in 1916 was to become the commonplace working holiday of the 1950s and 1960s.

Dulcie Deamer's adventures, constructed in her 1965 unpublished autobiography as a harum-scarum romp befitting the future denizen of

Kings Cross and Queen of Bohemia, provide a glimpse of an early twenti-eth-century woman 'on the road'.[62] She set off on her travels as an eight-een-year-old bride and wandered with her husband for eight years, inter-mittently returning to Australia and producing and discarding children. Deamer's first contact with the world beyond New Zealand and Australia was India, where the sights on her itinerary included brothels, the burn-ing of a twelve-year-old widow, and anti-British bomb-throwing. China followed, where she added the witnessing of an execution to her expand-ing and diverse travel experiences. After this beginning, England left her cold — literally and metaphorically — and the family moved on to New York where Dulcie Deamer became part of that great human cargo unloaded for over half a century at the immigration clearing house on Ellis Island. She had to pass through wire enclosures 'where one was examined for proof that one was free of certain obvious diseases, not deaf-and-dumb, and possessed of a certain amount of cash'.

If Dulcie Deamer's restlessness had taken her to strange places, Mary Gilmore's social commitment took her even further off the beaten track. A teacher by profession and radical in her politics, Gilmore sailed from Sydney in 1896 for Paraguay to join William Lane's socialist Utopian set-tlement, Cosme, where she taught the children, organised the library, edited the daily paper, married another colonist, the shearer William Gilmore, and gave birth to a son with the assistance of a nurse 'who was drunk before his birth till a week after'.[63] The settlement at Cosme went the way of all Utopias, and Gilmore and her family left, but it took them two years to earn the fares back to Australia. During this time, she lived in Buenos Aires while her husband 'went shearing in the Argentine', and endured a 31-day voyage down the South American coast to Gallegos on a leaking boat; water ran short and her son caught measles and was dependent on the ministrations of a doctor who was kindness itself, but who suffered from melancholia and loss of memory and dared not trust himself to do anything but pray. Gilmore also worked as governess to 'the most awful girl that ever lived' and gave English lessons. While she was on her own in Gallegos, war threatened between Argentina and Chile, and 'living among people who were only semi-civilized' she slept every night with 'an axe, two or three carving knives, and a siren whistle' under her pillow.

Once the patterns were established, women continued to go overseas to develop their talents as artists, musicians, actors, dancers and writers, to acquire higher degrees and professional qualifications, and to partici-pate in international sporting events.[64] Christina Stead and Florence James left for London in the mid-1920s to establish themselves as writers. Anne Dangar and Grace Crowley journeyed to France to hone their tal-ents as painters.[65] The questions that now need to be explored are those of the circumstances that made travel by women in pursuit of their own goals possible from the late nineteenth century, of the barriers they had to overcome, of the ways in which they negotiated or failed to negotiate their way through constraints, of what they were seeking and what they were escaping, of what they made of new places and experiences, of how they saw travel as changing their lives, and of the narrative patterns that they adopted to tell their stories. There are both common answers and answers that can only be found in the narrating of individual lives.

Interlude

Annie Duncan

Among the Australian women who acquired professional qualifications overseas in the last decade of the nineteenth century, the career choice of Annie Duncan was somewhat unusual; she trained to become a factory inspector in London. Her story, told in her 1934 memoirs, is another example of the ways in which enterprising women could deploy travel to create new lives.[1] Duncan was born in 1858, the daughter of a Glasgow doctor who had emigrated to Australia in 1838. Her early life was typical of time and class; as a young woman she helped run the house for her widowed father, read, played the piano, took singing lessons, practised her German and archery, and engaged in amateur theatricals. When her father died, the twenty-year-old Annie Duncan and her sister went to live with an aunt. She later claimed that she had never been much attracted by the idea of marriage.

> I was much more excited by the thought of following out some career by which I could earn my own living. I remember saying to some friend of my father's who must have said something about marriage that 'I intended to be an old maid and reform the race of old maids', and this was about the time of my coming-out.[2]

Her sister, who was more conventional, married in 1884. For the next eight years, far from striking out for a career, Annie Duncan fulfilled the role of the unmarried daughter and sister, that of family carer. She lived with her sister, helping with the children and the housekeeping, first in Adelaide and then in Launceston after her brother-in-law was appointed headmaster of Launceston Grammar School. In 1892 when her sister was becoming less dependent on her help, the 34-year-old Duncan decided to go to London, in the first instance to meet a brother who had settled in South Africa. With hindsight, she portrayed her departure as a turning point in her life and as the end of 'early youth'.

Her first voyage begat in Annie Duncan 'the passion for travel that still possesses me'. She revelled in the strangeness, 'the riot of colours' of the Eastern ports, but did not much enjoy the voyage itself. In Britain she met her brother, visited other relatives, enjoyed concerts and plays, and like countless other women took up brass rubbing. London 'gripped her heart'; the 'everlasting tarara boom-deay' of the street organs, the straw-berry sellers calling their wares in the high summer, the late post that arrived at 11.00 p.m. She crossed the Channel to spend a week in Paris and carried away memories of the life-size crucifixes glimpsed from the train in Normandy, the cracking of the long whips by the coach drivers of Paris, and new foods such as 'the sprigs of sow-thistle on the salad'.

Annie Duncan's financial situation became precarious in the wake of the 1893 bank crashes in Australia; like Dora Ohlfsen she was faced with the choice of either going home or finding work to prolong her time abroad. Despite her hatred of the English winter, her susceptibility to bad colds, and her longing for her family, she chose the latter alternative: 'I was quite determined to cut out a career of some sort, and be beholden to no one for my living'.[3] Annie Duncan decided to become a factory inspector and began attending lectures at the National Health Society and Royal Sanitary Institute, where her fellow students ranged from young plumbers to the Duchess of Bedford. Her choice of profession was influenced by her having some contacts in the area, and by her belief that factory inspection offered good prospects for women, particularly as it was not an overcrowded occupation; 'a person without any particular influence might hope to achieve something by hard work'. On the successful completion of her courses, Duncan took up a position as inspector of laundries and workrooms in the London district of South Kensington; she believed that she was only the third woman to be appointed to such a post. Thus her London became the shadow side of that of fashionable travellers and expatriates as she tried to secure proper ventilation and safer working conditions in the sweated labour shops of the 'haughty Court dressmakers'. Annie Duncan tried too hard, and her appointment was not renewed. She later observed that it was easier to get regulations obeyed in Sydney than in London where she had no power to compel employers 'to do what was commonly humane'.

The next stage in Annie Duncan's time in Europe was more conventional. After a holiday in Switzerland, she went to Paris for three months to study French. She took lessons with the woman who ran her pension, learnt to shop in the markets and to prepare food, attended a course of lectures at the Sorbonne on Spanish literature, and watched the funeral processions of Louis Pasteur and Alexandre Dumas.

In 1896, four years after she had left Australia, Annie Duncan decided to come home. Since her brother-in-law had taken up the position of headmaster of the King's School in Sydney, it was to that city that she returned, and she was appointed as a factory inspector in the labour and industry branch of the New South Wales Department of Public Instruction.[4] Looking back on her four years overseas, Duncan rightly felt that she had gained much.

> I was 37 and had learnt a great deal during my four years stay, had stood on my own feet, 'paddled my own canoe' without much help from anyone belonging to me, & was fitted out with a good profession.[5]

In her work she had found sisterhood in the generous-spirited help she had received from other women. She had also acquired a deep love for London. Recalling her emotions when she arrived in England on her second visit in 1914 she wrote:

> And now I was once more on English soil and going to see beloved London again, and my heart sang within me. During all the seventeen years that I had been in Sydney I had dreamt of England, and thought if I could see it once more, I should die happy. And now that day had come.[6]

Annie Duncan was typical of women travelling to acquire skills and qualifications at the end of the nineteenth century in that she was a no-longer-young spinster for whom independence rather than marriage was a goal. Her trip overseas had allowed her to make the transition from dutiful daughter and sister to independent, self-supporting woman.

CHAPTER 4

Travel and Independence

*Rebel daughters seem to abound. This world is so big
and so full of wonderful things to see and learn.*[1]

Mary Gaunt, who grew up in a family of five boys and two girls on the
Ballarat goldfields, traced the wanderlust that took her to exploring Africa
at the beginning of this century to her emigrating ancestors and to childhood games and reading.[2] The curios brought home from China by her
grandfather intensified her determination to travel; wander fever was in
her blood, the lure of the unknown was irresistible. Childhood passed.
Mary Gaunt's brothers took off 'a-roving in other lands' and she learnt that
her desire for equal independence was unwomanly, likely to spoil her
chances of marrying, and that travel was 'a most improper desire for a
young lady'.

> Our world was bounded by our father's lawns and the young men who
> came to see us and made up picnic parties to the wildest bush round
> Ballarat for our amusement.[3]

Despite Mary Gaunt's protestations, her early life had not been excessively restricted; she was the second woman to enrol at the University of
Melbourne, although she did not graduate. When she left university, she
faced the problem of making a living:

> what was to become of me? and not only me, but hundreds of other girls,
> too, girls of the upper middle class, who have no provision made for them
> in case they do not marry.[4]

With the encouragement of Edward Ellis Morris, who was a professor
of language and literature at the University of Melbourne, Mary Gaunt
turned to writing, dramatising the struggle of the single woman to find
dignity, self-sufficiency and independence in her novel *Kirkham's Find*,
and appropriating the adventures of her brothers to provide other
themes.[5] In 1890, at the age of 29, she went to England, Europe and
India, possibly in search of opportunities and outlets for her writing, but
she came back after one year. Mary Gaunt did marry, in 1894, but the
death of her husband six years later left her a childless widow. 'Penniless,
homeless and alone', she refused the obvious path of returning to her
parental home: 'Was I not free, free to wander where I pleased, to seek
those adventures that had held such glamour for me in my girlhood?'[6]
Thus Gaunt left Australia and became an expatriate, living first in London

and then on the Italian Riviera until 1940, when Mussolini's entry into the war forced her to flee Italy. She died in Cannes in 1942. In Europe, Mary Gaunt had realised her youthful ambitions for independence. She had supported herself — if not in great comfort and with increasing difficulty in old age — for over 40 years by her writing, travel books, novels and journalism.

Mary Gaunt had also achieved her childhood dreams of exotic travel. In 1907 she explored the west coast of Africa, travelling for 400 miles up the Gambia River. She appears to have been the second woman, after Mary Kingsley, to journey 'alone' in Africa — alone except for the seventeen African carriers and three servants. In 1912 Gaunt published her account of her adventures, *Alone in West Africa*. Her travels in China in the follow-ing year — north from Peking by mule cart to visit the hunting palaces of the Manchus — produced *A Woman in China*.[7] She intended on her second trip in China in 1914 to follow the old caravan route to Russia, but when bandits blocked the way, she travelled to Vladivostok and then across Siberia to Russia, returning to Britain through Sweden and Norway in the first weeks of the war. The excitement of dodging brigands was paralleled only by that of trying to smuggle her dog in and out of Sweden.[8] Her last travel book described a trip to Jamaica that she made in 1919.[9]

The titles of Mary Gaunt's first two travel books suggest that in associ-ating her travel with her gender, she was staking out a special and extraor-dinary position for herself, as well as looking to the market. Certainly her travels link her to her better-known British sisters like Mary Kingsley, Gertrude Bell and Marianne North. Consistent with the public image constructed by other early women explorers, Gaunt maintained the most conventional of feminine appearances as camouflage for her still 'unlady-like' adventuring. An Australian writer, Alice Grant Rosman, who inter-viewed Gaunt for *Everylady's Journal* in 1912 referred to 'her charming manner' that was in 'delightful contrast to the somewhat manly type one usually associates with adventure in wild countries'.[10]

Mary Gaunt's departure from Australia and her subsequent travels met her need to explore the world in the manner of her brothers, furnished material for her writing, and provided her with a life somewhat more interesting than that of a widowed daughter caring for aging parents. While her life was distinctive in the extent of her travels and in her success in supporting herself, the steps in her translation from sheltered and restricted young woman in rural Victoria to independent London-based writer relate very much to social change in the Australian colonies of the late nineteenth century.

From the 1880s, linked demographic, economic, political, and educa-tional developments opened up new opportunities for women and were in turn fuelled by the new agendas of middle-class women reformers. The considerable surplus of males over females for the first century of white Australia's history meant that few women in the colonies remained unmarried. By the 1880s, however, there were fewer men available in urban Australia as potential husbands for young women, so unmarried adult women became an expanding component of the Australian population; by 1921, some 19.5 per cent of women aged between 35 and 40 were still unmarried.[11] From the late nineteenth century, urban middle-class Australia contained a growing group of women without occupation, means of support, or destiny. At the same time, middle-class women began to enter the public world as social activists, campaigning for education, for the vote and participation in the political arena, and for social reform in areas that affected their gender — prostitution, temperance, divorce, child welfare, and women's working conditions.[12] Social circumstances, and pressure from women themselves, began, through education and training, to open up the possibility of more independent lives. Women were also making claims for greater movement in space as they agitated for dress reform and took to the bicycle.[13]

The painter Alice Muskett, who lived in Paris for most of the time between 1892 and 1912, summed up her feminist credo in her 1913 novel *Among the Reeds*; every woman should be trained for a craft or profession, should be helped to forge self-reliance, and should have a place of refuge.[14] To these three rights, Muskett added a fourth, that a woman should be made love to at least once in her life. This may explain why she did not publish her novel until 1933 — and then under a pseudonym — and why she chose to make the Latin Quarter of Paris her home for so long.

Because marriage was no longer woman's automatic destiny, there were opportunities for women who, like Annie Duncan, did not wish to or did not marry to shape more independent lives, to forge their own livelihoods, abroad as well as at home. The young Katharine Susannah Prichard knew that she wanted to be a famous writer and so resolved not to fall in love or marry.[15] For unmarried women, to travel abroad was to escape — permanently or temporarily — social and family pressure. To be unmarried in a society without a spinster culture was to bear a stigma, to be an old maid, to be, in Annie Duncan's words, 'a plain failure', and in many cases to live as a patronised and degraded family drudge.[16] Gladys Marks wrote home to her father from Paris at the beginning of 1914 that 'sometimes I think I'll really end here; it's a better place for old maids than Sydney'.[17] In a chilling passage in Christina Stead's *For Love Alone*, which rings as true for the 1890s or the 1950s as it does for the 1930s, Teresa Hawkins confronts her gendered fate after her cousin Malfi's wedding — suburban marriage or spinsterhood — and 'those who did not get a man were worse off'.

There was a pane of glass in the breast of each girl; there every other girl could see the rat gnawing at her, the fear of being on the shelf. Besides the solitary girl, three hooded madmen walk, desire, fear, ridicule.[18]

For women who wanted to hone their talents to a high level or to make a living, going abroad was also a means of moving beyond the reach of censorship. Grace Rusden was passionately devoted to music, but, fearing the opposition of her older brother with whom she lived, she took secret lessons. Confronted with his criticism and teasing after he learnt of her initiative, she began to speak of moving to England, where she might pursue her interests without interference from family or friends.[19] In the 1860s it was not possible for Grace Rusden, the sister of the clerk of the Executive Council of Victoria, to escape. But a generation later, Miles Franklin evaded the conflicting demands of her desire for self-realisation in a life of writing and of the social pressures to conform to gender norms by removing herself to another place when she left for North America in 1906.[20]

While the late nineteenth century witnessed the opening up of new opportunities for independence and travel for women, it was still only the few who could take advantage of them. The constraints of age, class, female decorum, patriarchal authority, and woman's role as universal carer still weighed heavily against the realisation of such ambitions. Lack of means made travel impossible for most women, and it was still family money that underpinned many of the journeys and the bids for independence. The women artists who journeyed to Europe in such numbers at the turn of the century, and who were to make such an important contribution to the development of art in Australia, were middle-class women travelling and living for the most part with the assistance of family money. Kate O'Connor, Dorrit Black, Norah Simpson, Bessie Davidson, Bessie Gibson, Jessie Traill, and Grace Crowley all had help from their families or from inherited wealth. It was her mother's estate that financed Stella Bowen's trip in 1914, and Margaret Preston was able to go to Europe in 1904 at the age of 29 because her mother's death had given her a small inheritance — but financial exigencies brought her back to Australia three years later, and she worked in a teaching position in Adelaide to save the money to return in 1912.[21] Less fortunate than most of her sisters was Marie Tuck; the daughter of a schoolteacher, she taught painting, worked for a florist, and saved carefully and was 40 before she realised her ambition to paint in France.[22] It was to take Christina Stead three years of punishing self-denial to finance her escape from Australia in 1928. But even the possibility of scraping and saving was restricted to the few.

Youth was the next greatest handicap for those desiring independence; the women for whom opportunities for independent travel were most available were those unencumbered by husbands and children, unmarried women old enough to be categorised as spinsters. It was 'the end of early youth' that it made it possible for the 37-year-old Annie Duncan to travel alone to Britain and to holiday on the Continent with friends. Nettie Higgins, leaving Australia in her early twenties with a chaperone for the voyage, implicitly recognised the greater freedom available to older women when she wrote to her future husband, Vance Palmer, that she wished that she 'could postpone the thing until I'm forty when I could be a maiden lady quite unattached'.[23] The Australian women writers who lived overseas at the beginning of the twentieth century departed, like Winifred James, in their late twenties, or they were widows, like Mary Gaunt, or separated from their husbands, like Tasma and Louise Mack. Of the more than 60 women artists who were in Europe bent on professional careers before the First World War, close to two-thirds were in their late twenties or older.[24] The vast majority of the younger women travelled with their families or with chaperones. Arrival at the safe age of 30, however, did not necessarily lead to independent travel. Painters Kate O'Connor, Bessie Gibson and Grace Cossington Smith made their first trips in this age group, but *en famille*; all were still living with their families in a condition of financial dependence.

Even when neither wives nor mothers, women's role as universal carers often stood between them and travel. Catherine Helen Spence went overseas for the first time in 1864 at the age of 40. She wrote in 1910 that she had hesitated about going.

> There was my mother, who was 72, and my guardianship of the Duvals to think about. I had also undertaken the oversight of old Mrs Stephens, the widow of one of the early proprietors of The Register.[25]

In 1905 Alice Henry finally realised 'the desire of her heart' to travel to England and North America when both her parents had died and her brother was about to marry.[26] Isabel Cookson, who received her Bachelor of Science from the University of Melbourne in 1916, and her doctorate from the same university sixteen years later, did not study overseas; 'as a young woman she was left to support and nurse her mother through a long illness and under strained financial circumstances'.[27] And after women had begun new lives abroad, family duties could still bring them home. Fanny Cohen, the future headmistress of Fort Street Girls' High School in Sydney, won the Barker Travelling Scholarship at the University of Sydney in 1911, but her studies in mathematics at Cambridge were cut short by the ill health of her mother, who had accompanied her to Britain.[28] The letters home of Gladys Marks are full of stories of her friends who like herself wanted to stay in Europe but whom family pressure was forcing home.

Nor did the progress of time necessarily erode the constraints on the travel of individual women. Grace Crowley left Paris in 1929, 'at a time when every opportunity for improvement in the art world seemed to be opening up for me', because her mother was ill. She later looked back on her years in Paris as the happiest in her life and wondered what would have happened had she stayed.[29]

Some families opposed the departure of daughters because of the loss of potential carers and fear for family reputation, or indeed for the welfare of the daughters, but for others, the decision of an aging, single daughter to establish a career and move away may have removed a financial burden, an embarrassing encumbrance, the more so if the daughter chose to be difficult, determined, eccentric. And there were families who positively encouraged their daughters' desires for fulfilling lives, or who even imposed the travel agendas. Edith Hepburn, the future poet 'Anna Wickham', acknowledged that she was eager to travel 'because of youth's universal desire for change', but she also represented her journey to Europe alone at the age of 21 to develop her singing voice as originating in her father's ambitions and his need to find compensation for the failures of his own life.

> I knew that somehow I had to get my parents into the news, fortify their self-respect with grand contacts and successful exploits. I had a general commission to know people so that my father, through me, could come nearer the famous society that delighted him. I was his only child, and the only object with whom he had a satisfactory love relationship. And his ambition to make an impression on the country that had ignored him was so strong that as the ship moved out from the Wharf, he called up to me, 'Punch, Anne, Punch', meaning that he wished me to write for that monumentally humorous paper.[30]

'Anna Wickham' was unusual — and the daughter of unusual parents — in her encouraged solitary departure to Europe.

There is no simple answer to the problem of why some women were able to overcome the obstacles to travelling abroad in search of qualifications and independence while others were not. Circumstances, the extent of opposition, personality traits, each played its part, as Drusilla Modjeska has shown in her discussion of Marjorie Barnard, whose opportunity to continue her brilliant academic career at Oxford was cut off when her father forbade her departure and she accepted his decision.[31] For Barnard, a timid woman lacking in confidence, the break was too big, too hard, but her failure was also a function of her gender. However, Janet Mitchell's story provides an example of how a young woman could negotiate for an independent life. Her older sister, Nancy, represented Janet as the delicate youngest child, brought up to be a lily of the field, but a lily determined to have a career.[32] A subtext in Janet Mitchell's own memoirs is the story of how she manipulated and persuaded her parents first to allow training for a musical career in Australia and then in wartime London, and finally to agree to her attendance at the University of London. Determination linked with delicacy, a highly strung nature, undisguised misery, violent fits of weeping, and twenty-page postal out-pourings could be powerful weapons in a family that placed high value on civilised intercourse. And by the time she wanted to enrol at Bedford College, it was 1919 and Janet Mitchell was 23 with no immediate prospect of marriage and with two unmarried older sisters. To allow her to remain in London attending university may have seemed opportune to her parents.

Western Australian painter Kate O'Connor provides another example of the bid for freedom of a strong-minded and determined upper-class woman.[33] In 1906, after a decade both studying and teaching painting in Perth, as she approached the age of 30, O'Connor finally set out on a trip to Europe with her mother and sisters. Rather than return to Australia, she demanded her share of the family annuity so that she could establish herself as a painter in Paris. While she made occasional trips home, O'Connor lived and worked in Paris until 1955, despite family pressure that she assume the role of the unmarried daughter and return to Perth to care for her mother. She was tough enough to hold out for her own agen-da. To resist the will of Jessie Lillingston (later Street), another upper-class woman who eventually broke with ideology as well as decorum, might well have been impossible. Despite family opposition, she had studied for a Bachelor of Arts at the University of Sydney. On her visits to Europe in 1911 and 1914 she had become active in the women's suffrage movement and began travelling on her own. As she rightly wrote to her future hus-band, Kenneth Street, from North America in 1915: 'rebellion has been my strongest feeling'.[34]

At the end of Miles Franklin's *My Career Goes Bung*, Sybylla decides to leave Australia. She notes that there is nothing particularly exceptional in her decision: 'Lady Jane's column is devoted to escapees. Sculptors, writers, singers, actors, painters, educationalists, politicians all depart inevitably'.[35] The departures of the woman writers — as indeed of women painters and of those who aspired to careers in other professions — had much in com-mon with the patterns of their male counterparts; surrender to the myth so seductively articulated by Henry James of Europe as 'civilisation', and to the ideology of colonial inferiority and metropolitan superiority, the belief that there were greater opportunities abroad, the desire for fame beyond the vil-lage, the need to be closer to publishers and larger markets, to participate in the intellectual and cultural centres.[36] Musicians went to study with recog-nised teachers, to learn of current developments, to acquire overseas experience. They enjoyed a musical life, hearing performances that they could only have dreamt of in Australia. Pianist Maude Puddy, who left Adelaide with her sister in 1906 and studied in Vienna until 1913, heard Fritz Kreisler, Wilhelm Backhaus, Artur Schnabel and Pablo Casals play and Mahler conduct all the Mozart operas.[37] Artists wrote home of their joy in seeing original paintings, both ancient masterpieces and the new. In an interview in 1961 Thea Proctor reconstructed her first sighting of impressionist paintings; 'it was a wonderful experience … we were absolutely excited by it'.[38] Impressionism was followed by post-impressionism, both thrilling and shocking to an artist trained to draw the figure realistically. Proctor's additional observation on the early importance of line in her own work is a reminder that when she left Australia at the beginning of this century, there were few reproductions in colour. Thus no one had any idea of the revolutionary use of colour by avant-garde painters in Europe. In the 1920s an art student wrote back to her teacher in Sydney of her first sight of the paintings of Cézanne: 'He is neither wild, mad, heavy nor dull. Dull! just the reverse. No reproduction has ever given any idea of this man'.[39]

Margaret Preston in the mid-1920s gave as the motive for her first trip in 1904 the desire 'to see really where she stood as well as to get some "finishing lessons"'.[40] She told of the odyssey, beginning in Munich and ending in Paris, which took her from rejection of the modernist paintings, which she saw as 'mad and vicious', to acceptance and to transformations in her own work. Thea Proctor, startled in Europe by postimpressionist canvases, was shocked when she arrived back in Sydney in 1921 'to see that Australian painting had not changed at all from the time I left in 1903, and the young painter seemed to be quite content to do imitations of Streeton'. Margaret Preston was even more scathing.

> The galleries are so well fenced in
> The theatres and cinemas are so well fenced in.
> The libraries are so well fenced in.
> The universities are so well fenced in
> You do not get bothered with foolish new ideas. Tradition thinks for you
> but Heavens! how dull![41]

These comments say something not only about the Australian art world of the 1920s, and the fear of the modern and foreign as contaminating, but also once again about the privileged and authoritative speech that travellers acquire by encountering the distant, the sacred, the centres. It was, after all, not only the provincialism of Australian painting that upset Thea Proctor, but also the angle at which women were wearing their hats.

Not all women were as open to the new as Preston and Proctor. Isobel Jacobs in an article in *Art and Architecture* in 1912 counselled aspiring artists against going to Paris where, *inter alia*, contemporary art inclined to sensationalism.

There is a well-known man there, Matisse who has a great following, who sells a great deal of extraordinary work, but who, I believe is experimenting as to how much an eager public will swallow of extravagance.[42]

And travel and encounter with the new did not necessarily revolutionise taste. Gladys Marks at the opening of the Autumn Salon in Paris in November 1913 saw 'the futurists and cubists and soi-disant modern pictures in general', and was not overly impressed.

Then the nudes! Oh my poor Greek and Roman Gods and goddesses is your reign over and are these to be the standards of beauty in the future? And then the indecencies and absurdities! Children at Kindergarten might have done some of the daubs.[43]

The producers and would-be-producers of artefacts of culture also voyaged to gather overseas endorsement, both for its own sake and as the means to recognition at home. Looking back in her 1963 autobiography, Katharine Susannah Prichard wrote:

My short stories and articles had been appearing in several Australian newspapers and magazines but I thought that an Australian writer would never be appreciated in our own country until she proved that her writing could evince some reception in England.[44]

When she won the Hodder and Stoughton prize for an Australian novel, she decided that she could return to Australia. Twenty years later, Florence James, determined to establish herself as a writer, was adamant in her letters home that she could not return until she had established her reputation in Britain: 'I know there's plenty of room at home to write, yet I *must* get a firm footing in the markets before it's the least scrap of good contemplating work in the colonies'.[45]

In addition to the reasons for going abroad that women writers and artists shared with men, there were other factors that were gender-specific. Recent work on Australian literary and art worlds at the turn of the century associated with 'radical nationalism' and the boys of the *Bulletin* and the Heidelberg school has suggested that these were unsympathetic and alienating environments for women, at least in Sydney and Melbourne — the story may have been different in Adelaide.[46] Literary groups such as the Casuals or the Dawn and Dusk Club met in pubs and bars, which were not spaces open to women. While Louise Mack received considerable encouragement from A.G. Stephens and good reviews for her first novel, *Teens*, and in her later life created a romantic image of her participation in a *belle époque* creative world, the encouragement was for the efforts of a pretty young girl, and Mack's position in the *Bulletin* literary world was very marginal. As one of two women in the Dawn and Dusk club, according to Arthur Jose, she 'was on the whole taken as a joke by her fellow Boy authors'.[47] John Le Gay Brereton later described Mack as a fluffy young chicken and the image that she cultivated was of a very feminine, over romantic, slightly dizzy individual.[48] But to what extent was this but another case of protective armouring? As Drusilla Modjeska has argued, the processes in Miles Franklin's decision to leave Australia are more complex than is suggested in *My Career Goes Bung*, but her experiences in the boys' world played their part.[49] And why did Alice Muskett, whose short stories affirm a woman's right to work, self-determination and equality in sexual relations, choose to spend most of her life between the ages of 25 and 50 in Europe?[50]

If women were trivialised and lampooned in the misogynist discourse of the world of the *Bulletin* and Bohemia, they were also excluded from the culture of the Bush, a masculinist culture of the frontier, the territory of the single man, the lone hand who rejected and fled the emasculating presence of women. In a letter from London to her mother in 1910, Nettie Higgins (later Palmer) described an evening in the company of Australian writers:

> We really had an Australian evening of it, though I felt rather out of it because I've been such a towny Australian all my life. They (Bean, Palmer) all knew what station life meant, and that's more of a sealed book to me than King George V's life at Buckingham Palace here.[51]

Higgins is confessing that Europe is more familiar territory for her than the bush; the irony is of course that it is her gender not her 'towniness' that excludes her; the legend of the bush was itself the creation of 'townies' and foreign to most men — her future husband excepted.[52] The two women who first penetrated this territory, Barbara Baynton and Miles Franklin, soon retreated — metaphorically and literally — and crossed the other frontier into overseas worlds. If women represented domesticity, gentility, morality, conventionality, they also stood for the effeminate culture of Europe, both as its transmitters via the gentility of the piano and the watercolour, and its supposedly second-rate reproducers in derivative and insipid tales of romance. While Henry Lawson was writing his short stories of men in the bush, Alice Muskett created hers of sophisticated women in the urban worlds of both Sydney and Paris. Hers were not part of the 'legend' and were ignored, but they point again to women's relegation to or occupation of the other frontier. If the nationalist strand in Australian culture and social life was masculine and masculinist, it may be that the cosmopolitan components were women's contribution.

Women artists faced problems similar to those of women writers. Adelaide Ironside was not alone in having her aspirations trivialised. Sir Winthrop Hackett wrote to Western Australian painter Kate O'Connor: 'Everybody here says what a brave girl you are to attempt to carve out your own destiny this way and I agree with them'.[53] Referring to her mother's forthcoming trip to Europe in 1913, Hackett asked if she was going to look after O'Connor. At that stage O'Connor was 37 and had been living alone abroad for the best part of seven years. Women artists were excluded from the high art of the period, the dominant pastoral mode, as Hilda Rix Nicholas was to find out.[54] They too had gender-specific reasons to pursue their studies far from home. Women might account for the majority of art students, but they were a minority of prize winners. Acceptance and recognition were much harder at home, and it was very much in the interest of the male artists to exclude and marginalise the women. They themselves were only beginning to emerge as professionals and the too prominent presence of women threatened their new status; 'done by women' and 'amateur' were virtually interchangeable terms. No doubt overseas residence and absence of reputation in Australia played their part in Dora Ohlfsen's failure to obtain work on Australian war memorials. But could a woman be given the commission for an equestrian statue of a general?

Exclusion from the dominant mode was to prove to have advantages as well as disadvantages. When they went into the art worlds of Paris and London, the women may have been more receptive; the new and different may be less threatening to those without a stake in the status quo. Accustomed to adjusting and hence to a more sensitive reading of cues, women may have been more responsive to new ideas, forms, and structures. It is now argued that it was returning women artists who introduced modernism into Australia, artists like Norah Simpson, Dorrit Black and Margaret Preston. Because first explored by women, modernism did not upset the pastoral genre, which continued to flourish in traditional styles.[55] Because the male art élite were committed to the old, there was space for women to appropriate the new and cast it in their own ways.

The experience of some of the women writers and artists in this period suggests that despite some very noisy male rejections of home, the escape motive may have been more important in women's journeys abroad. And travelling alongside the women who went abroad to pursue careers and the cultivation of their talents were others who no doubt feigned ambitions in order to escape. More constrained at home, women had more reason to flee and more to gain by flight. Even if the societies into which the women moved had as many constraints on women as there were at home, the constraints did not press so heavily when they were not locked into kin and neighbourhood networks, into ascribed identities and roles. The letters of Gladys Marks are also full of expressions of the joy of living beyond the eyes of the village, in an anonymous Paris where she and her friends could dance in a ring around Rousseau's statue without raising eyebrows, where no one knows you or your relatives: 'It is so fine to be among that strange polyglot mass of students and wear your old suit without wondering what uncle this or cousin that will say'.[56]

Much of men's travel, in the context of the *Bulletin,* the Bush and the *Lone Hand*, was represented as flight from hearth and home, yet domesticity weighed more heavily on women. To move far away was a means to escape the fate of joyless marriage, family drudge, universal carer. Kathleen Pitt (later Fitzpatrick) wrote of her mother's sadness when her overseas trip in the 1920s came to an end; she had 'nothing to look forward to but the resumption of the role of suburban housewife which she had always detested'.[57] To travel to Europe was not only to make a bid for independence, it was also to flee from the mundane to what literature and travel writing represented as the romantic and the exotic. Those whose lives are restricted and confined can compensate with rich dreams and fantasies, and women travelled in their imaginations long before they climbed gangways. In Sydney, Christina Stead's Teresa Hawkins dreamt of a shadowy married future in 'some coast town overseas, in some mysterious unseen spot where perhaps they spoke a foreign language'.[58]

Teresa Hawkins's departure from Sydney was also for the isles of Cythera, the place where love was not taboo, where secret desires were realised, and in London she found sexual fulfilment and freedom. *For Love Alone* is a story of the 1920s and 1930s. The extent to which the women of the previous generation were also fleeing puritanical moral codes and seeking sexual freedom is a problem to which there is little answer. Whatever their motives, the conventions of the time enjoined reticence about private life. We must await the 1930s for hints and the 1970s for explicit tales of horizontal travelling. What the late-nineteenth-century women aspiring to achievement recorded in their diaries, autobiographies, letters and interviews related to a public discourse — their professional aims, ambitions, struggles. And perhaps they should be taken at their word.

Since the very act of going overseas to establish an independent career was still considered questionable, many of the women appear, like Mary Gaunt, to have deliberately emphasised their conformity and propriety. The title of Margaret Thomas's tale of her travels, *A Scamper Through Spain*, suggests not only frivolity, but also innocent pleasure, not danger and defiance. And the women who wrote about their lives in *fin-de-siècle* Paris created images above all of conventionality and domesticity.

The dominant image of the artist at the end of the nineteenth century was still that of the outsider — passionate, eccentric, unconventional — and the Paris of the artists was the colourful, romantic, exotic, risqué place of George du Maurier's popular novel, *Trilby*.[59] In Tasma's novel, *The Penance of Portia James*, Portia flees London and her marriage to find solace and help from Anna Ross in Paris, who had fascinated her on the ship to Europe. And this Paris was murky, menacing. Anna Ross was a woman from a good English county family, but in her blood coursed that of a remote 'Amerindian' ancestress; she was dark, high-cheekboned, faintly *sauvage*, a painter who looked at the world with her own eyes, 'a solitary woman with male brains'.[60] Anna lived and worked, with little regard to convention, in an attic studio in the heart of the Latin Quarter. Portia had been in Paris before, but the only time she had crossed the river was on a shopping expedition to the Bon Marché. The left bank was 'terra incognita', a physical and moral environment that she found noisy, disordered, confusing and menacing. Portia was more frightened in the Latin Quarter than she was riding alone through the Australian bush — where presumably the danger was clean and physical, not murky and moral. She is dragged by Anna into the artistic life, into dinners in crowded, noisy, smoke-filled student restaurants where she is subjected to the male gaze, and into working as a model first for Anna and then for others.

> Her visit to the painter, Delstanche, had not been altogether as satisfactory to herself as to Anna. She had been made to take her hair down, and to show her neck and arms in all their summer whiteness; and though she had done as much times out of mind for the past week while she had been posing for Anna, to do so on the present occasion had seemed a formidable ordeal.[61]

On her return from a sitting in the Luxembourg Gardens, Portia is accosted by 'a Frenchman of the méridional type with swarthy skin and piercing black eyes', and is saved — presumably from a fate worse than death — by the fortuitous arrival of two English gentlemen with whom she is acquainted. Fascinated and repelled by the world of Anna, Portia eventually settles for safety and convention and returns to London and her disastrous marriage.

It is doubtful if painter Bessie Davidson's father had read *The Penance of Portia James*, but he knew that Paris was no place for a respectable young woman. Bessie was permitted to study art in Europe if Germany and not Paris was her destination. Bessie initially complied, but after a few months she did move to Paris where she spent the rest of her life.[62] Perhaps Mr Davidson should have read Winifred James's article, 'An Australian Girl in the Quartier Latin', published in *New Idea* in the same year that Bessie left. The author described her visit to the studio of a friend.

> It is common knowledge that the student can-cans his way to knowledge through a succession of wild nights spent in lurid cafes, unfrequented by the simpler Philistine.
>
> But it was the quiet side of life that I saw, and when the curtains were drawn and the lamps lighted, it was not difficult to imagine oneself miles from Bohemia, and back in the atmosphere of practical British domesticity.[63]

Alison Rae and Alice Muskett wrote about their life in Paris for the Australian press in terms of their ten-hour working days in the schools and of the tea parties in their studios, bohemian only for the art and book talk and the serving of Russian tea with lemon.[64] The Latin Quarter that Ada Holman portrayed in the first decade of this century was also very different from *Trilby*. She wrote from Paris of the taming of the Latin Quarter that was now given over to hard work rather than hard drinking and this domestication was the result of an invasion by women — there were now almost as many girl students as men and they came from all nations, with 'a fair sprinkling of Australians'.[65] It was now becoming normal, she continued, for the girls to be on their own sharing rooms, but mothers — particularly of the American variety — were still very much present. The invasion of the women had led to a new seriousness in the Latin Quarter, and to less attention to personal adornment. This was particularly noticeable among English and Australian women. Christobel Ballantyne Bollen visited Bessie Davidson in Paris in 1913 and found that her studio conformed to romantic expectations: 'it is just like studios you read about, a big, high room, with paintings and reproductions everywhere, and a bed covered with a fur rug to make it like a settee', but 'the Latin Quarter is much too respectable, not nearly as wicked and gay as I expected'.[66] The Latin Quarter was now rendered respectable for the wowsers and worried mothers — at least in discourse. Living in left-bank studios, drinking Russian tea, visiting 'cafes dancing with bright lights', watching the models 'flitting like bright butterflies', 'men with black locks falling on the shoulders', beautiful girls with 'full almond-shaped eyes' and children 'in slouch hats and buckled leggings', may have been romance enough.[67]

Yet Alice Muskett's short story of the love affair of two desperately poor foreign artists in 'Paris à la Bohème' suggests alternative lifestyles, as does 'Anna Wickham's' autobiography, which she wrote as 'a piece of housekeeping' prior to her intended suicide in 1937.[68] 'Wickham' who had set off for Europe carrying her parents' frustrated ambitions accepted a proposal of marriage shortly after her arrival in London in 1905. When her fiancé came to visit her in Paris where she was studying singing, they became lovers: 'I was interested in sex, feeling that love was somehow in my part in la vie de bohème, and my role as expatriate student'.[69] But does 'Wickham's' 1930s confession reveal any more than the reticence of the women at the turn of the century? It too may be following convention.

If silent on private lives, the turn-of-the-century women were more vocal when appropriating another plot of travel narratives, the myth of Dick Whittington, the poor unknown who arrives in the big city and after long struggles meets success. The protagonists in the 'Australian girl makes it in London' novels of Louise Mack and Winifred James are overwhelmed by the obstacles at the centre of the world, obstacles that with perseverance and courage they surmount to achieve success. Barbara Baynton told Vance Palmer of how she had 'hawked' her book from one publisher to another and had so many refusals she thought of putting it on the fire.[70] Mary Gaunt recalled her early days of struggle in London when she lodged alone in two dull rooms and wrote and wrote and editors returned and returned: 'I found London a terrible place in those days'.[71]

Women who travel go on different journeys, and one woman can embark with multiple goals, agendas and storylines. Teresa Hawkins's Cythera was not only the place where love was not taboo, but where women's talents 'could burst forth with primeval force'.[72] What is clear from the stories of the women who travelled to acquire qualifications, experience and reputation, is that these were goals in themselves and the means to more independent, self-sufficient, autonomous lives. Women like Annie Duncan, who had acquired professional qualification or experience, 'paddled their own canoes'. In 1913 Gladys Marks wrote home about her friend Doris who had lived alone in Vienna for six years studying music; she was 'a big brained experienced woman of the world now in addition to being a fine artist and won't brook loss of independence'.[73] But her father had just arrived and in London he would not let her go out alone at night and was insisting on her returning home. The story of Doris illustrates both the rewards of and the obstacles to independent lives overseas.

Interlude

Winifred James

The interconnections of being single, needing to make a living, and moving beyond Australia are illustrated in the life and career of writer Winifred James. Her life story also touches on other themes, those of women and imperialism, and women and citizenship, and of representations of the world beyond Europe,

In 1903 the 29-year-old Winifred James departed for London.[1] Her age with its attendant status of spinster rather than young girl made it possible for her to travel alone. She was the twelfth child of the Yorkshire-born Gertrude James and her Cornish Wesleyan minister husband. Winifred James's mother died soon after she was born and she was brought up by her grandparents. Confronted with the problem of having to make her own living, she first ran a teashop in Adelaide and then typically looked to a career in the arts. She first considered the stage, but diffidence and self-consciousness dissuaded her from acting and from her next choice, singing. She then turned to the more private art of writing.[2] After her stories began to be published locally, she looked to London for literary success. Two years after her arrival in London, her novel *Bachelor Betty* was published and sold well.

James remained in London supporting herself by writing — journalism, novels, travel books, essays and belles-lettres, including the extraordinarily sentimental, but extremely successful imperialist text, *Letters to my Son*.[3] She published vignettes of her travels in France, Italy and Corsica in the traditional female literary form of letters in *Letters of a Spinster*.[4] In 1912 James embarked on a trip to the West Indies, Haiti and Panama, recounting her experiences in another travel book, *The Mulberry Tree*. While in Panama, she met the American merchant, Henry de Jan, who was head of a fruit growing and exporting company in Almirante and they were married in London in 1913.

Winifred James's marriage took her from her antique-collecting, bridge-playing club life in London to its very antithesis, a Panamanian settlement of twenty whites, only two of whom were women, and some three hundred 'niggers and chinamen'. Domestic conditions were primitive, her home a four-roomed 'box'. She was also tormented by isolation, mosquitoes and malaria, and irritated by lazy 'niggers', whom she felt had neither the inclination nor the need to live in accordance with the Protestant ethic or the spirit that had forged the British Empire.

Winifred James's accounts of her experiences in central America produced two more books of travel, *A Woman in the Wilderness* and *Out of the Shadows*.[5]

Until 1922 James commuted between Panama, North America, London and Spain, where her husband was appointed as an American diplomatic attaché in 1918. Four years after the appointment, she left her husband and returned to London. The marriage was dissolved in 1927 following three years of expensive dispute, claim and counter claim in courts in London, New York and Panama.[6] In his divorce petition, Henry de Jan named an English planter as alienating his wife's affections; she later claimed that her husband displayed the symptoms of a dual personality.[7] Vignettes from her global if not her extramarital wanderings in these years were published as *Gangways and Corridors* in 1936.[8] After the collapse of her marriage, James established herself in 'a delightful three-storied house just on the border of Chelsea' and set up in the antique business. Alarmed by the onset of war and in ill health, she returned to Australia in 1939 at the age of 63, having lived abroad for 34 years. She died two years later.

Winifred James's novel *Bachelor Betty* is the story of a young Australian girl who journeys to London to establish herself as a writer, and with little more than her courage and capacity for hard work triumphs in the great overwhelming metropolis. The theme of the novel is the problem of the single woman who must support herself. Betty has no objection to marriage, indeed there is 'not one woman in a hundred who chooses single life because she prefers it'; like all women she 'secretly wanted to be petted and nursed and fussed over'. Her problem is that of the woman who has not found the ideal mate, who faces the choice between an unsuitable marriage contracted out of desperation or the uncertain life of a single woman, between 'cramping dependence and tremendous isolation'.[9]

When Betty has her work first accepted for publication, she experiences the orgasmic ecstasy of creative achievement.

> Sometimes I have the most entrancing dreams. I am flying through space touching nothing yet full of confidence and fearing no fall. It was in that state I left the office and found my way home. There was no pavement under my feet, my body had no weight, and I was not conscious of any action. I was simply being propelled by some joyous invigorating power.[10]

But was literary orgasm enough for a woman? Betty thought not, but if one cannot find the right man, then work and independence have their value and satisfactions. And women who could support themselves did not need to make unwelcome and unsuitable marriages, and this was 'an advancement in morality'.

In the novel that James published in the following year, *Patricia Baring*, set exclusively in Australia, the heroine voices her protests against the double standard in sexual morality and the limited opportunities for women, their imprisonment in the role of Penelope. Her betrothed goes off to India for two years, while she waits at home.

> He is a man, he has the excitement of his business to make the days slip by unnoticed. He is seeing new lands, making fresh interests. He is not *waiting* through the days and weeks and months and years, he is *living* them; and each day although it may not be filled with pleasure, is filled with happenings. With a woman it is so different.[11]

At this point art was to prefigure life. When marriage led Winifred James to the role of wife in a lonely, isolated settlement in Panama, she portrayed her husband's life as more bearable because he had an occupation, the outlet of work.

> At last I could bear it no longer. My body was ill with it. That and the heat and the isolation and the niggers we couldn't get, and the ones we got who wouldn't work, the monotony and the eternal difficulties with food, and the insistent ugliness of everything to do with mankind, made me unable to see anything straight. If I could have kept shop like William, I should have been interested all day too.[12]

In giving notice of the publication of *Patricia Baring*, the *British-Australasian* described Winifred James as a firm believer in the principle laid down by Herbert Spencer, that every man has the freedom to do all that he wills, provided that he does not infringe on the equal freedom of other men — except that Winifred James's claim was not for every *man* but for every *woman*.[13]

The Panama that Winifred James constructed in her writings is a menacing, threatening land reeking of sensuality and sexuality.

> There is something horribly sinister in the relentless destructive force of the place; in the dreadful hanging silences of the forest walls that rise around us. The great trees are alive and watching, but they never talk as other trees do. The dank green creepers that hang festooned from their branches are like so many motionless snakes: the parasites and orchids that cling in their crevices seem to me, no matter how beautiful they be, like lice upon a body. This blind watchful hovering monster only remains powerless so long as *you* are moving. Stop for a moment and you know that it is coming ever so invisibly towards you.[14]

All that could save the white person from the 'obscene embrace of the jungle' was eternal vigilance, a life of clockwork regularity, meticulous tidiness, an unswerving standard of excellence, no half-measures, the virtues that made the Empire.

Winifred James's childhood, like that of other women of her time, class and place, was saturated with images of Britain.

> As a child sitting in the darkness under high starlit skies, I knew primroses. When the name England was said I saw primroses. And when they spoke of primroses I longed for the England I had never seen; the England that was an ache in the blood from the time that thinking became a conscious thing.[15]

Her passionate attachment to Britain did not, however, carry rejection of her place of birth; Bachelor Betty waxed indignant about English misconceptions of Australia and the *Home* told its readers in 1923 that James was 'at heart an Australian'.[16] But Winifred James also identified herself totally as a Briton and espoused imperialist and British racist ideologies. Britain was the protector, promoter and policeman of civilisation, a role she held by moral right.

> England is the guardian of the world, and nothing but the inability of her people at home to realise the greatness of their charge can take this power from her. It should be to every man, woman and child, to every statesman and stevedore, a sacred charge; for on the integrity of each Britisher depends the safety, not only of themselves, but of the whole world to-day and to-morrow as well. Someone in this welter of self-determination must take charge. The vast number of little peoples managing their own internal affairs well enough while they stay at home, will only be well behaved as long as they feel a superior power above them.[17]

Her imperialist mentality is also clear in her volumes of belles-lettres, *Letters to My Son* and *A Man for Empire*, which might be read as an attempt to instil right values in the imperial young.

> I used to feel that if I could have made a man for England I should have made a man for all the world. It was not given to me. And yet, perhaps through you …
>
> Take good care of her, my darlings. Nothing so great will be yours again if you should lose her.[18]

The ardent imperialist did not produce a son for the Empire, nor even a husband, and she found it disappointing that Henry de Jan as an American citizen could not defend the Empire in 1914. Far more galling was that the fact she herself was not allowed to engage in war work in Britain and had to register with the police. The British Naturalisation Act 1870 deprived women who married foreigners of their British nationality. Women who lost their own nationality on marriage could also become stateless if the government of their husband's country refused to grant nationality. This issue was taken up by women's organisations in Australia and was regularly on the agenda of the conferences of the International Council of Women.[19] In the wake of the enormous displacement of peoples after the First World War, problems of nationality became an important item at the meetings of the Assembly of the League of Nations. By the mid-1930s women in the United States and the Soviet Union were able to retain their nationality on marriage, but women in Britain and the Empire lagged behind, despite their constant agitation. Winifred James, whose feminism was tempered by her insistence on femininity, waged her own campaign to regain her British nationality after her divorce. Her case became famous in February 1933 when she appeared in court for refusing to register with the police in London as an alien, and street demonstrations were organised by the Women's Guild of the Empire in her support.[20] The case against James was dismissed and in the same week the Home Office issued an order exempting British women married to foreigners from the necessity of registering with the police. In 1935 Winifred James was given a naturalisation certificate in an individual act of dispensation.[21] But the problem remained for other women, and it was not until after the Second World War that they were given the option of retaining their own nationality, but only after marriage to Germans, Italians and Japanese had created heartbreaking problems for some Australian women.

In press interviews given during her time overseas and on her return to Australia, Winifred James constructed a narrative, similar to that of *Bachelor Betty*, of the young Australian girl who arrived in London and through her grit and determination, hard work and perseverance, achieved early success and never looked back.[22] The fragmentary private notebooks that Winifred James kept in the 1930s tell a story different from that constructed for the public record. Written in a time of deep depression, the entries focus on illness, the problems of her failed marriage, and poverty, and thoughts of suicide. There are other narratives in the life of the woman who headed her notebooks 'Sex Education'. In the public record, Winifred James, like so many women who went abroad to find fame and fortune, fitted her journey into archetypal storylines that created positive images for the audience back home and possibly also for herself, to give meaning to her wanderings.

CHAPTER 5

Travel and War

*You look down on the roofs of Sarajevo, mosques with
their coloured domes and slender white minarets — so
many minarets and tall green poplars thrusting their
delicate points neatly and sharply into the blue sky. At
the rounded reddish tiles and blurred outlines of the
older low sunk Turkish houses, the sharp outlines of the
concrete and Byzantine-decorated brick of the tall modern buildings, the whole picture divided in two by the silver Miljaska crossed by ten bridges.*[1]

The Australian men who went to war in 1914 were driven by a wide range
of imperatives. Duty, patriotism — both imperial and national — and
social pressures were all important, but for the 'six-bob-a-day tourists',
enlistment also provided the opportunity to escape drab, confining lives
and for adventure and overseas travel.[2] It was war that provided the best
and only opportunity for most men to travel beyond Australian shores.

In 1914 women were caught up in the same emotions and longings as
men. They too wanted to do their bit for the Empire on which the sun
never set. As Sister R.A. Kirkcaldie, who served as a nurse in France,
wrote of her enlistment in 1914: 'The Empire was in peril. At once, the
thought of all of us was: "What can we do to help?"'[3] But the women who
wanted to take an active role in the defence of the Empire faced powerful
obstacles formed by the dictates of what was considered desirable and fit-
ting for their gender. Women had to be spared the hardships and horror
of the front; their jobs were to guard the home fires, provide comforts,
raise money, maintain morale, and knit socks. Nevertheless, many
Australian women became involved in the overseas theatre of war, saw
new parts of the world, and took the opportunity that war provided to
experiment with new and different ways of living.

Unlike the men, the women who travelled to war were for the most part
middle- and upper-class women who had the means to finance their war
service or who had been trained in the professions of medicine and nursing.
The stories told by some point to the range of the overseas war experience of
Australian women. In their narratives, the focus is usually on the adventure
rather than the horror of war.

War was adventure — and good copy — for the first Australian woman
to become involved in action, that irrepressible inventor and mythologiser
of self, Louise Mack. After the success of *An Australian Girl in London*,

Mack's career overseas included six years in Florence, where she had edited the English-language *Italian Gazette*. On the outbreak of war, she took off from London for Belgium as a war correspondent, but her first foray into war hardly covered her with glory.[4] The party of journalists she had joined had only been on Belgian soil for six hours when they heard rumours that the Kaiser had ordered that Channel crossings be halted and newspaper correspondents shot on sight. Mack and company beat a swift retreat. Undaunted, she decided to return to Belgium for a longer sojourn, taking all her possessions, including her latest manuscript for Mills and Boon. To the manuscript, the suitcase and couple of trunks containing enough clothes to see her through all seasons, she soon added a canary and a parrot that she rescued in Aerschot. The clutter did not prevent Mack from travelling around Belgium and staying in German-occupied Brussels before moving on to witness the invasion and fall of Antwerp. She remained in that last city after its German occupation at some risk to her own life and more to those of the Belgians forced to hide her. Mack eventually crossed the border into the Netherlands in the guise of a peasant and made her way back to Britain. She then wrote her instant account with a speed equal to that of later Gulf War journalists. Before the end of the year, Louise Mack had finished *A Woman's Experiences in the Great War*, become a public figure, and begun giving dramatic — and embellished — renditions of her adventures, first in Britain and then up and down Australia after she came home in 1916.[5] *A Woman's Experiences in the Great War* is told in the style of a breathless adventure story, with elements of the schoolgirl's ripping yarn, the intrepid self-possession of the Victorian lady explorer, and the jingoistic and sentimental patriotism that would have appealed to her boss, Lord Northcliffe. While the gulf between the living and the telling of the story may be even wider than usual in the case of Louise Mack's account of her sensational war experiences, she had set out to do something unusual for her gender and she had done it.

Other Australian women who were in Europe in 1914 also found ways to deploy their talents in the war effort. Painters Iso and Alison Rae joined a Voluntary Aid Detachment at a military camp at Etaples, and Dora Ohlfsen joined the Italian Red Cross. The musicians did their bit; Elsie Hall played for the troops in France, while her fellow pianist Una Bourne gave concerts in Britain for the Red Cross.[6] Ethel de Lissa, who had studied at the London School of Economics and was familiar with several European languages, worked on censorship of the foreign press with the Ministry of Information in London.[7] Jessie Traill first served as a VAD nurse in London and then with the Queen Alexandra nursing service in Rouen in France, and became so involved in the fate of one small village that she returned there after the war and contributed to its rebuilding.[8] Bessie Davidson, who had gone back to Australia in 1914, immediately turned around and

Ros Pesman, Avila, Spain, 1964 (Author's collection).

Gladys Marks (University of Sydney Archives).

Social life on-board ship in the nineteenth century (Photographic Collection, National Library of Australia, Canberra).

Deborah Hackett in Court dress (Battye Library, Perth, 1913B).

Cover for Ena Lilley's *A 'Possum Abroad* (R. S. Hews & Co., Brisbane, 1901).

Louise Mack (Photograph Collection, Mitchell Library, Sydney).

Winifred James (Winifred James, *The Mulberry Tree*, G. Bell & Sons, London, 1913).

Mary Gaunt in her cart at Christiansborg, West Africa (Mary Gaunt, *Alone in West Africa*, T. Werner Laurie, London, 1912).

'Two Australian Girls in Olden Lands', Florence Finn and friend (Florence Finn, *Pigmies Among Potentates or Two Australian Girls in Olden Lands*, Renwick, Pride, Nuttall, Melbourne, 1912).

Margaret Preston, Australia (1875–1963), *Self Portrait* 1930, oil on canvas, 61 × 50.8 cm. Gift of the artist at the request of the Trustees 1930 (Art Gallery of New South Wales).

George Lambert, Australia (1873–1930), *Portrait of Miss Thea Proctor* 1903, oil on canvas, 91.5 × 71 cm. Purchased under the terms of the Florence Blake Bequest 1961 (Art Gallery of New South Wales).

Hilda Rix Nicholas, Australia (1884–1961), *Poster: Salon des Beaux Arts c.* 1913, hand coloured soft ground etching, 39.9 × 29.1 cm. Gift of Rix Wright, the artist's son 1976 (Art Gallery of New South Wales).

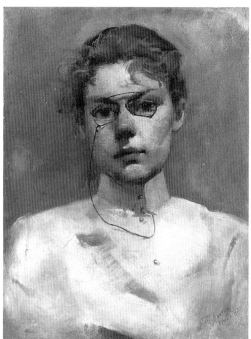

Julian Rossi Ashton, Australia (1851–1942), *Study of Alice Muskett* 1893, oil on wood, 33.4´× 25.5 cm (Art Gallery of New South Wales).

sailed again for France, joining the French Red Cross and becoming matron of a hospital for severely wounded soldiers.[9]

It was in the medical service that women went most obviously to war, and this is where their war experience is best documented.[10] Already at the turn of the century some sixty Australian nurses had sailed for South Africa to join the Australian forces fighting in the Boer War. Among their number was Agnes Macready who had sent back accounts of her experience to the *Catholic Press*.[11] Fourteen years later, in 1914, 25 nurses left Albany for Cairo as the first contingent of the Australian Army Nursing Corps. But the Australian Army Nursing Corps by no means accounts for all the women who worked as nurses and medical assistants in war zones. There were women who took themselves to Britain and joined the Queen Alexandra Imperial Medical Nursing Service and Australian women nursed with the Red Cross in France. It has recently been estimated that more than 2500 Australian women nursed overseas between 1914 and 1918,[12] seeing service in Egypt, the Middle East, Afghanistan, India, Britain, France, Italy, Russia and the Balkans, and on hospital ships and transports.

If women were now accepted in war zones as nurses, their presence as doctors was not welcome; in 1914 neither the Australian nor the British army would enlist women doctors for overseas service.[13] Therefore women created their own medical units or attached themselves to the Allied forces in Europe. Helen Sexton, who graduated in medicine from the University of Melbourne in 1892, was travelling in Europe when war broke out. With the assistance of friends, she set up a small field hospital in France, the Hôpital Australien.[14] Other women joined the hospital units established from Britain. Prominent among these was the Scottish Women's Hospital, a service with strong feminist connections, which maintained fourteen medical units on foreign soil under the command of Dr Elsie Inglis, leader of the Scottish wing of the National Union of Women's Suffrage Societies.[15]

One war zone where women were particularly conspicuous in the medical services was the Balkans. It was an assassination in the Serb city of Sarajevo that had triggered the first declaration of war, but by the autumn of the following year, Serbia's allies were totally absorbed on other fronts. Serbia was, however, still of prime concern to the Triple Alliance, and in 1915 the German–Austrian offensive joined by Bulgaria pushed further and further down the Balkan peninsula. Disease was added to war with the outbreak of a virulent typhus epidemic. To treat its wounded, diseased and dying, Serbia had only some 420 doctors, of whom it is estimated no fewer than 125 died in the typhus epidemic of 1915.[16] Thus, women made a critically important contribution in the Serb war zone, not only with units of the Scottish Women's Hospital, but also with the Serb Relief Fund and the Red Cross, and as individual volunteers in hospitals or with the Serb army. The most famous of all the women in Serbia was the English woman Flora Sandes, who joined and fought with the Serb army as a soldier.[17] Not quite as challenging to convention in their behaviour as Flora Sandes, the Australian women worked with the retreating Serb forces as medical practitioners, nurses, orderlies and ambulance drivers. Their number included Miles Franklin who from the United States in 1915 had felt 'the call of blood'.[18] She had crossed to Britain where, in July 1917, she joined a unit of the Scottish Women's Hospital and worked as an orderly for six months at a field hospital, headed by another Australian, Dr Agnes Bennett, on the front at Ostrovo, north-west of Salonika. Franklin wrote on her return to London that her involvement in war had been 'a lovely and happy experience' and that she 'never expected to be so happy again as I was there'.[19] Her feelings of a heightened sense of being alive in the Serb war zone were to be echoed by other women.

Also among the women combating typhus in the Serb army was Elsie Dalyell, a graduate from the University of Sydney who was in London on a fellowship at the Lister Institute of Preventative Medicine when war broke out. In 1915 she went to Serbia with a unit of the Scottish Women's Hospital, a unit run 'on clean British lines'.[20] In the midst of the problems and the suffering with which she had to deal, Elsie Dalyell found moments of enjoyment and exhilaration.

> It has all been good. I have felt splendidly fit all the time, and we are in a wonderful situation — the beauty round us takes one's thought from the wretchedness and misery we grapple with, and I think that saves the situation altogether. We are on a high plateau, the River Vardar runs through the plain below, and there are foothills about two miles off which lead up to the hoary Balkans themselves, and the nearer mountains are twenty miles away, but in this clear air it seems like five. The line of dazzling snow against a clear blue sky is the most wonderful sight I have yet seen.[21]

Among her adventures was the unforeseen end to a picnic in the countryside when Dalyell and her two friends were captured as spies by 'a wild Serb soldier'. In her story, British sang-froid coped admirably and, despite a forced march, she 'enjoyed the experience'. Dr Dalyell left the Balkan front in 1916 for France, where she worked as a bacteriologist with a unit of the Scottish Women's Hospital, housed in the twelfth-century abbey of Royaumont. By the end of that year, necessity had overcome the distaste of the army command for the employment of women doctors and Elsie Dalyell added Malta to her war itinerary. From there she was transferred to Salonika, where she remained until the armistice when she was sent with the army of occupation to Constantinople.

Agnes Bennett was succeeded as head of the Scottish Women's Hospital unit at Ostrovo by another Australian, Dr Mary De Garis, one of the first woman medical graduates of the University of Melbourne. By that time the unit comprised 70 tents and 200 beds. Skills of improvisation were much needed; to combat the bitter winters they 'wore an amazing collection of cardigans, furs or sheep vests, great-coats and mackintoshes, sometimes all at once'.[22] In summer the problem was the abundance of flies, wasps and particularly mosquitoes. Malaria was an ever-present reality, affecting most of the women who served on the Balkan front. Both Agnes Bennett and Mary De Garis were forced out of Serbia by the extent of their suffering from malaria. Miles Franklin also fell victim to the disease. In her memoirs, Mary De Garis gave vivid descriptions of the day-to-day vicissitudes of running a hospital in primitive conditions, and also of her enjoyment of her life in a remote, but colourful, frontier world.

> The social life of the unit was extremely interesting. In the first place it was a camp of women (about forty-five to fifty in number), most of us over twenty-five, but few over forty-five, set down in a foreign country, surrounded by men's camps, mostly foreign too. It was a cosmopolitan life, many nationalities being there. We saw very few English during my first twelve months in the country, but had as visitors Serbs, French, Russians and Italians: and as patients, in addition, Greek soldiers, Macedonian civilians (who might be Roumanian or Turk) and a few black French colonials.[23]

With patients and visitors, the women celebrated May Day, Kossovo Day and individual saints' days, the celebrations taking on a somewhat multicultural character with sack races and Serbian dancing. While recognising that without language one cannot expect to have any intimate knowledge of people, Mary De Garis expressed considerable affection and admiration for the Serb men both as fighters and patients, although her viewpoint was fuelled by British paternalism and presumed superiority. Her sentiments and attitudes were shared by another Australian woman, Olive King, who arrived in Serbia as an ambulance driver in 1915.[24]

The Balkans were not Olive King's first taste of the exotic. Born in Sydney in 1885, the daughter of Sir Kelso King, a wealthy and socially prominent businessman, she had been taken to Germany with her sister and a chaperone to finish her education, and had studied the usual music, china-painting, language and literature at Dresden. On her return to Sydney, Olive King did not take kindly to the social round that was the life of a young woman of her class. Romantically inclined, she formed a series of attachments to men whom her father considered unsuitable. Thus he regularly dispatched her overseas. In the years before the war, in the company of a chaperone, Olive King travelled widely in Asia, America and

Europe; in 1910 with three male companions — and without the chaperone — she climbed Mount Popocatapetl in Mexico.

War provided Olive King, who was in Britain in 1914, with the chance
to escape the constraints of convention and class and the opportunity to
realise her dream 'to be in the thick of things'. While she shared fully in
the jingoism of the time, it was also a desire for adventure that drove her
into the war. In 1918, she wrote to her father from Serbia of the longing
she had always had for travel, exploration and the pioneering life.[25] And
adventures she indeed had. Before joining the Scottish Women's Hospital
unit, Olive King had driven her own sixteen-seat ambulance with the
Allies' Field Ambulance Corps in Belgium. The organisers of this expedition were reputedly suspected of spying and returned hastily to England,
leaving King and two other drivers behind. They were arrested and
released just ahead of the invading German army. Olive King then joined
the Scottish Women's Hospital, working in France before travelling to
Salonika by ship to join a medical unit on the front at Gevgelija on the
Greek border. In December 1915, as the Austrian and Bulgarian armies
overtook the retreating Serbs and the hospital at Gevgelija was evacuated,
King wrote that once again she had only just escaped in time, getting herself and her vehicle onto the last train out of Gevgelija before the station
was bombed. With Serbia occupied by the enemy, the Allied forces
regrouped at the Aegean port of Salonika. Olive King joined the Serb
army as a driver attached to the medical headquarters and remained in
Salonika until the end of the war.

The war situation allowed full play for Olive King's initiative, physical
energy and impatience with convention. She transported hospital stores
and equipment to the front, and brought back the injured and dying
along primitive and dangerous routes. Merely keeping her ambulance on
the road was a major and time-consuming undertaking, and she came to
do much of the repair work herself. In August 1917, when a large part of
Salonika was razed by fire, Olive King portrayed herself as being in 'the
thick of it' as she drove back and forth across the city evacuating people,
or stood on a rooftop extinguishing sparks with a hose. Her letters home
gave vivid descriptions of the incidents she had witnessed. Below the
rooftop where she had held her hose was a courtyard full of wine-barrels.

> Soon after dawn the wine-barrels burst, the street beside the stores ran with
> wine, six or eight inches deep in the gutters, & overflowing in a trickle all
> over the street, like blood. Dagoes & the soldiers of two of our Allies threw
> themselves down, & lying full-length in the gutters, drank & drank. A few
> hours later they could be seen lying everywhere, a horrid mess beside them,
> sleeping it off.[26]

As the war moved into its final stages and the Serb army drove back the
invaders, Olive King became increasingly distressed by the terrible plight

of the soldiers. She appealed to her father for financial help from Sydney to set up canteens, and his committee raised £10 000. It was in the devastated capital of Belgrade that she opened the first Australian Serb canteen. Despite enormous problems in obtaining and transporting supplies and protecting them from theft, seventeen further canteens were established, selling food, blankets, clothing, and other necessities. On foraging expeditions for her canteens, she travelled from Fiume in the north to Constantinople in the south. For her work in Serbia, Olive King was awarded the Serb silver medal for bravery, the gold medal for zealous conduct, the Samaritan Cross, and the cross of the Order of St Sava, the last personally bestowed upon her by King Alexander.

Olive King's war was not all work. Salonika, always an exotic city of mosques, synagogues and churches, inhabited by people of many nationalities and creeds, became during the war a frontier city into which refugees and Allied troops poured. Off duty, King was occupied in the usual middle-class diversions — dining, dancing and bridge-playing — but her amusements took place in a much freer, less constrained, and more spontaneous atmosphere than that of prewar Sydney. She learnt Serbian and socialised with the Serb officers, falling in love with a liaison officer with the British army. The relationship came to an end when the officer was sent to the Serb legation in London, although they remained friends and corresponded for many years.

Like other women in the Serb war zone, Olive King expressed attachment to the land and the people.

> I see the sunrise every day & the dawn too, generally, & its really worth seeing here. This morning all the near hills looked like great folds of wine-coloured velvet, & the snow-peaked mountains behind were all rosy & glowing in the light. This is just the loveliest place, the mountains are glorious, & the air so fresh & invigorating.[27]

But King was also thoroughly endowed with a sense of British racial superiority. Thus in the context of the fire of Sarajevo, she declared with pride that the Tommies were not among the looters.

> It gives you a glow sometimes to realize you belong to the only nation that is trusted & respected wherever it goes. Hated & feared by some, but always honoured and never despised.[28]

And while King formed close friendships with Serbs, became totally involved in their war, and was critical of Allied policy and actions in the Balkan theatre, the Serbs were in the end inferior: 'they are for the most part, such simple, childish, dear, kind, bungling, blundering things'.[29] Olive King's attitudes were based not only on a sense of race, but also of class. Thus she was rather sniffy about some of her fellow-countrywomen, complaining about the accents and lack of style of the Australian nurses.[30]

As was the case with Miles Franklin and so many of the other women who worked with the Serb forces, King's war experience was for her an exhilarating, life-enhancing and liberating experience. She later recalled:

> That first winter in Salonika was a never-to-be-forgotten time of mud, floods, discomfort and hard work. All the same it was real good fun, and we enjoyed it like a sort of rough and tumble picnic.[31]

She took the momentous and symbolic step of cutting her hair, an event she reported to her father with some trepidation.[32] The improvised, unorderly, spontaneous way of life in the war zone fitted her 'gypsy' temperament.

> It is queer how one changes. If anyone has a streak of the vagabond in them, the war has developed it to such an alarming extent that the problem of finding some sort of occupation when we're obliged to quit the Balkans, or wherever we are, is an appalling prospect for thousands of vagabonds. I always knew I was a gypsy but you wouldn't believe me. Now, however, I know it, past all possible denying, & as some day we will have to close the canteens, it's coming on me with a sort of cold horror. 'What shall I do then?' Live in London, with all one's interests in shops & theatres? Or in Sydney going to teas and luncheons, playing tennis at the Golf Club, getting new dresses for the Races, & always being gossiped about & disapproved of? — Absolutely impossible, either prospect. I shall have to find work of some sort, but where I am my own boss & not tied down by either discipline & convention.[33]

The wish to escape the conventional social life of her gender and class became a recurring theme in King's letters after the war ended and she faced the prospect of her repatriation. She hoped that perhaps her father might buy her a 'station' where she could be independent. And she reiterated that she was no longer the same person.

> I shall go home as a perfect stranger. I can feel myself how enormously I have changed. Besides I left you a girl, I go home a woman nearly middle-aged & very experienced in a million different ways. It isn't only with short hair, no interest in clothes, broad shoulders, & increased (much increased) weight, I look different. I am different. When I try to look into myself, I can't see any point between the girl that left home & the woman that's going back, except two. These two are — I love you all as much as ever & in spite of everything I still feel 16. Otherwise I am entirely changed.[34]

The love for her father was to prove stronger than the transformation of self.

Olive King came back to Sydney in 1920 and did not leave again for 25 years, except for a brief return visit to Belgrade in 1922 to attend the wedding of King Alexander. Despite the longings expressed in her letters for a different way of life and despite the extraordinary life she had led in Serbia, King returned to her father's house. The energy, organisational ability and initiative that in Serbia had been deployed in alleviating suffering and misery were now poured into the Girl Guide movement. Between Olive King's desire for a life of independence, adventure and nonconformity lay her love for her father and her obedience to his wishes. There were British women who stayed in Serbia, who married men they had met during the war, but Olive King's relationship with her Serb liaison officer came to nothing. Her letters to her father during the war were filled with adoration for and devotion to him. This woman already in her thirties addressed her father as 'my dearest old Sweetheart Daddy' and ended them 'ever your loving little Sweetheart'. In some ways the letters read more as those to a lover than to a father. Despite the independence and self-reliance of her life in Serbia, once she was home King deferred willingly to her father and his superior wisdom. The war had given Olive King the rare opportunity to pursue for a moment that exciting, vagabond existence for which she had yearned. But the role of dutiful daughter was an equally powerful force in her life .

If family obligations constituted one of the greatest obstacles that stood between women and their desire for adventure and travel, ironically it was these same obligations that gave many women the opportunity to cross the seas during the war. In 1916 Florence Sulman, daughter of the architect John Sulman, sailed for England with her younger stepbrother Geoffrey, who had been rejected as medically unfit for the Australian army, but who hoped that by going to Britain he might find a way of doing his 'bit'.[35] He was accepted into the Royal Flying Corps and killed on a training flight in 1917. While Florence Sulman also did her 'bit' in England, visiting the wounded in hospitals and helping with occupational therapy, as well as making clothes for a Quaker relief fund, her real function was to take care of her brother. She wrote to her mother when her brother joined the Flying Corps:

> I have *tried* to tell Father all I know, and I am sure you will realize what a very difficult position I have been in lately. It was all very well for Geoffrey to say that I was not responsible for his actions, I had to try to think of some way of influencing him, to get advice from others he would listen to.[36]

Two weeks later, after he had moved north for training, she wrote that she had 'always felt happy to keep him under my eye, and will now do my best to be free whenever he feels inclined to honour me with a visit'.[37] When Geoffrey moved to Oxford for further training in January 1917, Florence Sulman took lodging in the city. After he died, she wrote home that her 'principal bit is finished'.[38]

Florence Sulman's letters are full of references to other Australian women who were in England to take care of husbands, fathers, sons and brothers. Queensland painter Vida Lahey finally realised her ambition to travel at the age of 34 when her family sent her to London to monitor the welfare of her three brothers and several cousins who were fighting in France with the AIF.[39] She had little opportunity to pursue her art ambitions as long as the war lasted, working at various times as a draughtsperson, a chauffeur for convalescent servicemen, and in the Anzac buffet. At the end of the war, she was finally able to follow her own agenda in the studios and galleries of Paris. Mary Edgeworth David, daughter of the geologist Edgeworth David, went with her mother to Europe after her father was injured in an accident in France.[40] They had to travel via Canada and, while waiting in Halifax for a ship to take them to England, Mary worked in a munitions factory. When she arrived in England she enlisted in the Women's Auxiliary Army Corps as a driver and later transferred to the Women's Legion.

When her husband, Norman Brookes, was sent to Cairo with the Red Cross in 1914, Mabel Brookes, accompanied by her baby and a nanny, sailed to join him, leaving an older child in Melbourne with her parents.[41] In Cairo, she made her home at Shepheard's hotel and joined the Red Cross as a helper, taking the wounded on outings, visiting hospitals, and serving cakes and tea at the canteen. Mabel Brookes's six months in Cairo were to provide the setting for three of her later novels, which all revolved around Australian women travelling overseas during the war.[42] She returned to Australia when her husband was posted to Baghdad, but in 1918 she followed him again, this time in a cargo ship carrying horses to Calcutta. There Mabel Brookes tasted the life of the Raj as the guest of the Comptroller of the Household of the Governor of Bengal, and while her husband played tennis with maharajas, she met poet Rabindranath Tagore, who had won the 1913 Nobel Prize for Literature.

Mabel Brookes was by no means unique in joining her husband in Egypt; Shepheard's hotel had its share of Australian women among its patrons. It was in Cairo that Margaret Chisholm met and married the first of her three titled husbands. Shepheard's hotel was also for four-and-a-half-years the headquarters of Mabel Brookes's sister-in-law, May Brookes, who transformed her apartment into 'something approaching ancient Egyptian splendour and beauty', although amidst 'all this melange of Egyptian splendour', 'her big Australian flag floated proudly from the centre of my balcony'.[43] An amateur singer, in 1914 May Brookes had spread her wings for the first time and set off for Egypt with her 'faithful maid' Lucy and her accompanist Mrs Billings. Her desire 'to do something' was fulfilled as she visited the wounded in hospitals, or took convalescents for drives by day and gave concerts for the troops by night. May Brookes's leisure-time activities, even if carried on against the backdrop of the desert, were not so very different from those of her life at home: golf, racing, musical evenings in her apartment attended by the scions of Victorian society — even if some of them were for the moment mere privates. She was in Cairo for the Armistice when the 'Australian high spirits of the soldiers found an outlet in many pranks', which included riding a donkey up the classic stairs of Shepheard's hotel. Other 'escapades' in Cairo that night were less harmless. And May Brookes discovered that once the enemy abroad had been quelled, the natives at home became restive, and from her British stance, Shepheard's proved a more dangerous abode in peace than it had been in war.

> Although Shepheard's had been constantly guarded during the war, we now felt strongly the danger of riotous Arabs — ruthless and treacherous, and who had commenced a ferocious attack on the British residents of all parts of Egypt.[44]

May Brookes left Cairo for a Europe still recovering from the devastation of war. Her train trip from Trieste to Paris she described as one of her worst experiences as a traveller: 'I was afraid to sleep, as at that time the train was packed with a very cosmopolitan crowd, some of them very evil specimens of humanity'.[45] But, once through the doors of another famous hotel, Claridge's in Paris, all became right in her world.

Less intentionally caught up in the war was Hilda Freeman. Born in the Ballarat district of Victroria, where she grew up to become a schoolteacher, Freeman travelled to London in 1910. She took up a teaching post with the Church Missionary Society at Limpsfield, attended summer courses at Oxford, and furthered her interest in theatre production.[46] In January 1914 Freeman set off for Germany to work as a governess. Two years later, she published a narrative of her nine months in Germany, the last two 'in the hands of the enemy'. The account was based on the diaries that she kept at the time, 'so that every event and dialogue in the book are literally and absolutely true, and in no way polished up for effect'.[47] Polished up for effect or not, Freeman wrote in the persona of an intensely patriotic Australian who also insisted upon a British identity, an exuberant, sensible Australian with strong opinions on how things should be, and loyal to fresh air and frequent baths.

Hilda Freeman arrived in Germany as an Australian and so, she alleged, found it very difficult 'to divest myself of my democratic habits', but she was in Germany 'to absorb Germanity, cultivate its point of view, wear its clothes, speak its language, and bow to its customs'.[48] This was not difficult during the first two months since she was staying at the British and American Governesses' Home in Berlin. But then she moved to North Germany, to the estate of the Baron von Klinggraeff near Neubrandenburg, where she was the only 'English woman' in the district. She became fascinated by the life on the baronial estate and by the extended family of grandmothers and aunts whom she regaled with her enthusiastic and patriotic accounts of life in Australia.

> I paint Australia in such luminous colours that it dances like a beautiful mirage over the horizon of the imagination of my hearers; upside-down, of course.[49]

Australia was also a place, she thought, where men believed women to be equal, in contrast to Germany where men were treated 'as if they are little gods', something that Freeman felt they were far from deserving.

At the end of June, Hilda Freeman's peaceful, bucolic life came to an end with the news of the assassination at Sarajevo. At first she paid little attention.

> But it does not interest me very much. Serbia and the Balkan Peninsula are associated in my mind with war and dissensions ever since I can remember anything about them at all, so it seems quite natural that they should have trouble again.[50]

And her attention was clouded over the next weeks when she became desperately ill with what was later diagnosed as malaria. Hilda Freeman was in hospital when Britain declared war on Germany. Thus in the first days of the war, she was bedridden, isolated, dependent upon the German press and hostile hospital staff for news of the war, and divided by the enormous abyss of the war from the German family for whom she worked and which had befriended her. Too ill to travel when she was discharged from hospital, Freeman returned to the family of Baron von Klinggraeff. Personal relations remained warm, but she lived in a world where conversation revolved around German victories and British atrocities, and where she refused overtures that suggested that being Australian was different from being English, or that Australia would only fight unwillingly. Freeman was repatriated to London at the end of September in one of the last exchanges of prisoners, and returned to Australia in 1915, where she published her account of her months in Germany and gave lectures on her experiences. In the following year she married a returned soldier who had been wounded at Gallipoli and they went to live in Grong Grong, NSW.

Hilda Freeman had left Germany in September 1914, but Ethel Cooper remained behind.[51] Born into the Adelaide establishment in 1871, Cooper was orphaned at an early age. Her first trip outside Australia was in 1879 when her grandmother took Ethel and her younger sister, together with a nanny, to England to visit relations. Back in Adelaide, music became Ethel Cooper's preoccupation. Stella Bowen recalled Ethel Cooper in Adelaide as an excellent pianist and composer: 'who also played the trombone for visiting orchestras and might often be seen, camouflaged by a black coat and man's tie, amongst the wind instruments at the Theatre Royal'.[52] Ethel Cooper was already showing the signs of being a modern woman. In 1897, she made her second trip to Europe, music and Germany her main targets. She left Australia again in 1903, and spent over three years in Europe, mostly in Leipzig. In 1911 Cooper returned to Leipzig where she felt at home in a world of musicians.

Ethel Cooper remained in Germany throughout the First World War, neither expelled nor interned. One explanation that she gave for this was that when war broke out she found herself helping the American consulate to facilitate departures, and her intention was to join the exodus. But when the first German wounded arrived in Leipzig hospitals, Cooper was asked to play the piano for them, and considering one wounded man the same as another, she consented, only to be arrested immediately afterwards on a charge of espionage. She was released 24 hours later, after her German friends intervened. But there was no chance then of her being allowed to leave Germany. So she remained.

Each week during the war years, Ethel wrote a letter to her sister. The letters written in the first year were smuggled out to Switzerland, but those written over the next three years remained in Leipzig, hidden first between the pages of the scores for Beethoven's string quartets and later in a cavity in a dining-room table. The letters coolly record the vicissitudes of the day-to-day life of an intelligent observant woman and her friends. One particular object of her concern and help was an eighteen-year-old pregnant English girl who had come to Germany with her German fiancé. After he was called up, Ethel helped arrange their marriage and gave the young woman emotional support and financial assistance before and after the birth of the child and following the death in action of her husband.

In Germany in August 1914 Ethel Cooper presented a very differently crafted persona from that of the enthusiastically and exuberantly Australian Hilda Freeman. She made few references to Australia in her travel letters, and place of birth does not seem an important component in the identity that she was fashioning. The image that she conveys in her letters in the early days of the war is that of a European woman who hated war, saw fault on both sides, maintained her personal friendships, and was impatient with the moral claptrap of war.[53] Nonetheless, Ethel Cooper was a loyal British subject and her imperial patriotism grew stronger as the war dragged on. When she heard gossip about new cyanide-gas bombs, she was desperate to send the news out. By 1917 Ethel Cooper's campaign to leave Germany intensified, but not unreasonably, given her familiarity with living conditions and morale, the German authorities refused her request for expatriation. While in no way harassed, she was the object of accusations of spying and occasional police attention. And there remains the faint question of whether Ethel Cooper was in fact a spy.[54]

The war lives of Ethel Cooper and Olive King underline again the role of travel abroad as escape and opportunity for women who might be best described as uncomfortable in the roles assigned to them by their gender and class, women who had chosen not to marry, women of strong personality and physical energy. For such women, war overseas could be as much an escape route from the mundane as it was for men. In the late 1930s, a small number of Australian women became involved in another European war when they went to Spain after General Francisco Franco led an army rebellion against the popular front government of the four-year-old Spanish Republic.[55] The women who volunteered to serve in Spain were motivated both by ideological convictions and the desire for more adventurous lives. Una Wilson, who had been nursing in a ward for old men at Lidcombe Hospital, told reporters shortly before she sailed that

> if we get captured and shot that's that. It's only a few years off your life and it's better than spending all your days in a private hospital. Danger is the spice of life, that and the feeling that we'll be doing something with real meaning.[56]

Another nurse in Spain at the time wrote :

> We have been through some tough time and it's only a fluke that we are alive. Who cares, anyhow, I don't, and if they don't pop me off this time just think of the almighty experience.[57]

The struggle to contain fascism in Spain failed, and when Germany invaded Poland in September 1939, Australia followed Britain into another European war. Again women took off for foreign shores as journalists, doctors, nurses, medical aides, and in other non-combatant roles in the army, navy and air force. Mary Kent Hughes's arrival in England in the spring of 1940 was not what she had visualised in her girlish dreams. Her first sight was not of white cliffs and green fields, but of wrecked ships and submarines. But she had come to apply for a commission in the British Army, not for a holiday.[58] Mary Kent Hughes finished up with the British army in Palestine, and it was of course in the Middle East, the Pacific and New Guinea, not in Europe, that Australian women in the armed services were to be most conspicuous in the Second World War, a war that this time reached Australia's own shores. Other women, like Hilda Freeman in 1914, were caught by circumstances. Among them were the women in occupied Europe including those who through marriage had lost their British citizenship and whose land of birth was at war with the land of their domicile, husband and passport. It is with some of their stories that this chapter concludes.

Vera Bockmann lived throughout the war in Nazi Germany.[59] Bockmann's great-grandfather had emigrated from Silesia in the 1840s and she grew up in the German-Australian community in South Australia. In 1926 the 23-year-old Vera Hoffman met Otto Bockmann, the chief wireless officer on a German ship berthed in Port Adelaide. Eighteen months later she married him in Hamburg, and surrendered her passport.

> I had to surrender my passport to the British Consulate the day before we were married. It was an uncomfortable experience, making me realise that I was losing something very precious. Being young, I light-heartedly managed to convince myself that one nation was as good or bad as another, and where on earth could one find more charming and lovable people than in Hamburg. Why, even two of Queen Victoria's daughters had married Germans. Henceforth I would be a German citizen.[60]

After her marriage Bockmann went to live first in Potsdam, and then in Berlin, where her son was born in 1938 just after 'Kristallnacht'. She had experienced emerging Nazism at first hand in 1931 when curiosity took her to a party rally and she watched a three-hour performance by Hitler. She was to glimpse him again in more subdued mode when he attended the memorial service for George V in the Anglican Church of St George in Berlin.

> For a brief moment I caught his eye. All the stories about magnetic eyes seemed substantiated then and there. They were the darkest, slatiest blue eyes I had ever seen. It seemed to me as though each eye had a different expression.[61]

Until the outbreak of war, Vera Bockmann found support for her life in a foreign land by seeking out her own kind and centring her social life on the American church where she met another Australian-born wife, Muriel Muhlen-Schulte, who had married her German husband in 1930 in Melbourne. The two women were to sustain each other in enemy territory during the long, difficult and dangerous war years.[62]

Hitler's magnetic eyes were not to protect Berlin from the consequence of his foreign policy and war, and in January 1944, the apartment block in which the Bockmanns lived was bombed. Evacuated for a time to Silesia, Vera Bockmann was back in Berlin to experience the Russian occupation, to learn to say 'Ja Anglichanka', to live with frightening rumour and the reality of hunger and malnutrition. In 1946 she returned to Australia where the family lived until 1953, when they moved back to Germany. Otto Bockmann died in 1971 and ten years later his widow joined the ranks of so many expatriate women in returning home in the face of the isolation of old age. Muriel Muhler-Schulte, who gave birth to her daughter in the midst of bombing raids in 1943, spent the last months of the war in the comparative safety of Alsace, but her husband never returned from the Russian front.

Vera Bockmann's story was one of survival; she made no contribution to the defeat of fascism. Other women did. Best known is the story told by Nancy Wake.[63] In 1932 Wake sailed from Australia for Europe via New York, a twenty-year-old would-be journalist. She later wrote of the feeling of exhilaration that ran through her as she stood on the deck, wondering what the future had in store for her. She could not have foreseen her future as a partisan in the French Resistance. After a stint in London, Nancy Wake moved on to Paris in 1934, and France was to be her home for the next twelve years. In her autobiography, she created images of a happy-go-lucky, cosmopolitan Parisian life of cafés and bars, but, true to her origins, since her apartment had no bathroom, she installed a bath in the kitchen and became known in the *quartier* as the 'mademoiselle with the bath'. Nancy Wake later traced her hatred of Nazism to her encounters and friendships in Paris with those fleeing Hitler's terror and to her first-hand observation of the violence of anti-Semitism in Vienna and Berlin in the mid-1930s. While on holiday on the Riviera, she met Henry Fiocca, a wealthy industrialist whom she married in 1941 — against the wishes of his family. She thus became a French citizen. For the brief period of the 'phoney war', Nancy Wake lived in Marseilles the luxurious life of the indulged wife of a wealthy man, but in the spring of 1941 her husband was called up and she joined a small voluntary ambulance in the north. The French surrender in June left Nancy Wake and her husband as citizens of Vichy France.

Nancy Wake's autobiography tells how she slowly, through her contacts with Allied prisoners, became more and more absorbed into underground activity in Provence, acting as a courier and organising the escape of prisoners. By 1943 she was under suspicion and knew that it was only a matter of time before she would be identified as the Resistance courier known to the Gestapo as 'the white mouse'. She decided to flee to Spain and hence to Britain, but escape proved no easy achievement. On the model of the spy hero, laconic in all circumstances, she described her adventures.

> For weeks now I had been subjected to more than my fair share of drama. I had been forced to flee from home, separated from my beloved husband and my darling Picon, made six fruitless journeys to the Pyrenees, been thrown into prison and kicked around, jumped out of a moving train, been fired at by a machine-gun, sprinted to the top of a mountain, lost my jewellery, walked for five nights, been starved for eight days, and infected with scabies.[64]

Nancy Wake eventually reached Britain where in time she was recruited by the Special Operations Executive, which had been formed to work with the Resistance forces in German-occupied Europe. In March 1944 she parachuted back into central France, where she co-ordinated Resistance activities, training Maquis groups and taking part in a number of engagements, on one occasion walking 200 kilometres to find a wireless operator to get a message through to London. After the German surrender in France, Nancy Wake returned to Marseilles and to the confirmation of the death of her husband at the hands of the Gestapo.

At the end of the war, Wake worked for a time with the Foreign Office and then in 1948 came back to Australia and tried to settle in Sydney. It was a mistake. She now felt more at ease in Europe, she was 'too cosmopolitan' for parochial Sydney, too exotic also for the Liberal Party of New South Wales, for which she stood as the only just unsuccessful candidate against another local internationalist, Herbert Vere Evatt, in the 1951 federal election. In the same year Nancy Wake returned to London and 'I felt as if a great load had been lifted from my shoulders'.[65] But she was eventually to return and settle in Sydney.

Nancy Wake narrated her wartime adventures and exploits with insouciance as a good yarn. Her style, reminiscent of Louise Mack, is that of the ripping schoolgirl adventure. She was not the only Australian woman who told a story about participation in the Resistance in Europe. Understatement was not in the repertoire of Doris Gentile, who created a record of perhaps the most fantastic wartime life of all Australian women who sailed for Europe.

Interlude

Doris Gentile

In 1925 Doris Gentile sailed from Sydney for Africa and began to create the record of an extraordinary life that she was later to represent as a quest for adventure and experience, a quest that had its origins in early childhood when, travelling along the road to Mount Hay in the Blue Mountains, she vowed 'to see what was at the end of all the roads in the world'.[1] Born Doris Dinham in Sydney in 1894, she worked as a journalist and copywriter and had published short stories and a novel before her departure.

In South Africa, Dinham worked as a publicity officer for the United Tobacco Company, published stories in local newspapers, explored the Kalahari desert, and then journeyed from Cape Town to the Congo. How she made the trip and with whom is difficult to fathom because there is a considerable degree of inconsistency in the stories that she told to the press under such headings as 'Sydney Girl in Cannibal Land', 'Alone Through Africa' and 'Lost for a Fortnight in the Wilds'.[2] Trekking, motorbike and capecart were given on various occasions as the mode of travel, and she claimed to have been unaccompanied on her journey except for native bearers. Doris Dinham told the correspondent of the *Sydney Morning Herald* that she had passed through cannibal villages, paddled her canoe among hippopotami and crocodiles, lost her way in the jungle and been chased out of one village by armed women.[3] Eight years later she was described in an article in the *Times* as a woman in the 'line of our great adventurers', who, accompanied only by native guides had ventured into places where no white person had ever been before and who had actually seen a ju-ju feast.

> On one occasion she just escaped being eaten by cannibals, and once met a cannibal who was a graduate of Brussels University and dressed in European clothes, but still proud of being a cannibal.[4]

Doris Dinham's African experiences provided her with the material for two novels, the first of which, *Black God*, was very widely and favourably reviewed and was nominated as Book of the Month in New York.[5] The novels are unusual for the period in that the protagonists are Africans. The name of the author was not, however, Doris Dinham, but D. Manners-Sutton, the name under which she usually published and that she claimed was an old family name.

After Doris Dinham had made her trek through Africa, she sailed to Europe, where she worked as a freelance journalist in London and studied languages and drama in Paris and Vienna and in various cities in Italy. In 1930 she added romance to adventure when in Taormina in Sicily she met Salvatore Gentile, whom she described at the time to her friend, the children's writer Ella McFadyen, as 'a Sicilian writer, as handsome as any picture of the magnificent Medicis' and as a grandson of the 'Duca di Cusa'. He took her dancing every night, sent her roses every morning, and pulled out a stiletto when Doris went out to coffee with a German student.[6] In 1934 Doris Dinham married Salvatore Gentile in Benghazi, Libya. By the time of the marriage, the handsome Sicilian poet had become a poor, greying, stout draughtsman with the Italian army, whose noble status seems very tenuous, although his wife's new visiting cards introduced her as the Contessa Dorina Gentile. Age was as flexible as social status in Doris Gentile's hands; her marriage certificate gave her age as 26, although she was born in 1894. Future documents fixed the anomaly by giving 1908 as her date of birth. At the end of 1934, Doris Gentile's daughter was born in Rome, and two years later, her son in London. Neither marriage to a Sicilian nor motherhood put an end to her travels. She was in Britain in 1939 when war broke out, but strangely in April 1940, just before Mussolini entered the war on the side of Germany, Doris Gentile returned to Sicily. The most fantastic part of her story was about to begin.

Nothing has been established about Doris Gentile's life in the first years of the war, but at some point she left Sicily and her husband, later claiming that he and his family were ardent supporters of Mussolini. She settled for a time in Genoa with her children and then in 1943, probably in the brief interlude between the overthrow of Mussolini and the German occupation of northern Italy, Doris Gentile made an unsuccessful attempt to cross the border into Switzerland.[7] Trapped in that part of Italy ruled after 1943 by Mussolini as the head of the German puppet regime, the Republic of Salò, the family found refuge in the village of Civiglio in the hills just above the lakeside city of Como.

> A village high above the town of Como. Small, unproductive, old, some of the narrow streets were cobbled, with a few shops, a Trattoria, three villas and a contrada with two or three small farms behind farmhouses and barns. High hills rose up behind the village, green in summer snowy in winter… Beyond the high hills was a road resembling a mule track and from there all the high points above the lake of Como could be reached.[8]

In the fragments for two autobiographical novels written in the early 1960s, 'The Sawdust Republic' and 'No Time for Love', as well as in random scrap entries in a notebook and in her children's memories are some

hints on Doris Gentile's life in Civiglio in these years.[9] She was utterly
without financial resources; the money that she had deposited in Barclay's
Bank in Rome was confiscated and her assets in Australia and Britain
frozen as enemy property.[10] She gave clandestine English lessons,
bartered her camera for food and burnt her books for warmth. Despite
these manoeuvres and the help of a peasant woman in the village, the
family was often hungry, malnourished and miserably cold.

This much can be established around Doris Gentile's life as a refugee in
wartime Italy. But she made other far more dramatic claims. In a letter to
her brother-in-law in Australia written in May 1946, in between news on
her children and conditions in England, she wrote:

> I'll never forget the day of the German surrender, you see I and a few col-
> leagues were the ones who brought it about. You wouldn't know me now,
> I'm a two gun woman in pants, that also knows how to throw bombs well
> and truly. Did you fight, you'll say? We did nothing else but fight.
>
> You see I had to choose at the outset whether I served my country or
> remained neutral and I chose my country, and it is only by the grace of God
> that I wasn't put against a wall and shot.[11]

The letter also mentioned that her eyes hurt her lot and this was the result
of torture by the Blackshirts. Doris Gentile elaborated on these claims in
'No Time for Love' and 'The Sawdust Republic'. The fragments tell the
story of an Australian woman living with two children in Civiglio at the
time of the Republic of Salò, who was known as the 'Signora Inglese' not
because she was English, but because that was her language. The narrator
insists that the story is fact not fiction, that nothing has been fabricated,
that she is giving the truth about a piece of history that has been often
written about 'with a penful of lies'; 'you are now hearing the truth for the
first time about a mess of lies'.[12] The events that she narrates 'could very
well have been fairytales, they did not seem real at the time'.[13] And her
truth is that the Australian Signora in Como fought with the partisans,
delivering and hiding arms and messages, that she was arrested and tor-
tured, that she was among the first to discover that Mussolini was fleeing
from Como, and that, in trousers and with her hair hidden under a cap,
she was with the partisans who confronted the Duce hiding in the back of
a German truck at the roadblock between Musso and Dongo on the
shores of Lake Como on 27 April 1945. The Australian Signora was also a
distant witness to the execution of Mussolini.

Doris Gentile did not finish her novels, so her story never entered the
public arena, and she made no official request for compensation or recognition. No corroborative evidence to support her story has yet been
found. There is no record of her presence among the partisans in available
British sources, or in the records of the Centre for the History of the

Resistance in Como, or in the memories of the few surviving local people who fought in the Resistance and with whom I spoke in the summer of 1994.[14] This lack of documentation renders her story implausible, but not necessarily impossible.

Much mystery still surrounds the capture and execution of Mussolini, mystery compounded of confusion, self-aggrandisement, fear, party politics, and the struggle in the spring of 1945 not only to defeat the Nazi-Fascists but also to control the future of Italy. Precisely who was present at the execution of Mussolini, and how and how many times he was in fact executed, are still questions on which there is no agreement.[15] The claimants to a role in the Duce's capture by now number in the hundreds, and even in the 1990s they still come forward.[16] Doris Gentile's story is by no means the most far-fetched. In the fragments of her novels, Doris Gentile made reference to her possession of information that was too dangerous to know, and this, together with fear, was the reason that she gave for her refusal after the war to discuss her life in wartime Italy. Some of those assumed at the time to be closely involved did meet violent 'unexplained' deaths in the first weeks of the Liberation, and there are still people connected to the events on the shores of Lake Como in the last week of April 1945 who will not talk about their experiences. It is known that Allied agents in northern Italy had contact with people of British nationality who were living in the Como area. And the role of British agents in the final days and hours of Mussolini is still unclear. It is believed in some quarters that the 'treasure' with which Mussolini attempted to flee Italy included not only the funds of the Republic of Salò, but also documents that were very damaging to Winston Churchill, so that British authorities as much as Italian interests had reason to have the Duce quickly and quietly eliminated and to muddy the waters.[17]

What part, if any, Dòris Gentile contributed to the Italian Resistance will now probably never be known. The woman who played with her social status and age, who, as the accounts of her African adventures suggest, could certainly tell a tall story, and who portrayed her life as a spirited search for adventure on a grand scale, had reason enough to invent a heroic life at the end of the war. In the eyes of her Australian friends and relatives she had married a Sicilian, a man who in fact had little claim to distinction. Once Mussolini entered the war on the side of Hitler, her husband was not only a 'dago', but also the enemy, and in 1945 a defeated and contemptuous enemy. And not only her husband; she too was an Italian citizen. In 1945 Doris Gentile was poverty-stricken, and in the years that followed her life was far from easy. In 1947 she migrated with her children to Canada, but that did not work out and back in England she published no further writing and became dependent on secretarial work for a living. A heroic and pivotal role in the downfall of Mussolini, a place in history, freed her from an inglorious past and present ignominy. While there remains the possibility that not all of Doris Gentile's tale is fabrication, the most dramatic elements must be regarded with scepticism. Yet there was much that was heroic in the mould of Mother Courage in Doris Gentile's securing of her own and her children's survival in 1943-45. And, to say the least, her traveller's tale is a good one.

CHAPTER 6

Travel and Reform

We suffragettes are one all the world over.[1]

Most tourists display little interest in the politics and problems of the societies through which they move. They are not travelling in the present, but in the past, and in the isolated, sanitised furrows of tourist land, a place of museums, hotels, shops and restaurants peopled by guides, waiters, porters and beggars. Poverty upsets the tourist when it manifests itself as dirt, smell and importunate beggars, and inconvenience, and language can cut the tourist off from the host society. Political comments on the whole are restricted to passing — usually jejune — asides, exemplified in the 1920s and 1930s in the widespread expressions of admiration for Mussolini, who had transformed Italy by rendering the picturesque and romantic efficient.[2] Tourists unwittingly stumble on and through *coups d'état*, riots, revolts and revolutions. Hilda Freeman related the story of two Scottish girls spending the last week in July on holidays in Berlin.

> We couldn't speak German but thought we could manage for a week. We went up to Unter den Linden one day, and followed a perfectly dense crowd to the Kaiser's palace. The Kaiser came out and spoke to the people. They hoched and hoched, and we hoched with them. Then we went down to the Crown Prince's palace, and he came out and spoke too. The people yelled and cheered, and so did we. We hoched again; but we've never hoched since. They were declaring war and we never knew.[3]

Accompanying those travellers whose eyes were fixed on monuments and ruins was a minority for whom the present was also the focus, who journeyed to understand and to change the world. By the end of the nineteenth century women were prominent in this group.

Among the first women for whom travel was linked to a commitment to reform was the South Australian writer and social activist Catherine Helen Spence. In 1865 she made her first journey from South Australia back to the Britain that she had left 26 years earlier at the age of fourteen.[4] By that time, she had already embarked upon the path into the public sphere that was to make her life so different from the nineteenth-century template of a woman's life. Spence later described herself as 'a new woman', 'awakened to a sense of capacity and responsibility', not only to the family and the household, but also to the state.[5] She supported herself by her writing, but she was also a preacher, public speaker, and parliamentary candidate, whose interests ranged from electoral reform to the rehabilitation of Francis Bacon as the author of the plays erroneously attributed to Shakespeare. The sphere of Spence's activities extended to the care of orphans, destitute and delinquent children, to the Unitarian church, and to the campaign for women's suffrage.

Almost half of Catherine Helen Spence's time in Britain on her 1865 trip was spent in Scotland visiting relatives and the scenes of her childhood. As in so many communities that must send their sons and daughters overseas, Spence's family pitied her for her exile. She herself had little regret.

> I can never forget the look of tender pity cast on me as I was sitting in our old seat in church, looking at seats filled by another generation. The paterfamilias, so wonderfully like his father of 1839, and sons and daughters, sitting in the place of uncles and aunts settled elsewhere. They grieved that I had been banished from the romantic associations and the high civilisation of Melrose to rough it in the wilds, while my heart was so full of thankfulness that I had moved to the wider spaces and the more varied activities of a new and progressive colony.[6]

When Catherine Helen Spence moved south, she was, like all tourists, enchanted by 'the great beauty of the English landscape', 'its undulations, its softness, its wonderful variety of mountain, wood, and shore', 'its perpetual verdure', and stimulated by the variety and opportunities of London.[7] But she also had other agendas in her travels.

> My interests have always been in people and in the things that make for human happiness or misery rather than in the beauties of Nature, art or architecture. I want to know how the people live, what wages are, what the amount of comfort they can buy; how the people are fed, taught, and amused; how justice is executed; how much or little liberty the people enjoy.[8]

From the record of her travels, she saw no sites, enthused over no monuments, and entered no galleries. Her Italy was different from that of most tourists: 'I visited at Siena a home for deaf mutes'.[9] In London, Spence gravitated to the circles of those interested in electoral reform. She was excited by the company and conversation of clever men and women, which made her 'wish for such things in Adelaide'.[10] Among the clever men and women she met were John Stuart Mill and George Eliot. The latter encounter was a disappointment: 'I felt I had been looked upon as an inquisitive Australian desiring an interview, and it was a failure'.[11]

Catherine Helen Spence made a second trip overseas in 1893 when she was approaching 70 years of age. Her first destination was Chicago and that great statement of modernity, the World's Fair. Part of modernity was the development both of progressive movements working to curb the excesses and injustices of unfettered capitalism and of feminism intent on modifying those of unfettered patriarchy; thus the World's Fair was also the site for a number of conferences with reformist agendas. One delegate tried to convey the excitement of the conference atmosphere in Chicago.

> What can I say in a few moments to give any idea of these great gatherings? I believe it is not an over-statement to say, the like has never been seen in the history of the world. For six months, part of the time with the heat most intense, the Art Palace of Chicago was thronged day and night with men and women interested in the reforms of the day, as well as the leaders of thought in the religious and scientific world.[12]

Spence attended the World Congress of Representative Women, the International Conference on Charities and Correction, the Proportional Representation Congress, the Single Tax Conference, and the Peace Conference. She then travelled around the United States and Canada for eleven months 'delivering over one hundred lectures', and meeting 'the most interesting people in the world'.[13] Spence was not only in North America to learn; she also went to teach the Americans and Canadians to vote.[14] She came from a colony that had introduced the secret ballot, and American reformers 'everywhere were eager to hear of a system of voting that would free the electors from the tyranny of corruption'.[15] It was not only the vote that interested Catherine Helen Spence: its form was of equal importance; she was a passionate advocate of the system of proportional representation and was in North America at the invitation of local advocates of the system to preach the cause.

The journeys of Catherine Helen Spence introduce another kind of travel engaged in by women from the late nineteenth century, that is, travel related to reform and to women moving into the public sphere and joining international networks for the advancement of women, for social justice, and for peace. They attended conferences, engaged in lecture tours, participated in feminist agitations and campaigns in other countries, and made their contribution to the cause of gender and social justice beyond their national borders. The women went to learn, but also to contribute. They journeyed not just as the passive recipients of the superior culture and manners of the old world, but to engage with the rest of the world as the denizens of a new society that they believed was more advanced in many important respects, and especially *vis à vis* the 'mother country'.

Like the women who first left Australia to secure training and experience, or to alleviate the suffering of war, the travelling feminists were mostly middle-class women with the means, the confidence, and the contacts to move easily in other worlds. But reform agendas did provide travel opportunities for middle-class women of modest background when their fares were paid by organisations and sponsors, and when their international networks provided accommodation. They tended to be older women without domestic responsibilities, widows and single women. Catherine Helen Spence was single and in her forties when she made her trip to Britain in 1865, Vida Goldstein was 32 when she went to a women's conference in Washington DC in 1902, and Alice Henry was almost 50 and finally free of domestic responsibilities when she left Australia in 1905. And things did not change. It was not difficult for Bessie Rischbieth, first as a wealthy, childless wife, and then as a wealthy widow, to be the most travelled Australian feminist of the interwar years. On the other hand, Jessie Street, whose appearances on the international conference circuits were eventually to rival those of Bessie Rischbieth, left Australia only twice between her marriage in 1916 and 1945, and both trips were family-based; one to visit her father, the other to chaperone her daughter.[16]

   The women's organisations that had emerged in Australia in the 1880s moved on in the next decade to link up with their counterparts in other countries and to become part of an international women's movement. Connections were first established through visits to Australia from over-seas reformers such as the 'missionaries' sent to Australia from the United States by the Woman's Christian Temperance Union (WCTU), which had strong feminist commitments, to establish branches in Australia; through the exchange of information; and then, increasingly, through Australian women travelling overseas.[17] In 1895 Susan Sager from Queensland attended the International Convention of the WCTU in London; four years later, Mrs John Thompson from Victoria visited England and North America, where she 'lost no opportunity of becoming acquainted with WCTU workers and their methods' and returned inspired with new ideas.[18] And if the WCTU had begun in Australia through the work of American missionaries, by the end of the 1890s Australian women were working as organisers overseas, which was a source of considerable pride.

> Australia's native and adopted daughters are not lacking in ability, and now that the advantages of higher education may be easily obtained, many of them will be as well equipped for even world-wide philanthropic service, as their sisters in other lands.[19]

Catherine Helen Spence was not the only Australian woman interested in reform who attended the World's Fair. Margaret Windeyer was there as a New South Wales Commissioner with the specific brief of taking care of the exhibits in the Women's Building.[20] The 26-year-old Windeyer, who was to be a lifelong campaigner for the rights of women and children, was unusual for her comparative youth, but she was also the daughter of a feminist mother. On arrival in the United States, she told stories of oppo-sition at home to her appointment, and she was the only foreign 'lady commissioner' at the fair. Her individual, if not bizarre, taste in dress, her vivacious and forthright personality, and her speech, to American ears 'the most astonishing of dialects', also contributed to the attention she received when she arrived in Chicago.

The women's exhibition in the Women's Building testified both to the diversity and commonality of women's experience, and to their capacities for organisation, and her six months in the Women's Building gave Margaret Windeyer strong feelings of solidarity and camaraderie with a wide and diverse range of women. She also attended a number of the conferences, including the World Congress of Representative Women and the Congress on Dress Reform. In her address to the Women's Congress — as one of over 600 speakers — Margaret Windeyer drew the experience of the women of the far-off 'newest nation' into the international network. During her time in the United States, she also established links with North American women's organisations and met some of their leaders.

The World Congress of Representative Women in Chicago was also the second quinquennial meeting of the International Council of Women (ICW); the first had met in Washington in 1888 on an initiative of the National Women's Suffrage Movement in the United States, and was attended by women from eight overseas countries.[21] In 1893 Australia still had no organisations affiliated with the ICW. The last speaker at the Chicago Congress called on the delegates to form National Councils of Women in their own countries, which would become part of the International Council, so that women could bind the whole world together in peace and unity. Three years after her return, at a meeting at Sydney Town Hall, Margaret Windeyer proposed the establishment of a National Council of Women of New South Wales. Her voyage to Chicago had played an important role in the integration of Australian feminists into an international network. The second National Council of Women in Australia was formed in Tasmania in 1900 by the peripatetic Emily Dobson.[22]

Australian women do not appear to have been represented at further conferences of the ICW until the Rome meeting in May 1914, when a delegation of six women participated — or rather did not participate. According to Gladys Marks, the Australian delegation was one of the weakest; the 'best of the lot' was the young Jessie Lillingston (later Street) but she was 'gagged', and every time Gladys herself wanted to speak she was squashed by the others.[23] The older women in the delegation were convinced that the Australian women must stay in the background and make no sound. Clearly not all Australian feminists were free of a sense of inferiority or thought that Australia was in a position to make contributions. Nevertheless, Gladys Marks found the conference an exciting experience; 'it's "no end" instructive to rub shoulders with thinking women of all nationalities. I try to meet as many as possible'.[24] She found the same satisfaction ten years later in 1924 when she was one of seven

Australian women at the Conference of the International Council of Women in Copenhagen.[25] True to her obsession with clothes and femininity, Gladys Marks noted at Copenhagen that the French women were very chic, but that most of the delegates, especially the Germans and Dutch, were dowdy. Like Winifred James, Marks wanted her feminists to be feminine; she was delighted at a meeting in Paris to find that the president of the French National Council of Women 'was intensely feminine'. Jessie Lillingston had also been excited in Rome by her meeting with women from other countries who were working for equal rights, and she made many lifelong friends.[26] In 1916 when she went to North America to link up with feminists and to find out more about prostitution, she utilised and fostered the networks that she had begun to build in Rome.

North America, as another new and progressive society, attracted Australian feminists from the time of Catherine Helen Spence's visit. She had opened up networks on which later visitors were to build. In 1902 Vida Goldstein, the leader of the Women's Suffrage Movement in Victoria, travelled to and through the United States to attend the first meeting of the International Suffrage Alliance in Chicago, where she was elected as corresponding secretary.[27] Goldstein carried with her several commissions from various political bodies in Australia seeking information on such issues as the American penal system, union organisation and industrial conditions, and about programmes for dealing with neglected and delinquent children. Landing at San Francisco, she made her way by train across the United States, stopping en route in Salt Lake City and Chicago. In the Mormon capital, she visited Utah State Prison and a Mormon temple. She was relieved to find only one wife in the Mormon household in which she stayed, but at the same time disappointed that she was thus deprived of an experience — and a traveller's tale. After the conference in Washington, where she was exhilarated by the camaraderie and fervour among the delegates, Goldstein went on to New York, before recrossing the United States to catch her boat in San Francisco. During her North American visit, she had addressed meetings, appeared before committees of the United States Senate and House of Representatives, visited prisons and orphanages, and sat in on juvenile courts. At the conclusion of her time in North America, she summarised her reactions.

> Although I have had a perfectly delightful visit, it has been real hard work all the time. Travelling on trains, living in one's trunks, speaking everywhere I went, visiting penal establishments, charitable institutions, schools, universities — you can draw a mental picture of what I have been through, and yet I don't think you will be able to form any idea of what the whirl and the rush has been. And you can't imagine what wholly delightful invitations for theatres, concerts and pleasure trips I have had to refuse, because with only a limited stay in each place, I have had to put work first and pleasure second.[28]

When Goldstein returned to Australia she had knowledge to impart, not on the latest fashions in dress or interior décor, but on labour organisation, industrial conditions, factory legislation, child protection, and the conditions of women, as well as some of the idiosyncrasies of American life, such as the taste for rocking chairs, spitting and tobacco chewing. Goldstein reported that American women were the freest in the world, despite the fact that the vast majority were unable to vote. She thought the American penal system far in advance of Victoria's, but the system of child welfare in South Australia superior to anything in America, and she was not impressed by the American political system. And, as was so often the case, the reception of her knowledge on her return was not always positive; she was accused of being excessively pro-American.[29]

In the first decade of the twentieth century, the forces of progressivism in the United States were achieving some success. Thus, when Alice Henry, furnished with introductions from Catherine Helen Spence, arrived in America in 1905, she too aroused interest as the citizen of a society that had earned the reputation of being 'the social laboratory of the world'.[30] Henry had been active in Australian progressive reform, and so was knowledgeable about government intervention in industry, about compulsory arbitration, and about a political party that had grown out of organised labour.[31] The possessor of relevant knowledge, and an accomplished public speaker, Henry soon found herself in demand on the lecture platform. She established contact with Hull House, the settlement house on the west side of Chicago. Founded by Jane Addams in 1889, by the time that Alice Henry arrived Hull House was a world-famous centre of progressive feminism. The settlement network led Henry to the National Women's Trade Union League (NWTUL), a semi-philanthropic body dedicated to the advancement of working women. She became secretary of the Chicago branch of the NWTUL, and in 1910 editor of its journal, *Life and Labor*, and settled in the United States. In the following years she lectured extensively for the League, contributed to its expansion, and published two books in the area of women and labour.

Alice Henry remained in North America until 1933, when at the age of 75 she faced the problem confronted by many single expatriate Australian women, that of care and comfort in her old age. Two years earlier she had written to a friend that she was thinking about returning to Australia; she dreaded the responsibility of an illness, and of a 'last illness which is sure to come some day'.[32] Thus, like Winifred James, Alice Henry came home; there was 'nothing else for it'.

On Henry's death ten years later, Frances Perkins, Secretary for Labor in the Roosevelt administration, wrote that the news brought not only a very real sense of the loss of a friend, but also the 'sense of gratitude for all the help that this Australian woman has given us in the United States'.[33] Alice Henry had made a significant contribution to feminism and progressivism in North America, but she had also gained much from her life abroad. She, like so many of her kind, had fretted in a land that was 'so distant from the centres of civilisation', so 'very cut off from the rest of the world', and that had, of necessity, 'the atmosphere of a small country town'. Her career as a journalist had been restricted by her gender, the outlets for her talents had been few. In North America she found greater opportunities to utilise her lecturing and writing skills, and to promote the ideas to which she was committed, on a scale and in a context unimaginable in Australia. Early twentieth-century Chicago was the fastest growing city in the United States, a seething and vibrant polyglot city whose factories, mills, and stockyards swallowed up the thousands of immigrants who were pouring in from all parts of Europe. Consequently, it was also a city that both embodied the most oppressive features of industrial capitalism and spawned a quest for their amelioration. Until she approached old age, Alice Henry found little reason to regret her decision to remain in Chicago. She visited Australia in 1926 and declared in a newspaper interview: 'I left Australia twenty years ago because I found no scope here for my work and I think that in a lesser degree the same thing applies today'.[34]

A year after she arrived in Chicago, Alice Henry was joined by the 26-year-old Miles Franklin, who remained in the United States until she crossed the Atlantic at the end of 1915 to make her contribution to the British war effort. Franklin also went to work with the NWTUL, becoming full-time secretary in 1910 and assistant editor of *Life and Labor* in 1912.[35] In the following year, she acted as press officer for the League during the great Garment Workers' strike in Chicago. She wrote back to Australia that year that she had been in 'big movements' and felt 'swallowed up'.[36] But Franklin, much younger than Alice Henry when she arrived in Chicago, and battling to establish herself as a writer by night while working by day, found her life at times bleak and lonely in the city of legendary winters, where 'the damp, ungracious rawness, laden with fine snow as sharp as salt' rose from Lake Michigan 'like an Arctic dragon's breath'.[37] A decade earlier, Vida Goldstein had not been overly impressed by Chicago; what she did remember was the dirt, the extreme cold and the breeziness and speed of the natives.[38]

Another of Alice Henry's credentials when she arrived in the United States was that she was 'up-to-date' with the suffragette campaign in England.[39] She had been present at the great protest meeting in Manchester in October 1905 after Christabel Pankhurst and Annie Kenny were released from Strangeways gaol following their arrest and conviction for disturbing the peace at a Liberal Party rally. For Henry, sisterhood was international and no group of women had the right to abandon the fight for women's suffrage until every woman in the world had the vote.

The militant campaign of the Women's Social and Political Union (WSPU) in Britain, the imprisonment of the suffragettes, the hunger strikes, and the subjection of the women to horrific forced feeding, aroused the sympathy of feminists everywhere, and Australian women in England participated in the struggle of these women to obtain the vote. Among the more conspicuous was Muriel Matters, who arrived in Britain in 1905. Two years later she joined the WSPU, and in the following year took the first 'Votes for Women' caravan on tour through the villages of southern England. Matters achieved fame in the following year when she chained herself to the iron grille in the ladies' gallery of the House of Commons. It was this grille, set in place to conceal women visitors, that Vida Goldstein saw as embodying 'the smallness of the English mind' and 'the true English conception of Woman, the mother of the race'.[40]After her arrest and conviction, Muriel Matters spent a month in an institution well off the normal tourist beat, Holloway prison. With an obvious flair for publicity, in the next year she flew over London in an airship inscribed 'Votes for Women' scattering handbills over the Houses of Parliament. In 1910 Matters made a return visit to Australia, lecturing on feminism and socialism and rallying support for the British sisters. Back in England, she participated in the establishment of a women's settlement in London's Lambeth slums, and after the First World War stood unsuccessfully as a Labour Party candidate for the House of Commons.

Other Australian women campaigned with the suffragettes while in Britain. Katharine Susannah Prichard joined the WSPU, Nettie Higgins — with some reservations — and Gladys Marks attended rallies while they were in London, painter Dora Meeson pasted notices on public hoardings and pillar-boxes, and Jessie Street sold the suffragette paper, *Votes for Women*, on street corners and did house-to-house canvassing.[41]They did so not as disadvantaged provincials, but as already enfranchised daughters conscious that they came from a more progressive and socially just society in which gender relations were more egalitarian. A contingent of Australian women marched in the Great Suffrage Procession of 1911 under a banner painted by Dora Meeson, 'Trust the women Mother as I have done'.[42] In May of that year Angelina Pearce noted in her diary of her trip to Europe that she had been invited to take part in the procession, whose Australian leaders included Lady Cockburne and Lady Macmillan.[43] Margaret Fisher, wife of the Australian Labour Prime Minister Andrew Fisher, led the Australian marchers, and Katharine Susannah Prichard carried a banner. It was Vida Goldstein who had organised the participation of the women from other countries in the procession.

Goldstein was by this time an internationally recognised feminist who had come to Britain as the invited guest of the WSPU and its leaders,

Emmeline Pethick-Lawrence and Emmeline and Christabel Pankhurst. On her arrival at Victoria Station in London, she had been greeted by an enormous crowd of WSPU members, and during her nine months in Britain she was the subject of much interest and adulation. Goldstein was a persuasive public speaker and she addressed public meetings across England and Scotland. Her first speech in London, given in the Albert Hall, drew an audience of 10,000, despite the fact that advertising of the meeting had been forbidden. Miles Franklin wrote home to Goldstein's mother that her daughter 'was the biggest thing that happened in the woman movement for some time in England'.[44] Her time in England brought Vida Goldstein into direct contact with the life-and-death struggle for the vote in which the British suffragettes were engaged. In November she was on the platform in the Caxton Hall at a meeting that ended in the streets and the arrest of 223 people. And her album of her time in England included photographs of the trees planted in memory of two suffragettes whose deaths had resulted from their suffrage commitment.[45]

While Vida Goldstein had journeyed to England to assist the English sisterhood, her contacts with the militants of the WSPU influenced the direction of her own feminism. She came to see oppression of women as deriving not only from capitalism, but also from the gender order and masculinity, and on her return to Australia she adopted a higher profile on sexual issues.[46] Her English experience had also made her more inter-nationalist in outlook and much of her energy in the years between her return and the outbreak of war was taken up in rallying support for the British suffragettes.

Vida Goldstein had long been a committed feminist when she arrived in Britain in 1911. For others, their time in Britain was a radicalising experi-ence.[47] It had been her encounter with the wretchedness of London's East End on a finishing trip to Europe in 1883 that had set Jane Addams on her search for a more useful life and to the creation of Hull House.[48] Twenty years later, Muriel Matters told a similar story. She had come to London from Adelaide as a 28-year-old actor and singer. While she had some con-tact with socialist ideas in Australia, it was in London that she underwent the political conversion that took her into radical politics and the suffrage movement, where she realised that 'I was a born agitator'.

> I had to cross the line to discover myself as an active agitator in this move-ment. Everything in this country conspired towards this discovery. The chill November days of mist and fog; the sordid general environment for the masses of the people, with extreme wealth and luxury on the one hand and bitter black poverty on the other;... the incessant grind from the street organs invariably wailing out hymns of petition; the raucous voices of street singers, and the endless beggars that met one's gaze and tugged at one's heart-strings from the corner of every street — these and other things too

numerous and too dreadful to be mentioned, work mightily on the spirit of all who, having eyes to see and hearts that feel, enter this capital of the world.[49]

Muriel Matters was by no means the only Australian horrified by the poverty at the heart of the Empire. Her reaction was common among Australians who ventured into the slums of the East End. Bitter condemnation of the wretchedness of the lives of Britain's poor, and the accompanying scathing critique of the society that tolerated so much misery, was also part of nationalist as well as socialist and feminist discourses.[50] The extent and depth of poverty was an important element in the attacks launched against Britain by *Bulletin* boys like Randolph Bedford.[51]

Scots-born South Australian writer and socialist reformer, Catherine Martin, who lived in Europe from 1890 to 1894 and again from 1904 to 1907, gave a different definition of exile, not those on the periphery of the Empire, but of those at its heart — exiled from civilisation.

> But so complete is the exile of London's poorest from civilisation, that after becoming for a little time used to the spectacle, it unconsciously corrupts your mind into resting on their possession of mere food and shelter, as something to be thankful for...
>
> It blunts and confuses the moral sense — the wilderness of hideous streets in district after district, divorced from every sight and sound that wakens any feeling of hope, of joy, of admiration...
>
> When you get away from these regions, they lapse as it were into forgotten cities of the dead — they are like some wild nightmare you have mistaken for reality …
>
> Could there in effect be anything more unreal than that one part of a Christian nation should consign another section of it, to a level so far below the physical condition of slaves that were bought and sold. [52]

Mary Gaunt, indulging in a diatribe against missionaries in West Africa, asked why a society that was infected 'with such ghastly festering sores at its own heart', that condemned 'little children to a life of utter hopelessness', should presume to try and impose its codes upon others.[53] Katharine Susannah Prichard believed that her experience of London poverty 25 years later was an important marker on her path to communism. She had lived in the slums at Worlds End in attempt to gain an insight into how the poor lived.

> There was a pub at the corner. Brawls resounded from it every night; fishmongers and vegetable hawkers yelled; barrel organs squalled, children shrieked and sang dancing around them. I could not get accustomed to the noise, nor to the stench of a poverty-stricken area: damp, decaying houses, urinous walls, accumulated filth in drains and rubbish bins on the pavement.[54]

Horror among the more socially committed at the slums of Britain was accompanied by biting condemnations of the British class system and the moral blindness of the ruling class. Alice Henry wrote:

> I never passed by those Park Lane mansions, but I seemed to see them built upon the wealth and misery of the world. And when I saw the armies of the unemployed, the product of their environment; when I saw the lifelong struggle to make ends meet — the best that life could give to all but a few Englishmen and women — and the poor, stunted lives that most of them lead in town or in country, I wondered that there could be found thoughtful men ready to condemn Australians for any social experiments they had made.[55]

Pattie Deakin, in Britain in 1907 as the wife of the Australian Prime Minister Alfred Deakin, was equally disgusted: 'I have seen and heard much that I never even dreamed was possible...That people who lead such lives, such examples, should still be classed as superior is to my mind revolting and criminal'.[56] Catherine Martin's *The Old Roof Tree; Letters of Ishbel to her half-brother Mark Latimer*, which purported to be written from an English cathedral town and from parts of Europe, and which contains reflections on art, religion, literature and the meaning of life, was an intervention in the British present. Her scathing attack was intended to inspire 'a more critical examination of the strange chaos of misery that underlies Britain's social system'. Her target was the clerical middle class, which she felt was so out of step with Christian teaching.[57]

It was not only feminists and social reformers who were offended when they encountered the British class system in its daily manifestations. Rose Scott Cowen, who grew up on a Queensland station and was sent in 1895 at the age of sixteen to spend a year with her English relatives, wrote of her distaste before the 'humble deprecating manner of the underclasses': 'I was used to men who were suntanned and outspoken not a poor old yellow humble worm'.[58] On a tour of Spain, Margaret Thomas reflected that 'in no country I have visited is there the absurd slavishness which is supposed to be the thing in England to keep the servants'.[59]

For feminist women, and for those of reformist bent, Australia, since it was not hidebound by class and tradition, was the better society. Gladys Marks attended a meeting of the Actresses Franchise League in London in 1913, where the problems of working-class women — sweating and subcontracting, denial of legal guardianship of their children, infant mortality — were discussed: 'Nobody in Australia can possibly realise the condition of things through defective legislation and administration in England. We're in advance of them in a hundred respects'.[60] In the face of an English attack on Australian socialism, Catherine Martin meditated on the inability of the English to introduce change into their own society:

Method and regularity and order are qualities that belong to the very bowels of morality in an old country where everything has been immemorially fixed by custom and habit and Party Government...

   In a new country, where man is so much an Arab of the desert, ready at a moment's warning to fold up his tent, and look for a fresh oasis, he is from the nature of things more ready to act on the emergency of the present, without looking up the records of dead yesterday. Indeed he often has none at which to look.[61]

Vida Goldstein made connections between Australia as a new, young society and the greater gains made by its women.[62] They had the vote 'because it is easier to overcome the anti-suffrage forces, ignorance, tradition, and prejudice in a young unfettered country'.[63] Despite the masculinity and misogyny of cultural worlds in Australia, it was a rhetorical convention to represent Australian women as the product of a society in which there was greater gender equality and freedom for women than was the case in Britain. The heroine in Alice Rosman's *Miss Bryde*

   belonged to a nation that out of its very youth, out of the significance and struggle of pioneering days and all they meant of gallantry shared labour and effort, had evolved a saner attitude on the eternal question of the sexes, recognising that in the fitness and equipment of its women, no less than of its men, lay the surest way to economic strength and prosperity.[64]

Mary Edgeworth David, who accompanied her father to Oxford in 1910, wrote that the two aspects of England that she could not cope with were snobbishness and the attitudes of men towards women: 'I had been accustomed all my life to being treated as an equal by my men friends'.[65] In her travel books, Mary Gaunt, in widely different environments, elaborated on the virtues — virtues born of necessity — of Australian women.

   Besides it is the custom of the country that a woman should stand beside her husband; has not married for a livelihood, men are plentiful enough and she has chosen her mate, wherefore it is her pleasure and joy to help him in every way.[66]

Informing Gaunt's writing is her feminist commitment to equality in relations between men and women, husbands and wives, what should be rather than what was.[67]

   Feminist and reforming women could be as interested in seeing the sights as any other traveller, but their agendas took them well off the usual scenic and social routes. While Catherine Martin delighted in the beauty, art and architecture of Venice, a highlight of her visit to the city that is the essence of fantasy and romance was her meeting with Italian radicalism in the *palazzo* of a *marchesa*.[68] The British 'notables' whom Ada Holman interviewed for her travel jottings were all reformers and suffragettes.[69] In

England, Katharine Susannah Prichard participated in Fabian socialist
meetings, and Alice Henry attended classes and meetings of the Workers
Education Movement and went to the London School of Economics to
hear George Bernard Shaw. But then George Bernard Shaw was as much a
conventional site on the tourist map of reformers as Voltaire had been in
the late eighteenth century — Nettie Palmer, before leaving Australia in
1909, listed a meeting with him as one of things she wanted to include on
her itinerary, Vida Goldstein lunched with him in 1911, Ada Holman
heard him speak in the Albert Hall in the same year, Gladys Marks went to
a lecture in November 1914, and Miles Franklin heard him discussing
politics in 1919.[70] The reformers visited slums, factories, orphanages,
prisons. Jessie Street's sojourn in Cairo on her way home in 1911 was
unusual for a woman in that it included a visit to a brothel frequented by
British army personnel, and her stay in New York in 1915 included a period as under-matron in a home for girls who had been arrested for solicit-
ing.[71] Miles Franklin's America included the shacks of the coalminers.

> During the day we saw for ourselves the terrible living conditions, the utter
> lack of sanitation as represented by choked drains, and the general desola-
> tion of the mining camps. The conditions throughout are so miserable that
> only the exceptional character can hold out against demoralisation.[72]

Sights of equal misery greeted the women who joined international
humanitarian agencies working among the displaced peoples of eastern
and south-eastern Europe at the end of the First World War. When the
armistice made it possible for Ethel Cooper to leave Germany, she
returned to Australia, but by 1922 she was back in Europe as a volunteer
worker with the Quaker relief organisations in Germany, Austria and
Poland. She was not the only Australian woman working with the
Quakers in Poland. Others included writer Joice Nankivell Loch and her
husband, Sydney Loch.[73] The Lochs had left Australia in 1918 and, after a
time in London, had moved on to Ireland in the last year of the civil war.[74]
After Ireland, they joined the relief teams working along the Stochod
River in the marsh areas of eastern Poland which, as a frontier zone
between the German and Russian armies, had become 'a vast soldier's
grave'. When the war ended, millions of Polish peasants who had been
forcibly deported east during the war streamed back, fleeing famine and
bearing typhus.

> We were do-gooders on a grand scale. Famine, typhus, dysentery, swarms
> of homeless in old army dugouts and trenches. People lived underground,
> very often partially underwater as snow heaped over their hovels melted
> with the heat of their stoves. Hundreds of people; thousands of people,
> until they stumbled into our dreams. Members of the mission typhus units
> stood week after week by their de-lousing stations, clad in rubber boots and

silver mackintoshes; earning for themselves the title 'silver ladies'. They lived in a world of steam, surrounded by stark-naked patients — some skeletons, some obese with the terrible obesity of starvation. Steam surrounded them, piles of hair was heaped round them, shaved from the patient. Yet the 'silver ladies' could laugh as they skimmed the scalded lice from the surface of the water, as they wielded clippers or pushed great hangers of clothing into field ovens.[75]

During her time in the refugee camps, Joice Loch came to an appreciation of Poland, both country and people. She was entranced by the beauty of the countryside in its different seasonal unfoldings.

> Poland has a haunting enchantment that few other lands have, from the hour when the hand of God pulls back the covering of snow to uncover the brilliant blue chionidoxia in that glamorous moment when the peasants race from their houses, shouting into the snow sky: 'A stork! A stork! and the first, longed-for bringer of summer folds his wings, weary from long flying, and glides down into the marshes still covered with snow that crackles under his weight, a sign for man and frogs.[76]

When the Quaker missions in Poland closed down, Ethel Cooper and Joice and Sydney Loch moved south to Salonika to work among more displaced people, Greek refugees fleeing Turkey, Armenians escaping from Smyrna, and victims of the Revolution and Civil War in the Soviet Union. According to the Lochs, Ethel Cooper's strong-minded and independent attitudes, and somewhat eccentric actions, were rather disconcerting, particularly her claims to have eaten the elephant in Leipzig Zoo during the war and to be a reincarnation of the Pharaohs, and the libations of wine she poured out on moonlit nights before the altar she had built to the Greek god Pan.[77] In 1932, after a decade of extensive travel in Europe, Ethel Cooper returned to Australia, but Joice and Sydney Loch remained in Greece, making their home in the Byzantine Tower of Pyrghos near the small village of Prosforion at the base of the Athos peninsula.

> Over a stretch of sea was the peninsula of Athos, and rising out of it a huge Byzantine tower, mystic, wonderful, gleaming blue-white in the full moonlight, or pink-stained white in the setting sun. A sentry on the land-frontier of the Holy Territory.[78]

While her husband pursued his fascination with the monasteries of Mt Athos, forbidden territory for women, Joice Loch became involved in the life of the surrounding villages and all the problems that result from barren land and under-employment. Noticing that some of the refugees were skilled rugmakers, she decided to try and build up a local rug industry, based on local wools and dyes and looking to the illuminated manuscripts of the monasteries for designs rather than imitating Turkish pat-

terns. By the end of the 1930s, the industry had been successfully established. Joice and Sydney Loch became involved once again in the thick of
humanitarian work when war broke out in 1939. They were asked by the
Quakers to return to Poland to administer the Polish Relief Fund, but by
the time they were able to leave Greece, Poland had fallen, and the Lochs
spent the war years assisting Polish refugees, first in Romania and then in
Cyprus and Palestine.

In the 1920s and 1930s women continued to travel overseas to attend
international conferences in pursuit of the promotion of women's interests and social reform. Before the war, Vida Goldstein, a committed paci-
fist, had also attended peace conferences while abroad. Peace movements
were closely linked to humanitarianism, and hence to charity, a recognised and established area of female activity, and their international networks and commitment to the cause of women's rights beyond national
boundaries furnished many Australian feminists with an international
outlook. The horror of the First World War had spawned new peace
movements and organisations, and feminist women were to provide one
of the most dynamic and radical elements in interwar organisations in
Australia dedicated to the outlawing of war.[79]

Six months after the signing of the armistice, Eleanor Moore left
Melbourne to participate in an international movement to prevent war
from ever happening again. Her destination was the first postwar conference of the Women's International League for Peace and Freedom
(WILPF), which derived from the Women's Peace Party in the United
States and various women's peace and suffrage organisations in Europe.[80]
Born in Melbourne in 1875, Eleanor Moore, on leaving school, had
attended a business college.[81] Frustrated by her gender in her wish to
become a court reporter, she worked for Hansard and then as a secretary
for the woolbrokers, Dalgety's. In 1905 the by then 30-year-old Moore
made a six-month trip to Europe with her sister Alice, a holiday financed
out of savings from her salary at Dalgety's. Looking back on her first trip,
she claimed that she was horrified not only by the appalling poverty in the
cities of England, and by class privilege and class deference, but also by
the all-pervading militarism in church as well as state. Ten years later
when the Sisterhood of Peace was founded in Melbourne, Eleanor Moore
was elected as the international secretary; she was also an executive member of the Australian Peace Alliance, which advocated a negotiated peace
and opposed conscription.

Eleanor Moore's journey to Geneva was a saga in itself and an instance
indeed of the tyranny of distance. Notification of the conference and May
as its date reached Australia on the last day of the February. Thanks to her
Dalgety connections, Moore was on board a ship five days later. Her fellow Australian delegates, Vida Goldstein and Cecilia John, who made

their arrangements at a more leisurely pace, did not arrive at the conference until the second week. When Moore reached London, she discovered that the conference had been moved from The Hague to Zurich. But on her arrival in Zurich in the middle of the opening session, she learnt that distance could confer distinction. Creeping into the assembly hall, Moore handed in her credentials. The proceedings were then interrupted when the chair, the omnipresent and indefatigable Jane Addams, called Eleanor to the platform to announce the arrival of the Australian delegate, who had journeyed for ten weeks to attend.

After the conference, Eleanor Moore spent some time in Europe while waiting for a passage back to Australia, attending summer schools at Oxford and Cambridge, lecturing in Manchester, staying with trade unionists in Paris, and working with the secretariat of the WILPF in Geneva. She began to appreciate cosmopolitan life at 'the centre of a harmonious international circle'; at a Christmas party, eight different languages were spoken in the room, and she met a Polish gentlemen who had command of six and had learnt his English from the novels of Charles Dickens.

On her return to Australia, Eleanor Moore became the paid part-time secretary of Australian Peace Alliance, and, in 1928, secretary of the Australian section of the WILPF. She travelled overseas again in 1928 when she represented the WILPF in the Australian delegation led by Bessie Rischbieth to the Women's Conference of the Pan-Pacific Union in Honolulu.[82] Moore saw the Pan-Pacific Union as part of the beginning of the slow process by which Australia would realise that it was a continent in the South Pacific, not an island off the coast of Europe. In Honolulu 'cosmopolitan' took on a wider significance, and Moore felt her insularity and the cultural and artistic impoverishment that was a consequence of the White Australia policy.

After 1919 it was the League of Nations that was the focus of peace movements. Sydney Loch failed in his pursuit of a position in the secretariat of the League of Nations, but Frank Moorhouse secured one for Edith Campbell Berry, the protagonist of his 1993 novel, *Grand Days*, which is set in the world of the League. There were no real-life counterparts to Edith Campbell Berry. In 1922 the League of Nations Union in Melbourne endorsed the principle that the Australian delegations to the League Assembly should include a woman.[83] But all the government would agree to was the appointment of women as 'substitute' delegates, and since the 'substitutes', unlike the officially endorsed male delegates, had to pay their own fares, the choice usually fell on women who were already in Europe for other reasons. Substitute delegates included academics like Freda Bage, who makes a brief appearance in *Grand Days*, Jessie Webb and Margot Hentze, feminist leaders like Bessie Rischbieth, and peace workers like Eleanor Moore and Alice Moss. If the men who governed Australia were little interested in increasing the presence of women at the League of Nations Assembly, they were hardly exceptional. According to Jessie Street, who attended meetings of the Liaison Committee of International Organisations in Geneva in 1938, there were few women delegates to the League from anywhere, and the male delegates were backward in their attitudes to women and their understanding of the problems arising from sex discrimination.[84] The only woman in Geneva in 1938 with high public profile was the 'heroine' of the Russian Revolution, Alexandra Kollontai, Soviet Ambassador to Sweden — and by then she had been marginalised in the Soviet power structure.

In addition to their role as substitute delegates, a number of Australian women did journey to Geneva in the interwar years, consulting and observing on the fringes. Muriel Heagney worked briefly in 1926 with the International Labour Office, where Eleanor Hinder also spent some time in 1931 in connection with her work on industrial and labour reform in Shanghai. Jessie Street's interest in social insurance took her to the Library of the League in 1930 and Janet Mitchell went to the Assembly in 1935 as 'temporary collaborator for Australia'; each year the League's information section invited between twenty and thirty men and women of different nationalities to visit Geneva, where they were given special facilities for studying the organisation of the League and access to all its public meetings. Janet Mitchell's time at the Assembly coincided with the Abyssinian crisis, and she heard Sir Samuel Hoare and Pierre Laval make their ringing — but as it turned out hollow — speeches pledging total commitment to collective resistance against unprovoked aggression. In her memoirs, Mitchell gave an evocative description of the time and place.

> The succeeding days were for me vivid with impressions. As I watched the lobbying in the Salle des Conversations, I saw how the work of the League was done — in apparently accidental, carefully-planned meetings between individuals. Here, by the cocktail bar, or in the discreet alcoves opposite it, one saw mainly the lesser fry — the representatives of small States, members of the Secretariat, pressmen waiting for their prey. The air buzzed with rumours of what the great men had said, what they were going to say, what they were saying even behind the closed doors of their suites in the Hotel Beau-Rivage or the Hotel des Bergues...
>
> It was an unnatural hot-house atmosphere, which by the force of suggestions made one see significance in the most trivial happenings: Mr Eden, walking with the Australian member of the Council, Mr S.M. Bruce, and stopping for a moment's talk with Litvinoff, was an International Incident.[85]

As the 1930s progressed, fascist powers loomed more threateningly on the international scene and communist and anti-fascist activists joined forces to combat fascism in organisations such as the Movement Against War and Fascism launched in Paris in 1932. Branches of the Movement Against War and Fascism had been established in Sydney and Melbourne in 1933, and Australian women in Europe participated in the struggle where it was happening.[86] Once again, some had taken their home-grown radicalism to Europe while others were radicalised *in situ*. During her third trip to Europe in 1935, Nettie Palmer, who was active in the Movement Against War and Fascism in Australia, attended the First International Congress of Writers for the Defence of Culture in Paris, where she corralled Christina Stead into the Australian delegation.[87] Patricia Thompson's anti-fascism developed in Europe. Looking back on her overseas trip in 1937, she portrayed the young secretary who left Australia as politically ignorant. From a fellow passenger on her ship who was a devotee of the Left Book Club she learnt that Adolf Hitler was not so much a man with a funny Charlie Chaplin moustache as a menace to world peace. In Europe she worked for a time as a stenographer at the League of Nations in Geneva, and then at the Left Book Club in London. Her working experience, together with the new friends she had made, turned her towards politics 'which had a decidedly pink tinge' and she became caught up in popular-front activities.

> As far as we could, in our own puny way, we tried to influence events by making ourselves part of the Popular Front. We marched behind Hewlett Johnson, the Red Dean of Canterbury with his snowy white hair and gaiters, who strode onwards carrying a great red flag. We called for resistance to Fascism. We helped to support Spanish orphans. We never missed Left Book Club rallies, calling for non-intervention in Spain, independence for India, Japanese quit China, Italians quit Abyssinia, Germany stop bullying the Czechs, or any other left-wing causes.[88]

It was in Spain in 1936 that the fascist menace became reality in a civil war that gripped imaginations and emotions as the great confrontation between democracy and fascism — or alternatively, between order in church and state and the red menace. Nettie and Vance Palmer had taken their daughters to Europe in 1935. The elder, Aileen, put her political commitment on the line when she joined a British medical team in Spain.[89] She was not the only daughter of a reformist mother to go to Spain. Ada Holman's daughter, Portia, who had remained in Britain after reading economics at Newnham College, Cambridge, and who went on to study psychology, medicine and psychiatry, worked at the British Hospital in Valencia in 1937.[90] And there were also the nurses who had sailed from Australia to serve with the republican forces.

Commitment to internationalism and social reform diverted some women from the well-beaten track to Europe — in the cases of Janet

Mitchell and Eleanor Hinder, to China. The track to China for both women began in another organisation with strong international links, the Young Women's Christian Association (YWCA). The early years of Janet Mitchell's story have been told — a highly strung young woman who challenged class and family codes to take up professional training first in music and then in the Arts Faculty at London University. When she returned to Australia in 1923 with her London University degree and the vague idea that she wanted to do something in the way of social work, her first job was as education secretary with the YWCA in Melbourne. Through its World Fellowship Movement, Mitchell became aware of 'the staggering difficulties in the way of women's progress in the Orient'.[91] In 1925 she was an Australian delegate to the first Conference of the Institute of Pacific Relations in Honolulu and came back impressed by the work of the YWCA in China and Japan. Although Mitchell came home with an increasing international awareness and 'in a mood of elation, for I had seen not only a new world but one in which I wanted to take an active part', her next career move was to become the organiser of the Government Savings Bank of NSW's Thrift Campaign. She then went on a study tour of similar organisations in North America.

The Government Savings Bank of NSW collapsed in 1931 and Janet Mitchell's options once again became open. She was invited to participate in the Australian delegation to the 1931 Institute of Pacific Relations Conference in Hangchow, which coincided with the Mukden incident and the Japanese invasion of Manchuria. Caught in a love-hate relationship with China, Mitchell decided to stay on after the conference, journeying to Manchuria as a freelance journalist. She settled in Harbin, where she made a living teaching English, mainly to the Russian refugees in which the city abounded. Mitchell witnessed the Japanese occupation of Harbin in February 1932, and the subsequent League of Nations Inquiry led by Lord Lytton. She left China sceptical about the future of the League. After a year as acting principal of the Women's College at the University of Sydney, she moved to London where she wrote a novel set among a Russian refugee community in Harbin, *Tempest in Paradise*. When Janet Mitchell wrote her autobiography in 1935 she was warden of Ashburne Hall at the University of Manchester.

Eleanor Hinder was born in Maitland in 1893 and after taking a science degree at the University of Sydney, taught for a short period before moving into welfare work when she was appointed welfare superintendent at the large Sydney retail store, Farmer and Co.[92] At the end of 1923, she was granted one year's leave of absence on full salary and a travel grant to investigate industrial welfare overseas. An invitation to view the efforts of the National YWCA to ameliorate the appalling factory conditions endured by women and children in China made Shanghai the first stop on her itinerary. Hinder wrote prophetically to her mother in January 1924:

> In a way it seems as if this is a laboratory at the moment of things directly concerned with my own education in the things I have come to see — it is a wonderful thing that I should have come.[93]

For the rest of her life she was involved in the struggle, against unbelievable odds, to improve the lives of women and children in China.

From Shanghai, Hinder went on to Japan and Europe. In Geneva she visited the International Labour Organisation (ILO) and in Oslo she was an Australian delegate to the Congress of the Federation of University Women. She came home via North America and New Zealand. At the beginning of 1926, Hinder returned to China on a two-year Rockefeller Fellowship to work with the YWCA on factory conditions in Shanghai, at that time a centre of both Chinese export and foreign missionary activity. She also played an instrumental role in forging the Joint Committee of Shanghai Women's Organisations into an effective lobby group. Hinder's work was already being disrupted in 1926, as it was to be for much of her future, by civil wars and rebellions, and in 1928 she left Shanghai, attending the Pan-Pacific Women's Conference in Honolulu before returning to Australia. In the following year, Hinder was a delegate for the Australian Council of the Institute of Pacific Relations at the Kyoto Japan Conference and from Kyoto went back to Shanghai where she freelanced, taking whatever work was available, including being special correspondent in China for the *Newcastle Morning Herald*.[94]

By 1931 the Chinese people faced new horrors with the Japanese invasion, and Shanghai was subjected to aerial bombardment. Since affairs in the area had come to a virtual standstill, Hinder left, travelling in the United States and Europe. In her absence from China she was offered the position of chief of the Shanghai Municipality's newly created Industrial Division, with responsibility for organising service to improve safety and hygiene in factories, mediation in industrial disputes, rent control and child welfare. She was to hold the post until 1942. Child labour, child protection and the problem of 'girl slavery', white and otherwise, became increasingly the focus of her attention. The aftermath of a generation of civil war and of the Japanese invasion added the care of refugees and orphans to her welfare commitments. In 1942 Eleanor Hinder was repatriated to London, where she joined the British Foreign Office, which sent her to Montreal to work for the ILO. Two years later, she was appointed as British representative on the Far Eastern subcommittee of the United Nations Relief and Rehabilitation Association (UNRRA) Technical Committee, thus embarking on a new phase in her life working with the United Nations.

Eleanor Hinder's life in China was sustained by a close and lifelong friendship with Viola Smith, a distinguished American lawyer working in the United States Trade Commission in Shanghai from 1929 to 1939, who was also deeply concerned with women's and welfare issues. When Hinder officially retired in 1956 and failed in her attempt to secure United States citizenship, the two women established a home in Sydney. Smith remained in Australia after Hinder's death in 1963, playing a considerable role in women's affairs, publishing in 1975 *Women in Australian Parliaments and Local Government Past and Present*.[95] Viola Smith might be seen, then, as a North American counterpart of Alice Henry and reminds us that the meetings and accidents of life create expatriates in Australia as well as abroad.

The women who journeyed as part of their commitment to social amelioration, feminism and peace had entered the public world and acted on an international stage. Their travel gave them access to like-minded people, the knowledge that distant though Australians might be from the centre, they were part of worldwide movements, and a sense of solidarity with women across the world. Ruby Rich, looking back in 1976 at the age of 88 on a lifetime of involvement in women's movements, social reform and travel, summed up what participation in international conferences had meant to her.

When we go to the International Congresses that I've been privileged to attend and of course other Societies have their International Congresses too, but those that I have been to, I not only have an opportunity of hearing others, sometimes of sharing with them the platform, but I also have that great privilege of getting to know women of other cultures, of other nations, but linked with me is that lovely feeling they have towards the cause that we both believe in, or try to help further, namely the status of women, the equality between women and men, for the betterment not just of women but of the family and humanity.[96]

Interlude

Dora Birtles and Irene Saxby

Between 1926 and 1938, there were just under 240 000 temporary departures from Australia.[1] Since some people travelled to Europe frequently, the number of departing was fewer than the number of departures, and Australia's travelling class still probably numbered somewhere around 3 per cent of the total population of seven million. Of the departures of the 1920s and 1930s, women account for 55 per cent, and of people in their twenties, as many as three-quarters were women.[2] In the years after the First World War travel became more organised, promoted and constructed by a developing tourist industry. Magazines like *Home* and *B.P. Magazine* featured articles and glossy advertisements associating the modern woman with travel, and travel with adventure, the romantic and the exotic. In 1935 the *Women's Weekly* established a Travel and Information Bureau and began organising tours.[3]

In his study of British literary travelling between the wars, *Abroad*, Paul Fussell has argued that in the 1920s travel became a metaphor for flight and freedom. His fugitives were British and male. In her gloss on Fussell, Billie Melman has taken his argument further to suggest that the metaphor was widely diffused beyond the circles of a literary élite and loomed large in both the romance fiction and journalese of the period.[4] The female traveller was a symbol both of the urge to escape that followed the First World War and of the modern woman, independent and free of restriction. The urge to escape from the confines of domesticity and patriarchy — both temporarily and permanently — and to sample life in more romantic and exotic places had been an agenda fuelling the overseas travel of Australian women from the first days that independent travel had become an option for them. In the 1920s and 1930s they found new ways of travelling.

As the first woman to be admitted as a solicitor in New South Wales, and as an active feminist and champion of the League of Nations, it was in part — but only in part — with her tongue in cheek that Marie Byles wrote in the introduction to her account of her 1928 travels that she felt a real duty laid upon her not to 'do' the regulation cathedrals and ancient buildings, not to attend the conferences of all the highbrow societies to which she belonged. Her aim was 'to ramble, tramp, hike, and climb mountains, learn about boats and simply enjoy life', and this was just what she did in Britain, Norway, Canada and New Zealand.[5] What Australia lacked for Marie Byles was 'real mountains'.[6] Her taste for mountains found her in 1938 in China, Tibet and Burma, where she came into contact with Buddhism, and thirteen years later she became a founding member of the Buddhist Society of New South Wales.[7]

Marie Byles had travelled to Europe by cargo boat; journalist Margaret Gilruth and a friend worked their way to London in 1931 as stewards on a Norwegian freighter, which took them to Egypt, Italy, Turkey, Russia, Holland and Germany.[8] Gilruth began her return trip by hiking across Europe to Brindisi. The account of her adventures in one British newspaper also made mention of the exploits of another Australian girl, Winifred Howard, who had worked as a greaser alongside a Chinese crew in the engine room of a tramp steamer that sailed from New York through the Panama Canal to China and then on to Arabia.[9] The same article referred to yet another Australian mode of adventurous travel; Jeanne Day of Adelaide had tried to reach Europe as a stowaway. 'Australia', the piece concluded, 'was becoming noted on this side of the world for the adventurous spirit and the roving nature of its young women'.

If women worked their way to Europe on cargo boats, the travel plans of three young woman who had met as students at the University of Sydney in the early 1920s were even more adventurous. In April 1932 the ten-metre Swedish-built cutter, *Gullmarn*, sailed for London from Newcastle with a crew of five: Dora Birtles, Joyce Metcalf, her husband, Hedley, and her cousin, Irene Saxby, and a Swedish sailor. The voyage aroused considerable attention because it was the first time that Australian women had participated in such a venture and because of prurient speculation about the possible consequences of the cohabitation of a group of men and women in such close quarters over a long period. The voyage continued to receive publicity since all the women wrote accounts for the press as a means of financing their travels. In 1934 Dora Birtles turned the material in her diaries and letters into her travel book, *North-West by North*.[10]

Joyce Metcalf was the daughter of Labor politician and judge, Sir George Beeby. Irene Saxby, whose father had been headmaster of both Newcastle and Sydney Boys' High Schools, had been a teacher of French in New South Wales country high schools before abandoning a profession that she disliked to study art. At the time of the voyage Dora Birtles was a 28-year-old married retrenched teacher. Brought up in Newcastle, she had met her poet-writer-Bohemian-radical husband, Bert Birtles, while a student. His love poem to Dora, 'Beauty', had so scandalised the university authorities that he was sent down. Dora's involvement in the poem and her own poetry led to her suspension from the university and departure from the Women's College.[11] Bert Birtles had no interest in joining the voyage of the *Gullmarn*, so Dora went alone. They were to take up their marriage again three years later when they met in Greece. Dora

Birtles wrote in *North-West by North* that one of the reasons for her departure was the need 'to escape the net of bondages that being long-married
implied and to find an individual freedom for a little time'.[12] These were
no doubt sentiments shared by many women. Dora Birtles and her marriage were unusual in that she was able to act in accordance with her feelings. She later wrote that she joined the crew of the *Gullmarn* not because
she wanted to be the first woman to undertake something, but because
the voyage was the 'cheapest and easiest way of travelling in a floating
home and seeing the world en route to London, a more shining beacon
for all of us than any Samarkand'.[13]

North-West by North tells of the voyage along the coast of Queensland
and through the waters of the then Dutch East Indies to Singapore. The
journey brought adventures enough and Dora Birtles was enchanted by
her mode of travel.

> For me it was the unadulterated joy to be alive, going somewhere, taking
> oneself with the hiss of the water past the bows and a wake like a comet
> pearling the darkness behind...[14]

But what is most notable about Dora Birtles's story is the focus not on
adventure, but on relationships. Indeed, because of this focus, her travel
book has been identified as following a 'feminine' storyline.[15] By the end
of the voyage, Dora Birtles knew as well as any postmodernist that subjectivity is unstable and in flux.

> Nothing is ever simple in real life. Had we been in a book the author could
> have built up our characters into consistent wholes and given us only the cir-
> cumstances that suited the parts we ought to have played, but in the day to
> day muddle of living a self-coherent person rarely exists, and character, the
> sterling and gold standard variety, goes down before the flow of personality
> over events. Character is a concept of moralists and is supposed to remain
> stable of march towards good or ill, whereas personality is fluid, and real.[16]

Following an archetypal storyline, Dora Birtles represented the voyage
as a period of self-testing and learning. She wrote that it was her first
chance to be quite independent and responsible for herself, and she learnt
what a petted and swaddled life she had hitherto enjoyed. She came to see
the months of morbid introspection on board the *Gullmarn*, and her inces-
sant desire for solitude, as the necessary corollary of her breaking away
from all intimate associations and moving towards autonomy.[17] The voyage was also Irene Saxby's 'first taste of freedom and adventuring'.
According to Dora Birtles, at the time of their departure Irene Saxby was a
woman who had never quite managed to grow up, who was possessed of
'an enchanting Peter Pan quality'.[18] When she stepped ashore in
Singapore, she was different: 'How brown she was among the other

women, how brawny her arms, how care-free and independent her every casual gesture'.[19] Her freshly ironed ribbons and muslins were no longer appropriate cladding, they belonged to a previous life; 'we were different women now'.

Beyond transformation in individuals, Dora Birtles's narrative tells of the disastrous impact of the voyage on personal relationships, of the fraying and breaking of the ropes of friendship and goodwill, of the ways in which quirks of personality, habits and mannerisms become magnified, begin to irritate, when people are confined without relief of escape, when lack of privacy is defined as having nothing of one's own except a toothbrush. In addition, there were quarrels about money and competition for publication of accounts of the voyage.

> So there we were, on a voyage that might have looped like the arc of a rainbow, off the humdrum earth to the other side of the world, a most wretched set of people tied together by circumstance, our antagonisms jangling like fire alarms when we encountered, having to be careful with each other as if our tempers and dislikes were marked, 'Fragile with care; Polite side up'.[20]

Already, by Brisbane, Dora Birtles had wondered whether she should go on:

> I had been doubting whether I ought to go on. I wanted to but we had smashed so much since we left; we had done all the things that ordinary, insensitive, prosaic, evil-wishing people had said we should. We had quarrelled over money, we had flown into senseless rages, we had been frightened of each other and jealous of amities and irritated to murder. We had made affection between the sexes illicit and we had made plain-speaking impossible.[21]

By Singapore, the voyage had foundered on human foibles and the participants went their own ways. Dora Birtles never saw Joyce Metcalf again, and Irene Saxby only once after 1933 — by chance on a bus to Sydney's Palm Beach in the 1960s. But the voyage did go on in Dora Birtles's imagination, and the writing of *North-West by North* two years later was a form of cathartic release: 'The whole experience could never have been settled for me until that was done. I have been incompetent to do anything for two years because of it'.[22]

The abandonment of the voyage in Singapore was but the end of one stage of the women of the *Gullmarn*'s adventures. Joyce Metcalf and her husband stayed with the boat and went on to trade copra along the Malay coast. Dora Birtles travelled on to China and Japan before working her way as a nanny to England. She then toured Europe with her sister, returned to England where she became London correspondent for the Newcastle *Sun*, and wrote her book. On its completion, she went out to

Greece in the middle of 1935 to meet her husband. The year that Dora and Bert Birtles spent in Greece was one of intense political agitation, which ended with the fall of democratic government and the establishment of the Metaxas dictatorship. Like all tourists in Greece, Dora and Bert Birtles went to the islands, but their agenda was somewhat different from that of the usual island hoppers. The island of their choice was Anaphi, a boat journey of some three days and four nights from Piraeus and a place of exile for Greek political prisoners. On Anaphi, the Birtles lived in a communist collective, established as much for survival as principle. Their experiences provided the subject for Bert Birtles's book, *Exile in the Aegean*, and for two of Dora's short stories, 'Prisoners' and 'Three Days in Averoff'.[23] Back in London, Dora Birtles became an active member of the women's section of the British Movement Against War and Fascism and followed in the footsteps of Muriel Matters in disturbing the dignity of the mother of parliaments when she stood in the gallery and threw peace leaflets down onto the members of the House of Commons during a speech by the pro-fascist Lady Astor. Dora Birtles did not follow Muriel Matters to Holloway prison, but was merely detained until the rising of the House.[24] Her disturbance of the House of Commons was not the only occasion on which she fell foul of the law of England. She was arrested on another occasion when she stood outside Australia House in a sandwich-board, which bore the proclamation BOYCOTT JAPANESE GOODS.[25] Dora and Bert Birtles returned to Australia just before the Second World War. Her life abroad had not dented the Australian identity of the woman who was to write *The Overlanders*, and to become the mother of two sons, Kanga and Jarrah.

Irene Saxby also earned her passage to Britain by working as a nanny. Her subsequent travels were to give her an even more adventurous and unusual life than that of her fellow sailors. In August 1933, through contacts she had made with the Quakers, Saxby accepted a teaching position at the Moscow Technicum for Foreign Languages.[26] She lived with a Russian family joining in the local life, skiing and skating in the winter, hiking and swimming in forest lakes in the summer, and attending the self-criticism sessions at her institute. Saxby returned to Australia in 1936 to see her family, 'but the Soviet Union and its people had too firm a hold on my heart', so she journeyed back to Russia where she remained until 1945. The Soviet Union of the treason trials of 1937 was rather different from the Soviet Union of 1933, and Saxby found that foreigners were suspect and work and accommodation difficult to come by. However, both eventuated in time. She shared the room of a Russian colleague in a third-floor apartment, occupied by several families, on Gorki Street. Thus, Saxby again merged into the life of the ordinary people around her, sharing their tribulations, terrors, deprivations and starvation during the Nazi siege of

Moscow in 1941. Her face and ankles grew puffy from malnutrition and vitamin deficiency, and she too received her allotment of land in the summer of 1942 to plant the seed potatoes that would feed her for the following winter. As far as she knew she was, apart from journalists and diplomatic personnel, the only British person living in Moscow in the early years of the war. Later, when the Australian Legation was set up in Moscow, Saxby became the archivist, and not surprisingly she did not always see eye to eye with the official Australian view of events.

At the end of 1994, in a retirement village in Sydney, Irene Saxby, then ninety-two, told me of her life in Moscow. Active in the anti-nuclear movement after she returned to Australia, and still committed to the ideals of social justice of a previous age, she talked of both the weaknesses and the strengths of the political system under which she had lived for ten years.

Irene Saxby's departure from Australia in 1932 conforms to familiar patterns in that it was a bid for freedom and a flight from the mundane. When I asked her in 1994 about teaching in Moscow at the time of the mass purges and of war, she replied that anything was better than teaching French in New South Wales high schools. Of her return to Australia in 1945 she wrote in 1982: 'so ended the most meaningful and adventurous part of my life'.[27] The reason for her return via a long circuitous journey just before the end of the Second World War was the terminal illness of her much-loved only sister. When her sister died, Saxby remained to assume the role of a dutiful daughter, and the woman who had lived through the siege of Moscow became her widowed father's housekeeper in Avalon, a family carer whom her male siblings regarded in the cold war anti-communist Australia of the 1950s as a traitor to her country and an embarrassment to her family. But Irene Saxby had been far from alone in both her interest and presence in the Soviet Union in the anti-fascist 1930s.

CHAPTER 7

Travel and Politics

We were like pilgrims approaching the promised land.[1]

After 1917 Russia was not a place where the traveller's eye was fixed on churches and museums, and after Lenin's death in 1924 a visit to only one monument was *de rigueur*, and that was his tomb in Red Square. What visitors to Russia had come to see was the present; it was the contemporary that elicited comment, whether the spectator was *engagé*, opposed or apolitical. Politics was the point of travel. Thus Audrey Blake reflected on the difference between the overseas trips that she made in 1937 and 1982. On the later visit to Europe, she had felt an intense need to see the treasures of the British Museum, the paintings of the great galleries, the works of the spirit.[2] In 1937, en route to Russia, where she was to represent the Australian Communist Party on the Young Communist International, and where her husband was to be attached to the Comintern, she had spent three months in London. At that time, they entered no museums, gazed at no pictures. Her life were dominated by politics. Another Australian pilgrim, Suzanne Abramovich, wrote that she went to the Soviet Union

> because I am more interested in observing the living hands of the present make and shape life as we live it, than growing sentimental over the ruined work of the dead hands of the past.
>
> We are living in the most interesting period in history, and to the intelligent traveller who wishes to understand the social tendencies of his generation, the Soviet Union is the most interesting country.[3]

The journeys of the Australian women were part of that 1930s political pilgrimage of western intellectuals to the Soviet Union, to witness and to bear witness to a new heaven and a new earth, a pilgrimage whose participants included not only British left luminaries like Sidney and Beatrice Webb, George Bernard Shaw and Harold Laski, but also their colonial dependants.[4] The political inclinations of the pilgrims covered all positions on the anti-fascist popular front: communist, Fabian, social democrat, Christian socialist, left-leaning liberal. Most of the Australian women who visited Russia and who have left accounts of their responses in letters, newspaper reports, and contemporary and later memoirs were typical pilgrims. Audrey Blake, Jean Devanny and Katharine Susannah Prichard were all members of the Communist Party before they reached the Soviet Union, while Dorothy Alexander (later Gibson) and Betty Roland joined on their return to Australia. Irene Saxby certainly had leanings towards communism, and Jessie Street was moving in the direction that would make her an official guest at Stalin's funeral in 1953. Suzanne Abramovich disavowed communist affiliations, but her account of her time in Russia was published by the Friends of the Soviet Union. Ada Bromham and Isabel McCorkindale went together as feminists, but Bromham's Christian socialist outlook was to take her in the 1950s to China in a peace delegation led by John Burton.

Pilgrimages are made to holy places. The Soviet Union was holy because it was the site of a vast attempt to create a brave new world, although what particular aspects of the new world were deemed brave varied from traveller to traveller or from one ideological commitment to another. The visits to Russia are one manifestation of travel in search of the lost paradise, of Utopia, of the 'world where the sun never sets and death is conquered for all time'.[5] For those disillusioned with capitalist society and its discontents, or who saw the Depression as evidence not only of the social evils of capitalism, but also of its imminent collapse, the socialist revolution in the East beckoned as the light on the hill. Seek and ye shall find. Something of the mesmerising power of the image of a new world in which self and society were made anew is conveyed in the reflections of Dorothy Alexander in 1935 after she had been teaching for a year in Moscow.

> This year in the Soviet Union was an altogether amazing year for me. Life was very hard and turbulent, all that was artificial, trivial and superficial was stripped away; what was valued harmonised with what seemed most valuable to me — and I felt that here was the main source for the strength and resistance to war and fascism.[6]

The fashion for making pilgrimages to the Soviet Union coincided with the years that saw the end of the first Five Year Plan and the beginning of the second. It was a time of momentous progress, when the foundations were being laid for an industrial economy, for a higher standard of living for ordinary Russians, and for vast schemes of health care and welfare. But these were also the years of enforced collectivisation, with the attendant famine, and displacement and deaths of millions of people, of the consolidation of power by Stalin, of the show trials and liquidation of the old Bolshevik leadership, and of arrests, deportations to labour camps and executions on a massive scale. Little of this underside appears in the travellers' tales.

A world that has witnessed the exposure of the events of the 1930s that began at the 20th Party Congress in 1956, and now the very collapse of the Soviet Union, finds it difficult to understand the pilgrims, their naïvety and self-deception, and the sleights of hand, the ethnic and intellectual arrogance with which they excused and justified actions and policies that would have been absolutely unacceptable in their own western liberal democracies. But the pilgrim texts are just the most obvious and well-documented examples of the traveller's tale emanating from the traveller, not the place.

The travellers arrived in Russia with the hopes, expectations, ideological investments, and public and private agendas that always accompany a journey. They had departed from societies in the midst of economic depressions in which there were few safety nets to protect the victims; in 1933 one-quarter of the Australian workforce was still unemployed. Convinced before arrival that the Soviet Union was, if not an ideal society in the making, then at least the site of a great social experiment, the perception of the travellers was obviously structured. But more than this, for the travellers to see or describe a place of starvation, of terror and gulags, was to confront delusion, to lose sustaining myths, to face fascist expansion, the enormous dislocation and suffering of the Depression, and the bankruptcy of liberal democracy with nowhere to go. As another of the 1930s pilgrims has written:

> I had set out to seek whatever would confirm my convictions and 'objectively' justify my enthusiasm. A traveler of this kind may sincerely believe that he wants to discover the truth; yet he is incessantly plagued by the sort of illusion he can never escape, because he creates it himself. And he creates it because he needs it, just as the deceived lover needs the delusion that he is loved ...[7]

A former member of the Australian Communist Party, Amirah Inglis, recently explained that to be a communist in the 1930s required discipline and obedience to the dictates of the Party, because only socialism could produce the just society.[8] 'Defend the Soviet Union' was the most enduring communist slogan, and communists self-censored what might conflict with their reality.

It is no doubt true that some of the writing of committed communists who visited the Soviet Union was deliberately and consciously manufactured, but it is unlikely that the majority of the pilgrims, that women like Katharine Susannah Prichard, were blatantly engaged in the production of propaganda. Rather, they saw what they wanted and hoped to see. The visits to the Soviet Union were certainly manipulated. Betty Roland wrote that during her stay Prichard was treated as an important person.[9] Jessie Street's tour, which included attending a session of the Supreme Soviet and meetings with officials, was organised by the Society for Cultural Relations with the USSR. None of the women appears to have known the language, so they were clearly dependent on interpreters and guides during the 'conversations' in which they felt themselves to be making 'real' contact with 'ordinary' people. Jessie Street was delighted with the person she described as our 'guide, interpreter and friend', who arranged for her to meet and 'talk' with local women.[10] What the women saw in the Soviet Union was no doubt 'real'; the question they needed to ask was whether it was typical.

The women were conscious that they would be accused of having been duped in their travels in the Soviet Union. So Katharine Susannah Prichard called her book *The Real Russia*. She emphasised that her journey was not 'a conducted tour', that she had wandered at will using Intourist in much the same way as elsewhere one used Thomas Cook, and that her conversations with other tourists confirmed that her experience was the norm.[11] Ada Bromham was determined not to be hoodwinked and to follow a route never before taken by a tourist, and Suzanne Abramovich dismissed the preposterous idea that Soviet institutions were 'window-dressed' for the benefit of innocent tourists. According to Abramovich, the Soviet government had far more pressing things to do than worry about sightseers;[12] she made it a rule to drop in to any institution without appointment.

The anxiety of the women to establish that their travellers' tales were authentic points to another factor that structured perception and text. They were convinced that it was 'the other side' that distorted and manipulated the image of the Soviet Union. In their view, the information in the capitalist press and emamating from western governments was nothing but anti-Soviet propaganda. Dorothy Alexander, writing home from Moscow in December 1934, asked her parents: 'What have the papers been saying about the murder of Kirov? And the shootings afterwards? Panic, and martial law and similar malicious twistings of the truth?'[13] Jessie Street claimed to have been continually amazed during her stay at her own ignorance about Soviet history, an ignorance that had been deliberately fostered in her own land. One outcome of her trips was her determination to spread 'the truth'.[14] The pilgrims were not misguided in their mistrust of other writing on the Soviet Union. As Pamela Travers, the creator of Mary Poppins, who was born and lived in Australia until she was 24, observed after her tour of the Soviet Union: 'Isn't it curious that nobody can even hear the name of Russia with equanimity? Those for it are fanatically for it, those against fanatically so'.[15] As has been pointed out in relation to British pilgrims, 'objective assessments' of the Soviet Union in the 1930s are difficult to find.[16] If the conviction that writing that portrayed the Soviet Union unfavourably was merely 'anti-Soviet propaganda' allowed the sympathetic traveller to ignore warning signs, so too did the sense of belonging to a beleaguered minority. To be a member of the Communist Party of Australia was to belong to a barely tolerated fringe group, to belong to a common front organisation was to be at best a naïve idealist, at worst a communist dupe. In the Soviet Union it was to be at one with the millions, with power, with the future, with history.

Irene Saxby was not the only Australian woman teaching in Moscow in the mid-1930s. The desire for adventure and experience, as well as political sympathies, also drew Dorothy Alexander to Russia. Her story comes to us through letters and articles that she wrote during her time in Moscow, her later recollections, and the loving biography created by her husband, Ralph Gibson.[17] Dorothy Alexander was born in Melbourne in the last year of the nineteenth century. The daughter of a businessman father, who moved in socialist circles and who was later to be a prominent member of the Movement Against War and Fascism, and of a conservative, home-centred mother, she graduated in Arts from the University of Melbourne in 1920 and looked to a career in education. Recalling her life as it was drawing to a close, she wrote that she fell tremendously in love at the age of nineteen, but that she was reluctant to marry; she was inexperienced and she wanted to escape the destiny of her mother, caught within the home, tied down and restricted.[18] There were too many things that she wanted to do; she wanted a different kind of world, a different sort of relationship between men and women, and she was fascinated by people of other countries, cultures, and religions.

Despite her urge for a more liberated life, it was with her parents and a friend that Dorothy Alexander made her first overseas trip in 1922. On her return to Melbourne, she became interested in new educational movements, teaching at an experimental progressive school for four years. In 1929 she made her second overseas trip, again with her parents, but she remained behind to spend a year at Cambridge. In England she became involved in the New Educational Fellowship and attended the organisation's world conference in Elsinore, Denmark, an experience that fired a lifetime commitment to international socialism and pacifism.[19] Alexander was back in Melbourne in 1931 with the hope of founding her own school. But a year later she sailed again for England with a new marriage, which did not survive the boat journey. She began teaching in London and her interest in progressive education took her into similar political circles. Alexander joined and worked with the British Movement Against War and Fascism and took a position in the school in Hampstead for the children of the staff of the Soviet Embassy. Her first attempt in 1933 to get to the Soviet Union failed through delays in obtaining a visa, but she was successful in the following year when she was invited to teach in the Anglo-American school in Moscow.

The letters that Dorothy Alexander wrote to her parents in her first months in the Soviet Union convey her sense of joy, amazement and gratitude that she was 'in this land of my dreams'.[20] The Kremlin enchanted her beyond expectation, and she was inspired by the great new town of

Kharkov with its magnificent buildings, 'in the finest modern style I've seen, quite devoid of decoration of course and with lots of glass and beautiful simple outlines … no dilapidation, all in repair'.[21] At her school in Moscow, she participated in the 1935 elections, which she portrayed as very democratic.[22] She anticipated that there would be critics of open voting at home, but she knew that at this stage of the dictatorship of the proletariat, the enemies of the proletariat could not be allowed to vote. And the enemies of the proletariat had struck in December 1934 when Kirov, leader of the party in Leningrad, was assassinated. Alexander went with the school to see his body lying in state, but after three hours standing in a queue in the fierce cold of December, they had to turn back. For Alexander the assassination was the work of a counter-revolutionary foreign-backed organisation.[23]

Dorothy Alexander clearly had no doubt that she was in the right place at the right time.

> Yes, it is truly a wonderful thing that I am here. Quite suddenly it strikes me. And always on the nights after the Leninism lectures when I come out on to the Red Square. Snow carpets it now and powders all the quaint cupolas of the old Cathedral at the far end.[24]

Nevertheless, she came back to Australia in July 1935, apparently in connection with her divorce, and was undecided about whether she would return to Moscow to teach the next year. As soon as she arrived in Melbourne, she was swept up into the anti-war movement, and worked for the Movement Against War and Fascism and the International Peace Campaign. In November 1935 she joined the Communist Party of Australia and in the following year married Ralph Gibson, one of the leading figures in the party and the anti-war movement.[25] The rest of Dorothy Gibson's life was to be lived in the world of the Communist Party and the movements for peace and disarmament. [26]

It was love — the following of a man — rather than politics that took Betty Roland to the Soviet Union. She fled marriage and Australia in 1933 when she ran away to Europe with Guido Baracchi, at that time a fervent Marxist who had been expelled from the Communist Party of Australia.[27] Soon after their arrival in Britain, Roland and Baracchi went to Russia with 21-day visas to deliver documents and to witness the May Day celebrations; they stayed sixteen months, working in the translation section of the Co-operative Publishing Society in Moscow and Leningrad, and sharing in the daily tribulations of the local people in their search for food and accommodation. Roland kept a diary while she was in the Soviet Union, which she later edited and published. Describing herself as petty bourgeois and politically naïve when she left Australia, Roland developed little interest in Marxist theory and practice while in the Soviet Union, where her life was centred on Baracchi. However, her diary does convey something of the romance and excitement of living in a Soviet Union coming to the end of the first Five Year Plan.

> So, life is not all toil and hardship in this summer of 1933 — far from it. There is a lot of gaiety and a strong surge of hope. 1932 was bad. There was a famine, one of the worst on record as the crops failed for lack of rain and what yield there was went largely unharvested by the rebellious peasants who resented collectivisation. This year things are different...
>
> All this is extraordinarily exciting, one has a sense of participating in a great historical event. The contrast between the optimism here and the pessimism of the outside world is striking. I remember the hopeless men who sat in Melbourne parks, heads bowed in their hands, waiting for the next handout from the soup kitchens.[28]

Roland and Baracchi marched in the May Day procession in Moscow in 1934, 'an exhilarating moment': 'Not even the most hardened sceptic would remain unmoved at the shouts of triumph from ten thousand throats, the clenched fists raised in the traditional red salute, the air of exultation'.[29]

In the later published version of her diary, Roland commented on some of the consequences of the economic upheaval of the time, the thousands of homeless, starving victims of collectivisation in the streets of the cities, the overcrowding and food shortages that came in the wake of rapid urbanisation. She also noted the privileges and luxuries enjoyed by the party élite of the classless society, in contrast to the people's daily struggle for food and shelter, the officially non-existent beggars and prostitutes, the presence of the members of OGPU, 'the state's chief instrument of terror, universally feared', the atmosphere of suspicion. She also foreshadowed the terror, to which some of her friends and acquaintances were eventually to fall victim. But the published version is not the original text of the diary.[30] Certainly her 1935 article, 'Motherhood Here and in the Soviet Union', which appeared in *Working Woman*, a publication of the Communist Party of Australia, admitted to no doubts.

In her descriptions of the people she met, the friends she made, the incidents and events of normal social life, Roland gives a sense of life in Moscow and Leningrad in the mid-1930s. She wrote not about a great social experiment, but about the struggle for existence, about work and leisure, joy and sadness, as she and her Russian and foreign friends had experienced them. Included among her friends and acquaintances were writer Freda Utley, whose Russian husband was to die in the salt mines of Siberia, and the American fellow travelling journalist, Anna Louise Strong, at the time editor of the English-language *Moscow Daily News*, a woman who did not impress Roland.[31] Far more impressive was Madame

Anitchkova, widow of a tsarist ambassador to Paris executed in the Revolution, who received Roland and Baracchi in the attic of a palace, the entirety of which had once been her home.

While they were in Moscow, Roland and Baracchi welcomed a house guest to their one-room home, a guest whom Roland described as 'a serene person with a soft voice and gentle smile', and who slept at night like Roland, under an umbrella to shade her from the naked bulb by which Baracchi worked at his translating. The house guest was Katharine Susannah Prichard, who had joined the Communist Party of Australia on its foundation in 1920, and who was 'tremulous with happiness' on reaching the promised land.[32] After Prichard left the Roland-Baracchi ménage, she travelled some thirty thousand miles through the Soviet Union, including Siberia, where she attended a writers' festival at Stalinsk. Roland saw Prichard again at the end of her tour. The person who had been 'tremulous with happiness' had been replaced by a thin, tired woman pinched with cold, sadly disillusioned, bereft of her former optimism; 'she had seen so much and learnt so much that she had never dreamt of, and her heart was sick'.[33]

No such disillusionment emerges from the account of her travels that Katharine Susannah Prichard published on her return from the Soviet Union.[34] A creative writer, she evoked a Utopian paradise in a series of wonderfully vivid images and vignettes of people and places; she wanted to record her experiences 'in splashes of colour, gouts of phrases like Walt Whitman would have'.

> Ancient buildings of dead beauty, slums of the middle ages, sullen rivers, dark pine forests, pink and white churches with gilded domes, wild waste places, ragged mountain ranges under perpetual snow, fretted scaffoldings stretching above them: new cities of glass and steel, dove-grey concrete, crowding in on them: a black mouldering village beside its striped fields: harvest fields flooded with sunshine, a kolkhoz (collective farm) village of new pine logs in a forest of golden birches.[35]

Prichard's Soviet Union was one of successful collective farms populated by happy, enthusiastic people.

> The happiest people I met in Russia or Siberia were the collective farmers, men and women. They were rejoicing after a record harvest, and busy with plans for the next season's sowing, more machinery, new houses, improvements to schools and clubs, winter courses of agricultural study for their udarniks (best workers) and brigadiers, the leaders of the field brigades.[36]

Everywhere she went, Prichard met and 'spoke' with local people, relating uplifting and heart-warming tales of the changes that the Revolution had wrought in their lives — before the Revolution, grinding

poverty, hunger, illiteracy, after the Revolution, economic security, education, fulfilling lives. Prichard gave many examples of the commendable
commitment to work and community, and described approvingly the
various techniques of shaming that secured co-operation and productivi-
ty — the wall sheets listing merit and demerit points, the films with close-
ups of lazy workers, the rallies organised by the Young Pioneers outside
factories to bail-up late or slack workers. She also described the Chiskas,
the public 'personal development reviews' carried out on Party members
to assess their continued fitness for membership with all its attendant
privileges.[37] These had been part of the daily life of Irene Saxby.

Moving about the same streets and squares as Betty Roland, Prichard 'saw'
no prostitutes or beggars, nothing but happy children swarming about
watched over by their devoted mothers. Prichard readily admitted that the
Soviet Union was not yet the workers' paradise — indeed she had been
asked by Soviet officials not to distort the picture — but the shortcomings
lay not in the new system but in the tsarist inheritance, the terrifying place of
the beginning. And surviving from the past were the enemies of the people,
the kulaks who with their 'knavish tricks' tried to sabotage progress.

A high point of Prichard's time in Russia was her participation in a literary conference at Stalinsk in Siberia. Already moving in that direction,
she embraced social realism and the credo that writers should abandon
the ivory tower and become absorbed into the working lives of the people. Prichard had much praise for the literary circles in which workers
studied the masterpieces of Russian and international literature, while at
the same time learning to turn the experiences of their own lives into literature; the rejuvenation of literature would come from the peasants and
the workers.[38] Drusilla Modjeska has underlined the importance of
Prichard's visit to the Soviet Union, both for the introduction and propa-
gation of social realism in Australia and for its impact on her own work.[39]
She also points to the discrepancy between the rosy picture of the Soviet
Union in Prichard's *The Real Russia* and Betty Roland's references to
Prichard's doubt and disillusionment.[40] What then of the discrepancy,
which depends on acceptance of Roland as a reliable witness? Did Roland
exaggerate the doubts — either in the diary at the time or in the later edit-
ing? Was it loyalty to an embattled party at home and to a Motherland
abroad increasingly exposed to Nazi Germany that constrained Prichard
from expressing her doubts? While overseas, Prichard suffered a terrible
personal tragedy when her husband, Hugo Throssell, committed suicide.
Perhaps she felt her absence from and neglect of him could only be justified by dedication to the highest — unflawed — cause. She later wrote:
'Only my belief in the need to work for the great ideas of Communism
and world peace helped me survive a grief so shattering'.[41] There is no
simple answer to the telling of the tale of journeys to Stalin's Soviet Union.

There may be no deliberate distortion in Prichard's writing; she saw what she wanted or needed to see. And if not the 'real Russia', she did create a wonderfully alive and rich traveller's tale.

Katharine Susannah Prichard also gave a rosy picture of the position of women in the Soviet Union, including that of the ex-prostitutes who were running a very successful textile factory in Novosibirsk, another indication of the way in which women responded to economic independence.[42] For Prichard, the abolition of all discrimination was the result of socialism, not feminism. Yet precisely because of the proclaimed advancement in the position of women there, the Soviet Union was of interest to feminists.

It was concern for the welfare of women and children that led Suzanne Abramovich, for example, to the Soviet Union at the end of the 1920s.[43] A suburban general practitioner in Sydney, she worked for six months at an Institute for the Protection of Mother and Child in Moscow and travelled for three. She took the position of women as the standard by which to judge progress. In the Soviet Union there was no longer a 'women's question' and a number of social problems had been solved by the granting of equality to women. The economic independence of women had raised the quality of marriage, since there was no longer any necessity for people to live together after the bonds of affection had gone; sex was rightly treated as a biological function, with the result that the prurience and innuendo so commonly associated with sex was eliminated. Women had complete freedom in matters of motherhood and the right to legal termination of pregnancy after due counselling; 'This to me is the true expression of the freedom of women in Russia'.[44] And for the women who chose to bear children, the system of maternal and child welfare was the finest in the world, one that did not deprive a mother of the right to rear her child, but that prevented an ignorant mother from undermining the health of a future citizen. Abramovich was, like others, impressed by the Children's Courts and the Children's Theatre in Moscow, and by the high cultural level. She recognised that there were shortcomings, such as the acute shortage of housing, but these were in direct ratio to the progress being made. Abramovich had seen a new world in the process of being built, a unique experience.

Isabel McCorkindale and Ada Bromham, well-known workers for the causes of both women and temperance, went to Europe in 1935 to attend the World Convention of the Woman's Christian Temperance Union in Stockholm and a conference of the British Commonwealth League in London. They made a visit to the Soviet Union and also came back convinced that women enjoyed absolute equality.[45] To criticism of the employment of women in heavy manual work, the women replied that this needed to be seen against the background of the millennia-long class and patriarchal exploitation and oppression of peasant women, whose heavy labour was now being justly rewarded, whose lives were now protected by illness and age insurance, and for whom the way was now open for better lives for themselves and their children.[46]

Bromham and McCorkindale felt some discomfort and embarrassment when faced with one aspect of equality of the sexes — the lack of segregation in railway sleeping-cars. Jessie Street, on her 1938 trip to the Soviet Union with her nineteen-year-old daughter, was equally disconcerted when she realised that they were to share their soft-class compartment with two army officers.

> We rang for the conductress and retired to the passage. Our cabin companions ushered Philippa and me in first and we got undressed and into the bunks. I put on the night light and said to Philippa to lie with her face to the wall. I then opened the door and they came in, and in a short time climbed up to their bunks. We had a peaceful night. I was first to wake up in the morning. They were all asleep, so I thought I would get dressed. I sat up and to my dismay there was a long mirror on the door and I could see the officer from head to foot asleep on the opposite bunk, and I knew he would have an equally good view of me. What could I do? I decided to dress quickly. I went out to wash and when I came back they were both dressing and Philippa was still in deep sleep.[47]

Having survived the experience, Street, whose temperament seems to have been inclined towards the prudish, contemplated British mores anew: 'I thought what a lot of phobias and inhibitions we have built up for ourselves in the English-speaking world and how much more natural and normal was the behaviour of the people in Russia'. Later Street noted that young girls were not accosted in the street, and that the vested interest in prostitution had evidently been eliminated. She then pondered whether promiscuity and prostitution were the creations of capitalism.

Natural relations between the sexes was not the only thing Jessie Street found to admire on her travels in the Soviet Union. She claimed in her memoirs that the idea for her visit had originated with 'simple working people' from the Society for Cultural Relations with the USSR in Sydney, who had offered to pay her fare from London to Moscow so that she could discover and tell them the truth.[48] In the typescript of an article entitled 'Impressions of Russia', written around 1939–40, she gave as the main reason for accepting the mission her wish 'to see what the status of women really was in that country', since she was sceptical about the claims made by enthusiasts that women had equality in Russia.[49] Her personal framework in approaching the Soviet Union was that of a woman who had worked all her life for equal rights, status, pay, and opportunities for women, and who resented the fact that in the capitalist world the vast majority of women when they married and had children were chained to the house.[50] From her first moments and her encounters with women working on the railtracks, as train drivers, as station attendants, as police, as tramdrivers, she was favourably impressed by the condition of women, by their enjoyment of equal pay, and by the provisions for illness, childbirth and childcare, which allowed women with families to take part in the economic development and public life of their country and to enjoy economic independence. Street found much else to admire, including the tomb of Alliluyeva, Stalin's second wife.

Writer Doris Hayball was another visitor who was disturbed by arrangements in railway sleeping carriages and who saw the woman issue as vital.[51] Like the other women, Hayball acknowledged the emancipation of women in the USSR, but she wondered whether women would maintain their position in the labour market and their economic independence once there was no longer a labour shortage. Hayball's perception of the position of women was indeed shrewder than that of her more ideologically committed contemporaries who wrote about the condition of women in the language of the Revolution, when the liberationist and egalitarian goals had included the emancipation of women and when their participation in the workforce was understood as the means to the economic independence that was the necessary prerequisite for genuine equality.[52] The massive entry of women into the workforce in the 1930s was the result of Stalinist policies that created an immense labour shortage. Stalin also stepped back from the collective and the communal with his new emphasis on the family as the unit of reproduction and socialisation. If Suzanne Abramovich had returned to Russia after 1934, she would have been sadly disappointed. In that year the right to legal termination of pregnancy was abolished, except in cases where a woman's life was threatened. Population growth had clearly become more important than women's rights.

Not all the Australian women who visited the Soviet Union went as converts. Hayball, who found much to admire in Nazi Germany, attended a theatre festival in Russia in 1937 and reported that her fellow thespians were very divided in their views and perceptions.[53] Hayball was not sure that communism would succeed and she found much to criticise; the shortages in housing, food and clothing, the petty, time-consuming bureaucratic procedures, the lack of attention to strict hygiene in the crèches, the black market in which she herself dealt when she bartered silk stockings with an impoverished aristocrat for antique lace and beading. And when she heard stories of sabotage and quick, wide-sweeping reprisals, she wondered if Stalin 'had, perhaps, gone a little mad, developed a persecution mania, shut up in the Kremlin, as he was at the time of my visit'.[54] On the boat going back to Britain she heard other members of the group talk of the undercurrent of spying and treachery. She herself did not know what to think, but since her visit she had learnt that some of the Russians in Moscow who had entertained her were now too worried about accusations of conspiracy to receive other foreign visitors. Pamela

Travers claimed that she went to Moscow merely to enjoy herself, and in her narrative she assumed the persona of the irreverent sceptic among the true — and excruciatingly dull — believers.[55] She struggled to find the right gesture before Lenin's tomb, since she felt that to kneel and cross herself might not be quite appropriate. She described the collective farm to which she was taken as a joke, a 'comic charade'. What she emphasised about the new heaven was its drabness, the dreariness of the people and their anaesthetised faces.

The women whose comments have been discussed by no means account for all of the women who were in the Soviet Union as tourists or pilgrims in the interwar years.[56] In her diary, Betty Roland referred to a Melbourne girl who had recently arrived and, proclaiming herself a sculptor, had been given a commission to carve a statue of Georgi Dimitrov, the hero of the Reichstag fire trials and general secretary of the Communist International.[57] And in Odessa, on their way out of the Soviet Union, she and Baracchi met a sad Australian couple who had been carried away by romantic idealism and had surrendered their passports in order to become Soviet citizens. They had nothing to complain about in the treatment they had received, but they were desperately homesick and already regretting their rash act.[58] Florence Cardell-Oliver, who visited the Soviet Union in the mid-1930s, later entered the Western Australian Legislative Assembly for the Nationalist Party. Her political attitudes are revealed in her 1934 pamphlet, *Empire Unity or Red Asiatic Domination?*.[59]

On their journeys to and from Russia, the pilgrims usually crossed Germany, their feelings towards which could be ambivalent — attracted to the place, repelled by the regime. Dorothy Alexander wrote of this ambivalence to her parents in August 1934.

> There is much to tell you of Hamburg. I think it is a most beautiful city and I wish I'd lived there, or somewhere in Germany for awhile, before these Nazis were born. We were there when the big conference was on in Nuremberg and yet they were everywhere — and everywhere we passed the boys and girls, out in brigades, glorious looking children with rucksacks and blankets on their backs and hats on their heads — brimful of zest of life and yet taught that the greatest glory is to die in battle — and they sing words about the blood gushing from the sword that pierces the Jew!!![60]

Betty Roland's train trip through Germany to Russia earlier in the same year had not been without its element of danger. After their flat in Leningrad had been broken into, and all their possessions stolen, she went to London to get more warm clothes. In London she was asked by Harry Pollitt, leader of the British Communist Party, to take books and documents back to Russia. She agreed, wanting to impress Baracchi and the bureaucrats of the British Party whom she felt looked down on her as a frivolous, petty bourgeois hanger-on. On the train she hid the books at her feet under a rug, the documents were in a trunk in the luggage van. When the German customs guard saw the hammer-and-sickle stamp in her passport and learnt that her destination was Moscow, he asked for her trunk to be opened.

> I now felt partly paralysed and my mouth and throat were dry. Slowly getting to my feet, I dropped the rug from my knees so that it concealed the parcel of books. Then, like one walking in a dream, I moved into the corridor and waited for the next development.[61]

The guard began searching the trunk, but then the train stopped, and the border guards alighted — her luck had held.

Other less politically conscious Australian women travelled in Germany, oblivious of Nazism. And some found much to admire. Miss E. Hadley, who was studying German at the University of Berlin, wrote home about a Nazi rally that she attended during the March 1936 elections — about the packed hall, the crowd outside pressing to come in, the standard-bearers, the banners, the flags, the music, the arrival of the party chiefs, 'Sieg-Heil' — 'really it is hard to find the words to describe the enthusiasm of the scene'.[62] Goebbels's speech, she wrote, 'was the most telling and perfectly constructed, and the most effectively-delivered speech that I have ever heard'.

> Then the Fuhrer rose, and if the enthusiasm had been wonderful before, it was now beyond description. The speech you have all read in your newspapers. You all know how he reiterated his reasons for the march of the troops into the Rhineland, how he spoke of the change from the previous regime of chaos to the order which now obtains throughout Germany, of the unity of the people, which now has one party instead of the thirty-three parties in 1932, of the decrease in unemployment from seven millions to one and a half millions, of the increase in manufactures and in production on all sides. Most of this was heartily applauded, but perfect avalanches of cheers and applause greeted his words on his fight for the restoration of honour and 'gleichberechtigkeit' (equality) among the nations. He was speaking to the world as well as to the German nation. It was a most remarkable experience, quite unforgettable.

After the rally, Hadley was impressed by the quiet efficiency of the SS men in dispersing the crowds. Walking the streets of Berlin, she found the enthusiasm of the people for the Führer overwhelming. After visiting the Women's Office of the German Labour Front organisation, she described in appreciative detail the work being done for girls and women. Little but place distinguishes Hadley's text from those of the pilgrims in Russia. But place was all-important by the mid-1930s.[63]

Interlude

Voyages and Ports

When they set off on their travels, 'the first of the strange kingdoms' that the women encountered was the 'limited republic' of the ship, a totally enclosed and isolated world.[1] While the voyage was a passage from one world to another, it was also a world in itself. And the ship could be the single place where women spent the most time on their travels.

Entrance into this new strange kingdom was preceded and accompanied by a series of well-defined rituals. The weeks before were absorbed in a series of farewell parties, the more social occasions being well-documented in the women's pages of the local press. For those travelling in style, in the days before the weighing of baggage and the disappearance of porters, packing was a large-scale operation, as Frances Maguire's memories of her family's 1910 trip suggest.

> Large trunks were brought up from the cellars to have their straps and locks repaired. A dressmaker arrived and was installed in the sewing-room where she surrounded herself with a fascinating assortment of silks and linens and muslins, sequins and silver beads and lace flounces. Enormous square hat-boxes of solid leather were bought to carry the 'merry Widow' hats then in fashion; canvas kit-bags held rolled rugs and cushions and the small pillow with special linen cover considered indispensable when sleeping in foreign hotel bedrooms.
>
> Then there was the furniture: cane lounges for sleeping on deck in the tropics and folding canvas chairs for daytime use, the kind that pinch your fingers when you try to erect them and collapse when you sit in them. Some people even took folding tables and a tea basket with cups and saucers and a kettle which could be boiled over a small spirit stove. This also could be used to heat the iron (for in this pre-nylon era all our linen, calico, silk and muslin underwear and blouses had to be ironed after washing). There was a special heavy leather case for Father's top-hat, and there were dressing-cases, one for each person. These were enormously heavy and were fitted with glass bottles, silver-backed hairbrushes, clothes-brushes, ointment pots, soap-boxes, mirrors, manicure sets, sewing kit, glove tongs and curling tongs for the hair, a tiny silver spirit-lamp for heating the tongs, and little compartments for the hairpins and combs.[2]

The departing were accompanied to the ship by an array of relatives and friends, and were regaled with flowers and fruit. As the ship pulled out, coloured streamers maintained lingering contact for a moment with those left behind.

> Our last sight of Sydney town was a very packed crowd on the wharf waving and waving. It was an extremely pretty sight as the streamers, hundreds of them, seemed to hang over the heads of the waving crowd and moved along as the crowd moved.[3]

One of the most common images of Australian travel is of the festoons of breaking streamers.

The cutting of the Suez Canal and the coming of the steamship in the 1870s eventually reduced the Australia–Europe run from some four months to little more than a month. The realisation by shipping companies of the potential in the passenger trade led to the building of the great passenger liners that turned the voyage from an exercise in endurance into one of pleasure, enjoyment, and romance. The length of the voyage was to remain much the same from the 1880s until the demise of sea travel in the 1970s, just as the rituals of shipboard life stayed remarkably constant — the crossing-of-the-line ceremony, the fancy dress gala, the sports events, the ship's concert.

> When it was the fancy-dress night there were hula girls parading and Camille, white-faced, clutching her scrap of bloody hanky, and ghouls with knives poking out of them, and hooded monks with bug eyes, and the old lady who was Queen Victoria every voyage.[4]

Even with ports of call, five weeks was a long period of confinement. Nancy Adams remembered the community of the ship as being 'engrossed in its self-containment: the sports and dances, the flirtations, the gossip, the quarrels and scandals'.[5] Louise Mack thought that there was nothing like the first hours at sea to bring out all the latent antagonisms between people, and Nettie Higgins, making her second voyage in 1914, wrote that she felt 'as if there are forty dramas being acted at once: some melodramas, lots of farces, one at least a diluted Maeterlinck, or Tolstoi realism'.[6] Thus the ship became a metaphor for hothouse life. Working on the Aragon front during the Spanish Civil War, Aileen Palmer compared the periods of inactivity to life on board ship, 'when people have nothing to do but gossip and fight'.[7] Conferences reminded Janet Mitchell of shipboard life; she remarked that 'when people are wrenched out of their natural environment, all their foibles come to the surface'.[8]

Paradoxically, life on the ship on the one hand mimicked and reproduced the hierarchies and formalities of life at home, and on the other created free space. Class and status were as important at sea as they were on land, hence the segregation of first, second and steerage class passengers. Mabel Brookes, travelling first class in the years before the First World War, created the image of a life at sea that was the continuation of life on land, 'an occasion rather like the Melbourne Cup'.[9] As Mabel Brookes implied, first class could also create the sense of family. Fellow passengers usually included many friends and acquaintances, particularly in the March and April sailings, which landed passengers in England for the social season of presentations at Court, the Chelsea Flower Show, Ascot, Wimbledon, Cowes. Class tensions simmered on the ship, and the more socially ambitious and insecure in second class were acutely conscious of their inferior position. And within first class, issues such as placement for meals could become the source of much chagrin and misery. Not all first class passengers felt comfortable. Pattie Deakin, travelling with her prime minister husband, 'liked the look of the second class passengers better than the first'.[10] But Jessie Lillingston, who stepped out of her class context when she travelled second class from Britain to the United States in 1915, was none too keen on the socially inferior at first hand: 'I am not appreciating 2nd class very much, but it amuses me vastly at times'.[11] She commented that most of her fellow passengers were 'of the servant type'.

Not all voyagers made the trip on the big liners. Some women preferred the greater peace of cargo ships. Marie Byles made her first overseas trip to Europe in 1928 on a Norwegian cargo ship as one of four passengers.

> How I pitied the unfortunate tourists on a passenger boat, where the lights of the saloon challenge the lights of the stars, and the music of the orchestra drowns the sad and solemn music of the sea, whose language you can understand only when you are alone at the fo'c'sle head of a cargo boat, where there is no movement but the gentle rise and fall of the ocean. On a passenger boat man makes for himself music, dancing and life, but he loses the music of the waves, the dancing of the moonbeams, and the life of the universe.[12]

Financial exigencies placed others on ships that were far from luxurious. Mary Brennan wrote of her 1914 voyage that her boat was filthy and 'overflowing with rubbish'; 'there was no such thing as service or change of sheets'.[13]

By the First World War ships may have looked like home, but life on board was a total contrast to normal daily life for most women, because of their freedom from domestic responsibilities. Ada Cambridge luxuriated in her leisure and in the rejuvenation that six weeks of inactivity and monotony brought: 'I ate, and slept, and basked, like a soul-less animal: I forgot there were such things as posts and newspapers, as dinner-planning and stocking-mending, as calls and committee meetings'.[14] 'Soaked and steeped and sodden in peace' she insensibly renewed and re-established her strength. Not all women revelled in such inactivity. Jessie Mitchell, accompanying her husband on a business trip in 1934, wrote home: 'We are both well but both hating this lazy life. I will be glad to get home again and have a good spring cleaning at 45 Findlay Av'.[15]

Ships, the sea and voyages were also archetypal liminal space, between places, no place. Stella Bowen recalled her voyage in 1914:

> The ship became a kind of buffer state between two worlds — a state where the stiff and amorous fledgling was able to try her conversational wings amongst strangers who had never been told that Stella Bowen was quite a dull girl! ...
>
> I had £20 a month, I was free, and I was beholden to nobody, but these precious gifts were but coins to be fingered lovingly and not as yet spent.[16]

Half a century later, the protagonist in Barbara Hanrahan's *Sea-green*, poised on the ship between what she is fleeing and what she is seeking, muses: 'Separated from the reality of all the past, I've seemingly turned into no one. Everything familiar has been blotted out by an expanse of crinkled blue'.[17]

Unstructured place, sea air, the rocking motion of the boat, all led to the clichéd association of ships with romance and sex, with 'the ship-board romance'. In the 1870s a Methodist parson, the Reverend David O'Donnell, worried about the behaviour of 'the frailer sex' on his ship.

> Still, allow me to say, and this in a very low whisper in every maiden's ear, that the sea air, or the motion of the ship, or the closeness of the quarters, or something else, does make a difference, even in the behaviour of some ladies, when at sea ... On every ship in which I have sailed, coquetry and flirtation have spread like an epidemic.[18]

Another parson, John Bunyan McCure, wrote in the same decade that ships were fearful places for young women because 'there are evil-disposed persons who are ready and anxious to take advantage of them to lead them astray'.[19] Despite McCure's self-constitution as a one-person vigilante squad, and his patrolling of the 'dark parts' of his ship, there was much wickedness afoot; married women were acting in shameful ways, 'yielding to those wretches who can only live upon the vices of others'.

The potential sexual threat to young girls meant that those who, like Nettie Higgins in 1910 and Stella Bowen in 1914, were allowed to travel alone were attached to chaperones for the voyage. Evelyn Costin, whose mother paid a fee to the widow of a sea captain travelling on the same ship to look after her daughter, found the motherly eye that was kept on her 'rather too stringent'.[20] But Jessie Street found her stringent motherly eye was necessary when she took her daughter to Europe in 1938.

> We are really having a pleasant trip and Philippa is enjoying herself very much. She has a very devoted follower — one of the cricketers — Fingleton

by name. I really got quite worried about things for a while. Board ship life offers so many opportunities and really P. is so young and inexperienced. After waiting until well past midnight one night I finally went on a hunt and dug them out and blew them up.[21]

Street relayed her worries about her daughter's shipboard romance to her husband to prepare him for the inevitable rumours, 'since there are so many people on board that we know'. As it happened, however, the romance lasted and Philippa Street later married Test cricketer Jack Fingleton. She was one of the many women who married men they met on board ship.

By the 1930s a shipboard romance was a ritual event of a voyage, hinted at and promised in travel brochures, an event to be invented if not experienced, an event that because of the shortage of eligible men was not available to everyone. Gladys Marks complained about the shortage of suitable bachelors on her ship in 1913, and the statistics on departures from Australia in the 1930s suggest that there were three times as many women in their twenties taking off for Europe as there were men.[22] Women also predominated in the exodus of the 1950s and 1960s; in her fictional account of her departure from Australia, Barbara Hanrahan noted that 'to be popular on the ship you had to be willing to iron… a shirt to iron was a badge that you had a man'.[23]

Christobel Bollen wrote home to her mother at the beginning of her 1913 trip that while there was not one nice man on board, everyone must be told that she was having a lovely time. But in time her letters became non-stop listings of her conquests, the ship's doctor, who on the night that they left Colombo had 'put his hand on my shoulder & suddenly pulled me over to him & kissed me about ten times all over my face', the purser, the first officer, the captain, and assorted husbands.[24] On her voyage in 1936 Ida Haysom made friends with a car salesman from Bondi who had joined the navy. They sat on the deck until 2.00 am; 'it was a most beautiful night with a lovely moon nearly at full'.[25] Her friend left the ship at Malta; 'we said goodbye in the shade of the old life boat where we had so many happy hours'. She concluded: 'my shipboard romance. Not an unusual thing to happen but it's a wrench at the end'. Florence James's shipboard romance lasted a little longer. Travelling via Cape Town on the long stretch up the African coast she became friendly with a young South African science student travelling to Cambridge. He was carrying out research into diseases among South African cattle, 'so you can imagine the interesting talks'.[26] The friendship continued and Florence James and her scientist met in Paris for the following Christmas.[27] The romance eventually died away when the friend's South African fiancée arrived in Britain and Florence James's complicated private life took another turn.

The sexual implications of the romantic attachments of Florence James are far from transparent, and the event of the 'shipboard romance' and its telling covered a wide range of activities from innocent flirtation to the steamy writhings in the officers' cabins on the Italian ships of the 1960s recorded in Barbara Hanrahan's *Sea-green*.

The voyage, if the first encounter with freedom, with a world beyond the eyes of the village, where the absence of both past and future made new adventures possible, was also, for most pre-multicultural Australians, the first meeting with the foreign and foreigners. Those who travelled on French and Italian ships were immediately exposed to different ways of eating as well as loving. Nancy Cato felt that her European trip had begun as soon as she embarked on her Italian ship.[28] Dymphna Cusack observed race hatred for the first time on her voyage to Europe in 1949 when 700 West Indians came on board in the Caribbean. She discovered that 'by inclination, temperament and opinion I was ranged on the side of the West Indians'.[29] This experience was the starting point for her novel *Sun in Exile*, the story of an Australian girl who on the ship to Europe meets, and eventually marries, a West Indian, and of the prejudice that they experience.

The voyage also took travellers to their first foreign places; on the Suez run to Colombo, Aden, the day trip to Cairo with its camel ride to the Pyramids and the Sphinx; on the Cape run, to Durban, Cape Town, Las Palmas. Colombo was for the majority the first experience of the world beyond Australia. Thus it was signalled in travel writing as 'our first foreign port', 'the first taste of a foreign land', 'my first glimpse of the tropics', 'the first glimpse of the Orient', a place where all 'was novel and strange'.

> I was all excited, this being my first glimpse of the tropics. I shall never forget the sensation of wild delight and excitement upon landing for the first time on this lovely island, and getting into a rickshaw and running through the Eastern streets past Oriental shops of dazzling colours, native girls with their pretty waist cloths and fragrant flowers in their dusky hair, the serious looking Buddhists, Hindoos and brahmins, the dear little sacred oxen in the old-world wooden wagon and the great thatched carts full of fruit and vegetables, with the hum and buzz of seething life all over.[30]

Most travellers enthused about their first encounter with the foreign, but Colombo was constructed as the 'other', remote and irrelevant to the real world. It was a place of scenes, dramas, pictures for the traveller's gaze; it was described as different, exotic, colourful, picturesque, chaotic, mysterious, tantalising, languid, dreamy, all the projections that make up Edward Said's Orientalism. There were two Colombos, that of the expatriate imperial ruling class, the Galle Face and Raffles hotel, the Cinnamon Gardens, Mt Lavinia, and that of the 'natives', 'of the cool, airy bungalows where one does live, and the loathly hovels where one doesn't live'.[31] The two worlds met when the tourists went shopping. Phyllis Downe, travelling in the late 1930s and staying with friends, was taken to shop in the native quarter. She was nervous to find herself the only white person among the milling natives, but the chauffeur provided security as the link between the two worlds.

> Goodness knows, he was as black as the ace of spades, but he was a tangible connection with the world we had left, the bright, gay, flower-filled world which seemed so remote in the heart of the native quarter.[32]

Natives 'swarmed', 'milled', 'yelled', 'gesticulated', 'pestered' — 'there is far too much of this pestering' — and when not picturesque or comical were described as dirty and smelly.[33] More than one traveller reported that the first thing she did on return to her boat was to have a bath.[34] The encounter with a world constructed as so totally different from home could be disturbing. In 1928 Mabel Dowling was glad to get back to the boat 'among things we could understand'; 'the native mind was beyond us'.[35] Her experience had made her realise more than she thought possible 'what it was to live in a clean, wholesome country'. Edna Kerr in 1959 learnt to appreciate something else after witnessing the poverty in Colombo, '"our" Land of Plenty', which caused her to ask ironically if 'all men were born equal'.[36]

CHAPTER 8

Travel and Discovery of the World

> Though he (an Australian) may have taken long bush
> rides, and made narrow escapes from death by thirst or
> starvation, he has not travelled in their sense of the
> word, for he has not seen antiquities, or stood on any
> world-renowned height to view a classical land.[1]

> There was nothing mythic at Sydney: momentous
> objects, being, and events all occurred abroad or in the
> elsewhere of books.[2]

While some women travelled specifically to Asia or the Middle East or
North America, and most made marginal contact with the non-European
world through the ports of call on their voyages, until the late twentieth
century it was Europe that was the traveller's goal. What did they make of
the new worlds they encountered? How did the place of departure inform
their perceptions? To generalise is to distort since each woman's voyage
was individual, but despite the increasing variety of ways in which women
travelled and the greater opportunities for independent journeying as the
twentieth century advanced there is much consistency in the travellers'
views of the world from the mid-nineteenth to the mid-twentieth century.
Britain was as much 'home' in the discourse of the 1930s as it had been in
the 1880s.

When they left Australia in the late nineteenth and early twentieth centuries, the women knew that they were colonials journeying from the
periphery to the centre, that as European people by race and culture, as
the descendants of immigrants, they were returning to the original home.
The trips took at one level the form of a pilgrimage to sacred sites of family, history and culture, to the places where 'things had really happened',
indeed to the 'real world'. Sacred sites could be family graves. Annie
Duncan, touring Scotland in the 1890s, went to Glasgow to see her
father's home and the family burial ground. She found the former, but the
latter had disappeared under the extension of a railway yard.[3] Eighty
years later, Connie Miller visited Ashton-upon-Mersey: 'I conversed quietly with a great aunt and two uncles in their eight-hundred-year old
graveyard sweet with lace flowers and singing birds'.[4] Sacred sites could
also be cultural and religious, and widely disparate. Painter Anne Dangar
disembarked at Marseilles in the1920s to make her pilgrimage to Aix —

revered as the birthplace of Cézanne.[5] For Sydney Anglican deacon, Clare
Davies, who made her trip to Europe in 1955, the sacred place was the
Tower of London, where she felt she was on holy ground when she
walked in the footsteps of the Reformation martyrs, Cranmer, Ridley and
Latimer.[6] But it was to the Baha'i holy shrines at Haifa in Palestine that
Effie Baker made her pilgrimage in 1924, and Winifred Stegar accompa-
nied her Indian camel-driver husband to Mecca in 1927.[7]

The women sailed to lands that were both known and unknown,
familiar and unfamiliar, to haunted places, to lands that already existed in
their imaginations.[8] They carried with them images, expectations,
knowledge and preconceptions that would frame and structure what
they saw and how they saw it.

> In her dreams she found such fairy cities, such seas and mountains, such
> sunsets! She named them Florence, Rome, the Adriatic, the Alps, the
> Mediterranean, London — all sorts of names.
>   Peggy's room was her world. She peopled it herself. She filled it with far
> countries. She lighted it with dreams.[9]

Like Louise Mack's Peggy, the women had travelled long before they
embarked on their journeys, had named their places, taken possession.
As one of the Rowe sisters wrote home more prosaically: 'it is so queer to
be in such strange countries about which I have read so often'.[10]

The images that the women carried with them were formed by family
memory, and an education steeped in English literature and European history, verbal and visual images. Amie Livingstone had an English governess, the daughter of an ambassador, who had lived in France, studied
music with Liszt, and who told her stories that rekindled longings for Paris
and Rome, Vienna and Prague, longings that had their origins in the pic-
ture-books she had devoured as a child living in the Victorian Alps.[11]
Travel writer Nina Murdoch, exploring Andalusia in the 1930s, wrote that
Spain had first entered her imagination through the culture of childhood;
'rain, rain go to Spain', 'the King of Spain's daughter', 'castles in Spain'.[12]
Dymphna Cusack, flying to Albania for the first time in the 1960s, recalled
the mood in which she had taken off.

> Here I was flying southward to that romantic land which had haunted
> me since my schooldays when I asked as my first entrance as Viola in
> *Twelfth Night*:
>   'What country, friends, is this?'
>   and the answer came.
>   'This is Illyria my lady'.
>   Far off in an Australian country town, the word glowed in my mind along
> with Samarkand and Rome, Isphahan and Peking, all seemingly unattain-
> able as dreams.[13]

Given a lifetime of preparation and expectation, the first response on arrival was often that of sheer incredulity at actually being there.

> Yes, Nan, life is worth living!
> I am actually in London, the anticipation of years an accomplished fact. Yours in a chronic thrill of delight.[14]

Gladys Marks on her first encounter with the art galleries of Florence could not believe that it was 'me looking at it all'.[15] A generation earlier Janey Rowe had written:

> I cannot now realize that we are really in Europe it seems to me like a perpetual dream, we see one thing and another that I have thought, and read of for so long.[16]

Edna Kerr, in Europe almost a century later, found it 'hard to realise that we are actually in these places', whether London, Stockholm or Vienna.[17] At the beginning of jet travel, artist June Davies wrote in her journal when she arrived in Athens:

> We then walked up to the PARTHENON, and these are the moments that have a light air of unreality about them … You have read about these places, know their histories, seen reproductions … and here you are.[18]

The new world that the women had entered was both real and unreal. It was the real world, real because its existence had been confirmed in works of literature and history. As V.S. Naipaul, another writer from the colonial periphery, has observed, 'no city or landscape is truly rich until it has been given the quality of myth by writer, painter or its association with great events'. Ida Haysom, camping in an English field covered with buttercups and daisies, knew that she was 'surrounded by real flowers'.[19] Buttercups and daisies were 'real' flowers because they were the flowers of her childhood reading and of poetry. Concepts of real and unreal could also become very mobile. For Alice Henry prior to her arrival, Torquay had been a picture-book and Reading an image on a box of biscuits, but when she confronted them with 'real people and real horses and real carts on real roads', they were 'more unreal than anything I had ever seen on the stage'.[20]

Because Europe had existed for the women on the pages of books long before it was encountered, it was often represented as pictures come to life. On arriving in Naples in 1934 on her first trip to Europe, Jessie Mitchell recalled that as a schoolgirl she had pored over the photographs in an atlas. She had always especially admired the photograph of the Bay of Naples, 'so you can well imagine my pleasure when I looked out of my window on the morning of May 16th and found this picture come to life'.[21] Berthing in Dunkirk in 1940, a woman working as a ship's surgeon wrote that the wharf labourers 'were men who might have stepped out of a coloured picture in a French travel-book — small and dark, with white skins and rosy cheeks, dressed in blue corduroys and the inevitable beret'.[22] Angelina Pearce placed herself in a picture when she had afternoon tea in a sidewalk cafe in Naples just as 'one sees people doing in pictures of foreign towns'.[23]

The real world was also a dream world. The Rowe sisters constantly referred to themselves as being in 'fairyland'. Lands and cities that had first existed for the Australian women in childhood stories, on Christmas cards and chocolate boxes, often continued to be represented within this framework. Una Falkiner thought that

> Scotland ought to be called fairyland, with its ferns and silver birches and firs and moss and lanes of vivid greenery that reflects much bright green colour and the foxgloves and daisies and dogroses in the hedge rows.[24]

Writing about her time in Dresden as a young girl, Nancy Adams came out from the Opera House into the snow to find that the buildings on the square 'were even more like the illustration of a fairy-tale than they were by daylight'.[25] This association stemmed from childhood; the earliest images of Europe were often illustrations in fairytales; the cities and forests of Europe were first mediated through the Brothers Grimm.

Fairyland was not the only imaginary land that the women entered. Places were also literature and history. When Katharine Susannah Prichard strolled through the Temple Gardens and the Inns of Court and along the Embankment to Westminster, 'it was like walking through history, all the romantic associations of poetry and the great names of English literature accompanied us'.[26] For Ethel Turner, Florence was English literature. She visited the Hotel Villa Trollope.

> We make a tour of the rooms to learn who have used them. This was Mr and Mrs Browning's room. Here in number 36 George Eliot wrote much of 'Romola'. In this one Nathaniel Hawthorne wrote 'Transformation or the Fawn'. Here in number 60 Thomas Hardy wrote 'Tess of the d'Urbervilles' and Mrs Burnett 'Little Lord Fauntleroy'... one of her books.[27]

The association continued. Nancy Cato believed that her passion to spend so much time in Italy in 1956 was probably due to romantic literature: 'Keats and Byron, Shelley and Mary Godwin, Henry James and Dante Alighieri'.[28]

Confrontation with dreams could prove both confirming and disillusioning. Sites were often for example not as big as had been imagined. When one woman saw Paternoster Row in London in 1881 she was surprised; when she had seen pictures in magazines and books she had imagined it was a very large place, but 'it was nothing but a lane not wider than our gateway at home'.[29] And surprise at the small size was a common response when women met the Pyramids. For June Davies in 1969, the Parthenon was not as large as the picture she had in her head. In her case, however, diminution did not mean disappointment since the fabled monument was 'more splendid than you imagine'; it was 'no let-down'.[30] But beauty is in the eye of the beholder. When Gillian Bouras arrived in Athens five years later, everything was 'drab and grey', and she almost wept 'in disappointment at the dreariness'.

> What had happened to the legendary light, to the 'shining, violet-crowned, divine' city? Even the first sight of the ruins was a shock. Quite uncon- sciously I had expected them to be isolated in tidy little sections of their own, not cheek by jowl with the visual pollution of the twentieth century Athens.[31]

The women could be aware of the fantasy element in their expecta- tions. In 1902 Louise Mack's Australian girl approached Rome by train from Naples.

> I had anticipated brown and grey ruins, and ruins, and ruins, and ruins. Here were green fields, and the fire of a million scarlet poppies, blazing from fields and roadsides. Except for the poppies and the great grey walls, I could have believed myself going from Launceston to Hobart...
>
>   I didn't expect to find marble emperors stalking about marble streets in purple state. But I didn't expect a railway station and buns and coffee at *Rome*! Trains at *Rome*![32]

Eliza Mitchell portrayed a similar response in her diary of her 1881 trip.

> We got in about four, and it did seem too dreadful to arrive in Rome by a train — to get into an everyday cab and look after luggage. It was altogether too modern and commonplace. No ruins, no Seven Hills — not visible at any rate — no Capitol, no Forum — or anything denoting antiquity! A wail of disappointment — but I wonder what I expected? The train to steam into the heart of the Forum?[33]

These responses remind us that the objective of travel is the past as much as the present, not just another place, but also another time, hence the fre- quency with which adjectives like 'old', 'ancient', 'quaint' and 'primitive' are deployed. And in their sightseeing, it was above all the past, and a romanticised past, that most Australian travellers sought. Real worlds were old worlds, had history. White Australia was young, history was something that, in the words of Ethel Turner, we 'crude unhistoried' Australians did not have.[34] Over and over the opposition is constructed — Europe as history, Australia as non-history. For Agnes Hay, what was striking about Australia was 'the absence of the past', that 'there is no his- tory except that which is being made'.[35] Young countries, Gladys Marks announced, did not have the romance and dignity of tradition — 'countries like people are the better for a past'.[36] A past, a history, was understood according to the list of Henry James; palaces, castles, manors, old country houses, thatched cottages, ivied ruins, cathedrals, abbeys, Norman and Gothic churches. Thus travel writer Nina Murdoch, in Europe in the 1930s, enthused:

> How can I tell to those who do not know, the exquisiteness of gooseflesh that arises from setting hand upon a wall built by Charlemagne a thousand years ago?
>
> Surely no people in the world should respond as eagerly to the romance of ancient things as we whose story is but a century old![37]

Nancy Cato landing in Naples saw lying on the porch of the Castel Nuovo a heap of stone cannon balls, 'not even very old, yet older than anything seen in Australia'.[38] Barbara Hanrahan's 1960s questing art student also landed at Naples: 'Dot said how you could feel it was Europe … cold slippery cobbles and it was a place so old and grubby, and I had never felt an Australian before'.[39]

Not all North Americans had wanted Henry James's European past, indeed many had fled, or were the children of fugitives, from that past. And there were women who recognised that Europe's history was a mixed blessing. Allison Howorth, making her European tour in the late 1930s, acknowledged that the traditions and history of old countries made them interesting from the tourist's point of view, but 'surely much of it is history that no new country wants'.[40] Much as she enjoyed seeing old castles in Britain, she was 'always conscious of the horrors' that had taken place there. The feeling could be even stronger on the Continent. Doris Gentile, after living under the Nazi fascist government of the Republic of Salò, wrote that when she was young she felt a pang of jealousy 'at those others, the lucky ones who lived in older civilized lands, who were busy with making of their history'.[41] But having been 'plunged headlong into a piece of lush and violent history' and forced to confront the 'cruelty of civilization', she was not so envious. Painter Janet Alderson, looking back on the large part of her life that she spent living abroad, reflected on the advantages of the absence of history: 'There's freedom in lack of history, a tremendous freedom in a lack of history, a tremendous advantage when you don't have anything to hold you back'.[42] This had also been the belief of the reformers of the early twentieth century. And there were always travellers who recognised that there were different kinds of history and that their own land was as ancient as any, 'if we would only take the trouble to find it out'.[43] But whether the possession of history was a good or a bad thing, the construct of Europe as old, Australia as new, framed the women's responses.

If Europe was history it was also culture, 'real' culture, and possessed

> art galleries where artists' work was hung and it mattered, where connois-
> seurs came to view pictures and Englishmen like Soames Forsyte came to
> buy them; a city where publishers accepted manuscripts and producers
> staged for the first time plays that would be famous.[44]

Thus the Australian women with various degrees of knowledge and
enthusiasm attended concerts and theatres and trudged through galleries
and museums, the sites where culture was acquired and consumed. By
the end of the nineteenth century galleries and museums were obligatory
rites on the ceremonial agendas that made up the tourist's track.[45]

> On Saturday I paid another visit to the National Gallery and spent three or
> four hours there. One really wants to spend months to know all the pic-
> tures. I have a few favourites and I go and sit in front of them and drink in
> their beauties for hours at a time. One never gets tired of looking at the
> works of Rembrandt, Cuyp, Greuze, Maes, Reni, Rubens, Rinsdael, Teniers,
> Bonheur, Constable, Gainsborough, Landseer, Romney, Turner, Vernet,
> Leighton, Graham, Alma Tadema, Dicksee, Fildes, Prinsep and others of
> the great masters.[46]

How could the colonial tourist not be overawed when, already conscious of her cultural deficiency, the objects of high culture were marked
off and endowed with an aura of the sacred. One early twentieth-century
tourist related her encounter with Raphael's *Sistine Madonna* in the gallery
in Dresden.

> Well may it be double starred in the guide book, and well may it be counted
> as one of Dresden's priceless treasures. It stands on a pedestal in a room all
> by itself. On entering this room you are at once struck by its perfect beauty
> and absolutely satisfying effect. In that room and in the presence of that
> exquisite picture, nobody speaks above a whisper. At least, no one did the
> whole time we were there, and I can quite believe that no one ever does.[47]

But even the need to heighten sensibility and fulfil the tasks of the
properly constructed tourist could break down — at least in the privacy
of diaries. How many of us have blanched when faced with yet another
Saint Sebastian 'doing the pincushion act with myriads of arrows'?[48]

> I have had an elegant sufficiency of scriptural pictures especially San
> Sebastians which I could never abide. The saint always looks so pleased and
> satisfied, tho' riddled with arrows.[49]

The irreverence of Florence Finn before Saint Sebastian was typical of
her representation of her responses to the icons of her culture. The statue
of Apollo driving the chariot in the British Museum was the climax of her
'Philistine mirth'; it was without legs, arms, head, torso and chariot and

confined to 'one horse's head broken off just behind the ears'.[50] But is mockery of self and object only the other side of breathless reverence?

For most Australians, Britain was the centrepiece of the trip to Europe until at least the last decades of this century. While many Australian women made temporary or permanent homes in the cities of Continental Europe, for most the experience of the Continent was a latter-day quick version of the Grand Tour. The result was that Europe was usually homogenised as the Continent, an outlook that derived in part from British insularity.[51]

It was with hearts brimming over with emotion that most Australians sailed up the English Channel.

> I will never forget my first sight of England as we neared Plymouth. A great lump came into my throat and tears to my eyes. Here I was a native Australian coming 'home', the home of my father and my grandfather and even as I write I am overcome by emotion even after years.[52]

Britain was above all the land of family origins, family sites, family history. It was the place known through the memories and nostalgia of parents and grandparents, through the familiar objects of childhood. Anticipating Sir Robert Menzies, 'London was the Mecca' of Winifred James's dreams.[53] London was also the centre of the Empire and hence also the pivotal point of the world. 'But most of all', wrote Ena Lilley, 'I love London because it is "The Heart of the World"'.[54] As the heart of the Empire, Britain was also the political, financial, and educational centre, the primary place of authentication and recognition. The history and historic sites of Britain, the Houses of Parliament, Westminster Abbey were the heritage not only of the Britons at home, but of the Britons overseas. It was their British nationality that gave Australians their place and status in the world, that is, the world beyond Britain. In Britain, their place and status was more problematic.

If one contrast between Australia and Britain was that of youth and antiquity, another was of colour, of dry arid green and real green. As they approached England the Australian women knew that the land was going to be green, green in a way no Australian could imagine, and the green would be divided by hedges and interspersed with primroses and buttercups, and when the Australian eye glanced up, it would see a thatched roof, spiralling smoke, a church spire or turret.

> English scenery was in her mind a jumble of green fields, buttercups and daisies — of picturesque wintry landscapes, with a robin in the foreground, and a spire in the distance, such as she had seen on Christmas cards, or on the wrappers which had enfolded their tea and sugar from Frazerville.[55]

But ships berth in the docklands of big cities, not in green fields, so romantic images could be shattered at the moment of arrival. Disappointment on arrival was a theme in the novels that took Australian women to Britain.[56] Henry Handel Richardson later wrote of her arrival at Tilbury:

> But for the ugliness of Tilbury and the low-lying flats surrounding it, I was not prepared. I had pictured the scene very differently. So this was England; England, too, the miles on miles of dismal slums through which we travelled to our sooty terminus.[57]

Kathleen Pitt (later Fitzpatrick) who made her trip 'home', four decades after Richardson, sailed up the west coast of England. From the deck she saw the 'actualisation of pictures seen in books' — 'hedges, church steeples, tiny fields'. But it was a different 'home' she saw when the ship docked at Liverpool in the middle of the 1926 General Strike. She confronted an England that was 'hideous and rather frightening, because sub-human types of people seemed to abound, people unlike any we had ever seen before, ragged, gaunt and grim'. The train journey south to London took Fitzpatrick through the industrial cities: 'dreadful black towns containing thousands of identical houses in identical streets, dwellings which did not seem designed for human habitation but as cells in great chunks of black honeycomb for worker bees.'[58] On her arrival in London in the 1880s Mrs Alfred Bennett lodged near Euston Square Station:

> But the first night in London was the most disagreeable of all our experiences up to this point. On looking out of the back window it seemed to me that London consisted of a huge field of nothing but crooked chimneys and their pots. It was not by any means a pleasant view of the great city.[59]

When Mrs Bennett moved into a South Kensington hotel, her response to London was far more positive, as were the reactions of the women whose London was the West End. And the English countryside away from the industrial towns splendidly conformed to expectations. Ida Haysom climbed the tower of Wickham College in Winchester and

> just couldn't speak, a lump was in my throat & I almost felt like crying. It was real England. Low green hills all around, copper beeches & other lovely trees, the college with its ruins, the cricketers, the old houses in the close.[60]

Yet one prevailing image of England was the London of Charles Dickens, the city of poverty, damp and fog. In Cicely Little's 1940s novel, *The Lass with the Delicate Air*, the protagonist arrived in London in the middle of a wet, cold April, and found a certain amount of satisfaction in the 'wetness, coldness and drabness of London, merely because it was living up to its reputation'.[61] Those expecting Dickensian images sometimes felt let down by the appearance of the sun. Nancy Cato, with her perceptions so influenced by her reading, was 'at first disappointed that the sun was shining and there was no London fog'.[62]

Once entered, London could not be possessed. The sheer size of that 'urban continent', the largest city in the world in the late nineteenth and early twentieth centuries, was overwhelming.[63] In Tasma's *Not Counting the Cost*, the Clare family, brought up by their mother to despise the place of their birth, approached the English coast in a state of 'jubilant excitement', meeting the promised land, beholding face to face, seeing with 'bodily eyes', the places familiar in imagination since as long as they could remember. But when the young Clares left the boat to find lodgings, expectations were shattered.

> 'London is too big', she said despondently. Her voice sounded weak and cracked with fatigue and underground railway smoke. 'And, oh, so dirty, you can't think, Eila! First we went over forests of houses with red roofs. I thought they would never end; and such miserable houses! Then we got to an enormous dark railway-station, with crowds and crowds of people. The air smelt so funny, and everything looked huge and dingy'.[64]

What the Clare family was also making its protest against was modernity and the society of strangers. But other women embraced the gifts of the world's greatest metropolis. For Ada Holman, it was the very modernity of London, the variety, range and excitement of the city, that was its attraction.

> Never to be bored, never to be left to one's own resources, never to have time to reflect on the issues of life and death is the modern ideal, only to be found in gigantic cities, of which London is the superlative.[65]

Nettie Palmer wrote home that since there was such variety in London, further travel was unnecessary.[66] The anonymity of the modern city was something that many women embraced.

> I revelled in my independence. I loved everything about London: most of all the feeling that no one knew me. I was too excited to be lonely.[67]

Perhaps most typical of the Australian responses to London was that of Ena Lilley.

> There one can satisfy most of one's ambitions and tastes. The old world offers artistic, scenic, literary, musical, and in fact, endless attractions that a new world lacks. There one can see the best and the worst of life; one's life is broadened and deepened, one's intelligence increased, one's sympathies sharpened, and one's soul-hunger enlarged and satisfied.[68]

If the mind maps of the Australian travellers constructed the world as the old and the new, the contrasts were by no means all to the disadvantage of the new. The old, as was clearly articulated by women of reformist bent, could mean not only culture and sophistication, but also rigid class structure and divisions, privilege and poverty, hidebound tradition, decadence, as opposed to the more open, flexible, experimental and progressive new societies.[69] Not only reformers, but more conservative women such as Ena Lilley, saw sights in the East End that horrified, that could never be erased from the mind.[70] There were other places and perspectives; Nettie Higgins wrote from Germany in 1911 that even in the poorest parts of Berlin she had not seen houses as squalid as those in Carlton.[71] But on the whole, the East End of London became the benchmark of poverty. When they arrived in the warmer climes of the Mediterranean, the Australians represented poverty and misery in the sun and warmth as more tolerable, as 'smiling poverty'. Thus Margaret Thomas in Spain wrote that 'nowhere is seen the sordidness and hopelessness of English poverty'.[72] Notions about the superiority of the British race inform such views since 'smiling poverty' was also regarded as more voluntary, linked to inertia and sloth.[73]

Poverty was associated with dirt, filth and smell; it was the smell of the slums that Ada Holman found so overpowering. But as for the rest of London, she was amazed and impressed by its cleanliness.

> exquisitely kept roads and footpaths, trees and gardens everywhere, cheerful broad houses, guiltless of spot or speck. There's no grime or grit anywhere. Debris is got rid of as if by magic.[74]

Her response was somewhat unusual. The travelling Australians identified their own land with light and cleanliness — of mind and body — and were all too prone to regard the rest of the world within these parameters. Travellers' tales from the 1950s of the English storing coal in the bathtub have a long history. Henry Handel Richardson, re-creating her reactions on her arrival in England, recalled the place of her birth as a land 'whichever its defects, was at least bright and sunny, and clean'. She also wrote of the reluctance of the Germans to wash, that is on an Australian scale.[75] Richardson's dismissal of Germans as dirty ran counter to commonplace perceptions of that land as clean and ordered, as Gladys Marks wrote from Berlin in May 1913:

> It is beautiful and it works like a great big machine, kept well oiled and unconceivably clean. I've never seen such cleanliness in town or inhabitants. I haven't yet seen a dirty or ragged creature. The poorest streetsweeper is neat, the very tram guards look newly clothed, bright buttoned — clean handed.[76]

Cleanliness was the first adjective used by Agnes Hay when she crossed to the Continent:

> I shall never cease to remember the impression made on me by the sight of this first Continental city that I had ever seen. Its scrupulous cleanliness, its white and green houses, its beautiful churches.[77]

The town was Antwerp. Travellers for whom Naples was the 'first Continental city' tended to resort to other adjectives. Irritated by quarantine procedures at Naples, Edith Doust found it 'so absurd that the dirty Neapolitans we saw should fear being contaminated by the crew of our clean and stately ship'.[78]

Cleanliness was linked to fresh air, and many Australian travellers told of their battles over the disposition of windows on Continental trains. Mary Grant Bruce, author of the Billabong books, making her European trip in 1927, recounted her experience on a train to Avignon. Her fellow travellers in the carriage were a 'fat Frenchman with a thin wife' who, since they occupied the seats next to the windows, controlled their movement.

> The carriage had been insufferably hot and airless when we entered it at Nice, where I had begged for an open window. They opened one grudgingly about eight inches from the top, but closed it with a decisive bang as soon as the train started, remarking that they had colds. It was horribly evident they had colds. They sniffed and snuffed and coughed and sighed, and cast malevolent looks at the door by the corridor, which we had determined should be shut only over our dead bodies.[79]

The Australian women may have wished for fresh air, but they were not so sure about the cold. When Annie Duncan arrived at Port Said on her homeward journey, she felt for the first time in four years 'thoroughly, completely and comfortably warmed through, and like an animal coming out of long hibernation'.[80] Una Falkiner constantly railed against the English climate in her 1929 diary. On her return to Australia she wrote:

> Oh how I love the Australian sunshine, golden, yellow, warm undiluted sun out of a clear clear heaven! All the sun at home seemed to show through five thicknesses of gauze, awfully soft and charming but not the clear warmth.[81]

Some visitors to Britain were critical of the formality of upper-class British life. Mrs Bennett, who paid close attention to the processes of the London season, was amused by the rigidity of the rituals.

> We had always been accustomed to look upon the English as a free people, but we found that in respect to the observance of conventionalities, they are less so than any other nation while, with respect to social matters, they are the veriest slaves. People in good society could not think of taking their infants or young children with them for a drive in the Park in the afternoon, though they could do so with impunity in the morning; neither would they go to the opera or the theatre during the season in a four-wheeler, out of season they would not mind a bit.[82]

Christobel Bollen in London in 1913 wrote home about her surprise at the extent of English conformity:

> on a certain day the men change from felt hats to straw & on a certain day people who think themselves quite the things, leave London, in fact every-

one seems to be ruled by what everyone else does, & the people who don't
follow the fashion are immediately thought of no importance'.[83]

Kathleen Pitt found the routine of gentry life stifling when she stayed with
relatives in Kent. She recognised that her distaste might stem in part from
the independence and comparative lack of discipline in her Australian
upbringing.[84]

Some women were offended by what they saw as the English lack of
hospitality in contrast to Australian generosity. An indignant attack on
English mores by 'Kangaroo Kate' in the *British-Australasian* pointed out
that while we received the English in Australia with open arms and asked
them to stay a month, 'they merely ask us to afternoon tea — and regret
that the tea is cold'.[85] Annie Duncan recalled that when she had written
to a cousin informing him of her arrival in England she received a 'chilly
reply' that did not 'conform to my Australian ideas of hospitality'.[86] The
editor of the women's column in the *British-Australasian* did her best to
explain to the visiting Australians the rules of and reasons for English
hospitality; whereas the hospitality of the bush was elastic, in England
people's visiting lists were so very, very large that timetables were inflexi-
ble, 'no sooner has a guest vacated a room than it is filled'.[87] Louise
Mack's Australian girl in London in time grew weary and impatient of
Australian informality and indiscriminate friendliness. At a party in
London, she found herself shrinking back from what she had been longing for — 'the gay, free chatter, the unstinted expressions of welcome, of
my fellow-countrymen'.

> I fear I have grown old and dull. There was something irritating to me in
> confronting those Australians en masse. I missed something to lean up
> against, something one gradually comes to need — the restraint and reserve
> of the English. [88]

The Australian girl's reaction belongs to the conventions of anti-tourism;
the speaker has settled in London, taken on the local colouring, become
one of the natives, and thus takes on a stance of superiority before those
who fail to hide their identity, who stand out, who are tourists.[89]

While Australians as colonials could feel a sense of inferiority in
Britain, they were also aware that the experience of the overseas children
of the Empire could be more extensive than that of those who had
remained at the centre. Ada Cambridge observed that 'the children who
go out into the world have, and must have, a wider grip on affairs than the
parent who stops at home'.[90] In making this point, Cambridge was of
course echoing Rudyard Kipling — 'What do they know of England who
only England know?'[91] It was sometimes argued that distance and longing
made Australian women more appreciative of Britain than the natives
themselves. Lady Rose, the English aristocrat villain in Sophie Osmond's
late-nineteenth-century novel *An Australian Wooing*, is 'almost as ignorant

of London as a South Sea islander', and is a woman with less culture and manners than her Australian protégée, whose education had opened to her a London of literature and history that she wanted to explore.[92] Elizabeth Marrable, heroine of 'Iota''s *Comedy of Spasms*, tells her mother that she likes being a colonial: 'I know more of England this minute than half the English girls I meet'.[93] After her pilgrimage to the statue of Peter Pan in Kensington Gardens, a sacred site for women brought up in the 1920s and 1930s on a diet of J.M. Barrie, Phyllis Downe wrote:

> Oh, English children and grown-ups, who take these things for granted, could never realise what it means to us to see them, to be in the midst of them — these things of which we have heard and read all our lives.[94]

When they travelled beyond Britain, the Australians often claimed a more informed perspective than the insular English tourists. In Spain, Margaret Thomas did not enthuse about the fruit; no doubt it lived up to its fabled reputation for people coming from Northern Europe, but Australians had tasted better and were disappointed.[95] Louise Mack's Australian girl was not impressed by Italy's legendary sun and light. She could understand the English delight, but Australians had no need to travel for such pleasures.[96] Florence Finn watched the sun set over the desert in Egypt, but 'hailing from a land of beautiful sunsets' did not 'rave' as did most of the others in the party when 'the sun slipped behind the hills'.[97]

Ada Cambridge, English born and engaging in her first return trip home after 40 years in Australia, displayed no regrets at the course her life had taken; food was better in Australian restaurants, the bulk of Australian women were better dressed than English women, and shopping in London made her realise how good Australian shops were.[98] Miles Franklin when she arrived in London in 1912 was aghast at the dowdiness of English women.[99] Emily Bennett thought that 'ladies in the colonies are quite as stylish and novel in their dress as in England' and that 'the shops of Sydney and Melbourne compare very favourably with the majority of those in London'.[100] Modern England offered no more than modern Australia. Such comments can be construed as defensive, but, on the other hand, perhaps we should recognise more clearly the extent to which late-nineteenth-century Australia participated in an international cultural and commodity market, and that Sydney and Melbourne were as up to date as Manchester and Birmingham.

The Australian women abroad identified their own land as having 'intelligent, unaffected and independent people', but more than that as having 'the gaunt, grey bush, the dazzling sunshine, clear skies'.[101] In the days before Vegemite, nostalgia was expressed through attachment to nature; Nettie Palmer hoarded eucalyptus leaves, Margaret Thomas after 30 years' absence from Australia wrote a poem, 'On Seeing Some Sprays of Wattle in London Streets',[102] and the scent of boronia, 'the most beautiful scent in the world to us', washed over Louise Mack's Australian girl.[103] In England nature was domesticated, controlled; in Australia, it was untamed, free. Thus the further — and selective — contrast of the gentle, nurturing English countryside with the wild threatening bush, the contrast of translucent, tender, subtle air with harsh burning light.

> Our country is so different, so very different. In place of luxuriant woods and gently rolling meadows we have great armies of silver gums that climb the mountains and march down into the gullies, waving their plumed heads and singing a song of eternal unrest. Here, everything is serene, calm, secure. There everything is gigantic, danger, distance, droughts, deserts.[104]

The Australians rhapsodised about the English countryside, more familiar than their own in representation, but much as they might love green fields and tinkling brooks, this was a landscape that was tidy, tight, tame — for some oppressive. Catherine Helen Spence believed that a carefully cultivated nature was also crippling and confining, and Henry Handel Richardson responded negatively to high hedges bordering narrow lanes:

> Having grown up in a country famed for its openness, I found them stuffy and oppressive. It may also be that the sense of smotheration they induced was associated with an asthmatic's struggle for air.[105]

But the highly cultivated nature in England gave a sense of time, of tradition, of history, of belonging.

> Whereas in Australia the emptiness and windswept isolation take away thoughts of human habitation, in England the air is enriched by the long occupation of men, the countless spirits that came and went and seem yet to remain in essence.
>
> Each country has its own geology, appearance, boundaries, buildings, enterprises, loyalties, customs, lore, speech, its sense of continuity in family life and abode — in this continuity so unlike Australia, where, restless people as we are, restless as the aborigine, properties and houses are continually changing hands.[106]

Maie Casey here touches something at the heart of the psyche of an immigrant people who imposed an alien way of life on the landscape, who seized a land they did not possess. This was a land that offered no messages, myths, comfort or sense of belonging to its conquerors.[107]

For most of the women who belonged to the circles of the travelling élite in the late nineteenth and early twentieth centuries, home was two places. To look askance at this double identity as something less than truly Australian is to define 'Australian' in an unnecessarily restrictive and impoverishing way. In Britain, most Australians displayed a strong sense of loyalty to the place of their birth or permanent abode. But they saw themselves — and often not uncritically — as also *belonging* to the place of their parents and grandparents, and of their culture. There were many positions along the spectrum whose end points were a strident anti-British Australian nationalism and conversion into a British identity and loss of origin. And place of birth was not necessarily a determining factor. No woman was more critical of Britain or identified more with Australia than Scots-born Catherine Martin, no woman more fervently imperialist than Australian-born Winifred James.

The concept and reality of Empire bridged the gap between the two homes, providing a common identity for metropolitans and colonials, Britons and Australians, but it was an identity felt and needed more by the colonials, the denizens of the periphery. Australians might see themselves as British, as the overseas sons and daughters of mother England, and might see Britain as a land as familiar as their own, but often their reception in their British home was not quite what they expected. Alice Henry found that her country 'was a matter of indifference' in Britain: 'They knew nothing of it and did not care. No wonder I had an inferiority complex on behalf of Australia'.[108] Ada Cambridge was annoyed that in the great English journals 'there was rarely so much as a mention of Australia, while every little tinpot dependency of a foreign power had its trifling affairs attended to'.[109] Because Australians saw themselves as family, because their imaginations were so steeped in images of Britain and its history, it came as a shock when they were treated as strangers, when they learnt that Australia was of little interest or relevance, that it had no equivalent place in the British imagination. Historian Kathleen Fitzpatrick, looking back over her life in the 1980s, wrote that it was in Britain in the early 1920s that she discovered her Australian identity. Brought up to think of England as 'home', she learnt that most English people regarded colonials as 'dreary provincials whom they would prefer not to know'.[110] In the long run these attitudes informed her own identity, 'not as a long-lost cousin of the people at "home" but as an Australian and a member of a new nation in the making'. Fitzpatrick was not alone in forging a stronger Australian identity while abroad.

Negotiating with Britain — the home that was not home, the foreign that was not foreign, where Australians were both the same and different, family and outsiders — was a difficult process. To move to Continental Europe was to become properly foreign, to remove identity problems. Thus Kathleen Fitzpatrick, despite the language barriers, felt more at ease in Paris and Rome than in London.

> That was, I suppose, largely, because our status on the Continent was not anomalous: we were foreigners pure and simple. In England we were not exactly foreigners but decidedly we were not English either but colonials, people of an inferior race.[111]

She also felt freer, that beyond actions that were forbidden by law you could do as you pleased, a feeling that reflects the liberty that is associated with being outside one's own society more than any understanding of the manners and mores of French or Italian life. Britain was not quite outside.

Australian women travelled the length and breadth of the Continent, but I have chosen to focus on Paris to explore their responses. For most women the French capital was a place of brief sojourn, an obligatory and much-desired stop on the Continental tour. But there were many who lingered, or remained there forever. From the late nineteenth century, Australian women had settled in Paris to study music and art. They were joined from the early twentieth century by women acquiring professional qualifications in the language and literature. Most women went as consumers of French culture, but Louise Hanson-Dyer, who made her home in Paris from 1927 until her death in 1962, was to make an important contribution to the musical life of France.[112] So to generalise about the responses of Australian women in France is to construct common models, not cover all experience.

When they went to Paris, Australian women constructed another set of opposites, London and Paris. Part of the contrast was the product of size. Much of the charm of Paris was its smaller and more human scale; the French capital did not overwhelm and dwarf in the way that London did. Tasma's Clare family fled London, which had become 'an unwieldy monster', for Paris, 'the embodiment of harmonious perfection'.[113] Kate O'Connor wrote that in London, one felt a unit, in Paris 'part of a great whole', and Ada Holman found that 'after the daedalian labyrinth of London, Paris is comparatively compact and manageable'.[114] Whereas for Katharine Susannah Prichard London 'had been strange and awe inspiring', Paris was 'curiously familiar and enchanting'.[115] Beyond its smaller size, Paris was lighter, less forbidding, less oppressive. Christina Stead wrote in a letter home in 1929 that Paris was

> far wealthier and gayer than London, and in point of beauty they cannot be mentioned in the same breath. London is crooked, narrow, mean, dirty and ill-conceived, Paris is a pearl of delicacy, brilliance and suavity ...[116]

More eloquent perhaps was the writing on Paris of painter Stella Bowen.

> I love and adore Paris. I love the way its quick and brilliant life runs openly on the surface for all to see. Every face in the street, every voice, every shape, is hard at it, telling its story, living its life, producing itself. In London the faces in the street have the air of having been locked up before being brought outside, as though a flicker of life would give away a secret to the enemy.[117]

London and Paris, Britain and France, were the contrast of work and play, of the real and the ludic worlds.

> Paris is delightful for a holiday, the outdoor life and gay insouciant air over everything is seductive and amusing, but London, with its crowds, its solidity, its wonderful mystery, its immensity and overpowering majesty, and its unlimited resources is impressively grand and eternally fascinating.[118]

Being an extension of home, Britain carried responsibilities — was serious. Paris, on the other hand, was recreation and pleasure — carnival. Thus the women felt freer and less restrained. Nina Murdoch, in her account of her time in Europe, wrote of her laziness in Nice, of lying in bed until half-past-nine.

> Yet there has been no furtive trying of my door handle to see if the stay-abed is moving. In a British country I should feel just a little guilty lying so, and the morning flying away. But not here![119]

'Gay Paree' was an invention of the British wishing to escape the constraints of home, and in a city that was gay the people were bound to be happy. Angelina Pearce was by no means alone in believing that 'everyone in Paris seems gay and happy': 'they have, indeed, learnt the art of always being happy and looking on the bright side of things'.[120] Katharine Susannah Prichard, wandering about on her first day in Paris, 'felt gay and light-hearted as if I were taking part in a comedy. Everybody was so friendly and amused by my French'.[121]

If Paris was pleasure and play, it was also romance. And sometimes the city met expectations. Escorted by a wealthy and cultivated companion, Prichard walked along the Left Bank, drove in the Bois, attended performances at the Comédie Française and the Moulin Rouge, and dined at Maxims. Other Parisian events included a reception in her honour, at which the cosmopolitan crowd included Albanian artists, Russian exiles, a professor from the Sorbonne and 'a golden-haired poetess in black velvet gown', and an escapade in the cemetery of Père Lachaise. A generation later when Christina Stead first went to Paris with William Blake, she was 'fed, sunned, dressed in grand chic, petted, educated, loved, indulged, taken (intelligently) all over Paris, musiced, champagned, cabareted, zooed, parked, taxied, walked and otherwise ambulated'.[122]

Romance for other women was in the imagination. Thus Nina Murdoch created herself in Nice.

> So I sit dreaming in the hotel garden among oleanders and palms, and loquat-trees and heavy-headed dahlias, soaking in the soft air of the Riviera on which comes delicately the faint, faint scent of magnolia like the bouquet, elusive and disturbing, of a paridisaic wine … And sitting a table or two away, a Frenchman in a strawboater … never takes his eyes from me in the hope that I may be feeling flirtatious on such a delicious morning. The patience of these Latins![123]

In a land of romance, different standards of behaviour applied. Winifred James was not offended by young men who stared at her in Corsica or Italy, although the same behaviour from Englishmen would have been unacceptable; 'an indignity under a grey sky becomes flattery under a blue'.[124] There is an arch innocence in the innuendoes of romance in the writing of Nina Murdoch and Winifred James, as there is in Gladys Marks's letter home complaining of her inability to have an adventure in Mediterranean lands.

> Do you know we can't get any adventures. Even when we go out alone it's like walking in Sydney. Why do people hold up Italians as awful examples? They're quite harmless.[125]

Another pair of opposites by which new worlds and old worlds were compared was that of innocence and decadence; the encounter of the innocent girl from a new society with the sophisticated, but corrupt, old world was a variant on the stock storyline of the country girl migrating to the city. It is a theme in Tasma's *Not Counting the Cost* when Eila meets her distant cousin, the hunchback Hubert de Merle.[126] Associations of decadence were artificiality, corruption, over-refinement. While Britain might be criticised for its old exploitative social systems, it was not normally associated with sexuality and sensuality. These, in the form of both raw passion and refined vice, were for Australians as indeed they were for the English attributes of the Mediterranean, of France, Italy, Spain. The Australian heroine of Anne Wilson's novel, *Two Summers*, after falling into the clutches of a sophisticated, wily Italian Count, had no problems in returning home and saying farewell to an 'alien, artificial world'.[127] Half a century later in her novel set in the last years of Fascist Italy, Doris Gentile referred to time and place as a 'lush piece of history' creating a world that was fetid, dark, stifled with passion, that cried out for open space, fresh air, wide vistas.[128] Another generation on, Barbara Hanrahan's protagonist in *Sea-green* sailed for Europe on an Italian ship and went to the cabin of an officer for seduction: 'I am far from anything open and simple and antipodean; this is the old, pagan world.'[129]

In most writing, the Continent was reduced to tableaux, pictures, scenes, to sites of monuments and cultural artefacts, to a series of characteristics, to the elements that were picturesque, quaint, odd, that conformed to and confirmed preconceived ideas. What fascinated Margaret Thomas in Madrid were the street scenes: 'in the lower quarters the life and movement are wonderful'. Apart from the street theatre of daily life, the only attraction of Madrid was the Prado Museum and its collection of the paintings of Velasquez.[130] If places were pictures and theatre, the local people became characters and strolling players. Thus the cavalcade that Ena Lilley watched in Naples included the laughing, old-fashioned, brown eyed children, the dirty old women foraging for rubbish in the dust heaps, the fruitsellers on the street corners, the black browed sullen men loafing about chattering and smoking … [131]

But the locals could also spoil the show; 'the place is full of curious archaeological and artistic treasures which cannot be sketched, because the inhabitants are so barbarous as to annoy and literally prevent your doing it'.[132] The local people were also inspected and judged from the superior viewpoint of the British race. Margaret Thomas wrote that the people of Madrid were

> ignorant, passionate and partly savage — above all, indomitably idle, but warm-hearted, affectionate, and disinterested to the last degree…
>
> The best we can wish them is that the civilizing steam-engine may soon penetrate to the remotest wilds of Spain bearing with it culture and prosperity.[133]

Half a century later Nina Murdoch gave her thumbnail sketch of Italians.

> The best and worst of the great mass of Italians is that they are such children, easily pleased, full of little importances, laughing, flying into a rage, strutting around blowing trumpets, waving flags, showing off, light fingered, joyous.[134]

In their reductionism and stereotyping of other worlds to sites and characters who were also national types, the women were doing nothing more than conforming to the norms of tourism.

Interlude

Stella Bowen

> *It lies upon me yet. It is something to do with the light, I suppose, and the airiness and bareness and frugality of life in the Midi which induces a simplicity of thought, and a kind of whittling to the bone of whatever may be the matter in hand. Sunlight reflected from red tiled floors on to white-washed walls, closed shutters and open windows and an air so soft that you live equally in and out of doors, suggest an existence so sweetly simple that you wonder that life ever appeared the tangled, hustling and distracting piece of nonsense you once thought it.*[1]

No Australian woman has written about France more lyrically than painter Stella Bowen who lived in Paris and Provence in the interwar years. Her France was somewhat different from that of her contemporary compatriates; she lived at the centre of the expatriate world of literary modernism.[2] She was there — at Rue du Fleurus with Gertrude Stein, 'a very commonsensible person, of a robust and earthy disposition, ever ready with domestic advice', with Edith Sitwell, whose portrait she painted, with Peggy Guggenheim from whom she borrowed money, with James Joyce, 'the most courteous and unassuming of guests', who stood godfather to her daughter, with Ernest Hemingway, who caricatured her as Mrs Braddocks in *The Sun Also Rises*.[3]

In 1914, the 21-year-old Stella Bowen sailed from Adelaide, travelling alone, but chaperoned, on the ship. Her widowed mother had recently died and Stella's departure was for the conventional one-year overseas trip. Raised in the genteel clerical circles of the city of spires, Bowen's initial destination was the home of the secretary of the Mothers Club in Pimlico. As it happened, the intended one year overseas turned into forever. A chain of circumstances led the young woman, who had been shown glimpses of life beyond Adelaide by her art teacher Rose Macpherson (Margaret Preston), to the Westminster Art School and to a flat in Pembroke Gardens. Ezra Pound came to a party in the flat and overnight Bowen was pitched 'into a milieu so unbelievably different from anything I had known or imagined, that I nearly exploded in the effort not to seem non-plussed'.[4] Through Pound, Bowen met the English writer Ford Madox Ford, with whom she was to live for ten years and who was to be the father of her daughter. Her relationship with Ford took Bowen in the 1920s to the Left Bank in Paris.

Stella Bowen's association with Ford and the parties that they gave made her part of the mythology of the lost generation. Possessed of enormous vitality and zest for living, Bowen loved dancing and she loved parties.

> I have always had a passion for parties if they are given with no ulterior motive other than that of pure enjoyment... A good party is a time and a place where people can be a little more themselves, a little exaggerated, less cautious and readier to reveal their true spirit than in daily life.[5]

While she may not have presided over a literary salon like Gertrude Stein or Natalie Barney, she and Ford did create some of the legendary parties of the period; the Thursday teas at the offices of the *Transatlantic Review*, the private dances at the *Bal du Printemps* in Rue du Cardinal Lemoine, and the parties that they hosted in the various Montparnasse studios and apartments where they camped. No doubt many of the guests came to the parties as part of Ford's network, but Bowen's gift for friendship, vivacity and gaiety played an important role in their success and reputation. She is remembered. And she went on giving parties after she left Ford, first in Paris and then in London, parties whose guest lists continued to include the beautiful and the damned — as well as the worthy. Fabian socialist reformer Margaret Cole, trying to recall in her autobiography where she might have met someone, listed as the likely places a WEA meeting, a popular front meeting, or a party at Stella Bowen's.[6]

The disintegration of Stella Bowen's relationship with Ford Madox Ford, which involved the writer Jean Rhys, also became the subject of legend — and of three novels by the other participants, Ford, Rhys, and Rhys's husband Jean Lenglet, a Dutch poet who wrote under the name of Edouard de Nève.[7] Bowen moved from representation by others to self-representation when she published her own memoirs, *Drawn from Life*, in 1940. Thus she was not only part of the legend, but one of its creators. And her inscription was in two media. To her evocative word images of the intelligentsia of the 1920s and 1930s must be added her portraits. Among her sitters were Pound, Stein, T.S. Eliot, Edith Sitwell, Yeats, Margaret Cole, and Stafford Cripps.

Stella Bowen's expatriate life was far from easy. Because of Ford's previous Catholic marriage, their relationship was blessed by neither church nor state, and her daughter was illegitimate. Her life was plagued by lack of money and by poverty, both while she was with Ford and after she left him. It was financial exigencies that drove her unwillingly from Paris to

Britain in the mid-1930s, and that played a considerable part in the writing and publication of her autobiography in the year after Ford died. That autobiography is the story of multiple journeys.

There is the literal journey that structures the autobiography and names the chapters. From Adelaide, Stella Bowen had moved to England, first to London and then into rural Sussex to live out with Ford the bucolic idyll, the simple and pure life of the amateur farmer. The dank and dark of England drove them at the end of 1922 across the Channel to the light and lightness of France, where for the next ten years Stella Bowen gravitated according to the season between the expatriate world of Paris and the coastal villages of Provence. A search for work and financial security took her to New York, New England and Vermont in 1932, and then back to England in the following year. Place both on the macroscopic level of region or city and the microscopic personal level was of central importance to Bowen, and much of her autobiography consists in the description and evocation of place, whether the landscapes of Provence, Tuscany and Umbria or a room in a rundown studio in Paris. In 1923 Stella Bowen joined Ezra and Dorothy Pound on a tour of central Italy. She arrived with her head full of images, expecting something 'soft and romantic'. The landscape that she found was both different and better.

> I had seen a hard country where everything had a lovely edge to it, and fell into marvellous formal patterns. Trees in serried rows and rocks in sequence and rivers in the exact position required to compose the picture. Old towns crowning symmetrical hills, with ramparts like a collar round the neck; bridges and towers and churches, their yellow-grey stone almost indistinguishable from the rocks upon which they stood, until a second glance revealed their keen, austere unblurred edges.[8]

The autobiography is also the story of her endless and fruitless struggle to find a permanent home, to create a haven of material and emotional security for her family.

> Do you think that if I get everything attended to before you come back that we shall be able to avoid messes for a long time? I mean trottings & scramblings. I should like to have all the material side of life fixed up in a thoroughly bourgeois fashion — & then I'll just *despise* it.[9]

Beyond the haven for the family, Bowen's search for place was also eventually a quest for a room of her own.

The journey from Australia to Europe was also constructed on several levels in the form of a female version of the *Bildungsroman*, the journey of self-development.[10] It is the story of the young provincial whose journey began in the provinces, in an Adelaide that was 'a queer little backwater of intellectual timidity — a kind of hangover of Victorian provincialism, isolated by three immense oceans and a great desert, and stricken by recurrent waves of paralysing heat'.[11] It was also a Garden of Eden,

> in which you remember bathing all day long in the bluest sea in the world, and eating all the fruit you could stomach — figs warm from the trees, grapes,...oranges, of course — and once you really start eating oranges there is no reason why you should ever stop — passionfruit, apricots, peaches and nectarines, all the fruits of the earth and no stint.[12]

In Europe the proverbial inexperienced provincial, 'the rubbishy young colonial', confronted the sophistication of the metropolis and engaged in a long quest to acquire and display the appropriate guise, knowledge and style, to achieve self-transformation.[13] Thus when some Adelaide relatives turned up in Paris sixteen years after Bowen had left Australia, she thought that she would be unrecognisable to them — 'that in sixteen years I had transformed myself completely'.[14] For Bowen, Adelaide was the symbol of the provinces, growing into the world was identified as shaking off Adelaide. The illegitimacy both of her relationship with Ford and of their daughter might indicate that Stella Bowen had shed Adelaide, but it was also a situation with which she was most uncomfortable and that she sought to conceal.

When Bowen cashed in her return ticket after she had been in London for one year, she cast off Australia just as surely as she cast off her accent in elocution lessons in London. She claimed that her only contact with the place of her birth after she left was the annual financial statement she sent home to her brother. Once she had finished describing her childhood in Adelaide, Australia is mentioned in *Drawn from Life* only as a place and symbol of provincialism. In the years after the publication of the autobiography, Australia was to come back into Bowen's life. At the end of 1943, she was appointed as an official Australian war artist with the temporary rank of captain, a position that was regularly extended until she was struck by illness in 1946, the cancer that put an end to her plans to take an exhibition of her paintings to Australia and killed her in the following year.[15]

The young 21-year-old who left Adelaide was also engaged in the process of growing up; as she wrote in *Drawn from Life*, she went to Europe to become an adult. And phrases such as 'I am still learning' or 'my education had received a shove forward' or 'a necessary part of an adult's education' recur throughout the autobiography. In their study, *The Female Hero in British and American Literature*, Carol Pearson and Katherine Pope, working within a Jungian framework, create a model of a woman's heroic journey to self-fulfilment in three stages.[16] The journey begins when the hero leaves the garden of innocence in search of freedom and unlimited possibility. During the second stage, the hero meets the powerful figure of the seducer and through this encounter is awakened into the world of experience. But the seducer turns out to be another captor, and the hero must slay the dragon of romantic love. The third stage begins when the hero separates from the seducer. She suffers the loss of illusion, but through the realisation that she must be her own saviour attains autonomy. In taking responsibility for her own life, the hero finds a new significance in work.

Journeying to the metropolis Bowen had met her seducer-prince. It is not difficult to cast Ford Madox Ford in this role, the famous writer and literary figure, the larger-than-life personality, twenty years her senior, the man to whom she wrote in 1919 that 'to have you really belong to me and to belong really to you is like coming home after a long exile'.[17] He certainly took Stella into a world of experience, gave her 'a remarkable and liberal education, administered in ideal circumstances', for which she proclaimed herself forever grateful, 'a privilege for which I am still trying to say "thank you"'. With the intellectuals, literati and artists, Bowen learnt to live among people who had replaced moral values with aesthetic ones, who did not regard themselves as having any obligations beyond developing their own egos and talents, who thought it 'quite all right to be dirty, drunk, a pervert, a thief or a whore', provided you had a lively and honest mind and the courage of your instincts.[18] But as Bowen was to learn, the mentor who initially served to rescue the questing woman, eventually became a barrier to self-development and autonomy. Thus, devoted as she was to Ford, Bowen became conscious of the loss of opportunity to develop her own talents, and when Ford began to look to other women to fulfil his needs, she embarked upon the last stage of her journey.

> To realise that there can be no such thing as 'belonging' to another person (for in the last resort you must be responsible for yourself, just as you must prepare to die alone) is surely a necessary part of an adult's education... But what a discovery it makes.[19]

Bowen had learnt that security built on others is a dangerous illusion, and this is the illusion that women are brought up to chase and to cherish. Falling out of love was as necessary a step in the attainment of wisdom as falling in love. And to liberate oneself from emotional dependence conferred the feeling of freedom, of integrity, 'of being a blissfully unimportant item in an impersonal world', 'of being queen in your own right', of experiencing 'true re-birth'. When Bowen left Ford, she moved from total devotion to and dependence on the great man to separation and self-reliance: 'but I couldn't have done it successfully without my painting'.[20] The remainder of her life was a continuous struggle to find the means to support herself and her daughter and to make a home, but her journey had achieved its goal of independence and autonomy. But the end of Stella Bowen's journey was something more. She is remembered as a woman of wonderful vitality, warmth and generosity, with a great capacity for making and maintaining friends. Artist Alice Halicka, who was a close friend of Bowen's in Paris, described her as the least egotistical person that she had ever known.[21] Australian historian Keith Hancock, who knew her in London in the later years of her life, described her as 'the most courageous, vital and harmonious personality that I have ever known', and wrote of her 'genius for living'.[22] This is the persona of the autobiography. In the last analysis, Bowen's most stylish creation was herself.

Stella Bowen's journey to Europe had given her a life unimagined and unimaginable in Adelaide. She portrayed its course and her expatriation as the product of chance, as without plan or purpose, a common thread in women's life stories. Carolyn Heilbrun has argued that women who wish a quest plot for their lives need to call upon events that accidentally, unconsciously transform their lives, change a conventional story into an eccentric one.[23] Chance is the protective colouring that hides the quest from the world — and from the self. Or if it is chance that turns trips into expatriation, that governs lives, do women's ways of telling stories allow its acknowledgment?

CHAPTER 9

Travel and Discovery of Self

*I wanted to move beyond the boundaries of myself, to
see, as Saul Bellow has written, if I was something other
than simply the product of an environment...In going to
Paris I longed not so much to reinvent myself or to leave
my country as to expand my known self, to blow apart
my known world.[1]*

It was not only to develop new talents, experience independence or find
new lands that women travelled; many, like Stella Bowen and Dora Birtles,
were also questing for new selves. The journey is not only an event, it is
also a metaphor. Journeys are both passages and rites of passage, the crossing from one state to another. A common expectation on the part of both
the traveller and the audience at home is that exposure to difference, to the
foreign, to the metropolis, will change the traveller. 'But how you have
changed' and 'But you have not changed' are common responses to those
who have returned from sojourns abroad. Stella Bowen had thought that
after sixteen years in Europe she would be unrecognisable to her Adelaide
relatives. Phyllis Downe was met when she arrived in London in 1939 by
an Australian friend who had already been there for some time; 'I didn't
recognise Midge, she looked so different — svelte and sophisticated'.[2]

The daughters of the élite and the socially ambitious had been sent to
Europe precisely to be transformed from colonial girls into genteel ladies.
In Paris with her companion William Blake, Christina Stead was equally
intent on metamorphosis from colonial caterpillar into European butter-
fly, elegant, *soignée*, chic — 'I am becoming the perfect Continental'.[3] In
these early days of growing confidence and of excitement in the trying out
of new, more sophisticated and enticing masks, she was anxious that the
new self be recognised and acknowledged at home. Thus she took a fellow Australian woman, who after three months in Paris was still 'simple,
colonial, unsophisticated', 'plus a strong accent' to the Casino de Paris,
complete with 'obscene wit' and 'beautiful naked bodies'.[4] The ines-
timably worthy Nettie Palmer was disconcerted when she met Stead in
Paris in 1935 by the latter's elegance, worldly air and accent — another
Australian had sacrificed her native speech. And the image presented to
Palmer was intended for export to Australia.[5] Stead's longing for transformation was mirrored in *For Love Alone* when Teresa Hawkins dreams of
her new life with James Quick, her employer and then lover in London.
He would make a woman of her, a brilliant woman, 'the Montespan of the

Nettie Palmer (Palmer papers, National Library of Australia).

Janet Mitchell (Nancy Adams, *Family Fresco*, Cheshire, Melbourne, 1966).

Joice Nankivell Loch working with a Quaker relief team among refugees (Joice Loch, *A Fringe of Blue: An Autobiography*, Murray, London, 1968).

Dora Ohlfsen before the war memorial 'Sacrifice', which she carved in Formia with Colonel Scipino of the Formia Memorial Committee. She is holding a plaque giving her 'freedom of the city' (Art Gallery of New South Wales).

Stella Bowen, *Self Portrait* (Private collection).

Grace Cossington Smith, Australia (1892–1984), *The Refugees* c. 1918, pencil drawing, 23.1 × 32.8 cm. Purchased with the Thea Proctor Memorial Fund 1972 (Art Gallery of New South Wales).

Australian girls in Rome, Indian style, in the 1950s.

Front cover (*Home*, December 1923).

Doris Gentile in Rome in the 1930s (Private collection).

Aileen Palmer (2nd from left), Barcelona, December 1936 (Aileen Palmer papers, National Library of Australia).

Dorothy Gibson at a school in the Soviet Union in the 1930s (Ralph Gibson, *One Woman's Life: A Memoir of Dorothy Gibson*, Hale & Iremonger, Sydney, 1980).

The ship sails (Holtermann Collection, Mitchell Library).

The trip to the Pyramids in the 1950s, Robin Porter.

Charmian Clift with her son on Hydra (Photograph Collection, National Library of Australia).

age', a Madame de Stäel, a Catherine the Great, 'no one who knew her would know her then; he would make her entirely over'.[6]

Travel was supposed to broaden the mind as well as smarten the appearance, as Gwen Hughes wrote:

> Travelling in foreign lands and learning to know their people should grow you wings of silver till you are no longer the crow that left home, nor yet a conquering eagle or a strutting peacock before the home folk, nor even a common domestic cock returning to strut the hen roost. No it's wings of silver the traveller should grow, illuminant with knowledge, for travelling with heart and mind open to learn should be transmutation of outlook, not from lead to gold, but from hard steel and concrete of every day modern living to wings of silver, the grey silver wings of a dove — harbinger of international good will and peace.[7]

Ida Haysom's thoughts on the last page of her travel diary, if less pretentious than the strictures of Gwen Hughes, are typical of the efforts of the travellers to sum up the impact of their wanderings and probably tell us more about the conventions of travel to which the women conformed than about individual evaluation of experience.

> It has been a wonderful experience, never to be forgotten. Our knowledge of the world and its people has increased and many of our conceptions and ideas have been greatly changed by our personal contacts.[8]

The transformation sought or undergone by the women who embarked on their overseas trips could go beyond style and outlook to include new understandings of self and the emergence of new selves, new forms of self-fulfilment. Self-discovery through an arduous search, as told in the journeys of Odysseus, Aeneas, and Columbus is a basic storyline of our civilisation. The archetypal journey is one where the young hero — and as is explicit in Joseph Campbell's work, the journeying hero was male — separates himself from the community and ventures into the world to encounter the challenges that allow him to forge his identity, to achieve manhood.[9] But once women became travellers, the archetypal narrative was available for the telling of their tales. They too could embark on a double journey where the experiences of leaving home, voyaging far away, placing themselves in new and challenging situations, engaging with alien modes of life, were also processes of self-testing, self-discovery, a revelation of purpose and future direction. This could also mean learning to cope with disillusionment and failure, of discovering limitations as well as possibilities.

Katharine Susannah Prichard, travelling on her own to London to establish her reputation as a writer, knew on arriving that her testing time had come.

> Gazing at the low-lying, green-filmed coast of England through a misty drizzle at dawn, and realizing all the tumultuous miles of sea between me and Australia, I felt homesick and afraid of what the future might hold. It seemed that I had left childhood and youth far behind; and must struggle now as an independent and adult person for the fruition of those hopes which had haunted me for so long.[10]

When the women were still young the trip coincided with and marked more dramatically the normal transition to adulthood. Henry Handel Richardson, who left Australia at the age of eighteen, later wrote that her three years in Leipzig 'stood for a definite break with the past'.

> From now on, instead of being merely a member of a family, I became a person in my own right. And a very different one from the aimless, ill-adjusted girl who had begun to feel herself the odd-man-out, and to judge people and things from that angle.[11]

Florence James's letters to her family narrate her first years in Europe as a process by which she developed her identity as a writer and as a woman. Engaged to be married when she left Australia, James came to represent her life at home as adaptation and conformity to the priorities of her fiancé. Having broken free, she now intended to develop her life according to her own agendas. She had crossed the world to 'reach a standard of values for my own life and the living which should be my own'.[12] Two years after she left Australia, Florence deployed a classic metaphor for change, the snake shedding its skin, to describe her enlightenment.

> It's curious. I feel as though I were snakes: I have sloughed off the skin of my girlhood & a romantic love that was so very fine in many ways. But underneath I have discovered something much richer & rarer, the possibilities of a woman. It is really I suppose the fruition of my two years of freedom. Suddenly I am full of new vigour, I want to write, write, write & my head is whirling with plans for work.[13]

Their travels placed women in new spaces, where often they were on their own, where they knew nobody and nobody knew them. While some may have found the experience frightening, it is striking how many revelled in both the anonymity and the challenge. When Winifred James's fictional persona Bachelor Betty arrived in London among all the 'strangeness', she felt free and confident.

> It does seem so funny to be in a perfectly strange place with altogether new people, and not a soul that belongs to your particular life up to now, within twelve thousand miles. It's like being born again when you're grown up; it's starting everything afresh.[14]

Alone in Harbin with no visible means of support during the Japanese invasion of Manchuria, Janet Mitchell felt liberated.

> And suddenly there swept over me the glory of lonely freedom. I had lost all
> security except what was in myself. I was on top of the world.[15]

The exhilaration conferred by the liberation of anonymity is a perennial
feature in stories that Australian women tell of their journeys. Thus the
language in a woman's letter of 1992 recalling an overseas trip of 1966–67
is hardly distinguishable from that of the women of her grandmother's
generation.

> As a 21 year old, my overseas trip in 1966–67 enabled me to break free of
> family ties for a while and at the same time 'live' some of my dreams. My
> most liberating moment was being totally alone in Paris living in a decrepit
> but charming hotel on the Left bank on the eleventh floor with pretty
> appalling schoolgirl French for communication. I was in a state of eupho-
> ria, having that feeling of 'no one looking over my shoulder'. It gave me a
> chance to discover myself, including the notions of romance that helped to
> motivate me.[16]

While self-discovery – development – transformation is a stock narrative line attached to travel, each woman has her own story. Three are now
briefly recounted: that of the young Nettie Palmer as told in her letters to
her family; that of her daughter Aileen Palmer, whose letters and unpublished drafts for novels a generation later reveal search for meaning for her
life in political commitment; and that of historian Kathleen Fitzpatrick
who in her autobiography recalled her time as a student at Oxford and its
impact on her self-definition.

When Nettie Higgins (later Palmer) graduated in French and German
from the University of Melbourne in 1910, her family offered her a trip
overseas. Their intention was for the trip to be a finishing experience, that
she should engage in cultural sightseeing, drink in 'the beauty of Italy.'[17]
While she did undertake the trip alone, she was chaperoned for the voyage. The protection of a chaperone had been advised by the friend who
was eventually to be her husband, Vance Palmer; he professed admiration
of her courage in venturing alone into the 'unknown heart of mysterious
Europe'.[18] But Higgins had her own ideas and plans.

Although Higgins portrayed the origins of her voyage to Europe as
lying in the initiative of others, she was engaging in a rite of separation
from her family. On the eve of her departure she wrote to Vance Palmer
that it was more 'horrid' for others than for herself.

> I'm glad to be going places where nobody will ever care if I live or die, and
> where I won't find my own photograph, literally or metaphorically, on
> every mantelshelf I see.[19]

The desire for a life of her own continued as a theme in her correspondence. As the voyage progressed, so did her sense of separation. She spec-
ulated that she was 'hard':

because it's a desperate thing to think too steadily about people in Victoria
who care for me more than I am able to care for anyone, I've almost come to
believe that those people don't belong to me except now and then when
something makes me write to them.[20]

Nevertheless, during the entire period of her stay she was punctilious in
her long weekly letters to her mother, and wrote regularly to her brother
Esmonde. The arrival of their return letters was of central importance to
her, as to so many questing daughters.

Doubtful before she left of her capacity for a life of sightseeing, in her
first months away Higgins interspersed tourism and visits to relatives
with attendance at public meetings and lectures. She also participated in a
summer school at the University of Marburg. During this time she lived in
a dense web of friends and acquaintances, especially after the arrival of
Vance Palmer. But she wanted more from her trip than the general cultural finishing her family had intended and was anxiously searching for
some purpose: 'I seem to have spent the last year in finding what I wanted
to do, and what some of my deficiencies were in that direction'.[21]

In January 1911, Nettie Higgins went to Berlin where she became a
student at the Institute of Phonetics, then run by an Australian, William
Tilly. Her intention in working for the diploma in phonetics was to gain
further qualification as a language teacher: 'I'll be more worthwhile in my
own self-confidence, and I think that awfully important in a teacher'.[22]
She had by then already agreed to marry Vance Palmer, although she was
not to inform her family of this decision until much later in the year. In
Berlin, Higgins was placing herself in an isolated and testing situation.
She lived at the Institute and the understanding was that students were
only to communicate in German, except in letters. Higgins took this
injunction with total commitment, even refusing to speak to Australian
friends who came to Berlin. Initially the rudimentary nature of her own
German meant that she was cut off from all but basic communication, and
her isolation was not eased by her preference for long solitary walks and a
feeling of lack of common interests with her fellow students. Higgins
recognised the importance of her experience of exile:

> this 'banishment' here's healthy in one way: it leaves one entirely without
> people to whom one is at all important. Nobody wants you for yourself, for
> nobody knows you except superficially: and nobody wants you on account
> of your relations for nobody knows your relations.[23]

But 'banishment' was also the experience of intense loneliness and introspection which she 'discussed' in her correspondence with Vance Palmer:
'you can't imagine how strange it is to have nobody to whom one can say
anything just exactly as you mean it'.[24]

Nettie Higgins's time of transition and experience of isolation in an unfamiliar place appears to have culminated in some sort of emotional crisis, reminiscent of literary models like that of Forster's Adela Quested in the grotto of Malabar, the moment of dissolution of self to achieve a new understanding and subjectivity.   .

> An unaccountable break-down came today when Mr Tilly was giving some of us a little oral exam. I collapsed as if I'd been six; and then remembered in surface things I'd been conscious of a good deal of loneliness lately, like a weight I couldn't shake off.[25]

It is not without significance that Nettie's 'breakdown' coincided with the arrival of spring, the season of rebirth, a spring that in Berlin was 'so visible and definite'. Involved in her crisis too was some kind of search for sexual identity. In recounting her breakdown to Vance Palmer, she added that Mr Tilly was 'a little too kind' and that this kindness was not dissociated from his consciousness of her as a woman.

> There's nothing bad about him and no possibility of it unless I were to make it very easy for him to be bad. And I won't do that. Only I wanted to tell you dear, not for you to worry about it, but because it's such a help to have a mate like you.

There is clearly more than one agenda in this story. When she was leaving Berlin at the end of May, Higgins wrote again that she now believed that Tilly's interest in her had been love. Her perception may have been accurate, but it may also have been the projection of a lonely woman in a highly emotional stage of transition, or of a young woman testing the waters. The interest of the director of the Institute was not the only 'adventure' that she reported to Vance Palmer. In Dresden for a three-day holiday, she explored the city in the company of a German who attached himself to her party on a steamer on the Elbe — a German who 'was nearly good enough for an Australian in his outlook': 'he liked me a lot, somehow and swore our friendship eagerly but not with anything tragic in it.'[26]

When in May 1911 the time came for Higgins to move on from Berlin to France for the second part of her preparation for the diploma, she was more settled, had begun to build up a social life. She felt that indeed she had changed. To her mother, she wrote that she had tried everything possible except family life, to Vance that she now had 'heaps of self esteem', 'a sort of trust in my own steadiness', that 'things happened and they changed me'.[27] Later in the year, after Higgins had passed her exams with considerable distinction, she commented again to her mother that travel had made her 'quite open-eyed and sensible'.[28]

Nettie Higgins's trip to Europe provided the context for her to separate from her family, to test herself in new and foreign environments, to try out new roles, to convert accomplishment into professional training, to establish herself as an independent woman. Sadly, it is arguable that the independence that she forged abroad did not survive her marriage to Vance Palmer and her return to Australia. Her time overseas was that brief moment for self before assumption of the gendered role of carer for others and protection and promotion of their talents. Thus Nettie Palmer became one of Drusilla Modjeska's 'exiles at home'.

A quarter of a century later, Nettie and Vance Palmer sailed again to Europe taking their two daughters, Aileen and Helen. Aileen Palmer's time in Europe, like that of her mother, is the story of a young woman's journey, search for identity and a life script, a journey that has been reconstructed with delicate sensitivity by Judith Keene from the fragments that make up Aileen Palmer's literary estate.[29]

Aileen Palmer's trip also followed her graduation in languages from the University of Melbourne. And just as her mother had wanted to do something more serious than spend all her time sightseeing, so too did Aileen Palmer. But whereas something serious for Nettie Higgins was the pursuit of academic qualification, for Aileen Palmer it was political activity. She had joined the Communist Party while a student at the University of Melbourne, and when the family arrived in London, she ignored art galleries in favour of participating in anti-fascist rallies and selling the communist paper, the *Daily Worker*.

> On Saturday I sold D.Ws (special Spain number) at mid-day, in the afternoon took Edith's friend, Peggy, distributing leaflets with me, posting them in the doors of houses in all the squares around these parts. In the evening went for a dry pub-crawl with another friend, and sold 26 D.Ws between us in one hour. Later this same friend came back, saying they were not selling D.Ws fast enough for the special drive, so she Peggy and I went and sold at Kings Cross Station till midnight. Sunday morning I leafleted and sold again, and in the afternoon Peggy and I went to the demonstration (in the Medical Aid Group followed by a loudspeaker).[30]

In one of the many draft fragments for an unpublished autobiographical novel, Aileen Palmer wrote that her mother lamented that she had brought two 'dummies' to Europe who were not making the most of art and antiquity. but she added:

> Still, a sense of the past affects us in different ways, and we weren't her contemporaries, but kids she'd brought up with a sense of the need to defend human rights in our time.[31]

Shortly after the family's arrival in Europe, Aileen Palmer moved to Vienna to improve her German, while her parents settled in the Catalan village of Mongat, fourteen kilometres north of Barcelona. In Vienna, Aileen Palmer came into contact with the opponents and victims of Nazism. When she moved on to Barcelona, through links with German-speaking exiles, she entered a network of young communists and partici-pated in political rallies, including one at which the future legend La Pasionaria spoke. In June she began working as an interpreter with the French team at the People's Olympics, an anti-fascist left-wing response to the Berlin Olympic Games. Aileen Palmer later tried to re-create the atmosphere of the last moments of democracy in Spain.

> When we went to Spain, it seemed a country of freedom, as the People's Front had just taken over the government, and women were let run around in short skirts and sandshoes, instead of all just being preserved on ice, for the tourists — an old spot of antiquity as it is now. Then I remembered that this was, after all, what I had come to Spain to experience: a sense of reawakening, ferment among the people that was said to be taking place in the country that had dreamed since the days of Don Quixote.[32]

In July 1936, after General Francisco Franco had staged his military insurrection against the government of the Spanish Republic, discretion seemed the better part of valour to Vance Palmer. Although of strong republican sympathies, he evacuated his family from Spain. His daughter was devastated; she desperately wanted to stay and left with great reluc-tance and only at her parents' insistence. Aileen Palmer had obeyed her parents, but the 21-year-old dutiful daughter had decided that the time had come to separate from the family and make her bid for independ-ence. While they lingered in Paris she went on ahead to London finding her own digs and hoping never again to hear, 'think how it would worry yer mother'.[33] And again one is reminded of the young Nettie Higgins's exultant anticipation of losing family and going to places where 'nobody will ever care if I live or die'. In London, Aileen Palmer threw herself total-ly into work with the British Committee for the Victims of Fascism. In the next month she went out to Spain as an interpreter and medical records keeper with the first medical unit that set up a hospital in the Aragonese village of Grānen, at the time under the control of an Anarchist group.

Human relationships were tense in Grānen, both within the hospital and between the hospital and the local commune. Nevertheless, this early period of the war was for Aileen Palmer a time of optimism and intense camaraderie, and her letters carry that same sense of euphoria and inten-sity of living that mark those of the women in Serbia in the First World War. In December, Aileen Palmer's unit was transferred south to join the Medical Services of the International Brigades, and for the next eighteen months, except for a month's leave in England, she was constantly on the move, in daily contact with death and destruction, desperately over-worked, desperately short of sleep. She was repatriated to England in

May 1938 and was caught — without regret — in Europe for the duration of the war. She spent the war in Britain working in London as an air-raid warden and ambulance driver during the Blitz. Her mother's illness and her sister Helen's summons brought her back to Australia in 1945 to assume the role of the dutiful daughter.

Despite the horror and the despair of her years in Spain and the failure of the just cause, Aileen Palmer later described her time in Spain as 'the springtime of my life', as a time when she was possessed by energy and drive, and most sustained by other people.[34] The emotions that she remembered are common, the exultation of a time when in danger and destruction, life is totally focused, totally directed, is given purpose and meaning. The same sense of purpose also underwrote her wartime life in London. As Judith Keene has argued, the Spanish Civil War was central to Aileen Palmer's personal development, 'the rock on which her political life was grounded'.[35] It was the depth of her political commitment to anti-fascist Spain that probably gave her the underpinning to sustain the drive to independence, to experience her 'first coming of age'. But Aileen Palmer had not escaped her parents.

As the daughter of Nettie and Vance Palmer, Aileen Palmer had lived from childhood in an environment that placed the highest premium on literary activity and achievement. She had grown up expecting and want-ing to write and thus was making her life in her parents' territory. In later introspection she wrote that she had 'to come of age' a number of times, and that perhaps she would not come of age in her own mind until she finished her book, 'a dutiful daughter's homage'.[36] From the early days of her repatriation to England in 1938, Vance and Nettie had urged Aileen to think of converting her experience in Spain into a novel. On her return to England, they were very happy to send funds for her support while she embarked on her writing career. As well as writing a short story and some poems, by November, Aileen Palmer had completed the first draft of her novel, 'Last Mile to Huesca'. In the course of revisions, her father inserted himself into her novel and hence into her past; on his suggestion, the pro-tagonists in the story set in a medical unit in Spain changed from a group of men and women to a young man from Queensland.[37] The manuscript, in whichever final version it was submitted, was not accepted for publica-tion. Judith Keene believes that the novel was at least as good as a number of similar works and attributes its failure to find a publisher to a changing political situation — Franco was in power, and public interest had shifted from Spain to the bigger war that was looming.

Aileen Palmer felt the novel's failure most of all for her parents, she felt she had let them down, and thus could never come of age. And her liter-ary estate is in large part composed of fragments and drafts of novels and short stories based on her family and her time in Europe. Back in Australia she lost purpose and direction, her mind drifting to the point where she spent much of the last 30 years of her life in a mental institution. Her writing suggests that her life had stopped when she came home; it was to Spain and the Blitz that she constantly returned: 'But life always takes you back to Barcelona. It is like a fatal motif in your life that you can never escape'.[38] The danger, the focus, the purpose of life in Spain and the Blitz transported Aileen Palmer away from her parents — and, more importantly, from herself. The pilgrim did not find holy ground again.

Nettie Higgins had found her journey to Berlin a challenging as well as an isolating experience. Loneliness and disappointment rather than exhilaration characterise the voyage of self-discovery and self-formation at Oxford in the early 1920s of Kathleen Pitt. While Nettie Higgins's journey has been tracked through the letters that she wrote at the time, Kathleen Pitt's story depends on the autobiography that she wrote almost 50 years later. Both women were graduates of the University of Melbourne and they also shared in serious purpose and scholarly ambition — not so much for place and preferment, but to do things well. The dream that accompanied Kathleen Pitt to Europe was that of Cambridge University:

> so off we went to Cambridge and found the 'Home' of our dreams in the peerless little city with its string of colleges, each like a jewel, laid out like a magnificent necklace on the green velvet of the 'backs'. What a marvellous place this would be to live in for two years.[39].

Cambridge in the flesh proved a bitter disillusionment. When she was interviewed by one of the keepers of the jewels, Pitt felt that she was treated with condescension and contempt; the response to her proffering of her University of Melbourne Bachelor of Arts was that American degrees were not much thought of at Cambridge.

If Cambridge proved too formidable for the colonial woman, on first encounter Oxford was less hostile. But the two years that the proud, but insecure, Kathleen Pitt, with her passion for literature and historical understanding, spent there reading history were far from happy. She felt doubly disadvantaged as a colonial and as a woman; she always felt the outsider. Her misery was compounded of cold, illness, bad food, loneliness, the cool indifference of her fellow students, poor tutors, the effort of completing the degree in two years, and a sense of social failure; 'during my two years at Oxford I never received an invitation to anything from an Oxford man'.[40] She found it difficult to adjust to the continuing discrimination against women and to the indifference of the gilded youth to the clever middle-class girls, an indifference confirmed in the memoirs of an Australian man at Oxford in the same period: 'We saw little of the women students. I never spoke to a woman student at Oxford apart from an occasional meeting or a Sunday tea party in a don's house'.[41] The background against which Pitt judged her social life at Oxford was what she recalled as the easy camaraderie of her days at the University of Melbourne where 'men students had quite liked the women students and mixed freely with them'.[42]

The account of another Australian woman who spent a year at Oxford in the early 1920s contradicts in some ways Kathleen Pitt's record. Future architect and writer, Mary Turner Shaw, was taken by her mother to be 'finished abroad', and decided after she arrived in London that she wanted to go to Oxford, which required a period with a crammer to gain entrance, since she had 'scorned' matriculation while at school in Melbourne. Her stay at Oxford lasted less than a year; she failed her first examinations. But the Oxford she had found 'was an unreal paradise peopled by far more articulate versions of the young men in blazers I had left behind': 'once again I was happily preoccupied in collecting from the letter rack envelopes bearing college crests and enclosing gracefully worded invitations to luncheons, teas, dinners, theatres and afternoons on the river'.[43] There were lectures and libraries, but 'there were also long summer days in punts on the river and winter afternoons dancing to a gramophone in somebody's room'. As a daughter of the Victorian squattocracy, Turner Shaw was probably more socially confident than Pitt, more at home with upper-class men, and she may also have been happy to play the role of decorative and diverting companion. Kathleen Pitt was looking for acceptance as an intellectual woman. Oxford was not strong on intellectuals in the 1920s.

Kathleen Pitt's autobiography represents her time at Oxford not only as social failure, but also and equally importantly as academic failure; the degree she took out was second not first class. Her experience did not live up to her expectations of herself nor did it conform to male narratives of Oxford as success, as time out in Arcadia. But Oxford influenced her life, and not only in negative ways; it introduced her to Henry James, whose writing was to become an abiding passion and informing element in her own writing, teaching and living. She also claimed that Oxford raised her political consciousness and took her into the left, and aroused her latent feminism. She 'learnt' too what true scholarship was and that if she herself did not have the potential, there was enough of 'that strange creature in me' to recognise, appreciate and foster the real thing.

> But essentially the Oxford verdict was just. I was not first-class, not an original or profound thinker and I would never set the Thames of scholarship on fire. But I was a worker, loved my subject, and had some imagination, some feeling for words, some gift for teaching. There was room, even in universities, for people with a vocation for teaching and now that I knew myself and my limitation I would never again aspire to a status beyond my capacity.[44]

Thus, the future academic who was a gifted writer invented herself first and foremost into an outstanding teacher and carer, a woman who generously fostered and promoted the talents and careers of her students. Many senior historians — male — successful in the academy as well as in the discipline readily express their admiration for and devotion to her.

Kathleen Pitt's experience of Oxford was then crucial in her formation of an identity that conformed to woman's role. It was her gender too that disposed her to accept outside classification and to blame herself for failure. Nettie Palmer's career was also that of carer, the guardian and champion of Australian literature and of its writers. She described herself as 'a very commonplace person'. Her letters to Vance Palmer as a young woman who had placed herself in a challenging and difficult situation in Berlin are full of self-doubt, denigration and deference. For the late-twentieth-century academic woman, there is sadness in reading Nettie Palmer's letters and Kathleen Fitzpatrick's autobiography, the more so when the latter is placed in the context of male recollection of salad days at Oxford. Any comparison can only be superficial since, for example, neither Keith Hancock nor Walter Crocker engaged in the public introspection or self-revelation, the laying bare of self-doubt and failure, of Kathleen Fitzpatrick's memoirs. Men rarely do. They tend to plot their life stories along other lines. The male record is far more of the externals of Oxford, indeed in Crocker's case that is all there is, the listing of the famous contemporaries, impersonal description. Hancock, like Fitzpatrick, was studious and purposeful, shy, status anxious, but he felt no sense of exclusion and he trod a charmed path, took the glittering prizes. Modest, certainly, but the record does not reveal self-doubt.[45]

In her odyssey of self-formation, Kathleen Pitt went to other places, made other discoveries. Places are haunted not only by individual nostalgia, but also by cultural memory, longing, desire. Dennis Porter, with a backward look to Freud, suggests that there is a sense in which a foreign country constitutes a giant Rorschach test, that we project onto places perhaps even more strongly than we project onto other people.[46] Unaware of Freud, Louise Mack had observed 'that places can change round', 'that land isn't a fixed quantity', 'that mystery and magic and romance can come out of our own brain and tinge anything you look at'.[47] Nowhere in Europe carries so dense a cluster of myths and associations as does Italy, the site of the Renaissance and of countless other rebirths, moments of insight, discovery.

> It was at Rome, on the fifteenth of October, 1764, as I sat musing on the Capitol, while the barefooted fryars were singing Vespers in the temple of Jupiter, that the idea of writing the decline and fall of the City first started to my mind.[48]

It was in a much less picturesque and romantic Roman space, the Piazza Esedra, that Kathleen Pitt experienced her moment of enlightenment and new self-knowledge Significantly, the day marked another rite-

of-passage, her twenty-first birthday. Pondering Horace's proposition
Caelum non animum mutant qui trans mare currunt, she recognised that the
immutable baggage we carry with us limits our capacity for development
and change, but also that travel does confront us with alternatives, other
ways, other values. In the Piazza Esedra looking towards Santa Maria
degli Angeli, her private revelation was her recognition of her affinity with
the classical rather than the romantic, apprehended in architecture, but
applying to all forms of culture and life, and symbolically representing
earth-bound, not sky-borne, stability not aspiration, 'scenes made to the
measure of man and humanised by his long habitation of labour in
them'.[49] Pitt associated the harmony of 'man' and nature as classical, but
once again it was also the longing of the denizen of the new society for the
security of a past, of tradition, of the sense of timelessness and belonging.

A generation later, Shirley Hazzard, portrayed herself as being transformed — reborn — in Italy; it was in Naples that she says she came to life
as a writer and a woman.

> It was a great revelation. It was like going to heaven. Bit by bit I began to have
> this great companion, the city of Naples, and of course to learn all sorts of
> things there — to change my way of looking at things, to enlarge my way of
> thinking about things. The year passed with as much interior development
> in me as the previous four or five years and perhaps even more. For one thing
> I became joyful ... really for the first time I knew what joy was. It became
> part of my life, I understood at last what that was . . . I should have said,
> when we were talking about changes that happened to me at Naples, I think
> perhaps the greatest single thing was the feeling of being restored to life.[50]

If Italy is a culturally endowed place of rebirth, we can have our
epiphanies anywhere — for Freud it was the Acropolis — and places
speak diversely to their beholders. Las Palmas in the Canary Islands as a
port of call was for Kathleen Pitt's family, for Florence James, and for many
other travellers in the 1920s, the first taste of Europe. After her ship
moored, Florence James 'spent the afternoon poking around the
squalidest town I've ever been into'. The Protestant James was disgusted
by 'the R.C. Cathedral'.

> It was big enough, massive, but tawdry inside, & the six fat monks chanting
> on one monotonous note before the high altar added no air of holiness, but
> made one think of the emptiness of the gold & silver within & the filth
> without. Where was God in the scheme?[51]

The impact of the Cathedral of Las Palmas was rather different on
Kathleen Pitt's sister, Lorna.

She recognised at a glance that the Cathedral of Las Palmas was centuries older than any building she had ever seen and that it was real Gothic, not a cold, deliberate nineteenth century imitation of it. The Cathedral, as it were, spoke to her, recognising her as an adoptive child of Europe, and she responded. In a sense Lorna passed out of our Australian lives, almost for ever, there and then at Las Palmas.[52]

Lorna Pitt was to marry an Italian and remain in Europe. Her story conforms to another journey pattern articulated by poet Peter Porter, that inwardly the traveller seeks a society that approximates more closely to the inner sense of self.[53] This is the dream of the person who does not fit at home, but it is also the alienation of the colonial, whose education and imagination has placed the real world elsewhere.[54] Educated by the sisters of the Sacré Coeur, studying European languages and culture at university, Lorna's first encounter with European culture was her return to Ithaca.

Interlude

Charmian Clift and Gillian Bouras

After 1948, the women who married foreign men on their travels no longer automatically lost their British nationality, although they were still liable to do so if they took out the nationality of their husbands.[1] Their children if born abroad had no right to British nationality or Australian citizenship. In marrying European, Middle Eastern and Asian men, the majority of the women were committing themselves to being no longer travellers, but aliens who must perforce adjust to societies of different languages and customs, gender and intra-family relationships.

> Another major area of adjustment was, naturally, that of mother-in-law and daughter-in-law relations. This, I quickly realised, resembled a mine field: the dangers, very real ones, were there, but they were hidden, and I was often unaware of the form they took. Conscious that I should not usurp Yiaia's place in her own home and kitchen, I was bewildered when she expected me to act as hostess to people I did not even know. When visitors came I was expected to wait upon everybody, even though I still felt a visitor myself. I was totally ignorant of her expectations, while she, I think, thought that daughters-in-law are, or ought to be, the same the world over. We did not, and do not communicate well.[2]

Thus began Gillian Bouras's life in Greece as a foreign wife.

The largest group of foreign wives were the women who met and married American servicemen in Australia during the Second World War. When the war ended, somewhere between 12,000 and 15,000 Australian women sailed to North America as war brides.[3] For the most part lower-middle- and working-class women, many still in or barely out of their teens, the war brides sailed to meet men they often hardly knew, to embark upon ways of life very different from those at home. The women adapted and failed to adapt, marriages survived and faltered. These are problems very much of individual circumstances. Foreign wives were in fact migrants facing many of the problems which migrants to Australia confronted and they adopted similar survival strategies. Thus Australian war brides in New York formed a club, and a group of Australian wives in Florence in the 1970s bonded together, organising dinners and picnics among themselves, creating a space where problems, grievances, regrets, loneliness, and feelings of homesickness could be aired among those who understood.

The postwar mass migration to Australia created other ways in which Australian women might become foreign wives. Gillian Bouras met and married her Greek husband in Melbourne in 1969. Over the next decade, Gillian and George Bouras made two trips to Greece to visit his family, and in 1980 they embarked with their two young sons on a six-month stay as a trial, to see whether they might settle. Six months stretched on and Gillian Bouras's home became a small village near Kalamata in the Peloponnese. Her third son was born in Greece. She has told the story of being a foreign wife within the narratives of migration and exile.

In moving to Greece, Bouras felt cut off from her past, her traditions, her identity. What she refused to lose was her language, and she was insistent that her children maintain their English. She could not bear the thought of having to communicate with them in any language other than her own. As a writer, she needed to remain totally anchored in the language in which she wrote. Consequently she would never speak Greek really well and so felt another kind of frustration; like all migrants she knew that intelligence and the ability to speak the official language are indissolubly connected in the bureaucratic mind.[4] And like all migrant mothers, she became on occasions an embarrassment to her adapting and conforming children. Yet in time, there was accommodation: 'I began to see that, although my world had shrunk in all sorts of ways, it had expanded in many others'.[5] There was also a realisation that one cannot go back to the place one left, as well as a growing appreciation of simple things:

> the sob of a donkey, the strangled yelps of what George calls 'trainee roosters', the colours, the rituals, the changes of seasons and the framework that the Greeks and the Orthodox Church have built upon them...and of the values of people who have nothing by the standards of the West, but who have much in terms of moral and spiritual values.[6]

She too came to have the 'Greek thing' and knew that she would never be free of it: 'for me, too, it would be a black and desolate fate to leave and never to return'.[7]

When Gillian Bouras became an expatriate in Greece, she was pursuing no dream, escaping no demons, fleeing no rejected home. She was simply doing what most women have done in history, following a man. Charmian Clift's journey to Greece conformed to another pattern, the flight from modernity, from civilisation and its discontents. This was a journey that gathered more and more participants with the intensification of industrialisation and modernisation, the journey that took D.H. Lawrence to Sicily, Sardinia and Mexico, the new-world fugitives of the 1950s and early 1960s to those parts of Europe relatively untouched by modernity, rural Greece, Spain, Portugal, the more remote parts of Italy, and their successors in the next generation to the villages of India. These were places where the living was cheap and the traditions of hospitality generous.

Charmian Clift's journey had begun in a flight to, not from, civilisation. London was her first destination. In 1963 expatriate writer Jack Lindsay reported that he had been told that some 32 000 Australians took off each year, that about half were persons who planned to stay abroad, and that a large proportion were members of the arts and professions.[8] Australia's intellectuals, writers and artists had long constructed themselves as fleeing a cultural desert, and the fugitives of the 1950s were but the latest generation to leave. Participants in that exodus included Peter Porter, Jill Neville, Cynthia Nolan, Sidney Nolan, Peter Finch, Pat Flower, Cedric Flower, Paul Brickhill, Loudon Sainthill, George Johnston and Charmian Clift. Looking back after her return to Australia in the mid-1960s, Charmian Clift recalled the mood of her departure.

> Australia, which we had left in the Jubilee year of Federation, seemed very far away. 'A cultural desert', we said (but only to other Australians), remembering it as being a distinctly unpleasant place in the immediate post-war years, more prosperous than it had ever been but paralysed by strikes..., cynical with the disillusionment of peace, and the taxi-drivers rapacious and the shop assistants rude and the licensing laws barbarous and creative nourishment scanty.[9]

She was later to have some second thoughts about her earlier perceptions of the place and the time that she left.

The exodus of the class of 1950 was no more peculiarly Australian than had been the departures of their parents and grandparents. The prevailing imperial and Eurocentric discourses still constructed the globe in terms of the centre and the colonies, provinces, villages. Canadians, South Africans, and West Indians flocked to London, another generation of Americans hung around the Left Bank of Paris. And to feel an outsider, an exile at home, to feel unrecognised, unrewarded, was still part of the identity of many artists as was the consequent search for 'home'.

> Expatriation is not 'outer', it is 'inner', not geographical but existential, it is a particular form of alienation, in which one feels displaced anywhere, and estranged from all others, who are recognised as normal.[10]

Unlike so many of the fellow fugitives from the cultural desert — and the established storyline — Charmian Clift and George Johnston did not embark upon a life of starvation in a garret when they arrived in London. Johnston went to London in 1951 as the head of the Associated Press office, which gave him and Clift a comfortable flat in Bayswater, a charlady, invitations to opening nights, book launchings and celebrity parties, and holidays on the Continent.[11] Although Charmian Clift was writing and publishing in London, her daily existence was very much that of the wife and mother, taking the children to Kensington Gardens and to sail boats on the Round Pond.

In November 1954, Johnston resigned his position and the family left London for Kalymnos, a barren island in the Aegean looking towards the Dardanelles, where the ever dwindling number of inhabitants made their precarious livelihood from sponge diving. A year later, they moved to Hydra, another barren Aegean island, but this time also picturesque, only forty miles from Athens and within sight of the Peloponnese. They bought a house on Hydra. Like Gillian Bouras, Clift's third child was born in Greece. Apart from a year spent in England in 1961, Clift and Johnston and their famiy lived in Hydra until 1964, when they migrated back to Australia. While in Greece, Clift wrote four books about Greece, two novels, *Honour's Mimic* and *The Sponge Divers*, and two travel narratives, *Mermaid Singing* and *Peel Me a Lotus*.

For Clift the move to the Greek islands was a declaration against the 'rat-race'.

> How to explain that we were civilisation sick, asphalt and television sick, that we had lost our beginnings and felt a sort of hollow that we had not been able to fill with material success. We had come to Kalymnos to seek a source, or a wonder, or a sign, to be reassured in our humanity.[12]

In their own relative poverty, and that of the villagers, Clift sought and found for a time the pre-industrial world, a life closer to nature, to the rhythms of the seasons, to the inevitable cycles of a life.

> Each day there is a little ceremony as a priest blesses each boat in turn as the empy barrels are loaded aboard, bidding it bring back good wine. The ritual, with its ancient implications, is somehow oddly reassuring.
>
> Dionysos is here, after all, and not in a dentist's chair in Athens. The old rhythm, the season's rhythm — of death, of resurrection, of growth, fruition, decay, and again resurrection — waxes and wanes in an inexorable cycle...to record the promise of joy implicit in those decks so anciently and beautifully murmurous with leaves.[13]

The simple peasant world gave her a life that was pared down: 'shedding so much we are stripped to our bare selves, lighter, freer, and impoverished of nothing but a few ridiculous little self-importances'.[14] And beyond this was the homecoming, on an island of sun, sea and sand, of the woman who had gown up wild and free on the south coast of New South Wales.

There is similarity in the responses of Charmian Clift and Gillian Bouras to the Greeces in which they lived: to the unfolding of the tasks of the seasons with their accompanying rituals; to the annual gathering and crushing of the olives in the Peloponnese; to the sailing and return of the sponge fleet on the islands; to the traditional customs of Christmas, Carnival, Easter, saints' days; to their encounters with the local people; to their poverty and fatalism; to their poverty and defiance through emigration; to the ceremonies of birth and death. Clift's third child was delivered by the local midwife and, while Bouras had a Caesarean section in an Athens hospital, the connections to the modern world were precarious. Confronted with the Greek way of death, the open coffin, the very public and uninhibited rituals of mourning, Gillian Bouras learnt that 'simple community has always known what the therapists have only recently begun to teach us. We must accept death: we must say goodbye in order that we ourselves can continue to live'.[15] In her village, it was the women who were the stage directors and protagonists in the ceremonies of death, women who knew nothing of going gently into the night, but who raged and raved. The paradox was the 'simultaneous acceptance and defiance of death'.[16] Watching an open coffin being carried through the lanes of Hydra, Clift was reminded that decay is inherent in all living things and that death is an event in life, as significant or insignificant as being born.[17]

In the writing of both Clift and Bouras, beyond the nostalgia for an Arcadian past, albeit a nostalgia that recognises the reality of grinding poverty — the maimed spongedivers who haunted the seafront at Kalymnos, the forced emigration of the sons of the Peloponnese — there is also once again that desire for belonging felt by an immigrant people whose way of life was imposed on their land rather than growing out of the soil, topography, rocks, seasons. Thus, while Bouras missed the Australian Christmas, she learnt new meaning in its winter celebration.

> I never thought of the Twelve Days of Christmas as being particularly ambiguous until I came to Greece. In the warmth and light of an Antipodean summer, it is easier to believe in all-pervading peace, love and good-will towards men, despite the many evidences of their scarcity. The Northern winter is stark, with the Birth the one ray of light penetrating the gloom. There is a sense of deadness, a feeling of life in abeyance, a physical and spiritual hibernation. Every Southerner should have a real Christmas, a Northern one.[18]

The northern Christmas was real not because it conformed to the Christmas cards of childhood, but because it conformed to the rhythm of the seasons. This longed-for harmony between nature and a people, which has been noted in the writing of earlier travellers, is a powerful and recurring theme in Australian writing from abroad.[19] It is to be found, for example, in the writing of Shirley Deane, who also forsook civilisation with her family in the 1950s and lived among peasant communities in Corsica, Southern Italy, Andalusia and Andorra.

Here, in southern Italy, the landscape is grand and vast, with its rocky crags, ravines and precipices, but on all sides traces of the hand of man are visible. For hundreds of years man has struggled with it, and conquered it. His handiwork is everywhere — every rocky crag, every pocket of earth, has its terraces of vines or olive trees, stretching wherever the eye can see into incredible, improbable places. By sheer length of centuries and weight of toil man has triumphed here, so one is at ease in the midst of grandeur. The landscape is humanized — not alien and untouched. Between man and the land there is mutual recognition and respect. Here, one is welcomed by the land as well as by the people.[20]

Much as Gillian Bouras longed for the company of her compatriots in her exile in Greece, her marriage tied her into the local community. She was caught in the gender relations that so overtly conferred power and prestige on men, and that circumscribed the lives of women. Charmian Clift, freely entering the local bars where the women of the island were never seen, was an outsider.[21] The presence of her children at the local school and their fluency in Greek, as well as her own daily interactions with the village, provided her with links into local life, but the language evaded her, and the tiresome official procedures to obtain residential permits in the climate of the troubles on Cyprus were a constant reminder of not belonging. The position of Clift as an outsider became more pronounced as more foreigners arrived in Hydra and an expatriate community was formed, which became the focus of her social ties.

When George Johnston took his family to Hydra, there were few foreigners on the island. The foreigners with whom the Johnstons mingled tended to be Australians such as Sidney and Cynthia Nolan, who followed them to Hydra for a time. But from the late 1950s, as Italy rushed into industrialisation and urbanisation, the fugitives, the drifters, the 'intellectual swagmen' from the over-developed world gravitated towards the Greek islands. Thus there emerged an expatriate community, which like all such communities fed on itself, copulated with itself, boozed with itself. Clift wrote of 'them', but she also realised that she was one of 'them', just as 'eccentric', just as tritely 'bohemian'.[22] They were her spiritual brothers, individuals who had retired from the rat-race, people who had the same cultural pattern, the same frame of reference, enjoyed the same jokes, shared the same concern about the trend of modern civilisation.

Yet I refuse to acknowledge them my spiritual brothers. For they have declared not only against the rat-race of modern life, but against life itself.
  They know no direction. They have lost all sense of wonder.[23]

In a sense, Clift was right in seeking to separate herself from the 'intellectual drifters'. While her Hydra narrative does conform in part to George Orwell's criticism of the works of expatriates like Henry Miller, in which people only drink, talk, fornicate, it also includes what Orwell saw as missing from Miller's writing, people working, marrying and bringing up children.[24] Clift's gender also placed her outside the expatriate writer/artist topos. She talked, drank and fornicated in an expatriate world, but in literature and experience this was a male world. The women in this world either did not write or, like the 'women on the left bank', avoided or were excluded from the male roistering.[25] Certainly Stella Bowen was involved in giving some of the legendary parties of that time and place, but, acutely conscious of her own illegitimate status and that of her child, she was intent on creating an oasis of stable family life, on respectability.

Slowly Clift and Johnston's dream of life on an island Arcadia turned sour when poverty was no longer choice, but necessity, when Clift faced the world of difference that lies between living simply because you choose to and living simply because you must. Poverty, the inability to make money from their books, Johnston's illness, alcohol, sexual infidelities and jealousies, the deterioration of the marriage, undermined and destroyed the dream. So, fifteen years after she had left Australia, Clift returned — as a migrant on a migrant ship.

Feeling something of a migrant, yet with memories of the place she had left, Clift was not sure about the answer to the comment that greeted her everywhere that the place had changed. Sydney was beautiful, with its tall skeletons of steel and concrete as romantic in its way as San Gimignano. Migration was making inroads, but 'the zestful and piquant influences of the Old World' appeared to have been rejected. The city still died in the evening and life retreated into suburbia, which to Clift appeared 'to be as stupefyingly dull as it was fifteen years ago, only more prosperous and therefore more smug'.[26] An outsider in Greece, Clift still self-defined as an outsider at home. Gillian Bouras, on the other hand, had created 'home' in two worlds.

CHAPTER 10

Travel, the Coronation, and Carnaby Street

I wanted to escape the things like suspender belts and lipstick and cotton-reel heels that had overtaken me in adolescence.[1]

The 1950s have been characterised as a time when women returned to the home, when their horizons contracted, when feminism and internationalism waned. Yet Australian women were still travelling to campaign for peace, for social justice, were still championing brave new worlds. Indeed, with the establishment of communist states in eastern Europe, and with the victory of the communist revolution in China, there were more brave new worlds.

Jessie Street packed her bags again in April 1945 and journeyed to San Francisco as the only woman adviser in the Australian delegation to the conference that founded the United Nations.[2] From there she went on to Toronto, to London, to the Soviet Union as an official guest, to Yugoslavia, to Germany, to Paris for the Women's International Democratic Federation Conference, and to Hyderabad as guest delegate to the All India Women's Conference. At the beginning of 1947, Street arrived in New York to attend the first session of the Status of Women Commission of the United Nations, where she was elected vice-president. She returned to New York in the following year for the second session, and while there participated in the revival of the Pan Pacific Women's Conference, the first meeting of which she attended in Honolulu in 1949. In the next year, the indefatigable Lady Street toured Scandinavia for the British Peace Council, and then attended the World Peace Conference in Warsaw, at which she was elected to the executive of the World Peace Council. She travelled extensively in Europe for the World Peace Council over the next few years and in 1953 was an official guest at Stalin's funeral. The pattern that Street had established in the immediate postwar years was to continue until her death in 1970.

Nor had her fellow campaigners from the interwar years put away their travelling cases; Bessie Rischbieth and Ruby Rich were still on the international conference trail in the 1950s. And Moscow had not lost its magnetism as the light on the hill for Dorothy Gibson. She returned to the Soviet Union in 1953 with her husband, who was seeking medical treatment for his asthma. Her experience in that year only served to deepen her sympathy for the people of the Soviet Union and their political system.[3] Nine years later, Dorothy Gibson was again in Moscow, this time for the World Congress for General Disarmament and Peace, where her fellow delegates included Jean-Paul Sartre and the Chilean poet Pablo Neruda. She made further visits in 1967 and 1971.

Among those who toured China was writer Dymphna Cusack.[4] While Cusack had visited Ceylon and India in 1935, it was not until 1949, when she was in her forties, that she embarked upon the European journey. She spent the next twenty years abroad, living after 1956 for the most part in the social democracies of Eastern Europe — the Soviet Union, the German Democratic Republic, Hungary, Yugoslavia, Albania. She was to write two travel books about her time in Eastern Europe, *Holidays Among the Russians* and *Illyria Reborn*.[5] A sympathetic, but not uncritically enthusiastic, champion of the communist system, Cusack's peregrinations through Eastern Europe had practical as well as ideological underpinnings.[6] Translations of her books had sold well in the communist bloc, and thus she had currency to use up.

Dymphna Cusack, like Catherine Helen Spence, travelled to understand people and social conditions. And like the reformist travellers of earlier in the century, she too noticed poverty and squalor, and was outraged. She spent the terrible European winter of 1955–56, 'the worst winter perhaps since Cicero', near the central Italian town of Formia, where she would have seen the war memorial that Dora Ohlfsen had carved. Cusack wrote of the terrible plight of the peasants, of unemployment, of poverty, of women 'who take off their shoes when they reach the asphalt to save them for the rough tracks'.[7] She was repelled by tourists prattling about picturesque poverty, and was appalled by the unconcern of the Italian rich for the suffering of the poor, by feudal attitudes that gave her a new perspective on social hierarchy in Australia. In Formia, Cusack was working on her novel *Picnic Races*. She later wrote:

> Italy was probably one of the best places I could have chosen to write *Picnic Races* because the contrast between the egalitarian attitudes of a small Australian country town — whatever its snobberies — was such a terrific contrast to the semi-feudal attitude of the Italian signori towards the peasants and workers.[8]

It was her anti-fascism, socialist commitment, and fears for the future that led to Cusack writing another novel while in Europe, *Heatwave in Berlin*, which had as its themes the survival and resurgence of Nazism and the culpable innocence of the new world. Like Gillian Bouras, Cusack's protagonist Joy married a European immigrant. Her German husband had arrived in Australia in 1950 claiming to have fled from Germany to

Austria in the 1930s. In 1960, at Joy's insistence, they visited her husband's family. In Berlin, Joy slowly and unwillingly discovers that her husband's wealthy and important family had been among the chief supporters of Hitler and were still fervent Nazis, and that her husband, albeit reluctantly, had been a member of the Hitler Youth, a sixteen-year-old conscript in the Wehrmacht, and a participant in atrocities. When she bitterly attacks her husband for his deception, he points to the self-deception of her insistent innocence and complicit ignorance.

> 'Till we came back here I loved that girlishness in you. That innocence of what the world really is — so unlike my own tormented soul. I loved even your very British talent for hiding your head in the sand when you can no longer avoid the ugliness before your eyes'.[9]

In the 1950s women clearly still travelled with social and political commitment and agendas, but, like Dymphna Cusack, they were women whose personae had been formed in the context of first-wave feminism and the struggle to destroy fascism and maintain peace in the interwar years. Before her death in 1954, Miles Franklin had looked in vain for the next generation of young women to take up the cause.[10] Women who grew up in the immediate postwar years and the 1950s were subject to the pressures of the cold war, to virulent anti-communism, and to the threat of nuclear war. They were the objects of an enormous propaganda campaign, which pushed them into early marriage and motherhood, into consumerism, into finding identity and obtaining status and respect in the role of good wife, mother, housekeeper and homemaker. In these circumstances, political commitment and feminism were weak among young women in the 1950s and early 1960s.

If they did not for the moment travel to change the world, the young women who embarked on overseas trips in the postwar years packed their trunks for many of the same reasons that had motivated their mothers and grandmothers — to see the sights, to acquire a little foreign language and culture, to be stamped with the overseas imprimatur, to be turned into ladies through European finishing schools and presentation at Court, to study art and music, to gain higher degrees and professional training, to have their talents developed, recognised, acclaimed and rewarded, and, increasingly, to go on holidays. The manner of their going had changed in that most were less curtailed, less chaperoned, enjoyed more freedom and independence. And the ways in which they could write about their experiences began to change even more. Travel as the romantic quest for love and as a journey towards the loss of innocence — sexual and otherwise — became more common and explicit as a female storyline, as illustrated in autobiographical novels like Jill Neville's *Fall-Girl* and Barbara Hanrahan's *Sea-green* and *Michael and Me and the Sun*.

My world was self-enclosed, a formal garden that never knew aphis or
mildew, canker or thrip or gall. At night, I slept soundly, chastely, in a room
scented with lavender in little bags, roses in a cut-glass vase.

I crossed the sea in a ship. And on the ship I lost something. Hands that
were cold ripped something precious away.

And now, in another country as snow flies at the window and icicles hang
from pipes, I falter — snared. It snows and I worry about the birds.[11]

The dominant responses and reactions of the women were much the
same as those of previous generations. Their educational formation and
family traditions were still predominantly British. They still moved in an
imperial and colonial world; culture and history were to be found in the
metropolis. Britain was still the main goal of travel, the centre of the world,
'a dream come true'. Literature still constructed imaginary places; the
romantic idea of London that the protagonist in Patricia Rolfe's novel, *No
Love Lost*, carried with her from Australia derived from lectures at university given by a professor who had 'once taken tea in Bloomsbury when the
Woolfs were there'.[12] There was still the 'tremendous thrill' of seeing the
places 'I've heard so much about and read about'.[13] In the years of Mr
Menzies, the Coronation and *the* Royal Visit, Britain loomed as large as
ever — and perhaps even more than in the interwar years — in the
Australian imagination. Women brought up on Anne Matheson's column
from London in the *Women's Weekly*, and on 'Crawfie's' *The Little Princesses*,
waxed enthusiastic over Royal rituals and sightings: to see 'the Queen and
princesses for the first time is really indescribable. They're all so beautiful
and gracious'.[14]

It was 1953 that was *the* year of royal fervour, and thousands of
Australians journeyed to Britain for the Coronation of Elizabeth II.

I prepared the lunch basket that night, and we had all the extra clothing —
coats, umbrellas and a waterproof sheet in readiness for the great day. We
must be in our seats in the Mall at 6am. Three-thirty to the minute we both
jumped out of our warm beds, dressed hurriedly, snatched some sort of
breakfast, filled our thermos flasks, and off we set up the hill to the Tube station. Everyone seemed to be up and about, all the houses showed signs of
activity.

On the first Tube at 5am for Victoria Station we felt in very high spirits,
but at the same time very cold and damp.

Leaving the station we walked with thousands (it seemed like millions)
down by the side of Buckingham Palace grounds and on to the Mall.

Finally the real day began.

Then came the glorious gold coach, and through the glass sides we could
see the Queen and the Duke of Edinburgh so well. Drawn by marvellous
grey horses, all exactly matching, it was indeed as though a fairy-tale had

come true. The harness on the horse carriages and the saddlery and the trappings on the mounted cavalry are beyond description here. Just as the Queen passed a glimmer of sunshine came through the clouds, which lit up the lovely golden coach. The footmen, coachmen, postilions and the wonderful horses made a sight we could never forget.[15]

In these immediate postwar years, admiration and affection for Britain were reinforced by the narratives of the Battle of Britain, of the gallant little island that had suffered so much in its lone stand against the demonic threat and reality of Nazi Germany. Recalling her visit to London in 1959, Jill Ker Conway wrote that to see St Paul's or to hear Big Ben was to be reminded of the years of her childhood when the family had clustered around the crackling radio to hear the impeccable BBC accent announcing 'This is London calling', 'in tones that conveyed British determination to resist the evils of Nazism to the end'.[16] Visitors to London encountered the vast craters gouged by bombs; they brought and received food parcels and queued for ration cards.

I first saw England in the early months of 1951 with late winter still gripping it harsh and the aftermath of the war still glumly apparent. We queued for everything, even Welfare State codliver oil and orange juice for the children, and people looked dank and shabby and terribly meek.[17]

Who could complain?

Beloved London, now shattered and burnt, is no longer the city of romance and adventure we knew, but it is a city of greater romance, of greater adventure, than we ever dreamed in the far-off days of five years ago. It is a city of pluck and determination, of steadfast courage in the face of continual disaster, a city whose unconquerable spirit has been an inspiration to the whole world.[18]

But Charmian Clift wondered how it was 'that these same meek people, meekly queuing, could have been capable of such heroism so very recently'. The 1959 self that Jill Ker Conway later constructed was more critical of the myths that she had absorbed in the wartime broadcasts of the BBC. Repelled by the British class system and its upper echelons in fashionable West End restaurants:

I would find myself gazing around at the other patrons, wondering which pink and well-fed face belonged to someone who had been all too ready to collaborate, too pro German to believe any of those ridiculous fabrications about the persecution of the Jews.[19]

War and its aftermath could influence travel and attitudes in Europe as well as Britain. It was to visit the grave of her brother, an RAF pilot shot down in 1942, that Edna Kerr visited Norway in 1959.[20] Jessie Traill, who

had witnessed the havoc wrought by the First World War in northern
France, returned in 1946 once again to encounter the aftermath of death
and destruction.

> Then there was that day in Rouen — my saddest day in France.
>   The whole of the city from the Quayside to the Cathedral is just one dev-
> astation of stones and rubble and no beauty of flowers to soften it.[21]

Edna Kerr was typical of Australian women in postwar Europe in feeling
uncomfortable in Germany, in wondering how the Germans felt about
their Führer and the devastation that they had wrought on the rest of
Europe. Few, however, were as explicit in their anti-German sentiments
as Mary Kent Hughes who was incredulous and utterly horrified when 'a
blonde beast' on her train in Germany informed her that Australia was
accepting German immigrants.[22]

Like their predecessors in Britain, most women in the 1950s enthused
over primroses and bluebells, buttercups and daisies.

> The South of England! Those magical words which for evermore will bring
> to my mind pictures of shadowy woods carpeted with bluebells, tranquil
> fields aglow with buttercups, age-old villages with thatched cottages, and
> hedgerows everywhere along the roadside studded with wildflowers.[23]

And as in the past, while admiring this enclosed, secure garden landscape, many of the women recalled with appreciation the less cultivated,
more austere and open landscape of home.

> The English country is really lovely especially seeing it for the first time.
> Everything is so green and it is all so tidy, the fields and trees are so very neat
> and it is all very perfect perhaps too perfect to one used to untidy Australian
> bush.[24]

The next generation, true to their origins in the land of Sunlight soap,
also complained about dirt, smells, and the non-Australian hostility to
fresh air and frequent bathing. Since Saturday was still the weekly bath
night in London, Friday night rush hour on the London underground
was something to be avoided by sensitive Australian noses. Edna Kerr
found it hard to become accustomed to the fact that in many countries 'a
bath is considered a luxury'. She would have liked to describe the variety
of toilets that she had visited, 'but such details would not be suitable for
general publication'.[25] But clean Australians were defeated by their
encounter with the bidet on the Continent.

> We decided to go to bed and had great fun deciding if the 'thing' in the bath-
> room was a la or not. Shaped a bit like one, quite low down but equipped
> with a plug and 2 taps, H&C which definitely flush. I said it was a W.C. but
> as there is also a place for soap Helen said its not. However we used it as

such and then the woman returned and said she'd show us 'la toilette' which is a dinky di la and goodness knows what the other thing is![26]

And if disturbed about European standards of cleanliness, the women still worried about their Australian accents and felt uncomfortable in a society in which class divisions were more obvious than at home, and in which their own position as colonials was uncertain.

While women continued to travel on diverse and varied journeys, the 1950s and 1960s are now particularly associated with one form, the working holiday.

> The year 1950 marked the beginning of 'The Great Adventure', a working holiday overseas. In these days when young people set off for a three week holiday overseas, travelling by air and sometimes carrying only a backpack, it is hard to imagine the excitement and mystique attached to an overseas trip then. Wartime austerity was easing in Britain and it seemed that the goal of most unattached young Australians was to save enough to travel by ship with the aim of working for a while before hitch-hiking around Britain and Europe.[27]

The mythology of the working holiday clusters around the 1950s and 1960s, but the event was well in place before the Second World War. From early in the century young Australian women had begun to travel in pairs or trios to see the world. Women with less money had found a means to travel as governesses, and in the 1920s and 1930s the working holiday became established as a mode of travel, although there were still many families who were critical and suspicious of such enterprise, or who forbade such adventures to their daughters. In her memoirs Dorothy Knox, the former headmistress of the Pymble Presbyterian Ladies College, recalled that when she decided to spend a year abroad in 1927 on a working holiday, it was not a common practice.[28] Janet Mitchell, in a 1931 article entitled 'Budgeting for Travel' provided an example of a business girl who was determined to travel.

> Picture a business girl earning four pounds a week, with no other resources, delicate and with one treasured dream — to go to Europe and earn her living there. When I first met her, she was living in one room in Darlinghurst, her total expenditure for food and clothing kept down rigidly to less than half her salary. It was in March that we met, and her goal was to sail in December. And sail she did, her total capital some £20, a few good introductions, and her personality.[29]

Writer Nancy Phelan went to England in 1938 in adventure mode. On arrival she immediately looked for work, becoming a waitress for tips only at the Quality Inn in central London before moving on to become a demonstrator for Pears soap in a series of Midland towns.[30] But in the

1930s jobs were not always so easy to find. Janet Mitchell's business girl did not immediately walk into a job. She 'had two or three weeks of intense anxiety, of wearying days and tormented nights' before finding work. Nurse Elizabeth Burchill, who arrived in London in the mid-1930s, had equal problems: 'Work was scarce. It was harder being alone. I did not have the knack of getting around the great metropolis to the best advantage and it was harder to cope with difficulties alone'.[31] Her attempt to place her name on the books of an exclusive nursing agency run by Noel Coward's mother failed, and it was only after walking miles each day seeking work, and when her money was almost gone, that an Australian introduction secured her work as a staff nurse in the Venereal Diseases War Unit at West London Hospital in Hammersmith.

What distinguished the postwar working holiday was the unprecedented number of young women with limited — often very limited — means who set out for Europe. Many, perhaps the majority, of the shoestring travellers were the first in their families to go overseas. They were embarking upon adventures beyond the expectations, if not the dreams, of their mothers and grandmothers. The new affluence of the postwar years allowed fledgeling nurses, teachers, secretaries, and physiotherapists to make the overseas trip. Cheap berths on the returning migrant ships meant that savings did not have to be great. Migration controls had not yet come into place in Britain, and Australians could still enter the mother country with all the rights of the native born. I was not alone in exercising my first vote in a British general election. But more important, there were no barriers to working. Jobs in hospitals, schools and offices, were plentiful and easy to come by because we all knew that the English did not know the meaning of work and efficient breezy Australians were in demand — at least for the jobs that no one else wanted.

In the departure of the thousands of young women in the 1950s and 1960s, there was much that was convention and fashion. If by her early twenties a woman had saved the fare and was not married, she took off. Their exodus was both a product and subversion of prevailing ideologies of womanhood and domesticity. Postwar Australia wanted its brides young, its wives fecund and in the home. At the same time as more Australian women were being educated, there was no commensurate expansion in opportunities to deploy their knowledge and ambition. Men were defined by occupation, women still by marital status. Society and culture remained firmly masculinist, even if its codes were transmitted by powerful domestic matriarchs. Thus away, abroad, over there, beckoned women with ambitions to be something other than wife and mother. And for those who had not yet learnt that women might have such ambitions, the trip promised a moment of independence before taking up the preordained destiny of home and Hills hoist.

It was women who predominated in the exodus of the 1950s and 1960s in circumstances that were both positive and negative. The trip to Europe was not quite such a prevalent convention for young men who had to establish careers and save the deposit for the home and Hills hoist. Their moments of liminality were briefer, but more frequent and long term — the pub and the club. But the option of a proper career, let alone of the pub and club, was less available to women, so they had little to lose by meandering off for a year or so. And because their destinies at home were more restricted and circumscribed, like their grandmothers and mothers they had more to gain abroad. If the men of Clive James's and Barry Humphries's time and place ridiculed and despised the Australia that they were leaving, women had even more reason to flee.

To refuse the suburban marriage was subversion, and it was also still failure. Far from abating in the wake of first-wave feminism and the progress of the twentieth century, the shame attached to spinsterhood revived with a vengeance in the postwar years. Artist Janet Alderson, who first left Australia in the 1960s and decided to move permanently abroad in 1972, recalled that Australia was not a good place for her because she was single.[32] The mothers of Barbara Hanrahan's questing women filled their weekly letters with news of the engagements and marriages of the local girls, and wondered wistfully when they could expect to be the mother of the bride. The mother of Patricia Rolfe's Victoria fussed that half of her daughter's schoolfriends were already married, that there would not be any suitable men left. So the overseas trip continued to provide the escape route for those who did not, could not, or would not make suburban marriages, and for those who did not, or did not want to, conform.

The nineteen-year-old Jill Neville travelled to London in 1951. In her novel *Fall-Girl*, the story of a young Australian woman in London in the 1950s, the protagonist is asked the usual question of why she had left Sydney. One answer to the question encapsulated much in a single image: 'I left because I didn't look good in a bathing costume'.[33] Her flat-chested body made her the butt of adolescent male taunting and linked her to the complaining, kill-joy 'old maid' next door. Her mother put down the neighbour's behaviour to frustration, but 'I knew that this had a lot to do with her flat chest'. Thus Neville's heroine also 'walked her way to London', scrimping and saving to move forever to a place where beaches were not important. Barbara Hanrahan's questing art student, Virginia, left Adelaide for a London where 'the sunburnt culture of health and youth and mediocrity she'd left was missing'.[34] The desire or need to escape the mundane continued as a powerful force fuelling women's travel.

The custom of the working holiday was to travel like Rolfe's Victoria with a friend or friends and a return ticket. The destination and base was

London, where groups of four or more rented basement and attic flats in
that area of London around Kensington and Earls Court soon labelled
Kangaroo Valley. At night the floors of the flats were often covered with
the bodies of other Australians who were passing through.

> If any Australian girlfriends of the others suddenly turned up in London,
> they slept on the floor in that room. Sometimes the flat was full of strange
> girls but Carolyn and Val and Peggy were saving to go on the Continent and
> extra girls were welcome because it meant that there were more of us to
> share the rent.[35]

The alternative to the open-house flat was the bed-sitter — which
required coins in the meter for heating and where the window ledge was
the refrigerator. Autumn and winter were spent in London working and
saving, and consuming unwholesome food, unwholesome because it was
cheap — and English. Thus the women worried about getting fat and did
get fat.

> Food is so foody here we eat up big on cakes and sweetstuff to make up defi-
> ciencies in meat. I get fat. I must not get fat.[36]

This London of the young Australians was a colonial world of the
Overseas Visitors Club, Australia House, the Down Under Club, the
Zambesi Club, and Kiwi House, of Australian dentists, of the search for
the Saturday-night parties in the flats of the children of the white
Commonwealth. Faye, Barbara Hanrahan's postal clerk, who lost her vir-
ginity on the voyage to the ship's hairdresser and thus received a free
'perm', lived in a flat behind Olympia, but she

> longed for the neon lights of the Earls Court Road where there was a party
> every week full of incredibly pleasant guys (Aussie and not just after one
> thing); where places had names like Kiwi Court and also Kangaroo.[37]

These were the parties wonderfully satirised by Patricia Rolfe in *No Love
Lost* at which Esme Birdwell lit fires of gum leaves and recited Henry
Lawson, and Australian males searched methodically, but in vain, for top-
ics of conversation beyond 'how to hitch-hike, the Down Under Club,
how beaut it will be to get back to good old Auz and where to buy good
old Auz beer in London'.[38]

Barry Humphries lampooned the sisters of Bazza Mackenzie for their
failure to establish real contact with the natives, but their lives in fact
touched and were touched at many points by the world around them; in
their jobs as temps and supply teachers, by weak tea in ABC and Lyons
cafes, by Wimpy Bars, by their forays into Marks and Spencers to buy
underwear — black not so much for allurement as to hide the effects of
London smog, by their first sightings of Indians, West Indians, Pakistanis,

West and East Africans, by the new sounds emanating from Liverpool, by the new haircuts from Vidal Sassoon, by the new geometric dresses from Mary Quant, by the BBC and *That Was the Week That Was*, by Portobello Road and street markets.

> Each night Virginia caught the Tube — Central Line from Holborn to Shepherd's Bush — and walked back the way she'd come. Sometimes she was in time for the market, and forgot her loneliness amongst black faces under flossy haloes of hair, lurid red meat in the Pak butcher's, green bananas, clove humbugs and liquorice torpedoes. She felt just the same as everyone else.[39]

The mid-1960s were the time of the Profumo affair, of Christine Keeler and Mandy Rice-Davies, when the British discovered sex, when the world discovered the Pill and Barbara Hanrahan's Australian girl in London 'lay awake in bed and wondered if anything was wrong with me. I still hadn't done it and I was twenty-three years old'.[40]

> Sex had got into my head: the sex of London, that had nothing to do with the Marriage Guidance Council, was always nagging at me. Sex was in those paintings I saw that day — sex had even got into the tin of frankfurters. Sex was in the newspapers and the surgical appliances shop; sex was in the underclothes ads on the Tube, in the dolly dresses, in pop songs.[41]

Patricia Rolfe's Victoria had her London affair — with an aging Australian expatriate — but it was not quite what she had been seeking. She had wanted to 'store up tender memories of a love affair in London, a window facing a square, cold and fog in the street and inside everything warm and safe'.[42] But Victoria, like so many of her predecessors, also revelled in the anonymity of London, where nobody cared about you; 'in a city of ten million, you could have a dozen love affairs and no one would find out'.[43]

With spring came the exodus from London. Cars and vans were hired to tour England. In the summer the vans moved to the Continent, while the more daring or indigent thumbed their way up and down the motorways of Europe. The goal was to go everywhere from Bergen to Barcelona, to gobble up everything in what was felt to be the one-off opportunity, to find the odd adventure with Giovanni or Juan, which could be later remembered and clothed in romance — or irony — for the telling. The car or van was usually stocked with Vegemite, baked beans, tampons, and all the other essentials of life of which backward foreigners were ignorant. Many of the travellers' tales from the 1950s and 1960s come from the experience of hitchhiking, then a common means of traversing Europe. Less dangerous than today, hitchhiking saved money, offered adventure and placed the participants daringly far outside the normal pattern of their lives.[44] They would hardly have hitchhiked at home.

While the young women may have been taking their time out, close contact was kept with home as postcards, letters and slides flowed south as witnesses to the trip, and the arrival of mail from home was a featured event in diaries. After a year or so it was time to go home. Emotions varied from anticipation, excitement and relief to reluctance and despair. What was still important was to demonstrate that one had changed, preferably by the acquisition of some patina of sophistication, or at least by arrival with shoes and bags from Italy, in new fashions to impress the out-of-date at home.

> I'd listen to them planning their routes on the Continent, and deciding what they'd wear when their ship docked at Sydney: the hat, the shoes, the gloves, the handbag — they were saving up, dreaming of every last detail for when they arrived home looking like different people.[45]

The model outlined above applies to many and to none. It is the model that became in time the subject of satire, such as with Barry Humphries's Debbie Thwaite.[46] The elastic number of physiotherapists sharing a basement flat in Kangaroo Valley, centring their lives in the Overseas Visitors Club and touring Europe in a Mini-Minor covered in sacred emblems was the latterday manifestation of the nineteenth-century Australian girl cracking her stockwhip and hollering 'Coo-ee' across Hyde Park. The meeting and mating of Australians in Kangaroo Valley, if a subject for satire, was neither new nor surprising. As early as the 1860s a character in Catherine Helen Spence's novel, *Mr Hogarth's Will*, commented on the tendency of Australians to cluster together 'even though they were not much acquainted in the colony'.[47] Immigrant groups, temporary and permanent cling together, provide solace, companionship, access to networks, housing and work, whether Italians in Leichhardt, Vietnamese in Cabramatta, or Australians in Earls Court.'

There are infinite variations on the theme of the overseas trips of the 1950s and 1960s. Many women, like Barbara Hanrahan's Faye, were miserable abroad. With insufficient savings or wages, they lived in squalid conditions far below the standard that they were accustomed to at home. They were lonely and homesick. Their lives centred around letters, those they wrote and those they received. Overseas was no fun, the British and the foreigners awful. But would home be any better? Others, like the mother and daughter whom Edna Kerr met while touring England, were making the trip strictly for status capital; they were bored and they could not rest because they had 'to get on with this travelling and get it over so that we can get home'.[48] And opposed to those whose Australian identity became more important and strident abroad was 'the sort of Australian who stayed in London, becoming more English than the English'.[49]

London was still 'home' and thus not a place for escape for the women who, like myself, crossed the Channel, not for a quick tour to see the sights, but to find new ways of speaking, living, and loving, in Paris and Rome, in Munich and Lisbon. We flocked to the institutes for foreigners in Perugia and Florence, the Alliance Française in Paris, the Goethe Institutes in Germany. We supported ourselves in the poor girl's version of the finishing school, the au pair job. Experiences as au pairs ran the full gamut from undreamt of conditions of luxury to equally undreamt of conditions of squalor, from freeloading to exploitation, sexual and otherwise. In Paris free accommodation could be gained in the tiny unheated maids' cells that lie under the roofs of those grand apartment buildings in the VI, XVI and XVII arrondissements in return for house-cleaning or child-minding. Giving English lessons to private students or in language schools — lessons which came with the assurance that the accent was of the most correct variety — was another standby for minimal survival on the Continent.

Patricia Hopper's diary tells the insouciant story of two Australian girls who rather haphazardly took au pair positions with French families in 1951.

> We will go to Brittany with them for 3 months' summer holiday and apparently all we have to do is keep the children happy and content … We couldn't understand if we are to live in Toulon or Toulouse, rather typical of us we don't even know where we are going! However it is a great chance and only 6 months so we will go and always be glad afterwards. Think of the French we'll know then.[50]

When the Australian girl from New England arrived in Brittany she found that the beach place of her French family was an estate of about ten acres, with three houses, a tennis court, an orchard, boats, and a private beach. With her *haute bourgeoisie* Madame, and the three not overly cooperative children who were in her charge, she learnt to cope with French customs and manners, with the rituals of handshaking and flirtation, with formal dinners at which seven wines were served and the parish priest was present. She learnt to appreciate French food. But her diary also records many moments of loneliness, her dependence on letters from home. In the midst of her new life, she remembered on 10 September that it was the night of the Bachelors' and Spinsters' Ball in Inverell.

Six months to two years may have been the norm for the working holiday, but there were other patterns. Some women, like Jill Neville's 'Fall-Girl', were intent on permanent expatriation when they left Australia. And as was the case for preceding generations, events could overtake inclinations. Sylvia Foley, the protagonist in Jessica Anderson's novel, *The Impersonators*, left Australia in the 1950s on a Greek ship: 'her first obsession was simply to get away'. But Italy once encountered seized her imagination:

> In Rome she was too impressed to speak. She could only shake her head. She almost cried. She had read about, yet had not expected, the impact of those visible layers of history.[51]

Over the following years she backpacked around Europe, married and divorced an Englishman, learnt languages, read history, became a tour guide, and organised her year so that in spring and summer she taught Italian in London and in winter she travelled. After twenty years away, she returned to Australia for a visit before settling permanently in Rome. Life again subverted life-plan, she fell in love and stayed.

If young women seized the overseas working holiday as the means to a moment of adventure and freedom before taking up their destiny as suburban mothers, Jill Ker Conway fled because she believed that she could not find a fulfilling life in Australia, that her gender would in Australia prevent her doing something that counted, serious work. The crisis came when she was not offered a traineeship with the Department of External Affairs. This rejection brought her face to face with discrimination, raised her consciousness, turned her ambitions to scholarly and academic life, and took her to another and more congenial place. She stayed away and became an expatriate, but one still constrained to do battle with the Australia that she believed had forced her out. Ker Conway has presented the story of her flight from Australia as unique. And it is in terms of her triumphant success abroad and in her ability to construct so articulate and elegant a story. Although text and ending may be distinctive, the components in her flight were less so. The need to escape a destructive, but dependent, mother, the search for vocation and a life story beyond the romantic quest and its realisation in marriage and children, either separately or in combination, fuelled the departures of both earlier generations and of other women in the 1950s and 1960s. Joan Freeman broke through the same gender barriers as Florence Martin when, at the end of the Second World War, she won a scholarship that took her to the Cavendish Laboratory at Cambridge where she gained her doctorate in nuclear physics.[52] She remained abroad, working as a scientist at the British Atomic Energy Research Establishment at Harwell. She too achieved great distinction.

It was not only the young who travelled in the 1950s and 1960s. The increased affluence of the postwar years gave opportunities to the middle-aged and more elderly women who had missed out on travel in their youth and who were finally free of domestic responsibilities. Florence Burke was born in 1896 and left school at sixteen to take up clerical work. Her family responsibilities lasted until 1950 when her 'last aunt' died and she was alone for the first time in her life. With encouragement from her friends, she decided to take an overseas trip. The joy of the older was no less than that of the young: 'I was going down Collins Street along near King Street, I didn't feel the pavement, I had wings on my heels. I didn't see anybody. I was going down to Thomas Cook's'.[53] Florence Burke left in March 1953. Trepidation characterised her departure and her arrival on the other side: 'I went on my own and I was a mouse, a shy mouse at that time'. But she too felt herself transformed. Painter Mary Macqueen went overseas for the first time at the age of 59 in 1971. Until then she had been involved in looking after her mother, her ill husband, and her son. Her mother died in 1968, her husband in 1970, and her son left home in 1971: '*I was fifty nine and free*'.[54] These stories remind us that life was slow to change for the majority of women, that the role of universal carer still belonged to them.

The thirty years that passed between the departure of Jill Ker Conway and the telling of the tale of her flight into exile witnessed the demise of Empire. In her autobiography, she represents her younger self as critical of imperialism; she felt anger when she encountered the plaques commemorating the bloody battles of colonialism, Lucknow and Mafeking, on the walls of England's cathedrals and village churches. In deciding on Harvard as her overseas academy, she was eschewing the sacred places of imperial education; but she was still choosing the side of the imperial rulers, of those who were to wage yet another colonial war in Vietnam.

Frances Letters, who graduated from university in the mid-1960s, had long felt the urge to leave home, to be 'where the action was'. She felt that the obvious place to go was South-East Asia.[55] Thus with a friend she spent a year hitchhiking through Malaysia, Thailand, Laos, Cambodia and South Vietnam. They were among the forerunners of the hundreds of thousands of young Australians who donned their backpacks to explore the countries of Asia as goals in themselves or en route to and from Europe.

If it was in the late 1960s that Asia became fashionable as a destination for travelling Australians, the story of Australian women in Asia and the Pacific is much, much older. From early days they had been present in the islands of the Pacific and Indian oceans as the women of sailors and traders. By the end of the nineteenth century, Papua, German New Guinea, South-East Asia, China and Japan were on the tourist map.[56] Members of the Australian upper classes like Ruby Madden, who attended the great durbar held by Lord Curzon in Delhi to celebrate the coronation of Edward VII in 1903, journeyed around the Raj staying with friends and relatives.[57] Jeanie Osborne met her Indian army officer husband while her family was in England for the education of her brothers. She was but one of many Australian women who made their homes in India as a result of marrying army officers whom they met on board ship or in

Britain.[58] From the late nineteenth century, the mission fields in India, as well as in China, Japan and the islands of the Pacific, had provided women with another way to move abroad and forge more independent lives.[59] Australian colonisation of Papua New Guinea created an expatriate society in which women played a significant role as wives, teachers, nurses as well as in the maintenance of racial barriers.[60] And Japanese entry into the Second World War was to take Australian women into the Pacific theatre as nurses, other army personnel, and prisoners-of-war.[61] The story of the travel and presence of Australian women in Asia and the Pacific is as varied and diverse and as worth the telling as that of their journeys to Europe.

As the sun set on the British Empire in the 1960s and 1970s, the Australian map of the world shifted and London's place as the magnetic centre waned. Britain began to look 'foreign' and not 'home' when Australians lost their automatic right on entry to a job, a vote, free dental care, and a social security card. They were confronted with visible signals of their foreignness the moment they set foot on 'England's green and pleasant land'; while Germans strolled through the gates marked 'British and EEC', Australian queued with the rest of the world beneath the sign 'Aliens'. Australia itself became 'foreign' under the impact of the postwar European and then Middle Eastern and Asian migration; the ancestral homes and family burial grounds of Australians now lie anywhere and everywhere.

Other changes in these decades dramatically affected the patterns of travel. The sexual liberation of the late 1960s and 1970s meant that middle-class women no longer had to cross the world to live the sexual lives that they chose; the power of the village gossips waned. The second wave of feminists took up the agendas that had fuelled the journeys into independence and autonomy of the women of the first wave. Travel no longer conferred the same privileged knowledge and status as it had in the past. Mass travel, package tours, brought travel somewhere overseas within the range of more and more Australians; trips became shorter, more frequent and more sanitised, and so the association of overseas journeys with rites-of-passage and pilgrimages became weaker.

Postlude

My story of women's journeys began in an attempt to situate my own life in the context of my predecessors by comparing my experience with that of Gladys Marks, who had set out on her adventuring 50 years before me. It ends in another comparison, with the trip of my elder daughter, who set off thirty years after her mother. The differences are marked. Whereas my solo departure was my first venture outside Australia, she had travelled to Europe on some five previous occasions in the baggage of her parents. One moment of joy on her trip in 1991 was to find with the instinct of a homing pigeon the house in Florence where she had lived as a seven year old. Whereas I had no relatives or connections on the other side of the world, she moved into a thick network of aunts, uncles, cousins and family friends. When I left Australia, chasing ancestors was not yet fashionable. Thus it did not occur to me to seek out family graves, which in any case were probably too remote to trace. My daughter in contrast journeyed to the sites of paternal family history, sites that lie not in Britain, but on the remote north-eastern coast of the Netherlands. Unlike her Anglo-Celtic mother, my daughter belongs to that third of Australian people who were born or who have a parent born outside the lucky country. But her mixed ancestry has its origin not in postwar migration, but in the postwar exodus of Australians to Europe; her mother is one of the thousands of Australian women who married on their travels. There are other differences. Whereas for my generation, the international phone call was something reserved for the gravest family occasions — marriage, illness and death — it is the only means by which my daughter communicates. No writer of letters or keeper of diaries, she will leave no written record of her travels.

My daughter lives in Paris, works for a French organisation, has a French partner. All three conditions are, like the events of my own overseas life, the outcome of chance as much as intention. She may or may not come back to live in Australia. That outcome too will probably be decided by circumstances. Identity is not a problem for my daughter. She has two family hearths, two passports, and moves with ease between them. Her sense of double identity separates her from my generation, but links her to her nineteenth-century immigrant and second-generation Scots and Irish maternal forebears who also saw themselves as possessing two homes. But unlike them she lives in the global village and talks to and commutes between Europe and Australia at will. The problem of whether she is or will become an expatriate is in these circumstances not an issue for my daughter or for her generation. That debate is now confined to an aging, if still voluble cohort, the leftovers of the 1950s and early 1960s.

In following the tracks of journeying women, I have made little distinction between trips for six months and trips forever. Some women left with the intention never to return and did not return; maybe they are Peter Porter's people born in the wrong place. Others married on the road, sought, or found without seeking, opportunities, options, work, careers, lifelong adventures that they believed were unattainable at home. And some, like Jessica Anderson's Nora Porteous, just tarried — and tarried.[1] They could, like Alice Henry, Winifred James, Christina Stead and Doris Gentile — and Nora Porteous — make the return journey at the end of their productive lives, forced home by the illness and isolation of old age. Or they could stay away forever, meld into other worlds. How many people know, for instance, that the grandmother of Italian film director Bernardo Bertolucci was an Australian. And does it matter?

For most of the women who made the overseas trip between 1870 and 1970, the main purpose was precisely that, a trip, from which they returned with diverse emotions and feelings. For some the trip had not fulfilled the dreams that they took with them, for others it had, but they were still glad to come home, to family, friends, normality. For Jessie Mitchell, there was 'no place like home — no people like the Australians, no country like sunny N.S.Wales'.[2] Travel could both confirm and undermine attachment to Australia and belief in its way of life. When Marjory Casson returned from her first overseas trip in 1949, she found a 'hard-faced people', 'old children'.[3]

If the trip for the vast majority was a matter of a few months or years before they settled back into life at home, the countless diaries and bundles of letters, the self-published travel books, the endless 'my trip' articles in the suburban and country press — my first encounter with the trip to Europe was in the *West Wyalong Advocate* — all bear witness to the significance of the overseas trip in the lives not only of women who made their mark in the public world, but also of ordinary Australian women. And it may just be that for the young, something of the significance of travel as a rite-of passage, a quest for self and the world remains. When I told my story of my departure to a young journalist, she claimed it as her story too. Perhaps travel, like revolution, will always lure with the prospect of rebirth, renewal, transformation.

Notes

1 Travel and Travellers' Tales

1 Suzanne Falkiner, 'A Sense of Territory', *Australian Book Review* 123, August 1990, pp. 24–9.

2 Beverley Kingston, 'The Lady and the Australian Girl: Some Thoughts on Nationalism and Class', in *Australian Women: New Feminist Perspectives*, Norma Grieve (ed.), OUP, Melbourne, 1986, pp. 27–41.

3 Paul Fussell, *Abroad: British Literary Traveling Between the Wars*, OUP, Oxford, 1980, pp. 16–17.

4 Hazel de Berg, conversations with Ruby Rich, 4 June 1975, NLA, Oral DeB 836, transcript, p. 11,054.

5 In 1953, 39 964 Australian residents made temporary departures overseas; in 1963, 112 427; in 1973, 638 141, Australian Bureau of Statistics, *Official Year Book of the Commonwealth of Australia*, vol. 42, 1956, p. 608; vol. 51, 1965, p. 285; vol. 60, 1974, p. 158.

6 Gladys Marks, undated letter to family from Paris, but November 1913, Gladys Marks papers, University of Sydney Archives, Acc.No.1/11, Group P 18, Series 2, Letters 1913–1924.

7 Georges van den Abbeele, *Travel as Metaphor:From Montaigne to Rousseau*, University of Minnesota Press, Minneapolis, 1991, p. xiii.

8 Dennis Porter, *Haunted Journeys: Desire and Transgression in European Travel Writing*, Princeton University Press, Princeton, 1991, p. 13.

9 Donald Denoon, 'The Isolation of Australian History', *Historical Studies* 22, 1987, p. 252. For some anthologies and studies of Australian overseas travel writing, see *Australians Abroad: An Anthology*, Charles Higham & Michael Wilding (eds), Cheshire, Melbourne, 1967; *Australians in America, 1876–1976*, J.H. Moore ed., UQP, St Lucia, 1977; *Travellers, Journeys, Tourists, Australian Cultural History* 10, 1991; *Wilder Shores: Women's Travel Stories of Australia and Beyond*, Robyn Lucas and Clare Foster (eds) UQP, St Lucia, 1992; *An Antipodean Connection:. Australian Writers, Artists and Travellers in Tuscany*, G. Prampolini and M.C. Hubert (eds), Slatkine, Geneva, 1993; *Changing Places: Australian Writers in Europe 1960s–1990s*, Laurie Hergenhan (ed.), UQP, St Lucia, 1994.

10 Alan Atkinson, 'The First Fleet Lives', *Push from the Bush* 27, 1989, pp. 49–52.

11 Loretta Baldassar, Visits to the Shrine: A Study of Migration as Transnational Interaction between the San Fiorese in Western Australia and Northern Italy, PhD thesis, University of Western Australia, 1995.

12 Margaret Tripp, Letters to her mother, 6 January 1872–27 April 1873, written during a voyage on board the SS *Belar*, the *Surat* and the *Malta*, and subsequently in England and France, SLV, MS 11539, Box 1721/11.

13 Henry Handel Richardson, *Myself When Young (An Unfinished Autobiography)*, concluded by O.M. Roncoroni, Heinemann, London, 1948, p. 74; 'Conversation with Janet Alderson', *Some Other Dream: the Artist, the Art World and the Expatriate*, Geoffrey de Groen (ed.), Hale & Iremonger, Sydney, 1984, p. 2.

14 Alan Lawson, 'Acknowledging Colonialism; Revisions of the Australian Tradition', in *Australia and Britain: Studies in a Changing Relationship*, A.F. Madden and W.H. Morris-Jones (eds), SUP, Sydney, 1980, pp. 135–44.

15 Louise Mack, *An Australian Girl in London*, Fisher Unwin, London, 1902, pp. 78–80.

16 Eleanor Moore, *Quest for Peace as I Have Known it in Australia*, Wilke & Co., Melbourne, 1949, p. 53.

17 See Mircea Eliade, *Patterns in Comparative Religion*, trans. Rosemary Sheed, Sheed & Ward, New York, 1958, pp. 380–3; Edward Shils, *Center and Periphery: Essays in Macrosociology*, University of Chicago Press, Chicago, 1975.

18 Florence Finn, *Pigmies Among Potentates or Two Australian Girls in Olden Lands*, Renwick Pride Nuttall, Melbourne, 1912.

19 Ernest Earnest, *Expatriates and Patriots: American Artists, Scholars and Writers in Europe*, Duke University Press, Durham, NC, 1968, p. 11. See also Janis P. Stout, *The Journey Narrative in American Literature*, Greenwood Press, Westport, Conn., 1983; William W.

Stowe, *Going Abroad: European Travel in Nineteenth-Century American Culture*, Princeton University Press, Princeton, 1994.

20 Stella Bowen, *Drawn from Life* (1941), London, Virago, 1984 (with a new Introduction by Julia Loewe). On the lure of the metropolis, Gillian Tindall, *Countries of the Mind: The Meaning of Place to Writers*, Hogarth, London, 1991, p. 47.

21 On gender and travel see, for example, Catherine Barnes Stevenson, *Victorian Women Travel Writers in Africa*, Twayne Publishers, Boston, 1982; Dea Birkett, *Spinsters Abroad: Victorian Lady Explorers*, OUP, Oxford, 1989; Sara Mills, *Discourse of Difference: An Analysis of Women's Travel and Colonialism*, Routledge, New York, 1991; Mary Louise Pratt, *Imperial Eyes: Travel Writing and Transculturation*, Routledge, New York, 1992; Mary Morris, 'Women and Journeys: Inner and Outer', in *Temperamental Journeys. Essays on the Modern Literature of Travel*, Michael Kowalewski (ed.), University of Georgia Press, Athens, Georgia, 1992, pp. 25–32; Janet Wolff, 'On the Road Again: Metaphors of Travel in Cultural Criticism', *Cultural Studies* 7, 2, 1993, pp. 224–39. The majority of these studies deal with the journeys of women from the centre to the periphery.

22 Winifred James, *Gangways and Corridors*, London, Allan, 1936, p. 39.

23 *The Odyssey*, quoted in *Taste for Travel*, John Julius Norwich (ed.), Macmillan, London, 1985, p. 406.

24 See, for example, Joan Druett, *Petticoat Sailors: Whaling Wives at Sea 1820–1920*, Heinemann, Auckland, 1983.

25 Annette Potts and Lucinda Strauss, *For the Love of Soldiers: Australian War Brides and the GIS*, ABC Books, Sydney, 1987, p. 15.

26 *Memoirs of Alice Henry*, Nettie Palmer (ed.), Melbourne, 1944, pp. 5–6. On Henry, Dianne Kirkby, *Alice Henry, the Power of Pen and Voice: the Life of an Austral-American Labor Reformer*, Cambridge, CUP, 1991.

27 Winifred James, *The Mulberry Tree*, G. Bell, London, 1913, p. 3.

28 See, for example, Julie Wheelwright, *Amazons and Military Maids: Women Who Cross Dressed as Men in the Pursuit of Life, Liberty and Happiness*, Pandora, London, 1989.

29 For Wollstonecraft, Richard Holmes, *Footsteps: Adventures of a Romantic Biographer*, Hodder & Stoughton, London, 1985; for Fuller, *The Woman and the Myth: Margaret Fuller's Life and Writings*, Belle Gale Chevigny (ed.), Feminist Press, New York, 1976.

30 James Buzard, *The Beaten Track: European Tourism, Literature, and the Ways to 'Culture' 1800–1918*, Clarendon Press, Oxford, 1993, pp. 139–52.

31 Marilyn Lake, 'The Politics of Respectability: Identifying the Masculinist Context', *Historical Studies* 22, 1986, pp. 116–31; Sue Rowley, 'The Journey's End: Women's Mobility and Confinement', *Travellers, Journeys, Tourists*, pp. 69–84.

32 E.J. Banfield, *The Torres Strait Route from Queensland to England by the British-Indian Steam Navigation Company's Royal Mail Steamer 'Chyebassa'*, T.Wilmett, Townsville, 1885, p. 3.

33 Joan Colebrook, *A House of Tall Trees*, Chatto & Windus, London, 1987, p. 236; James, *The Mulberry Tree*, p. 75; Marie Byles, *By Cargo Boat and Mountain: The Unconventional Experiences of a Woman on a Tramp Around the World*, Seely, Service & Co., London, 1931, p. 10.

34 Jessica Anderson, *Tirra Lirra by the River*, Macmillan, Melbourne, 1978.

35 Jill Ker Conway, *The Road from Coorain*, Alfred Knopf, New York, 1987; *True North, A Memoir*, New York, Alfred Knopf, 1994.

36 See, for example, her 1960 essay, 'Why I Left', *Independent Monthly*, December 1994 / January 1995.

37 Porter, *Haunted Journeys*, p. 9.

38 Stevenson, *Victorian Women*, p. 5.

39 Drusilla Modjeska, *Exiles at Home: Australian Women Writers 1925–1945*, Sirius, Sydney, 1981.

40 Morris, 'Women and Journeys'. p. 28.

41 I am grateful to Kerri-Ann Cousins for this story.

42 Mary Marlowe, *Kangaroos in Kingsland: Being the Adventures of Four Australian Girls in England*, Simpkin Marshall, London, 1918, p. 17.

43 (Maude Jessie Harvie), *Madge's Trip to Europe and Back*, George Robertson, Melbourne, 1911, p. 93.

44 Letter of Jessie Mitchell, 1 May 1934, Jessie Mitchell papers with family.

45 Amirah Inglis, *Australians and the Spanish Civil War*, Allen & Unwin, Sydney, 1987, p. 126.

46 On travel diaries, see Andrew Hassam, '"Farewell to Old England, and now for a new life and a new journal": Emigration Narratives', *Journal of Australian Studies* 36, 1993, pp. 23–35.

47 Gladys Marks, letter to family, 16 February 1913, Gladys Marks papers, Series 2.

48 Letter from S. Wynyard to author, November 1992.
49 Annotated Bibliography of Australian Overseas Travel Writing, Ros Pesman, David Walker and Richard White (eds), compiled by Terri McCormack, ALIA Bibliographies on Disk, Canberra, forthcoming [1996].
50 Millicent Millear, *The Journal of a Wandering Australian*, Melville & Mullen, London, 1902, preface.
51 Harvie, *Madge's Trip to Europe,* Preface.
52 Margaret Gilruth, *Maiden Journey; The Unusual Experiences of a Girl on Board a Tramp Ship,* Jonathan Cape, London, 1934, p. 7.
53 Mary Gaunt, *Reflection — in Jamaica*, Ernest Benn, London, 1932, pp. vii-viii.
54 Catherine Robinson, *The Green Paradise: The Story of a Woman's Journey in the Amazon and the Argentine*, Arthur Barron, London, 1936, p. 5.
55 On the autobiographies and autobiographial constructions by Austrtralian women, Joy Hooton, *Stories of Herself When Young: Autobiographies of Childhood by Australian Women*, OUP, Melbourne, 1990; 'Autobiography and Gender', in *Writing Lives: Feminist Biographies and Autobiographies*, Susan Magarey (ed.), University of Adelaide, Adelaide, 1992, pp. 25–42; 'Women's Life–Writing: Power and Alterity', in *Shaping Lives. Reflection on Biography,* ed. Ian Donaldson, Humanities Research Centre, Canberra, 1992, pp. 117–32.
56 Clare Davies, *This is My Life*, C. Davies, Sydney, 1965.
57 Ada Carnegie, *Yesteryear: Memoirs of My Trip Abroad Nearly Sixty Years Ago*, Hawthorn Press, Melbourne, 1966, p. 18.
58 Ibid., p. 74.
59 See also Richard White, 'Passing Through. Tuscany and the Australian tourist', *An Antipodean Connection*, Prampolini and Hubert (eds.), pp. 167–171.
60 Mary Kent Hughes, ibid., pp. 168–9.
61 Peter Brooks, *Reading for the Plot: Design and Intention in Narrative,* Random House, New York 1984, p. 3. See also Philippe Lejeune, *On Autobiography* Paul John Eakin, (ed.), trans. Katherine Leary, University of Minnesota Press, Minneapolis, 1989; Katherine R. Goodman, 'Poetry-Truth: Elisa von Recke's Sentimental Autobiography', *Interpreting Women's Lives: Feminist Theory and Personal Narratives*, Personal Narratives Group (ed.), Indiana University Press, Bloomington, 1989, pp. 118–218; George C. Rosenwald and Richard L. Ochberg, *Storied Lives: Culture, Politics and Self Understanding*, Yale University Press New Haven, 1992; Paul John Eakin, 'Writing Biography: A Perspective from Autobiography', *Shaping Lives*, Donaldson (ed.), pp. 195–209.
62 Finn, *Pigmies Among Potentates,* pp. 29–30.
63 Ida Haysom, diary, 12 May 1936, SLV, MSB128A.
64 Doris Hayball, *Sidelights on the Soviet: A Plain, Unvarnished Tale of a Trip to Russia and its Great Theatre Festival*, G. Batchelor, Melbourne, 1939, p. 91.
65 Doris Gentile, Notebook, n.d., Gentile papers, ML, ML MSS 2897.
66 Dora Birtles, Odd-Jobbing One's Way Round the World, typescript, Dora Birtles papers, Mosman Municipal Library, Box 4g5.
67 Denoon, 'The Isolation of Australian History', pp. 252–60.
68 Nicholas Jose, ' The Dream of Europe: *For Love Alone, The Aunt's Story* and *The Cardboard Crown'*, *Meridian* 6, 2, 1987, p. 113.
69 Kirkby, *Alice Henry*; Hazel Rowley, *Christina Stead: A Biography*, Heinemann, Melbourne, 1993; Jim Davidson, *Lyrebird Rising, Louise Hanson-Dyer of L'Oiseau-Lyre 1884–1962,* MUP, Melbourne, 1994; Patricia Clarke, *Tasma: The Life of Jessie Couvreur*, Allen & Unwin, Sydney, 1994.
70 Frank Moorhouse, *State of the Art: The Mood of Contemporary Australia in Short Stories*, Penguin, Ringwood, 1983, p. 2.

Interlude Antecedents

1 Mary Reibey, journal 1820–1821, ML, MSS 2132, p. 12.
2 Grace Black, diary, 1852, SLV, MS 8996, 59(a).
3 Jane Murray Smith to her mother, Mrs James Ford Strachan, 2 August 1864, letters from Robert and Jane Murray Smith, typescript copy, SLV, H15968.
4 Jane Murray Smith to her mother, 16 January 1865, 10 April 1864, ibid.
5 Jane Murray Smith to her mother, 19 March 1864, ibid.
6 For the travels of Sarah Wentworth, transcripts of the Wentworth papers held at the Historic Houses Trust of NSW, ML, A868; Carol Liston, *Sarah Wentworth: Mistress of Vaucluse*, Historic Houses Trust of NSW, Sydney, 1988; *The Grand Tour: The Colonial*

Discovery of Europe, Catalogue of exhibition at Elizabeth Bay House, Historic Houses Trust of NSW, 1993.

7   Liston, *Sarah Wentworth*, p. 62.
8   For the travels of Hannah Rouse, Caroline Thornton, *Rouse Hill House and the Rouses*, C.R. Thornton, Doolands WA, 1988; *The Grand Tour.*
9   Mary Stawell, *My Recollections,* R. Clay & Sons, London, 1911, p. 154.
10 Helen Rutledge, *My Grandfather's House: Recollections of an Australian Family,* Doubleday, Sydney, 1986, p. 20.
11 Jane Murray Smith to her mother, 8 November 1863, letters from Robert and Jane Murray Smith.
12 Elizabeth Dixon, *Journal of a Voyage from Sydney to London in the Barque 'Standerings'* (1842), Blackie & Son, London, 1946, p. 44.
13 Mrs A.A.C. LeSouef (Caroline Cotton), Journal of a Voyage to London from Melbourne, n.d., copy, SLV, MS 9096, MSB 571. For other accounts of voyages to Europe by sailing ship see Letters of Robert and Jane Murray Smith; Mattie McCracken, Diary of a Voyage on a Sailing Ship from Melbourne to India, *c.*1875, SLSA, Cudmore papers, PRG 189, series 3; M. Cameron, diary kept on a passage to England in ship 'Sobraon', 1878, copy, SLV, MS 9517, MSB469; (Eliza Kent) 'Abstract of the Journal of a Voyage from New South Wales to England', *Athenaeum*, August 1908, pp. 5–10, 99–103.
14 Janet Mitchell, *Spoils of Opportunity*, Methuen, London, 1938, p. 23.
15 Janet Mitchell, 'Why I am a Catholic', *This City of Peace: Being the Conversion Stories of 23 Converts to the Catholic Church*, Marjorie Hardy (ed.), Melbourne, 1949, pp. 102–3.
16 M.L. Skinner, *The Fifth Sparrow: An Autobiography,* SUP, Sydney, 1952, pp. 70–4.

2   *Travel and Status*

1   Shirley Hazzard, *The Transit of Venus*, Penguin, Ringwood, 1981, p. 37.
2   Nancy Adams, *Family Fresco*, Cheshire, Melbourne, 1966, p. 101.
3   K.S. Inglis, 'Going Home: Australians in England, 1870–1900', in *Home or Away? Immigrants in Colonial Australia*, David Fitzpatrick (ed.), Australian National University, Canberra, 1992, p. 106. Alice Grant Rosman in an article for *Everylady's Journal*, 6 October 1913, reported that rumour had the number of Australians in Britain at 25 000. Rumour appears in this case to have been accurate.
4   Ibid., p. 122.
5   Amie Livingstone Stirling, *Memories of an Australian Childhood 1880–1900*, Schwarz, Melbourne, 1980, p. 159.
6   *200 Australian Women: A Redress Anthology,* Heather Radi (ed.), Sydney, Women's Redress Press, 1988, pp. 43–5.
7   Inglis, 'Going Home', pp. 106–7. See also Eric Richards, 'Return Migration: Migrant Strategies in Colonial Australia, *Home or Away?*, Fitzpatrick (ed.), pp. 64–100.
8   George Farwell, *Squatters Castle: The Story of a Pastoral Dynasty. Life and Times of Edward Ogilvie 1814–96,* Lansdowne Press, Melbourne, 1966.
9   Jessie Street, *Truth or Repose*, Sydney, Australian Book Society, 1966, p. 9.
10 Inglis, 'Going Home', p. 106.
11 Beverley Kingston, *My Wife, My Daughter, and Poor Mary Ann: Women and Work in Australia,* Nelson, Melbourne, 1975, pp. 24–6,139; Kingston, 'The Lady and the Australian Girl', pp. 27–41; Leonore Davidoff, *The Best Circles: Society, Etiquette and the Season*, Croom Helm, London, 1973.
12 Rozsika Parker and Griselda Pollock, *Old Mistresses: Women, Art and Ideology*, Routledge Kegan & Paul, London, 1981, p. 99.
13 Kingston, 'The Lady and the Australian Girl', p. 32
14 Bowen, *Drawn from Life*, p. 25.
15 Rosa Praed, *Mrs Tregaskiss: A Novel of Anglo-Australian Life,* Chatto & Windus, London, 1896, pp. 30–1.
16 Lady (Eliza) Mitchell, *Three Quarters of a Century*, Methuen, London, 1940, pp. 41–67.
17 Ibid., p. 113.
18 *British-Australasian*, 30 July, 10 September, 19 November 1908.
19 Richardson, *Myself When Young*, p. 74.
20 Maie Casey, *Tides and Eddies*, Joseph, London, 1966, p. 21.
21 Margaret Gifford, *I Can Hear the Horses*, Methuen-Haynes, Sydney, 1982, p. 22.

22 *Women, the Arts and the 1920s: Paris and New York*, Kenneth Wheeler and Virginia Lee Lussu (eds), Transaction Books, New Brunswick, N.J., 1978, p. 58.

23 *My Dear Miss Macarthur: The Recollections of Emmeline Maria Macarthur*, Jane de Falbe (ed.), Kenthurst, NSW, Kangaroo Press, 1988, p. 58.

24 Mabel Brookes, *Memoirs*, Macmillan, Melbourne, 1974, p. 35.

25 Mrs Richard Armstrong, 'Our Italian Friend', *Centennial Magazine* 2, 8, March 1890, p. 653.

26 Penne Hackforth Jones, *Barbara Baynton, Between Two Worlds*, Penguin, Ringwood, 1989, p. 92.

27 Adams, *Family Fresco,* p. 105.

28 Gifford, *I Can Hear the Horses,* p. 23.

29 *British-Australasian,* 13 February 1913.

30 Katharine Susannah Prichard, *Child of the Hurricane: An Autobiography,* Angus & Robertson, Sydney, 1963, p. 116.

31 Dulcie Deamer, The Golden Decade, typescript, ML, ML MSS 3173.

32 Mrs Leonard W., Matters, *Australasians Who Count in London, and Who Counts in Western Australia*, Truscott, London, 1913, p. vii.

33 Ibid., 135

34 Caroline Simpson, 'Margaret Chisholm', *ADB*, vol. 13, John Ritchie (ed.), MUP, Melbourne, 1993, pp. 423–4. A copy of the marriage certificate is held with the files of the Australian Dictionary of Biography.

35 Maureen E. Montgomery, *'Gilded Prostitution': Status, Money and Transatlantic Marriages, 1870–1914*, Routledge, London, 1989.

36 'Colonial', 'Titled Colonials v. Titled Americans', *Contemporary Review,* June 1905, pp. 860–9. The figures applied to women from all British colonies, not just from Australia.

37 Edward Duyker and Coralie Younger, *Molly and the Rajah: Race, Romance and the Raj,* Australian Mauritanian Press, Sydney, 1991.

38 Kingston, 'The Lady and the Australian Girl', p. 39.

39 Mary Turner Shaw, 'Education of a Squatter's Daughter', in *The Door Half Open: Sixteen Modern Australian Women Look at Professional Life and Achievement,* Patricia Grimshaw, (ed.) Hale & Iremonger, Sydney, 1982, pp. 292–3.

40 Brookes, *Memoirs*, p. 40.

41 Amy Lewis, Paths to Happiness: A Mosaic of Scenes and Portraits, typescript, NLA, MS 6147.

42 Jane Connors, 'Ruth Bedford', *ADB*, vol. 13, p. 148.

43 Rosa Praed, *Christina Chard: A Novel,* Chatto & Windus, London, 1894.

44 Anonymous diary, Maritime Museum, Sydney.

45 Catherine Johnson, interview with Barbara Cullen, 10 November 1987, NSW Bicentennial Oral History Collection, transcript, NLA, Oral TRC 2301, INT 128.

46 A.S.H. Weigall, *My Little World: Reminiscences*, Angus & Robertson, Sydney, 1934, p. 216.

47 Diane Langmore, *Prime Ministers' Wives: The Public and Private Lives of Ten Australian Women*, Mc Phee Gribble, Ringwood, 1992, pp. 26–7.

48 Jessie Mitchell, letter, 25 July 1934, Jessie Mitchell papers.

49 *SMH,* 11 February 1905. For further examples, Inglis, *'Going Home'* pp. 110–15.

50 *British-Australasian*, 22 September 1910.

51 Lilley, *A Possum Abroad,* pp. 18–38.

52 *British-Australasian*, 16 January 1913.

53 Hackforth Jones, *Barbara Baynton,* p. 95.

54 David Marr, *Patrick White: A Life*, Random House, Sydney, 1991, pp. 76–7.

55 Essie Wood, *Yachting Days and Yachting Ways,* Walter Scott, London, 1892. Written in the form of a diary, the book covers a voyage in the Mediterranean, April-May 1892.

56 Brookes, *Memoirs,* pp. 43–51.

57 Ibid., pp. 53–9.

58 Teresa Pagliaro, An Australian Family Abroad: The Rowe Letters 1873–1874, MA thesis, Monash University, 1981.

59 Janey Rowe to Fanny O'Leary, 2 April 1874, ibid., p. 67.

60 Pagliaro, introduction, ibid., p. xliv.

61 Janey Rowe to Denis O'Leary, ibid., p. 247.

62 Ibid., p. 252.

63 Pagliaro, introduction, ibid., p. xlv.

64 Adams, *Family Fresco*, pp. 102–103.

65 Ethel Kelly, *Twelve Milestones*, Brentano's, London, 1929, p. 214.

66 Allison Howorth, *Coo-ee England: A Travel Diary*, George Batchelor, Melbourne, 1937, p. 160.
67 Mabel Brookes, *On the Knees of the Gods*, Melville & Mullen, Melbourne, 1918, p. 64.
68 Rosa Praed, *An Australian Heroine*, Chapman Hall, London, 1880, p. 210.
69 Ada Cambridge, *In Two Years Time*, Bentley, London, 1879, p. 178.
70 Winifred James, *Bachelor Betty*, Constable, London, 1907, p. 55.
71 Sophie Osmond, *An Australian Wooing: A Story of Trade, a Gold Mine and a Ghost*, Garden City Press, Letchworth, 1879, pp. 126–7.
72 Cambridge, *In Two Years' Time*; Praed, *Christina Chard*.
73 Cambridge, *In Two Years' Time*, p. 190; Ethel Karr, *The Australian Guest*, Remington, London, 1886, p. 55.
74 Richard White, *Inventing Australia*, Allen & Unwin, Sydney, 1981, pp. 63–84; Kingston, 'The Lady and the Australian Girl', pp. 27–34.
75 See Mary Helms, *Ulysses' Sail: An Ethnographic Odyssey of Power, Knowledge and Geographical Distance*, Princeton University Press, Princeton, pp. 131–71.
76 *SMH*, 26 August 1914.
77 Frances McGuire, *Bright Morning: The Story of an Australian Family Before 1914*, Rigby, Adelaide, 1975, p. 129.
78 *Bulletin*, 7 March 1890.
79 Louise Mack, *Girls Together*, Angus & Robertson, Sydney, 1898, p. 31.
80 Bowen, *Drawn from Life*, p. 27.
81 *British-Australasian*, 26 November 1908.
82 *The Grand Tour*, p. xiii.
83 Liston, *Sarah Wentworth*, p. 72.
84 Rutledge, *My Grandfather's House*, p. 28.
85 Inglis, 'Going Home', p. 120.
86 Gifford, *I Can Hear the Horses*, pp. 55–8, 63–74, 81–92.
87 *Home*, 1 June 1922.
88 Ros Bowden, interview with Hazel Hollander, 16 December 1987, NSW Bicentennial Oral History Collection, NLA, ORAL TRC 2301, pp. 8–9.
89 Eliza Mitchell, *Three Quarters of a Century*, p. 120.
90 Adams, *Family Fresco*, p. 81.
91 Janet Mitchell, *Spoils of Opportunity*, p. 33.
92 Street, *Truth or Repose*, p. 9.
93 Bowen, *Drawn from Life*, pp. 22–3.
94 Hazel de Berg, conversations with Ruby Rich.
95 Tasma, *A Knight of the White Feather. Incidents and Scenes in Melbourne Life*, Heinemann, London, 1895, p. 12.
96 Clarke, *Tasma*, pp. 68–81.

Interlude   Adelaide Ironside

1 On Adelaide Ironside, Janine Burke, *Australian Women Artists 1840–1940*, Greenhouse Publications, Melbourne, 1980, pp. 18–23; Jill Poulton, *Adelaide Ironside: The Pilgrim of Art*, Hale & Iremonger, Sydney, 1987. Poulton's text includes extracts from the letters of Ironside held in the Mitchell Library, Ironside papers, ML MSS 272/1, Lang papers, ML Doc 1873.
2 On women artists in Rome, Margaret Farrand Thorp, *The Literary Sculptors*, Duke University Press, Durham, N.C., 1965; Karen Petersen and J.J. Wilson, *Women Artists: Recognition and Reappraisal from the Early Middle Ages to the Twentieth Century*, New York University Press, New York, 1978; Dolly Sherwood, *Harriet Hosmer American Sculptor 1830–1908*, University of Missouri Press, Columbia, 1991.
3 Adelaide Ironside to John Dunmore Lang, London, 7 December 1855, Poulton, *Adelaide Ironside*, p. 51.
4 R. Pesman Cooper, 'Sir Samuel Griffith, Dante and the Italian Tradition in Nineteenth Century Australian Literary Culture', *Australian Literary Studies* 14, 1989, pp. 199–215.
5 Adelaide Ironside, 'Thought for the Australian League', *People's Advocate*, 1 April 1854. On Australian perceptions of the Risorgimento, R. Pesman Cooper, 'Garibaldi and Australia', *Teaching History* 16, 1982, pp. 62–6
6 Ironside to Lang, 12 December 1855, Poulton, *Adelaide Ironside*, p. 53.
7 (Edward Ogilvie), *Diary of Travels in Three Quarters of the Globe by an Australian Settler*, vol. II, Saunders & Otley, London, 1856, p. 281.

8 Poulton, *Adelaide Ironside*, p. 55.
9 Ironside to Lang, August 1861, ibid., p. 73.
10 Ibid., p. 65.
11 Ibid., p. 88.
12 Sherwood, *Harriet Hosmer*, p. 177.
13 Transcripts of Wentworth papers, Historic Houses Trust of NSW, pp. 45, 129.
14 Poulton, *Adelaide Ironside*, p. 66.
15 Pesman Cooper 'Garibaldi and Australia', p. 63.
16 On an expatriate and artist life in Rome, Sherwood, *Harriet Hosmer*; Thorp, *The Literary Sculptors*; Paul R. Baker, *The Fortunate Pilgrims, Americans in Italy 1800–1860*, Cambridge, Mass., Harvard University Press, 1964.
17 Sherwood, *Harriet Hosmer*, p. 59.
18 Poulton, *Adelaide Ironside*, p. 56.
19 *Letters and Memoirs of Harriet Hosmer*, Cornelia Carr (ed.), John Lane, London, 1913, p. 67.
20 Robert Browning to Harriet Hosmer, 21 February, 1858, ibid., p. 121.
21 Burke, *Australian Women Artists*, p. 19.
22 Parker and Pollock, *Old Mistresses*, pp. 100–1.
23 Ironside to Lang, 3 November 1860, Poulton, *Adelaide Ironside*, p. 69.
24 Ironside to Lang, February 1863, ibid., p. 96.
25 Ironside to Lang, 3 November 1860, R. Pesman Cooper, 'Australian Visitors to Italy in the Nineteenth Century', in *Australia, the Australians and the Italian Migration*, Gianfranco Cresciani (ed.), Franco Angeli, Rome, 1983, p. 138.
26 Sherwood, *Harriet Hosmer*, p. 172.
27 Parker and Pollock, *Old Mistresses*, p. 100.
28 'Chat with Sculptress', undated and unidentified news cutting, Mary Gilmore papers, NLA, MS 125.
29 Margaret Thomas, *A Hero of the Workshop and a Somerset Worthy Charles Summers, Sculptor*, Hamilton, Adams, London, 1879. On Thomas, Kenneth Scarlett, *Australian Sculptors*, Nelson, Melbourne, 1980, pp. 640–3.
30 In *Coo-ee. Tales of Australian Life by Australian Ladies*, Mrs Patchett Martin (ed.), R.E.King, 1891, London, pp. 257–267.
31 On Cowan, Scarlett, *Australian Sculptors*, pp. 132–6, Kerri-Anne Cousins, Theodora Cowan (1869–1949): The Career of an Australian Woman Sculptor, BA(Hons), thesis, Australian National University, 1989.

3   *Travel and Aspirations*

1 Ella Mc Fadyen, *Everylady's Journal*, 6 April 1913, p. 202.
2 Anne Wilson, *Alice Lauder, A Sketch,* Osgood, London, 1893; Rosa Praed, *The Ghost*, Everett, London, 1903.
3 'Our Song-birds in London. More Bars than Crumbs', *Lone Hand*, 1 May 1907, p. 105; Nellie Melba, 'Music as a Profession', ibid, 4 February 1909, p. 358.
4 *New Idea*, September 1902, p. 115.
5 *Bulletin*, 28 June1902 (as Gouli-Gouli).
6 Hackforth Jones, *Barbara Baynton*, p. 78.
7 Kingston, *My Wife, My Daughter and Poor Mary Ann*, p. 132.
8 Alice Grant Rosman, ' Girls who go to London Town', no 3, 'Stage-Struck Pilgrims from Australia', *Everylady's Journal,* 6 June 1913, p. 330. For some details on stage careers overseas of Australian actors, see Hal Porter, *Stars of Australian Stage and Screen*, Rigby, Adelaide, 1965.
9 'Actresses and Their Work', *The Australasian Stage Annual*, 5, January 1904.
10 For Nellie Stewart, Nellie Stewart, *My Life's Story*, John Sands, Sydney, 1923.
11 Mary Edgeworth David, *Passages of Time: An Australian Woman 1890–1974*, UQP, St Lucia, 1975, pp. 72–73.
12 Mary Marlowe, *That Fragile Hour: An Autobiography,* Lionel Hudson (ed.), Sydney, Angus & Robertson, 1990; *Kangaroos in Kingsland.*
13 Ada Holman, *My Wander Year: Some Jottings in a Year's Travel*, William Brooks & Co., Sydney, 1914, p. 19.
14 For the experiences of one Australian pianist studying in Stuttgart, London and Berlin in the 1880s and 1890s, Elsie Hall, *The Good Die Young: The Autobiography of Elsie Hall*, Constantia Publishers, Cape Town, 1969.
15 Holman, *My Wander Year.*

16 Clarke, *Tasma*, p. 84. Clarke's Bibliography contains a list of Couvreur's newspaper arti-
    cles.
17 Ibid., p. 101.
18 Mrs L.W. Matters, p. 11.
19 Ann Galbally, 'Australian Artists Abroad 1800–1914', *Studies in Australian Art*, ed. Ann
    Galbally and Margaret Plant (eds), Department of Fine Arts, University of Melbourne,
    1978, pp. 58–66.
20 This group has been constructed from the details in lists and biographical material in
    Vida Lahey, *Art in Queensland 1859–1959*, Jacaranda Press, Brisbane, 1959; Nancy
    Benko, *Art and Artists of South Australia*, Lidums, Adelaide, 1969; Rachel Biven, *Some
    Forgotten, Some Remembered: Women Artists of South Australia*, Sydenham Gallery,
    Adelaide, 1976; Burke, *Australian Woman Artists 1840–1940*; Caroline Ambrus, *The
    Ladies Picture Show: Sources on a Century of Australian Women Artists*, Hale & Iremomger,
    Sydney, 1984; Victoria Hammond and Juliet Peters, *Completing the Picture: Women
    Artists and the Heidelberg Era*, Artmoves, Melbourne, 1992; Victoria Hammond, *A
    Century of Australian Women Artists: 1840s-1940s*, Deutscher Fine Art, Melbourne,
    1993; Jane Hyland, *South Australian Women Artists 1890s-1940s*, Art Gallery of South
    Australia, Adelaide, 1994; press articles from the period on Australian artists abroad.
21 Burke, *Australian Women Artists*, p. 3.
22 Margaret Thomas, 'Paris Art Schools and Australian Students', *Literary Opinion*, August
    1891, pp. 51–2; Grace Joel, 'Australian Artists in London', *Art and Architecture*, 1906, p.
    101. Alison Rae, 'Australia Artists in Paris', ' Notes from Paris', *Australasian*, 14 March, 4
    July 1891. Iso Rae is noted in Hammond and Peters.
23 On women artists in the late nineteenth and early twentieth centuries, Ambrus, *The
    Ladies Picture Show*, pp. 13–21; Hammond and Peters, *Completing the Picture*.
24 *Jessie Constance Traill, 1881–1967*, Maitland Art Gallery, Maitland, 1985.
25 Bruce James, *Grace Cossington Smith*, Craftsman House, Roseville, NSW, 1991,
    pp. 24–5.
26 The main press sources for Ohlfsen's biography are in the newscutting file at the Art
    Gallery of New South Wales, including *Sydney Mail*, 10 June 1908, *The Triad*, 10
    September 1921. See also the *British-Australasian*, 20 August 1908.
27 Exhibition Albert Buildings Sydney, November 1920, Catalogue; 'A Place in the Sun';
    Sun News, 8 August 1926.
28 *Sydney Mail*, 10 June 1908.
29 Doris Dinham to 'Cinderella' (Ella McFadyen), 19 January 1932, Doris Gentile papers,
    privately held.
30 Dora Ohlfsen to Sir Robert Garran, 7 January 1932, Garran papers, NLA MS 2102,
    series 5/40.
31 Ibid. 5/49.
32 Hilda Rix Nicholas, 'An Artist's Life in Paris', *Home*, March 1922, p. 24. On foreign
    women artists in Paris, Charlotte Yeldham, *Women Artists in Nineteenth Century France
    and England*, Garland Publishing, Vol.1, New York, 1984, pp. 40–62.
33 Elizabeth Huton Turner, *American Artists in Paris 1919–1929*, Ann Arbor, UMI Research
    Press, 1988, p. 9.
34 On Nourse, Mary Alice Heekin Burke, *Elizabeth Nourse, 1859–1938: A Salon Career*,
    Smithsonian Institution Press, Washington, 1983.
35 For a description of painting in Etaples, Elsie B. Rix, 'An Artist's Colony in Picardy',
    Home, March 1922, p. 88.
36 Turner, *American Artists in Paris*, p. 9.
37 Stirling, *Memories of an Australian Childhood*, pp. 165–8.
38 Hilda M. Freeman, *An Australian Girl in Germany: Through Peace to War (January-
    October 1914)*, Speciality Press, Melbourne, 1916, p. 311.
39 For more detailed information on some Australian women graduates studying over-
    seas, Farley Kelly, *Degrees of Liberation: A Short History of Women in the University of
    Melbourne*, University of Melbourne, 1985; Alison Mackinnon, *The New Women,
    Adelaide's Early Women Graduates*, Wakefield Press, Adelaide, 1987; Ursula Bygott and
    K.J. Cable, *Pioneer Women Graduates of the University of Sydney 1881–1981*, University of
    Sydney, Sydney, 1985; the *Magazine* and the *Newsletter* of the Women's College,
    University of Sydney, and entries in the *ADB* index under academic, teacher, scientist,
    medical practioner, missionary.
40 Stawell, *My Recollections*, p. 192.
41 Patricia Horner, 'Susannah Williams', *ADB*, vol. 12, John Ritchie (ed.), MUP,
    Melbourne, 1990, p. 506; W.V. Hole & A.H. Treweeke, *The History of the Women's
    College within the University of Sydney*, Angus & Robertson, Sydney, 1953.
42 Bygott & Cable, *Pioneer Women Graduates*, p. 35.

43 For Nettie Palmer, see here, pp. 187–90; for Margaret Bailey, Margaret Lundie, 'Magaret Bailey', *ADB,* vol. 7, Bede Nairn and Geoffrey Serle (eds), MUP, Melbourne, 1979, p. 138.
44 Mackinnon, *The New Women,* pp. 204–205.
45 Jacqueline Bell, 'Freda Bage', *ADB*, vol. 7, p. 131.
46 R.W. Home, 'Florence Martin', *ADB* vol. 10, Bede Nairn and Geoffrey Serle (eds.), MUP, Melbourne, 1980, p. 427.
47 M. Hutton Neve, '*This Mad Folly': The History of Australia's Pioneer Women Doctors*, Library of Australian History, Sydney, 1980.
48 Judith Godden & Meredith Foley, 'Isla Blomfield', *ADB*, vol. 13, p. 206.
49 Janet Mitchell, *Spoils of Opportunity*, p. 58.
50 Beverley Kingston, 'Yours Very Truly, Marion Phillips', *Labour History* 29, 1975, pp. 123–31.
51 For women and sport, Marion K. Stell, *Half the Race: A History of Australian Women in Sport,* Angus & Robertson, Sydney, 1991; Dennis H. Phillips, *Australian Women at the Olympic Games 1912–1922*, Kangaroo Press, Sydney, 1992.
52 Phillips, *Australian Women at the Olympic Games,* pp. 18–20.
53 Ibid. , pp. 22–9.
54 Ibid., p. 29.
55 Richard White, *Inventing Australia*, pp. 115–16.
56 Buzzard, *The Beaten Track,* p. 58.
57 Thomas, *A Scamper Through Spain and Tangier*, pp. 208–9.
58 Violet Chomley papers, VSL, MS12478, Box 3299/8 (d).
59 Finn, *Pigmies Among Potentates*, p. 33.
60 Mary Brennan, with Elaine McKenna, *Better Than Dancing. The Wandering Years of a Young Australia*n, Greenhouse Publications, Melbourne, 1987, p. 79.
61 Ibid., p. 160.
62 Deamer, 'The Golden Decade'.
63 For Gilmore in Paraguay, *Letters of Mary Gilmore*, ed. W.H. Wilde and T. Inglis Moore (eds), MUP, Melbourne, 1980, pp. xxii–xxiv, 17–23. On William Lane's utopian colonies in Paraguay, Lloyd Ross, *William Lane and the Australian Labor Movement,* Hale & Iremonger, Sydney, 1980.
64 For some indication of 'professional travel' in the 1920s and 1930s, see the previously cited works of Mackinnon, Kelly, Bygott, Porter, Phillips, Stell, Hylton, Burke, Hammond and Peters, and Mary Eagle, *Australian Modern Painting between the Wars, 1914–1939*, Bay Books, Sydney, 1990; Barbara Mackenzie, *Singers of Australia: From Melba to Sutherland*, Melbourne, Lansdowne Press, 1968; the 1920–1940 issues of the *Magazine* and the *Newsletter* of the Women's College of the University of Sydney; Alison Turtle, 'The First Women Psychologists in Australia, *Australian Psychologist* 25, 3, 1990, pp. 239–55. For autobiographies of some of the women: Marjorie Lawrence, *Interrupted Melody: An Autobiography*, Invincible Press, Sydney, 1949; Gladys Moncrieff, *My Life of Song*, Adelaide, Rigby, 1971; Dorothy Gordon Jenner, *Darlings, I've Had a Ball,* Ure Smith, Sydney, 1975; Vera Summers, *Personalities and Places*, V. Summers, Perth, 1978; Dorothy Knox, *Time Flies: The Memoirs of Dorothy Knox,* Rigby, Adelaide, 1982; Kathleen Fitzpatrick, *Solid Bluestone Foundations and Other Memories of a Melbourne Girlhood*, Penguin, Ringwood, 1986; Anne Kerr, *Lanterns over Pinchgut*, Macmillan, Melbourne, 1988; Mark Cranfield, interviews with Hope Hewitt, 20 January–23 April 1982, NLA Oral History Program, ORAL TRC 1114.
65 For Crowley and Dangar in France, Grace Crowley papers ML, ML, MSS 3252 (typed transcripts Australian Dictionary of Biography, Canberra); extracts from their letters published in *Undergrowth*, 1927.

Interlude   *Annie Duncan*

1 Reminiscences of Annie Duncan, SASL, PRG 532.
2 Ibid., book 1, p. 143.
3 Ibid., book 2, p. 131.
4 *Gentle Invaders — Australian Women at Work 1788–1974*, Edna Ryan and Anne Conlon (eds.), Penguin, Ringwood, pp. 43–45.
5 Reminiscences of Annie Duncan, book 2, p. 229
6 Ibid., book 3, p. 32.

4   *Travel and Independence*

1   Gladys Marks to her father, 28 October 1913, Marks papers, series 2.
2   Mary Gaunt, *Alone in West Africa*, T. Werner Laurie, London, 1912, p. 2. On Gaunt, Joan Gillison, 'Two Invincible Ladies. Louisa Anne Meredith and Mary Gaunt', *Victorian Historical Journal* 50, 2, 1980, pp. 95–103; Ian F. McLaren, *Mary Gaunt. A Cosmopolitan Australian: An Annotated Bibliography*, University of Melbourne Library, Parkville, Vic., 1986; Sue Martin, '"Sad Sometimes, Lonely Often...Dull Never": Mary Gaunt, Traveller and Novelist', in *A Bright and Fiery Troop: Australian Women Writers of the Nineteenth Century*, Debra Adelaide (ed.), Penguin, Ringwood, 1988, pp. 183–97; Patricia Clarke, *Pen-Portraits: Women Writers and Journalists in Nineteenth-Century Australia*, Allen and Unwin, Sydney 1988, pp. 189–93; Birkett, *Spinsters Abroad*.
3   Gaunt, *Alone in West Africa*, p. 3.
4   Later interview in *Sydney Mail* in Clarke, *Pen Portraits*, p. 190
5   Dorothy Jones, 'Water, Gold and Honey: A Discussion of Kirkham's Find', in *Debutante Nation,* ed. Susan Magarey, Sue Rowley and Susan Sheridan (eds), Allen & Unwin, Sydney, 1993, pp. 175–84.
6   Gaunt, *Alone in West Africa,* in Sue Martin, '"Sad Sometimes, Lonely Often … Dull Never"', p. 191.
7   Mary Gaunt, *A Woman in China*, T. Werner Laurie, London, 1914.
8   Mary Gaunt, *A Broken Journey*, T. Werner Laurie,London, 1919.
9   Gaunt, *Reflection — In Jamaica*.
10   Alice Grant Rosman, 'An Australian in West Africa', *Everylady's Journal*, 6 June 1912, p. 339.
11   Graeme Davison, *The Rise and Fall of Marvellous Melbourne*, MUP, Melbourne, 1979, pp. 193–195.
12   On first-wave feminism, Farley Kelly, The 'Woman Question' in Melbourne 1880–1914, PhD thesis, Monash University, 1982. On women and reform, see Chapter 5.
13   Penny Russell, 'Recycling Femininity; Old Ladies and New Women', *Bodies*, ed. David Walker, with Stephen Garton and Julia Horne (eds), *Australian Cultural History* 13, 1994, pp. 31–51.
14   'Jane Laker' (Alice Muskett), *Among the Reeds*, Cassell, London, 1933, pp. 60–1, 75–7. On Muskett, Suzanne Edgar and Dorothy Green, 'Alice Muskett', *ADB*, vol. 10, p. 652–3.
15   Prichard, *Child of the Hurricane*, p. 65.
16   Reminiscences of Annie Duncan, book 1, p. 143.
17   Gladys Marks to her father, Paris, 5 September 1914, Marks papers, series 2.
18   Christina Stead, *For Love Alone*, Angus & Robertson, Sydney, 1990, p. 74 (first edn, 1945).
19   Penny Russell, *A Wish of Distinction, Colonial Gentility and Femininity,* MUP, Melbourne, 1994, pp. 87–9.
20   Modjeska, *Exiles at Home,* p. 31.
21   Bowen, *Drawn from Life,* p. 29; Margaret Preston, 'From Eggs to Electrolux', *Art in Australia,* 1927, no pagination; on Preston, Elizabeth Butel, *Margaret Preston, The Art of Constant Rearrangement*, Ringwood, Penguin, 1986.
22   Alfreda Day, Marie Tuck: 1866–1947, unpublished manuscript, Art Gallery of South Australia Research Centre, 1993.
23   Undated letter, but mid-October 1910, Palmer papers, NLA, MS1174/1/236.
24   For identification of group see here, Chapter 2, note 20.
25   Catherine Helen Spence, *An Autobiography*, reprinted from *Register*, Adelaide, 1910, p. 34. On Spence, Susan Magarey, *Unbridling the Tongues of Women: A Biography of Catherine Helen Spence*, Hale & Iremonger, Sydney, 1985.
26   Kirkby, *Alice Henry*, p. 57.
27   *200 Australian Women*, p. 182.
28   Cliff Turney, 'Fanny Cohen', *ADB,* vol. 8, Bede Nairn and Geoffrey Serle (eds.), MUP, Melbourne, 1981, p. 51.
29   Hazel de Berg, interview with Grace Crowley, 1966, NLA , Oral DeB 173.
30   'Wickham, Anna' (Edith Hepburn), 'Fragments of an Autobiography', *The Writings of Anna Wickham*, R.D.Smith (ed.), Virago, London, 1984, p. 120; On Wickham, Hooton, *Stories of Herself when Young*, pp. 195–7.
31   Modjeska, *Exiles at Home*, p. 26.
32   Adams, *Family Fresco*, p. 145.
33   P. AE. Hutchings and Julie Lewis, *Kathleen O'Connor: Artist in Exile*, Fremantle Arts Centre Press, Fremantle, 1987, pp. 38, 64.

34 Jessie Lillingston to Kenneth Street, 5 July 1915, Jessie Street Papers, NLA, MS 2683/1/21.
35 Miles Franklin, *My Career Goes Bung*, Georgian House,Melbourne, 1946, p. 233.
36 See Andrew Gurr, *Writers in Exile. The Identity of Home in Modern Literature,* Harvester Press, Brighton, 1981, pp. 1–32.
37 Caroline Pilgrim, 'Maude Puddy, Adelaide Pianist of Distinction', *South Australian Homes and Gardens*, 1 August 1949, p. 24.
38 Hazel de Berg, interview with Thea Proctor, 25 September 1962, transcript, NLA , deB 26.
39 Myra Cocks to Julian Ashton, 5 September 1925, *Undergrowth*, January–February 1926.
40 Preston, 'From Eggs to Electrolux'.
41 Preston, 'Why I Became a Convert to Modern Art', *Home*, June 1923, p. 20.
42 'Art Abroad — A Review by Isobel Jacobs', *Art and Architecture* 9, 1912, p. 420.
43 Gladys Marks to her father, 20 November 1913, Marks papers.
44 Prichard, *Child of the Hurricane*, p. 111.
45 Florence James to her mother, 1 November 1928, Florence James papers, ML, ML MSS 5877/9.
46 Richard White, *Inventing Australia*, p. 100; Modjeska, *Exiles at Home*, pp. 16–42; Susan Sheridan, '"Temper Romantic" Bias Offensively Feminine": Australian Women Writers and Literary Nationalism', in *A Double Colonization: Colonial Post-colonial Women's Writing*, Kirsten Holst Petersen and Anna Rutherford (eds), Dangaroo Press, Oxford, 1986, pp. 49–58; Lake, 'The Politics of Respectability', pp. 116–31.
47 Richard White, *Inventing Australia*, p. 59.
48 Nancy Phelan, *The Romantic Lives of Louise Mack*, UQP, St Lucia, 1991, p. 92.
49 Modjeska, *Exiles at Home,* p. 31.
50 Alice Muskett, 'The Fete Night', *The Australian Magazine*, 29 April 1899, pp. 87–92; see also 'The White Witch', *Lone Hand*, July 1907, p. 264; 'Playing the Game', ibid., January 1908, pp. 316–19.
51 Nettie Higgins to her mother, 18 November 1910, Palmer papers; Deborah Jordan, 'Nettie Palmer: Australian Women and Writing 1885–1925', PhD thesis, University of Melbourne, 1982, p. 144.
52 Graeme Davison, 'Sydney and the Bush: An Urban Context for the Australian Legend', *Historical Studies*, 18, 1978, pp. 191–209.
53 Hutchings and Lewis, *Kathleen O'Connor,* p. 46.
54 John Pigot, 'Decadent, Savage and Primitive: Hilda Rix Nicholas and Modernism', *Journal of Australian Studies* 32, 1992, pp. 27–33; Jeanette Hoorne, 'Misogyny and Modernist Painting in Australia: How Male Critics made Modernism their Own', ibid., pp. 7–18.
55 Ibid.; Bernard Smith, *Australian Painting 1788–1970*, OUP, Melbourne, 1971, p. 198; Ian North, *Dorrit Black 1891–1951*, Macmillan and Art Gallery of South Australia, Melbourne, 1979.
56 Gladys Marks to her mother, Paris, January 1914, Marks papers, series 2.
57 Fitzpatrick, *Solid Bluestone Foundations,* p. 11.
58 Stead, *For Love Alone*, p. 224.
59 On images of Paris, Joanna Richardson, *The Bohemians: La Vie Bohème in Paris 1830–1914,* Macmillan, London, 1969; Patrick Brantlinger, 'Bohemia versus Grub Street: Artists' and Writers' Communities in Paris and London', *Mosaic* XVI, 1983, pp. 25–42.
60 Tasma, *The Penance of Portia James*, Heinemann, London, 1891, p. 86.
61 Ibid., pp. 222–3.
62 Preston, 'From Eggs to Electrolux'.
63 *New Idea,* 6 April 1904, p. 902.
64 Alison Rae, 'Australian Artists in Paris', Alice Muskett, 'A Day at the Atelier Colarossi', 'Varnishing Day at the Champ de Mars', *The Daily Telegraph*, 24 February, 2 March, 22 August 1906. See also Margaret Thomas,'Paris Art Schools and Australian Students', pp. 51–2. The accounts of women like Rae and Thomas are but personal versions of the general late nineteenth-century representation of the respectability and acceptability of Paris for women art students. See Clive Holland, 'Lady Art Students' Life in Paris', *Studio* 30 October 1903, pp. 225–33.
65 Holman, *My Wander Year,* pp. 136–137.
66 Christobel Bollen to her family, 16 May 1913, Bagot papers, SASA, PRG 278.
67 'O'C', 'Paris in the Latin Quarter', *West Australian*, 17 May 1913, in Hutchings and Lewis, *Kathleen O'Connor,* p. 295.
68 Muskett, 'The Fete Night'.
69 'Anna Wickham' (Edith Hepburn), 'Fragments of an Autobiography', p. 132.

70 Hackforth Jones, *Barbara Baynton,* p. 80.
71 Clarke, *Pen Portraits*, p. 192
72 Stead, *For Love Alone*, p. 189.
73 Gladys Marks to her family, 22 October 1913, Marks papers, series 2.

Interlude   Winifred James

1 For the outline of the life of Winifred James, Sally O'Neil, 'Winifred James', *ADB,* vol. 9, Bede Nairn and Geoffrey Serle (eds.), MUP, Melbourne, 1983, p. 470, and the file of newspaper cuttings held by the Australian Dictionary of Biography.
2 *British-Australasian*, 10 September 1908.
3 Winifred James, *Letters to My Son,* Hodder & Stoughton, London, 1910.
4 Winifred James, *Letters of a Spinster*, G. Bell & Sons, London, 1911.
5 Winifred James, *A Woman in the Wilderness*, Chapman & Hall, London, 1915; Winifred James, *Out of the Shadows*, no imprint, London, 1924.
6 *Times*, 26 June, 5 August, 5 September 1924 and 3 May 1927.
7 Notebook headed Sex Education, Winifred James papers, VSL, MS11624, Box 1833/10.
8 Winifred James, *Gangways and Corridors*, Allan, London, 1936.
9 Winifred James, *Bachelor Betty*, p. 7.
10 Ibid., p. 233.
11 Winifred James, *Patricia Baring,* Constable, London, 1908, p. 327.
12 James, *Woman in the Wilderness*, p. 133. 'William' is the name given to her husband in the book.
13 *British-Australasian*, 10 September 1908.
14 Winifred James, *Out of the Shadows*, p. 14.
15 Winifred James, *London is My Lute*, Chapman & Hall, London, 1930, p. 198.
16 *The Home*, 1 December 1923.
17 Winifred James, *Out of the Shadows*, p. 94.
18 Winifred James, *A Man for Empire*, Chapman & Hall, London, 1930, p. 15.
19 The Australian Federation of Women Voters, *The Nationality of Married Women*, Sydney 193?; Married Women's Association, *Nationality of Married Women: Position of Women under British Nationality Laws and a Short account of Efforts to Procure their Reform*, London, 1945; Ada Norris, *Champions of the Impossible: A History of the National Council of Women*, Hawthorn Press, Melbourne, 1978, pp. 175–180.
20 *Argus*, 4 February 1933; *Times*, 7 February 1933.
21 *Argus*, 9 July 1935.
22 *Home*, December 1923; *SMH* Supplement, 16 January 1940.

5   Travel and War

1 Gwen Hughes on Bosnia 1935–38, 'Balkan Fever', unpublished typescript, Gwen Hughes papers, uncatalogued, SLV, pp. 72, 117.
2 See Richard White, 'The Soldier as Tourist: The Australian Experience of the Great War', *War and Society* 5, 1987, pp. 63–77.
3 Sister R.A. Kirkcaldie, *In Grey and Scarlet*, A. McCubbin, Melbourne, 1922, p. 9.
4 Phelan, *The Romantic Lives of Louise Mack*, pp. 154–76.
5 Louise Mack, *A Woman's Experience in the Great War*, Fisher Unwin, London, 1915.
6 Peter Burgis, 'Elsie Hall', *ADB*, vol.9, p. 162; 'Una Bourne', *ADB*, vol. 7, p. 358.
7 *Magazine of the Women's College*, November 1920, p. 38.
8 Jessie Traill papers, VSL, MS7975, Box 795/1(a).
9 Jane Hylton, 'Bessie Davidson', *ADB*, vol. 13, p. 576.
10 See Patsy Adam-Smith, *Australian Women at War*, Nelson, Melbourne, 1984; Jan Bassett, *Guns and Brooches: Australian Army Nursing from the Boer War to the Gulf War*, OUP, Melbourne, 1992.
11 ADB files.
12 Melanie Oppenheimer, 'Gifts for France: Australian Red Cross Nurses in France, 1916–1919', *Journal of Australian Studies* 39, 1993, pp. 65–78.

13 On doctors and the war, Ann M. Mitchell, 'Medical Women and the Medical Services of the First World War', *Festschrift for Kenneth Fitzpatrick Russell*, Queensberry Press, Melbourne, 1978, pp. 91–112; Farley Kelly, *Degrees of Liberation*, pp. 74, 95–103.

14 Hutton Neve, 'This Mad Folly', p. 161.

15 Ann Mitchell, p.103; Monica Krippner, *Quality of Mercy: Women at War in Serbia, 1915–18*, David and Charles, Newton Abbot, 1980, p. 22.

16 Ann Mitchell, 'Medical Women', p. 104.

17 Flora Sandes, *Autobiography of a Woman Soldier, A Brief Record of Adventure with the Serbian Army*, Witherby, London, 1927.

18 Miles Franklin to Eva O'Sullivan, 23 September 1913, *My Congenials: Miles Franklin and Friends in Letters*, Jill Roe (ed.), Angus & Robertson, Sydney, vol. 1, p. 97. For the details on Franklin's war service, see editor's notes, p. 103.

19 Miles Franklin to Alice Henry, 26 February 1918, ibid., p. 123.

20 'Dr Dalyell', *The Magazine of the Women's College*, November 1920, pp. 37–41; 'Extracts from a Serbian Letter by Dr Dalyell', ibid., November 1915, pp. 10–13. For the experiences in Serbia of another Australian doctor, Laura Hope, see Mackinnon, p. 57.

21 'Extracts from a Serbian letter by Dr.Dalyell', p. 38.

22 Kelly, *Degrees of Liberation*, p. 76.

23 Mary C. De Garis, *Clinical Notes and Deductions of a Peripatetic, Being Fads and Fancies of a General Practitioner*, Baillière, Tindall & Cox, London, 1926, p. 159.

24 *One Woman at War: Letters of Olive King 1915–1920*, Hazel King (ed.), MUP, Melbourne, 1986.

25 23 June 1918, ibid., p. 104.

26 29 August 1917, ibid., p. 60.

27 12 November 1915, ibid., p. 16.

28 29 August 1917, ibid., p. 60.

29 21 September 1917, ibid., p. 64.

30 29 August 1917, ibid., p. 53.

31 Ibid., p. 20.

32 20 July 1916, ibid., p. 32.

33 21 November 1919, ibid., pp. 169–70.

34 6 June 1929, ibid., pp. 202–3.

35 Letters of Geoffrey and Florence Sulman, typescript copy, ML, MS A1387.

36 7 September 1916, ibid., p. 221.

37 23 September 1916, ibid., p. 252.

38 3 July 1917, ibid., p. 643.

39 Bettina MacAulay, *Songs of Color: The Art of Vida Lahey*, Queensland Art Gallery, Brisbane, 1989, p. 16.

40 Edgeworth David, *Passages of Time*, pp. 70–81.

41 Mabel Brookes, *Memoirs*, pp. 70–81.

42 Mabel Brookes, *Broken Idols*, Melville & Mullens, Melbourne, 1917; *On the Knees of the Gods*; *Old Desires*, Australasian Authors' Agency, Melbourne, 1922.

43 May Brookes, *Wild Flowers and Wanderings under the North Star and Southern Cross*, Imprimerie Française de l'Edition, Paris, 1925, pp. 38,43.

44 Ibid., p. 52.

45 Ibid., p. 60.

46 Freeman, *An Australian Girl in Germany*; Hilda M. Freeman, *Murrumbidgee Memories and Riverina Reminiscences: A Collection of Old Bush History*, B. Niccol, Emu Plains, 1985.

47 Freeman, *An Australian Girl in Germany*, Foreword.

48 Ibid., p. 9.

49 Ibid., p. 53.

50 Ibid., p. 81.

51 *Behind the Lines. One Woman's War 1914–18. The Letters of Caroline Ethel Cooper*, Decie Denholm (ed.), Collins, Sydney, 1982. Biographical information from introduction.

52 Bowen, *Drawn from Life*, p. 19.

53 15 February 1915, Denholm, *Behind the Lines*, p. 59.

54 Ibid., pp. 2–3.

55 Amirah Inglis, *Australians and the Spanish Civil War*; Judith Keene, *The Last Mile to Huesca: An Australian Nurse in the Spanish Civil War*, SUP, Sydney, 1988.

56 Amirah Inglis, *Australians and the Spanish Civil War*, p. 157.

57 Keene, *The Last Mile to Huesca*, p. 4.

58 Mary Kent Hughes, *Matilda Walzes with the Tommies*, OUP, Melbourne, 1943.

59 Vera Bockmann, *Full Circle: An Australian in Berlin 1930–1946*, Decie Denholm (ed.), Wakefield Press, Netley, SA, 1986.

60 Ibid., p. 31.
61 Ibid., p. 77.
62 Muriel Muhler-Schulte, 'Biography of Hans Joachim Muhler-Schulte 1908–1945', typescript, VSL, MS 12419, Box 3294/2.
63 Nancy Wake, *The Autobiography of the Woman the Gestapo Called the White Mouse*, Sun Books, Melbourne, 1986; Russell Braddon, *Nancy Wake. The Story of a Very Brave Woman*, Cassell, London, 1956.
64 Wake, *The White Mouse*, p. 83. Picon was her dog.
65 Ibid., p. 176.

Interlude   Doris Gentile

1   My attempt to tell a story about Doris Dinham Gentile is based on the very random collection of personal material held in the Mitchell Library, ML MSS 2897, and papers held by the family. For a brief outline, Ian Moffat, 'Mother Courage', *Australian*, 13 October 1973.
2   Press clippings, Gentile papers, ML.
3   *SMH*, 30 September 1929.
4   *Times*, 4 February 1934.
5   D. Manners-Sutton, *Black God*, Longmans Green, London, 1934. Press clippings of reviews in Gentile papers, ML. On the Book of the Month award, Dinham to 'Cinderella' (Ella McFadyen), 9 May 1934, Gentile papers with family. The second novel was *Last Secret*, Longmans Green, London, 1939.
6   Dinham to 'Cinderella', 6 May 1930, 25 March 1931, Gentile papers with family.
7   Notebook, Gentile papers, ML.
8   The Sawdust Republic, fragments of a novel, no pagination, Gentile papers, ML.
9   The manuscripts of both novels are with the Gentile papers, ML. The dating of the novels derives from Gentile's references to the death of Enrico Mattei, the leading entrepreneur in postwar Italy and former partisan leader, which occurred in a plane crash in 1961, and from the collection in the Gentile papers of Italian and English newspaper cuttings dating from that time, which discuss the Republic of Salò and the death of Mussolini. The drafts mainly consist of typed sheets of various kinds of paper, including half sheets and scraps, with the odd handwritten page. The pages are not numbered and are stored in folders with no sequence. Nor is there necessarily any sequential narrative on individual pages. Thus any single page may contain partial and incomplete descriptions of incidents, reflections on experience, on fascism, on life, on history, on why and how the protagonist's life had brought her to this particular pass. There is much overlap between the two, but all the material is fragmentary, partial, elliptical.
10 Correspondence relating to Gentile's requests to regain her property and her nationality after the war is held by the Australian Archives, ACT Regional Office, series A 1066/1, Item 1C45/20/1/2/33.
11 Letter from Ben Rhdyying, Yorkshire, 18 May 1946, Gentile papers with family.
12 Gentile, No Time for Love.
13 Gentile, The Sawdust Republic.
14 On the resistance in the Como region, Gianfranco Bianchi, *Antifascismo e Resistenza nel Comasco*, Istituto comasco per la storia del movimento di liberazione, Como, 1975; Francesca Lodolini, *Incontro con il mondo resistentiale comasco attraverso una fonte inedita*, Istituto comasco per la storia del movimento di liberazione, Como, 1987.
15 While no discussion of the death of Mussolini is uncontaminated, for a recent summary of current views, Fabio Andrioli, *Appuntamento sul lago*, Milan, Sugarco Edizioni, 1990. On the thesis that there were in fact two executions of Mussolini, Franco Bandini, *Vita e morte segreta di Mussolini*, Mondadori, Milan, 1978.
16 '"Il Duce l'ho ucisio io". Bluff o rivelazione?', *La Repubblica*, 8 September 1994.
17 Andrioli, *Appuntamento sul lago*, pp. 275–93.

6   Travel and Reform

1   Vida Goldstein, quoted Janette M. Bomford, *That Dangerous and Persuasive Woman: Vida Goldstein*, MUP, Melbourne, 1993, p. 124.

2 R. Pesman Cooper, 'Australian Tourists in Fascist Italy', *Journal of Australian Studies* 17, 1990, pp. 19–31.
3 Freeman, *An Australian Girl in Germany*, p. 311.
4 On Spence, Magarey, *Unbridling the Tongues of Women*.
5 Ibid., p. 12.
6 Spence, *An Autobiography*, pp. 33–4.
7 (C.H. Spence), 'An Australian's Impressions of England', *Cornhill Magazine* X111, 1866, pp. 112, 115–18.
8 Spence, *An Autobiography*, p. 76.
9 Ibid., p. 77
10 Ibid., p. 37.
11 Ibid., p. 42.
12 Australasian Woman's Christian Temperance Union, *Minutes of the Second Triennial Convention*, Brisbane, 1894, p. 58.
13 Spence, *An Autobiography*, p. 74.
14 Magarey, *Unbridling the Toungues of Women*, p. 159.
15 Spence, *An Autobiography*. p. 70.
16 Kate White, 'Bessie Rischbieth, Jessie Street and the End of First-Wave Feminism in Australia', in *Worth Her Salt: Women at Work in Australia*, M. Bevege, M.James and C. Shute (eds.), Hale & Iremonger, Sydney, 1982, pp. 319–29; Penny Russell, 'Jessie Street and International Feminism', in *Jessie Street: Documents and Essays*, Heather Radi (ed.), Women's Redress Press, Sydney, 1984, p. 183.
17 On the international connections of the Woman's Christian Temperance Union, Ian Tyrrell, 'International Aspects of the Woman's Christian Temperance Movement in Australia: The Influence of the American WCTU, 1882–1914', *Journal of Religious History* 12, 1983, pp. 284–304, and *Woman's World, Woman's Empire: The Woman's Christian Temperance Union in International Perspective*, University of North Carolina Press, Chapel Hill, 1992.
18 Tyrrell, 'International Aspects', p. 291.
19 Australasian Woman's Christian Temperance Union, *Minutes of the Third Triennial Convention*, Brisbane, 1897, pp. 50–1.
20 Martha Sear, 'A Great Embroidery of Love': Margaret Windeyer, the World's Columbian Exposition 1893 and the Origins of the National Council of Women, unpublished paper. I am grateful to Martha Sear for allowing me to use her material.
21 The International Council of Women, *Women in a Changing World: The Dynamic Story of the International Council of Women Since 1888*, Routledge & Kegan Paul, London, 1966, pp. 3–40.
22 On Emily Dobson, see here, p. 24. Branches were formed in Victoria in 1901, South Australia, 1902, Queensland, 1903 and Western Australia, 1911. The International Council of Women, *Women in a Changing World*, p. 230; Ada Norris, *Champions of the Impossible*.
23 Gladys Marks to her family, undated letter, (but May) 1914, Marks papers, series 2. In her memoirs, written in the 1960s, Jessie Street gives Geneva as the site of the conference, but it is clear from Gladys Marks's letter and her references to Street, whom she knew at university, that the ICW Congress was in Rome. Jessie Street, *Truth or Repose*, p. 58.
24 Ibid.
25 Gladys Marks to her family,11 May, Copenhagen 30 May, London 8 June, ibid.
26 Jessie Street, *Truth or Repose*, p. 58.
27 On Vida Goldstein, Lyn Henderson, *The Goldstein Story*, Stockland Press, North Melbourne, 1973; Bomford, *That Dangerous and Persuasive Woman*.
28 Bomford, *That Dangerous and Persuasive Woman*, p. 43.
29 Ibid.
30 For Alice Henry in America, Kirkby, *Alice Henry* .
31 Ibid., p. 2.
32 Ibid., p. 207
33 Dianne Kirkby, 'Alice Henry and the Women's Trade Union League: Australian Reformer, American Reform', in *Worth Her Salt*, Bevege, James and Shute (eds), p. 244.
34 Kirkby, *Alice Henry*, p. 193.
35 For Miles Franklin in Chicago, *My Congenials*. vol. I, pp. 57–100; Verna Coleman, *Miles Franklin in America. Her Unknown (Brilliant) Career*, Sydney, Sirius Books, 1981.
36 Miles Franklin to Isabella Goldstein, 13 October 1911, *My Congenials*, vol.1, p. 69.
37 Coleman, *Miles Franklin in America*, p. 82.
38 Bomford, *That Dangerous and Persuasive Woman*, p. 36.
39 *The Memoirs of Alice Henry*, p. 34.

40 Bomford, *That Dangerous and Persuasive Woman*, p. 105.
41 Prichard, *Child of the Hurricane*, p. 178; Jordan, Nettie Palmer, pp. 126–131; Gladys Marks to family, 9 October 1913, Marks papers, series 2; Dora Meeson Coates, *George Coates: His Art and His Life*, J.M. Dent and Sons, London, 1937, p. 43; Jessie Sreet, *Truth or Repose*, p. 39.
42 Bomford, *That Dangerous and Persuasive Woman*, p. 109.
43 Angelina Pearce, *A Memento of Our Trip to Europe*, Adelaide, no date, p. 26.
44 Miles Franklin to Isabella Goldstein, 13 October 1911, *My Congenials*, vol. 1, p. 69.
45 Bomford, *That Dangerous and Persuasive Woman*, p. 113.
46 Barbara Caine, 'Vida Goldstein and the English Militant Campaign', *Women's History Review* 2, 3, 1993, pp. 363–73.
47 For Bessie Rischbieth's travel to England as a radicalising experience, Kate White, 'Bessie Rischbieth, Jessie Street', p. 320.
48 Coleman, *Miles Franklin in America*, p. 83.
49 Muriel Matters, 'My Impressions as an Agitator for Social Reform', in Mrs L.W.Matters, *Australians Who Count in London*, p. 162. See also 'Australian Women in Politics: An Interview with Miss Muriel Matters, *British-Australasian*, 9 February 1911; 'Miss Muriel Matters: Australia's Suffragette', Women's World, *Herald*, 21 June 1910.
50 Richard White, 'Bluebells and Fogtown: Australians' First Impression of England, 1860–1940', *Australian Cultural History*, 5, 1986, pp. 54–56.
51 Randolph Bedford, *Explorations in Civilization*, S. Day, Sydney, 1914.
52 Catherine Martin, *The Old Roof-Tree: Letters of Ishbel to her Half-Brother Mark Latimer (August-January)*, Longmans Green, London, 1906, pp. 168–9. On Catherine Martin, Margaret Allen, 'Catherine Martin: An Australian Girl?', in *A Bright and Fiery Troop*, Debra Adelaide, (ed.) pp. 151–165.
53 Gaunt, *Alone in West Africa*, p. 394.
54 Prichard, *Child of the Hurricane*, p. 177.
55 *The Memoirs of Alice Henry*, p. 29.
56 Langmore, *Prime Ministers' Wives*, p. 33.
57 Catherine Martin, *The Old Roof-Tree*, p. 84.
58 Rose Scott Cowen, *Crossing Dry Creeks 1879–1919*, Wentworth Press, Sydney, 1961, p. 70.
59 Thomas, *Scamper Through Spain*, p. 101.
60 Gladys Marks to her family, letter, 28 October 1913, Marks papers, series 2.
61 Catherine Martin, *The Old Roof-Tree*, pp. 104–5.
62 On constructions of Australia as a young and new society, Richard White, *Inventing Australia*, pp. 47–51.
63 Bomford, *That Dangerous and Persuasive Woman*, p. 109.
64 Rosman, *Miss Bryde*, p. 25.
65 Edgeworth David, *Passages of Time*, p. 77.
66 Gaunt, *Alone in West Africa*, p. 167.
67 Sue Martin, '"Sad Sometimes…"',pp. 184–185.
68 Catherine Martin, *The Old Roof-Tree*, pp. 246–249.
69 Holman, *My Wander Year*, pp. 64–73.
70 Nettie Higgins to Vance Palmer, November 1909, Palmer papers, NLA MS1174/1/243; Bomford, *That Dangerous and Persuasive Woman*, p. 109; Gladys Marks to her family, 13 November 1914, Marks papers, series 2; Miles Franklin to Alice Henry, 12 December 1919, *My Congenials*, vol. 1, p. 141.
71 Street, *Truth or Repose*, p. 40.
72 Miles Franklin to NWTUL Executive Board, Chicago, 30 October 1911, *My Congenials*, vol. 1, p. 69.
73 For the overseas life of Joice Loch, Joice Nankivell Loch, *A Fringe of Blue: An Autobiography*, Murray, London, 1968; Sydney Loch, Autobiography, typescript, NLA, MS 2948; Joice Nankivell Loch and Sydney Loch, *The River of a Hundred Ways: Life in the War-Devastated Areas of Eastern Poland*, George Allen & Unwin, London, 1924. Other Australian women in Poland included the trade union organiser, Muriel Heagney and nursing sister, Lilian Foster. For Heagney, Newspaper cuttings relating to Muriel Heagney, NLA; for Foster, *A Biographical Register 1788–1939*, ed. H.J. Gibbney and Ann G. Smith (eds), Australian National University, Canberra, 1987, vol. 1, p. 239.
74 Joice Nankivell Loch and Sydney Loch, *Ireland in Travail: The Personal Experience of Two Independent Visitors in 1920–21*, Murray, London, 1922.
75 Joice Loch, *A Fringe of Blue*, pp. 71–2.
76 Ibid., p. 72.
77 Ibid., pp. 97, 109. Sydney Loch's portrait of Ethel Cooper is more sympathetic than that of his wife.

78 Ibid., p. 113.
79 Carol Rasmussen, *The Lesser Evil? Opposition to War and Fascism in Australia 1920–1941*, History Department, University of Melbourne, 1992, p. 14.
80 On the Women's International League for Peace and Freedom, Johanna Alberti, *Beyond Suffrage: Feminists in War and Peace, 1914–1928*, Macmillan, London, 1989; Harriet Hyman Alonso, *The Women's Peace Union and the Outlawry of War, 1921–1942*, University of Tenessee Press, Knoxville, 1989.
81 For Eleanor Moore, Eleanor Moore, *The Quest for Peace*; Mimi Colligan and Malcolm Saunders, 'Eleanor Moore', *ADB*, vol. 10, p. 564.
82 For other women whose activity in peace movements took them overseas, see the entries in the *ADB* on Alice Moss, Cecilia John, and Edith Waterman, and see Hazel de Berg, conversations with Ruby Rich.
83 Norris, *Champions of the Impossible*, p. 45.
84 Street, *Truth or Repose?*, p. 62.
85 Mitchell, *Spoils of Opportunity*, p. 272.
86 On anti-fascist movements in Australia and on Australians and the Spanish Civil War, Robin Gollan, *Revolutionaries and Reformists: Communism and the Australian Labour Movement*, ANU Press, Canberra, 1975; Frank Farrell, *International Socialism and Australian Labour: The Left in Australia 1919–1939*, Hale & Iremonger, Sydney, 1981; Rasmussen, *The Lesser Evil?*; Amirah Inglis, *Australians and the Spanish Civil War*; Judith Keene, *The Last Mile to Huesca*.
87 Hazel Rowley, *Christina Stead*, pp. 169–74.
88 Patricia Thompson, *Accidental Chords*, Penguin, Ringwood, 1988, p. 139.
89 See here, pp. 190–3.
90 Student Register, Archives of the Women's College, University of Sydney.
91 Janet Mitchell, *Spoils of Opportunity*, p. 60.
92 For Eleanor Hinder, Frances Wheelhouse, *Eleanor Mary Hinder: An Australian Woman's Social Welfare Work in China Between the Wars*, Wentworth Press, Sydney, 1978, Letter from E.M. Hinder, *Newsletter of the Women's College* 2, 1933, p. 10.
93 Wheelhouse, *Eleanor Mary Hinder*, p. 9.
94 *Newsletter of the Women's College*, 1932, p. 8.
95 For an appreciation of Viola Smith, see Hazel de Berg, conversations with Ruby Rich, pp. 133.85 – 133.91.
96 Ibid., p. 133.83.

Interlude   Dora Birtles and Irene Saxby

1 Richard White, 'Overseas', in *Australia 1938*, Bill Gammage and Peter Spearritt (eds.), Fairfax, Syme and Weldon, Sydney, 1987, p. 438.
2 Ibid., p. 441.
3 *Women's Weekly*, 15 June 1935. I am grateful to Bridget Griffen-Foley, Macquarie University, for drawing my attention to the Women's Weekly Travel Bureau.
4 Billie Melman, *Women and the Popular Imagination in the Twenties: Flappers and Nymphs*, Macmillan, London, 1988, p. 95.
5 Byles, *By Cargo Boat and Mountain*, p. 10. On Marie Byles, Heather Radi, 'Marie Beuzeville Byles', *ADB*, vol. 13, pp. 325- 6.
6 Byles, *By Cargo Boat and Mountain*, p. 17.
7 Marie Byles, *Journey into Burmese Silence*, Allen & Unwin, London, 1963, pp. 15–16.
8 Margaret Gilruth papers, SLV, MS7983; Gilruth, *Maiden Voyage*.
9 *News-Pictorial*, 22 December 1931.
10 Dora Birtles, *North-West by North: A Journal of a Voyage*, Jonathan Cape, London, 1935. Her shipboard diaries and letters are bound together as 'The Cruise of the *Gullmarn*', NLA, MS 8305. Other papers, manuscripts and newspaper cuttings are held by Mosman Municipal Library, NSW. The names of the boat and the participants are disguised in *North-West by North*.
11 Deidre Moore in *Northern Herald*, 27 February 1992.
12 Birtles, *North-West by North*, p. 73.
13 Birtles, introduction to 1985 Virago reprint of *North-West By North*.
14 Quoted in 'Face to Face', *Sydney Morning Herald Good Weekend*, 23 May 1987.
15 Mills, *Discourse of Difference*, p. 97.
16 Birtles, *North-West by North*, p. 286.
17 Ibid., p. 332.

18 Birtles, diary, 31 May 1932, 'The Cruise of the *Gullmarn*', pp. 33, 102.
19 Birtles, *North-West by North*, p. 427.
20 Ibid., p. 354.
21 Ibid., p. 73.
22 Ibid., p. 57
23 Bert Birtles, *Exiles in The Aegean: A Personal Narrative of Greek Politics and Travel,* Victor
    Gollancz, London, 1938. Dora Birtles's short stories were published in *Coast to Coast,*
    1944 and *Australian New Writing,* 1946.
24 Len Fox, 'Writers of the Thirties', *Overland* 127, 1992, pp. 10–12.
25 Deidre Moore in *Northern Herald*, 27 February 1992.
26 This account of Irene Saxby's time in Russia is based on two articles that she published
    in the 1930s, 'Rambling Round Moscow' and 'Holidays in the USSR', *The Soviets Today,*
    November 1934, July 1937; on the account of her time in Russia, which she wrote in
    the early 1980s, Irene Rush, 'My Years in Russia', typescript, NLA, MS 8316; and on a
    conversation with Irene Saxby Rush in November 1994.
27 Rush, 'My Years in Russia', p. 230.

7   *Travel and Politics*

 1 Betty Roland, *Caviar for Breakfast*, Collins, Sydney, 1989, p. 4.
 2 Audrey Blake, *A Proletarian Life*, Kibble Books, Malmsbury, Vic., 1984, pp. 136–137.
 3 Suzanne Abramovich, *So This is Russia!!*, Friends of the Soviet Union, Sydney, 1930,
    p. 1.
 4 On political pilgrimage to the Soviet Union, Neal Wood, *Communism and British
    Intellectuals*, Gollancz, London, 1959; David Caute, *The Fellow Travellers: Intellectual
    Friends of Communism,* Yale University Press, New Haven, 1972, revised edn, 1988;
    Paul Hollander, *Political Pilgrims: Travels of Western Intellectuals to the Soviet Union,
    China, and Cuba 1928–1978*, OUP, New York, 1981; Michael Davidson, *American
    Writers in the Soviet Union*, Mercury House, San Francisco, 1991. On the Soviet Union
    and the Australian left, Rasmussen, *The Lesser Evil*, pp. 31–40.
 5 Manes Sperber, *Man and His Deeds*, McGraw Hill, New York, 1970, p. 2.
 6 Dorothy Gibson, 'A Soviet School in Moscow', Ralph and Dorothy Gibson papers, NLA,
    MS 7844, series 2, box 4, folder 21.
 7 Sperber, *Man and His Deeds*, p. 3.
 8 Amirah Inglis, 'The Woman Who Loved Russia and Hated Children', review of Hazel
    Rowley, *Christina Stead. A Biography*, *Voices* 3, summer 1993–94, p. 116.
 9 Roland, *Caviar for Breakfast*, p. 68.
10 Jessie Street, *Truth or Repose*, p. 146.
11 Katharine Susannah Prichard, *The Real Russia*, Modern Publishers, Sydney, 1934, p. 6.
12 'Australian Woman in the Soviet Union', report of the address of Ada Bromham to a
    meeting of the W.C.T.L., Perth, 12 June 1935, *The Soviets Today*, August 1935;
    Abramovich, p. 1.
13 Letter 6 December 1934, Gibson papers, series 2, box 2, folder 4.
14 Street, *Truth or Repose*, pp. 149, 154–5.
15 P. L. Travers, *Moscow Excursion*, Reynal & Hitchcock, New York, 1934, p. 6.
16 Neal Wood, *Communism and British Intellectuals*, quoted in Rasmussen, *The Lesser Evil,*
    p. 38.
17 Ralph Gibson, *One Woman's Life: A Memoir of Dorothy Gibson*, Hale & Iremonger,
    Sydney, 1980.
18 Autobiographical note, Gibson papers, series 2, box 4, folder 21.
19 Kelly, *Degrees of Liberation*, p. 95.
20 22 July 1934, NLA MS7844, series 2, Box 4, Folder 4.
21 29 July 1934, ibid.
22 5 January 1934(5), ibid.
23 6 December 1934, 5 January 1934 (5), ibid.
24 17 January 1934 (35), ibid.
25 John Sendy, *Ralph Gibson: An Extraordinary Communist,* Ralph Gibson Biography
    Committee, Melbourne, 1988.
26 For the later activities of Dorothy Gibson, see here, pp. 205–6.
27 Roland, *Caviar for Breakfast*, pp. 143–7.
28 Ibid., p. 61.

29 Ibid., p. 139.
30 Modjeska, *Exiles at Home*, p. 146.
31 Roland, p. 27. While Freda Utley looms large in Roland's diary, Roland is not mentioned in Utley's memoirs. Freda Utley, *Lost Illusion*, Chicago, Regnery, 1948.
32 Ibid., pp. 65–6.
33 Ibid., p. 86.
34 Prichard, *The Real Russia*, The text was first serialised in the Melbourne *Herald*.
35 Ibid., p. 1.
36 Ibid., pp. 13–14.
37 Ibid., p. 84
38 Ibid., pp. 246–257
39 Modjeska, *Exiles at Home*, p. 143.
40 Ibid., p. 147.
41 Ric Throssell, *Wild Weeds and Wind Flowers: The Life of Katharine Susannah Prichard*, Angus & Robertson, Sydney, p. 76.
42 Prichard, *The Real Russia*, p. 135.
43 Abramovich, *So This is Russia!!*; Interview, *The Soviets Today*, February 1934.
44 Abramovich, *So This is Russia!!*, p. 7.
45 'Women in the Soviet Union', report of address of Isabel McCorkindale to meeting of United Associations, ibid., June 1935.
46 Isabel McCorkindale, 'The Woman Manual Worker of the USSR.', ibid., June 1937.
47 Street, *Truth or Repose*, p. 152.
48 Ibid., p. 131.
49 Street papers, MS 2683/4/1322
50 Street, *Truth or Repose*, p. 147.
51 Hayball, *Sidelights on the Soviet*, p. 13.
52 On women in the Soviet Union, Gail Warshofsky Lapidus, *Women in Soviet Society: Equality, Development and Social Change*, University of California Press, Berkeley, 1978, pp. 95–122.
53 Hayball, *Sidelights on the Soviet*, pp. 192–4.
54 Ibid., p. 80.
55 Travers, *Moscow Excursion*, pp. 6–8, 54, 61, 95.
56 Other women who travelled to the Soviet Union included Muriel Heagney, who visited Russia in 1924, and Mrs Moroney, who spent six weeks in the Soviet Union in 1934, *Working Woman*, February 1935.
57 Roland, *Caviar for Breakfast*, p. 32.
58 Ibid., p. 139.
59 F. Cardell-Oliver, *Empire Unity or 'Red' Asiastic Domination*, E.S. Wigg & Son, printers, Perth, 1934; David Black, 'Dame Annie Florence Cardell-Oliver', *ADB*, vol. 13, p. 365.
60 22 August 1934, Gibson papers, series 2, box 4, folder 22.
61 Roland, *Caviar for Breakfast*, p. 128
62 *Newsletter of the Women's College*, 1936.
63 For another very favourable account of Nazi Germany, Doris Hayball, 'Continental Contacts', in which she wrote about the 'Hitler whom the Germans know and love — seen through their eyes — pictured with their own words — the Hitler who brought them out of the depths, the Hitler who WILL have a clean nation, the Hitler who exacts from jealous enemies respect for the beautiful land that they love and of which they are proud'.

Interlude   Voyages and Ports

1 Finn, *Pigmies Among Potentates*, p. 14.
2 Maguire, *Bright Morning*, p. 125.
3 Mabel Dowling, diary, 3 April - 7 August 1928, ML, ML MSS 4249.
4 Barbara Hanrahan, *Michael and Me and the Sun*, UQP, St Lucia, 1992, p. 5.
5 Nancy Adams, *Family Fresco*, p. 102.
6 Mack quoted in Phelan, *The Romantic Lives of Louise Mack*, p. 107; Nettie Higgins to Vance Palmer, at sea, 21 April 1914, Palmer papers, 1174/1/105.
7 Aileen Palmer to her family, 22 December 1936, NLA, Aileen Palmer papers, MS 6759, Box 1, Folder 10.
8 Janet Mitchell, *Spoils of Opportunity*, p. 154.

9 Mabel Brookes, *Memoirs*, p. 29.
10 Langmore, *Prime Ministers' Wives*, p. 26.
11 Jessie Lillingston to Kenneth Street, 15 April 1915, Street papers, 2683/1/5.
12 Byles, *By Cargo Boat*, p. 37.
13 Brennan, *Better Than Dancing*, p. 162.
14 Cambridge, *The Retrospect*, Stanley Paul, London, 1913, p. 16.
15 Jessie Mitchell to her family, 1 May 1934, Jessie Mitchell papers.
16 Bowen, *Drawn from Life*, pp. 30–31.
17 Barbara Hanrahan, *Sea-green* (1974), Fontana, Melbourne, 1980, p. 18.
18 The Reverend D. O'Donnell (Wesleyan minister), *Vignettes from a Tourist's Notebook*, Carey and Page, Adelaide, 1886, p. 92.
19 John Bunyan McCure, *Life in England and Australia: Reminiscences of Travel and Voyages over One Hundred Thousand Miles or Forty Years in the Wilderness*, Robert Banks, London, 1876, p. 260.
20 Evelyn Costin, *Shadows on the Grass: An Autobiography from 1901 to 1978 with its Adjacent History*, Edgewaters, Apollo Bay, Vic., 1981, p. 164.
21 Jessie Lillingston to Kenneth Street, 9 April 1938, Street papers, 2683/1/600
22 Gladys Marks to her family, 7 February 1913, Marks papers, series 2; Richard White, 'Overseas', p. 437.
23 Hanrahan, *Michael and Me and the Sun*, p. 1.
24 Christobel Bollen to her mother, 27 March 1913, Bagot papers.
25 Ida Haysom, diary, vol. 1, 3 April 1936.
26 Florence James to her family, 14 October 1927, James papers, ML, ML MSS 5877/9.
27 Florence James to her family, 7 May 1928, ibid.
28 Nancy Cato to author, 29 September 1993.
29 Dymphna Cusack, draft for autobiography, Cusack papers, NLA, MS 4621/9/243.
30 Lilley, *A Possum Abroad*, p. 8
31 Gilruth, *Maiden Voyage*, p. 35.
32 Downe, *Wind on the Heath*, p. 42.
33 M.D.B., 'A Day at Colombo', *Australian Nurses' Journal*, 15 March 1909, p. 108.
34 Anonymous diary of an overseas trip, March–August 1939, ML, ML MSS 5148.
35 Mabel Dowling, diary, 3 April–7 August 1928, ML, ML MSS 4249.
36 Edna Kerr, Here, There, Everywhere, typescript, SLV, MS 12101, box 2590/4(b), 8 March 1959, p. 6.

8   *Travel and Discovery of the World*

1 (Spence), 'An Australian's Impressions of England', p. 118.
2 Hazzard, *The Transit of Venus*, p. 37.
3 Duncan, Reminiscences, Book 2, p. 200.
4 Connie Miller, *Memory Be Green*, Fremantle Arts Centre Press, Fremantle, 1980, p. 160.
5 Anne Dangar to Julian Ashton, 8 April 1926, in *Undergrowth*, May-June 1926.
6 Clare Davies, *This is My Life*, p. 22.
7 Graham Hassall, 'Euphemia Baker', *ADB*, vol. 13, p. 93; Winifred Stegar, *Always Bells*, Angus & Robertson, Sydney, 1969.
8 For an interesting discussion of one Australian's Britain as a land of the imagination, Judith Brett, *Robert Menzies' Forgotten People*, Macmillan, Sydney, 1992, pp. 129–55.
9 Louise Mack, *Children of the Sun*, Melrose, London, 1904, pp. 40–241.
10 Pagliaro, 'An Australian Family Abroad', p. 24
11 Stirling, *Memories of an Australian Childhood*, pp. 43, 130.
12 Nina Murdoch, *She Travelled Alone in Spain*, Harrap, London, 1935, p. 12.
13 Dymphna Cusack, *Illyria Reborn*, Heinemann, London, 1966, p. 1.
14 Harvie, *Madge's Trip to Europe*, p. 26
15 Gladys Marks to her family, 28 March 1913, Marks papers, series 2.
16 Janey Rowe to Fanny O'Leary, Florence, 20 May 1874, in Pagliaro, 'An Australian Family Abroad', p. 103.
17 Kerr, Here, There, Everywhere, p. 57.
18 June Davies, journal, 1969–70, p. 11, typescript, VSL, uncatalogued.
19 Haysom, diary, 16 May 1936.
20 *The Memoirs of Alice Henry*, p. 27.
21 Jessie Mitchell, Diary, Jessie Mitchell papers.
22 *Newsletter of the Women's College* 9, 1940, p. 19.

23 Angelina Pearce, *A Memento of our Trip to Europe*, p. 11.
24 Una Falkiner, diary, July 1938, p. 101, ML, ML MSS 423.
25 Adams, *Family Fresco*, p. 82.
26 Prichard, *Child of the Hurricane*, p. 117.
27 Ethel Turner, *Ports and Happy Havens,* Hodder & Stoughton, London, 1912, p. 76.
28 Nancy Cato to author, 29 September 1993.
29 M. Hudson's Trip Through America, England and the Continent, January-October 1881, ML, ML MSS 1948, 24 June 1881.
30 June Davies, journal, p. 11.
31 Gillian Bouras, *A Foreign Wife,* Penguin, Ringwood, 1990, p. 49.
32 Mack, *An Australian Girl in London,* p. 74.
33 Eliza Mitchell, *Three Quarters of a Century,* p. 55.
34 Turner, *Ports and Happy Havens,* p. 27.
35 'Anglo Australian', (Agnes Grant Hay) *After-Glow Memories*, Methuen, London, 1905, p. 247.
36 Gladys Marks to her family, 29 January 1914, Marks papers, series 2.
37 Nina Murdoch, *Seventh Heaven,* Angus & Robertson, Sydney, 1930, p. 2.
38 Nancy Cato to author, 29 September 1993.
39 Barbara Hanrahan, *Michael and Me and the Sun*, p. 8.
40 Howorth, *Coo-ee England,* p. 151.
41 Gentile, 'No Time for Love'.
42 De Groen, 'Conversation with Janet Alderson', p. 5.
43 Howorth, *Coo-ee England,* p. 158.
44 Dora Birtles, 'Lovely, Lousy London', typescript, novel, p. 4, Dora Birtles papers, Mosman Municipal Library, Box 2g5.
45 Ervin Goffman, quoted in Dean MacCannell, *The Tourist: A New Theory of the Leisure Class*, Schocken Books, New York, 1976, p. 42.
46 Lilley, *A Possum Abroad,* p. 31
47 Harvie, *Madge's Trip to Europe,* p. 61.
48 Finn, *Pigmies Among Potentates*, p. 156.
49 Chomley, Diary, 15 May 1903.
50 Finn, *Pigmies Among Potentates*, p. 157.
51 See also Richard White,'Passing Through', pp. 165–6
52 Isabel Mackenzie, notes for an autobiography, Isabel Mackenzie papers, 1923–72, ML, ML MSS 2996/1. Mackenzie, an art teacher, recorded her recollections of her 1936 trip *c.*1968. On Australians in Britain, Richard White, 'Bluebells and Fogtown', pp. 44-59.
53 Winifred James, *London is My Lute*, p. 198.
54 Lilley, *A Possum Abroad,* p. 119.
55 Praed, *The Australian Girl,* p. 113.
56 See, for example, Tasma, *Not Counting the Cost,* p. 162, and Praed, *The Australian Girl*, p. 115.
57 Richardson, *Myself When Young,* p. 87.
58 Fitzpatrick, *Solid Bluestone Foundations,* p. 186.
59 Emily Anne (Mrs Alfred) Bennett, *Vignettes of Travel,* George Murray & Co., Sydney, 1886, p. 52.
60 Haysom, diary, 12 May 1936.
61 Cicily Little, *The Lass with the Delicate Air*, Angus & Robertson, Sydney, 1948, p. 82.
62 Nancy Cato, to author, 29 September, 1993.
63 'Urban continent' are the words of Dora Birtles, 'Lovely, Lousy, London', p. 22.
64 Tasma, *Not Counting the Cost*, p. 162; see also Praed, *The Australian Girl*, p. 115.
65 Holman, *My Wander Year,* p,17.
66 Nettie Higgins to her mother, 19 January 1911, Palmer papers, 1174/1/387.
67 Janet Mitchell, *Spoils of Opportunity*, p. 46.
68 Lilley, *A Possum Abroad,* p. 119.
69 Richard White, *Inventing Australia*, 48–49; 'Bluebells and Fogtown', pp. 54–55.
70 Lilley, *A Possum Abroad,* p. 117.
71 Nettie Palmer to her mother, 5 April 1911, Palmer papers, 1174/1/463.
72 Thomas, *A Scamper Through Spain*, p. 115.
73 See Roslyn Pesman Cooper, '"Majestic Nature — Squalid Humanity": Naples and the Australian Tourist 1870–1930', *Australian Cultural History*, 10 (1991), pp. 51–2.
74 Holman, *My Wander Year,* p. 12.
75 Richardson, *Myself When Young,* p 66.
76 Gladys Marks to her family, 6 May 1913, Marks papers, series 2.
77 'Anglo Australian', *After-Glow Memories,* p. 245.
78 Edith Doust, Children's Letter Competition, *Parthenon*, 1 August 1889.

79 Mary Grant Bruce, diary, November 1927, VSL, MS9975, box 1309/3.
80 Duncan, Reminiscences, vol. 2, p. 234.
81 Una Falkiner, diary, 5 July 1929.
82 Bennett, *Vignettes of Travel*, pp. 68–69.
83 Christobel Bollen to her family, 5 August 1913.
84 Fitzpatrick, *Solid Bluestone Foundations*, pp. 68–9.
85 *British-Australasian*, 17 September 1908, p. 12. See also Alice Grant Rosman, 'How to "Do" London', *Everylady's Journal*, 6 January 1914, p. 23.
86 Duncan, Reminiscences, vol. 2, p. 97.
87 *British-Australasian*, 27 October 1910.
88 Mack, *An Australian Girl in London*, p. 286.
89 On anti-tourism, Buzard, *The Beaten Track*, pp. 4–7.
90 Cambridge, *The Retrospect*, p. 30.
91 K.S. Inglis, 'Going Home', p. 130.
92 Osmond, *An Australian Wooing*, p. 119.
93 'Iota', (Kathleen Caffyn), *A Comedy of Spasms*, Hutchinson, London, 1895, p. 184.
94 Phyllis Downe, *Wind on the Heath*, Georgian House, Melbourne, 1946, p. 81.
95 Thomas, *A Scamper Through Spain*, p. 111.
96 Mack, *An Australian Girl in London*, p. 107; see Roslyn Pesman Cooper, 'The Past: Australians and Tuscany, 1850–1950', *An Antipodean Connection*, pp. 135–55.
97 Finn, *Pigmies Among Potentates*, p. 71.
98 Cambridge, *The Retrospect*, pp. 33–5.
99 Miles Franklin to Isabella Goldstein, letter, 13 October 1911, *My Congenials*, vol.1, p. 70.
100 Bennett, *Vignettes of Travel*, p. 73.
101 Lilley, *A Possum Abroad*, p. 119.
102 Margaret Thomas, *A Painter's Pastime*, Greening, London, 1908 , p. 106.
103 Mack, *An Australian Girl in London*, p. 282.
104 James, *Bachelor Betty*, p. 82.
105 (Spence), 'An Australian's Impressions of England', p. 112; Richardson, *Myself When Young*, p. 68.
106 Casey, *Tides and Eddies*, pp. 15,17.
107 See Nicholas Jose, 'Nuovo Mondo', *Age Monthly Review*, April 1988; Simon During, 'Postcolonialism', in *Beyond the Disciplines. The New Humanities*, Australian Academy of the Humanities, Canberra, K.K.Ruthven (ed.), 1992 and for further examples, see here, pp. 202–3.
108 *The Memoirs of Alice Henry*, p. 29
109 Cambridge, *The Retrospect*, p. 31.
110 Kathleen Fitzpatrick, 'A Cloistered Life', in *The Half-Open Door*. Patricia Grimshaw (ed.), p. 25.
111 Fitzpatrick, *Solid Bluestone Foundations*, p. 194
112 Davidson, *Lyrebird Rising*.
113 Tasma, *Not Counting the Cost*, p. 172.
114 Hutchings and Lewis, *Kathleen O'Connor*, p. 290; Holman, *My Wander Year*, p. 133.
115 Prichard, *Child of the Hurricane*, p. 138.
116 Christina Stead to Nellie Molyneux, Paris, 1 March 1929, *Web of Friendship: Selected Letters (1928–1973). Christina Stead*, R.G. Geering (ed.), Angus & Robertson, Sydney, 1992, p. 12.
117 Bowen, *Drawn From Life*, p. 87
118 Lilley, *A Possum Abroad*, p. 119.
119 Nina Murdoch, *Seventh Heaven*, p. 5.
120 Pearce, *A Memento of Our Trip*, p. 63
121 Prichard, *Child of the Hurricane*, p. 138.
122 Christina Stead to Nellie Molyneux, 2 April 1929, *A Web of Friendship*, p. 16.
123 Nina Murdoch, *Seventh Heaven*, p. 9.
124 Winifred James, *Letters of a Spinster*, p. 144.
125 Gladys Marks to her family, 10 March 1913, Marks papers, series 2.
126 Margaret Harris, 'The Writing of Tasma: The Work of Jessie Couvreur', in *A Bright and Fiery Troop*, Debra Adelaide (ed.), pp. 165–82.
127 Anne Wilson, *Two Summers*, Harper, London, 1900, p. 317.
128 Gentile,'No Time for Love'.
129 Barbara Hanrahan, *Sea-green*, p. 41.
130 Thomas, *A Scamper Through Spain*, pp. 50, 26.
131 Lilley, *A Possum Abroad*, p. 12.
132 Thomas, *A Scamper Through Spain*, p. 85 (Toledo).

133 Ibid., pp. 201–22.
134 Nina Murdoch, *Seventh Heaven*, p. 27. For some discussion of Australian attitudes of superiority in Italy, Pesman Cooper, "'Majestic Nature — Squalid Humanity'", pp. 46–57.

Interlude   Stella Bowen

1 Bowen, *Drawn from Life*, p. 147.
2 This narrative of Stella Bowen's life derives from her autobiography, *Drawn from Life*; from *The Correspondence of Ford Madox Ford and Stella Bowen*, Sondra J. Stang and Karen Cochran (eds), Indiana University Press, Bloomington, 1993, and from Arthur Mizener, *The Saddest Story: A Biography of Ford Madox Ford*, World Publishing Company, New York, 1971; and Alan Judd, *Ford Madox Ford*, Collins, London, 1990. On Bowen's painting, Hammond, *A Century of Australian Women Artists*, pp. 32–4, Hyland, *South Australian Women Artists*, pp. 20–3.
3 For women on the left bank, Shari Benstock, *Women of the Left Bank, Paris, 1900–1940*, University of Texas Press, Austin, 1986.
4 Bowen, *Drawn from Life*, p. 35.
5 Ibid., p. 125.
6 Margaret Cole, *Growing up into Revolution*, Longmans Green, London, 1949, p. 168.
7 Jean Rhys, *Quartet*, Harper & Row, New York, 1957 (first published 1928 as *Postures*); Ford Madox Ford, *When the Wicked Men*, Horace Liveright, New York, 1931; Edward de Nève, *Sous les verrous*, Paris, 1933 (edited English translation by Jean Rhys, *Barred*, Desmond Harmsworth, London, 1932).
8 Bowen, *Drawn from Life*, p. 97.
9 Bowen to Ford, 25 November 1926, *The Correspondence of Ford Madox Ford and Stella Bowen*, p. 236.
10 On women and the Bildungsroman, *Fictions of Female Development*, Elizabeth Abel, Marianne Hirsch and Elizabeth Langland (eds.), University of New England Press, Hanover, 1983, pp. 3–15; Dana A. Heller, *The Feminization of the Quest-Romance: Radical Departures*, University of Texas Press, Austin, 1990, pp. 1–21.
11 Bowen, *Drawn from Life*, p. 31.
12 Ibid., pp. 10–11.
13 Bowen referred to herself as a 'rubbishy young colonial' in a letter to Ford, 5 April 1919, in *The Correspondence of Ford Madox Ford and Stella Bowen*, p. 65.
14 Bowen, *Drawn from Life*, p. 175.
15 On Bowen as an Australian war artist, Lola Wilkinson, 'Stella Bowen: Australian War Artist', *Art and Australia* 28, 4, 1991, pp. 493–7.
16 Carol Pearson and Katherine Pope, *The Female Hero in British and American Literature*, Bowker, New York, 1981.
17 Stella Bowen to Ford, 23 April 1919, *The Correspondence of Ford Madox Ford and Stella Bowen*, p. 97.
18 Bowen, *Drawn from Life*, p. 119.
19 Ibid., p. 168
20 Stella Bowen to Janice Biala, 31 July 1945, Ford Madox Ford papers, Carl A. Krober Library, Cornell University.
21 Quoted in Mizenger, *The Saddest Story*, p. 346.
22 Clement Christesen, notes of interview with Keith Hancock, Clement Christesen papers, NLA MS 5019.
23 Carolyn G. Heilbrun, *Writing a Woman's Life*, The Women's Press, London, 1989, p. 48.

9   *Travel and Discovery of Self*

1 Susan Johnson, *Australian Book Review*, August 1994, p. 39.
2 Downe, *Wind on the Heath*, p. 75.
3 Christina Stead to Nellie Molyneux, Paris, 1 March 1929, *A Web of Friendship*, p. 12.
4 Christina Stead to Gwen Walker Smith, 25 May 1930, ibid., p. 26. For a fictional account of an Australian woman's quest to become European, Frank Moorhouse, *Grand Days*, Picador, London, 1993.

5 Hazel Rowley, *Christina Stead*, pp. 170–8.
6 Stead, *For Love Alone*, p. 454.
7 Gwen Hughes, 'Balkan Fever'. Gwen Hughes was a journalist who published six cookery books. She travelled extensively in Czechoslovakia and Yugoslavia between 1934 and 1938, developing a strong interest in folklore and collecting traditional costumes. I am grateful to Shonar Dewar of the Victorian State Library for this information, and for bringing my attention to the papers of Gwen Hughes.
8 Ida Haysom, diary, 1 December 1937.
9 Joseph Campbell, *The Hero With a Thousand Faces*, Pantheon, New York, 1949. For the gender specificity of Campbell, Heller, *The Feminization of the Quest–Romance*, pp. 1–3.
10 Prichard, *Child of the Hurricane*, p. 114.
11 Richardson, *Myself When Young*, p. 98.
12 Florence James to her father, 8 July 1928, Florence James papers, 5877/9.
13 Florence James to her family, 6 November 1929, ibid.
14 James, *Bachelor Betty*, p. 49.
15 Janet Mitchell, *Spoils of Opportunity*, p. 4.
16 Christine Stevenson to author, 27 November 1992.
17 Nettie Higgins to her mother, 9 March 1911, quoting from a letter from her aunt, Palmer papers, 1174/1/429.
18 Jordan, 'Nettie Palmer', p. 130.
19 Nettie Higgins to Vance Palmer, 3 February 1910, Palmer papers, 1174/1/268.
20 Nettie Higgins to Vance Palmer, early March 1910, ibid., 1174/1/288.
21 Nettie Higgins to her mother, 19 January 1911, ibid., 1174/1/387.
22 Ibid., 1174/1/389.
23 Nettie Higgins to her mother, 5 April 1911, ibid., 1174/1/462.
24 Nettie Higgins to her mother, 19 January 1911, ibid, 1174/1/387.
25 Nettie Higgins to Vance Palmer, undated but late March/early April 1911, ibid., 1174/1/453.
26 Nettie Higgins to Vance Palmer, 26 April 1911, ibid., 1174/1/485/.
27 Nettie Higgins to her mother 25 May 1911, to Vance Palmer, 22 April, 28 May 1911, ibid., 1174/1/539, 487, 539.
28 Nettie Higgins to her mother, 28 September 1911, ibid., 1174/1/637
29 Judith Keene, 'A Spanish Springtime: Aileen Palmer and the Spanish Civil War', *Labour History* 52, 1987, pp. 75–87, and 'Aileen Palmer's Coming of Age', in *Crossing Boundaries: Feminisms and the Critique of Knowledge*, Barbara Caine, E.A. Grosz and Marie de Lepervanche (eds.), Allen & Unwin, Sydney, 1988, pp. 180–91.
30 Aileen Palmer to her family, 19 July 1938, Aileen Palmer papers, 6759, series 1, box 1, folder 1. 'D.W.' refers to the Communist newspaper, the *Daily Worker*.
31 Aileen Palmer, fragment, 'One Foot in Yesterday', ibid., series 5, box 7, folder 54.
32 Aileen Palmer, fragment, ibid.
33 Aileen Palmer, fragment, 'Coming of Age', ibid., series 1, box 1, folder 38.
34 Keene, 'A Spanish Springtime', p. 87.
35 Keene, 'Aileen Palmer's Coming of Age', p. 181.
36 Aileen Palmer, fragment, 'Coming of Age'.
37 For a discussion of the novel, Keene, 'Aileen Palmer's Coming of Age', pp. 186–7.
38 Aileen Palmer, 'Coming of Age'.
39 Fitzpatrick, *Solid Bluestone Foundations*, p. 187
40 Ibid., p. 206. See also, Fitzpatrick, 'A Cloistered Life', pp. 120–33.
41 Walter Crocker, *Travelling Back: The Memoirs of Sir Walter Crocker,* Macmillan, Melbourne, 1981.
42 Fitzpatrick, *Solid Bluestone Foundations*, p. 206.
43 Shaw, 'Education of a Squatter's Daughter', p. 293.
44 Fitzpatrick, *Solid Bluestone Foundations*, p. 210.
45 Keith Hancock, *Country and Calling*, Faber & Faber, London, 1934, pp. 79–103
46 Dennis Porter, *Haunted Journeys,* pp. 11–12.
47 Mack, *Children of the Sun*, pp. 281–2.
48 This version of Gibbon's inspiration to write of the decline and fall of the Roman Empire is from Memoir E, *The Autobiographies of Edward Gibbon*, John Murray (ed.), Murray, London, 1897, p. 302.
49 Fitzpatrick, *Solid Bluestone Foundations*, p. 197.
50 'The Transit of Hazzard: Jan Garrett interviews Shirley Hazzard', *Look and Listen*, November 1984, p. 39; Giovanna Capone, 'Shirley Hazzard and the *Bay of Noon*', *Australian Literary Studies* 13, 2, 1987, pp. 172–84. On Hazzard and Italy, see also Laurie Hergenhan, 'The "I" of the Beholder: Tuscany in Contemporary Australian

Literature', in *An Antipodean Connection*, pp. 33–50. It is worth noting that on another occasion, Hazzard wrote that 'it was in Tuscany that I became a writer'. Shirley Hazzard, 'The Tuscan in Each of Us', ibid., p. 81.

51 Florence James to her family, 14 October 1927, Florence James papers, 5877/9.
52 Fitzpatrick, *Solid Bluestone Foundations*, p. 184.
53 Bennett, *Spirit in Exile*, p. 41. See also Tindall, *Countries of the Mind*, p. 180.
54 Gurr, *Writers in Exile*, p. 31.

Interlude   Charmian Clift and Gillian Bouras

1 Commonwealth of Australia, *Nationality and Citizenship Act 1948*, in United Nations Commission on the Status of Women, *Nationality of Married Women*, United Nations, New York, 1950, pp. 28–29.
2 Bouras, *A Foreign Wife*, p. 28.
3 Potts and Strauss, *For the Love of Soldiers*, p. 14.
4 Bouras, *A Foreign Wife*, p. 124.
5 Ibid., p. 190.
6 Ibid.
7 Ibid., p. 23.
8 Jack Lindsay, 'The Alienated Intellectual', *Meanjin* 92, xxii, 1963, p. 55.
9 Charmian Clift, 'News of Earls Court — Fifteen Years Ago', *The World of Charmian Clift*, George Johnston (ed.), Collins Sydney, 1983 (first edn.1970), p. 56.
10 George Johnston, *Clean Straw for Nothing*, quoted in Gary Kinnane, *George Johnston: A Biography*, Nelson, Melbourne, 1986, p. 225. On expatriates and place, Tindall, *Countries of the Mind*.
11 For the details of their overseas life, see Kinnane, *George Johnston*.
12 Charmian Clift, *Mermaid Singing* (1956), Angus & Robertson, Sydney, 1992, p. 11.
13 Charmian Clift, *Peel Me a Lotus* (1959), Collins, Sydney, 1988, p. 166.
14 Ibid., p. 90.
15 Bouras, *A Foreign Wife*, p. 127.
16 Ibid., p. 128.
17 Clift, *Peel Me a Lotus*, p. 91.
18 Bouras, *A Foreign Wife*, p. 107.
19 See here, pp. 172–3 and Ros Pesman, 'Some Australian Italies', *Westerly* 39, 4, 1994, pp. 95–104.
20 Shirley Deane, *Rocks and Olives: Portrait of an Italian Village*, John Murray, London, 1954, p. 13. See also her other travel books, *Tomorrow is Manana: An Andalusian Village*, John Murray, London, 1957; *The Road to Andorra*, John Murray, London, 1960; *The Expectant Mariner*, John Murray, London, 1963.
21 Clift, *Mermaid Singing*, p. 98.
22 Clift, *Peel Me a Lotus,* p. 127.
23 Ibid., p. 128.
24 Tindall, *Countries of the Mind*, p. 163.
25 Benstock, *Women of the Left Bank*.
26 Charmian Clift, 'On Being a Home-Grown Migrant', in *Trouble in Lotus Land,* Nadia Wheatley (ed.), Angus & Robertson, Sydney, 1990, pp. 101–2.

10   Travel, the Coronation, and Carnaby Street

1 Barbara Hanrahan, *Michael and Me and the Sun*, p. 50.
2 For Jessie Street's post-1945 travels, see Heather Radi, 'Chronology of a Life Well Spent', in *Jessie Street: Documents and Essays*, Heather Radi (ed.), pp. 1–6.
3 Dorothy and Ralph Gibson papers, 7844, series 2; Ralph Gibson.
4 See Dymphna Cusack, *Chinese Women Speak*, Angus and Robertson, Sydney, 1958. For other women in China, Helen Palmer, *Australian Teacher in China*, Sydney, Teachers' Sponsoring Committee, 1953; Myra Roper, *China: The Surprising Country*, Heinemann, London, 1966.
5 Dymphna Cusack, *Holidays Among Russians*, Heinemann, London, 1954.

6 Dymphna Cusack papers, NLA, MS 4621/9/210.
7 Dymphna Cusack, 'Italy the Romantic', *Overland* 7, 1956, p. 14.
8 Norman Freeman with Dymphna Cusack, *Dymphna Cusack*, Nelson, Melbourne, 1975, p. 101.
9 Dymphna Cusack, *Heatwave in Berlin*, Heinemann, London, 1961, p. 219.
10 Modjeska, *Exiles at Home*, p. 2.
11 Barbara Hanrahan, *Sea-green*, pp. 158, 207.
12 Patricia Rolfe, *No Love Lost*, Macmillan, London, 1965, p. 17.
13 Patricia Hopper, diary of a trip in 1951, privately held.
14 Ibid., 7 June 1951. The former royal governess Marion Crawford's *The Little Princesses* was a bestseller, as were other books on the royal family, books in a somewhat different vein from latterday counterparts.
15 Alice Nettleton, *Two Eyes and a Passport,* John Andrew, Sydney, 1956, p. 74.
16 Conway, *The Road from Coorain*, p. 108.
17 Charmian Clift, 'On England, My England', *SMH*, 21 May, 1968, *Being Alone with Oneself, Essays 1968–1969*, Nadia Wheatley (ed.), Angus & Robertson, Sydney, 1991, p. 30.
18 Downe, *Wind on the Heath*, p. 8.
19 Conway, *The Road from Coorain*, p. 208.
20 Kerr, 'Here, There and Everywhere', 16 April 1959, p. 17.
21 Jessie Traill, 'France Re-visited', Jessie Traill papers, SLV, MS 7975, box 795/4 (a)
22 Kent Hughes, *Matilda Walzes On*, Heinemann, Melbourne, 1954, pp. 88–89.
23 Downe, *Wind on the Heath*, pp. 81,90.
24 Hopper, Diary, 10 June 1951.
25 Kerr, 'Here, There and Everywhere', p. 77.
26 Hopper, diary, 10 July 1951.
27 Helen Caterer, *People, Places and Blankets Galore: Fifty Years of Memorable Encounters*, Helen Caterer, Myrtle Bank, SA, 1990, p. 30.
28 Knox, *Time Flies*, p. 20.
29 *B.P. Magazine*, December 1931, p. 15.
30 Nancy Phelan, *The Swift Foot of Time: An Australian in England 1938–45*, Quartet Books, Melbourne, 1983, pp. 5–80.
31 Elizabeth Burchill, *The Paths I've Trod*, Spectrum, Melbourne, 1981, p. 38.
32 De Groen, 'Conversation with Janet Alderson', p. 3.
33 Neville, *Fall-Girl*, Panther, London, 1967, p. 14,
34 Hanrahan, *Sea-green*, p. 111.
35 Hanrahan, *Michael and Me and the Sun*, p. 24.
36 Hopper, diary, 30 May 1951.
37 Hanrahan, *Sea-green*, pp. 120,122.
38 Rolfe, *No Love Lost*, p. 116.
39 Hanrahan, *Sea-green*, p. 113.
40 Hanrahan, *Michael and Me and the Sun*, p. 65.
41 Ibid., p. 134.
42 Rolfe, *No Love Lost*, p. 174.
43 Ibid., p. 182.
44 Jeannie Douglass, 'Women's Travel Narratives of the 1950s', in *Memory and History in Twentieth Century Australia*, Kate Darian-Smith and Paula Hamilton (eds.), MUP, 1994, Melbourne, pp. 234–6.
45 Hanrahan, *Sea-green*, p. 27.
46 Barry Humphries, 'Debbie Thwaite', in Barry Humphries, *A Nice Night's Entertainment: Sketches and Monologues 1956–1981*, Granada, Sydney, 1981, pp. 44–7.
47 Catherine Helen Spence, *Mr Hogarth's Will* (1865), Penguin, Ringwood, 1988, p. 165.
48 Kerr, 'Here, There and Everywhere'. p. 106.
49 Rolfe, *No Love Lost*, p. 135.
50 Patricia Hopper, diary, 15 June 1951.
51 Jessica Anderson, *The Impersonators*, Macmillan, Melbourne, 1980, p. 47.
52 Joan Freeman, *A Passion for Physics: The Story of a Woman Physicist*, A. Hilger, Bristol, 1991.
53 Florence Burke in *Good Talk: The Extraordinary Lives of Ten Ordinary Australian Women*, Rhonda Wilson (ed.), Ringwood, Penguin, 1985, p. 42.
54 Mary Macqueen, 'Living Line', *Half Open Door*, Patricia Grimshaw (ed.), p. 86.
55 Frances Letters, *The Surprising Asians: A Hitch-hike through Malaysia, Thailand, Laos, Cambodia and South Vietnam*, Angus and Robertson, Sydney, 1968, Preface.

56 For the travel writing of Australian women beyond Europe, Pesman, Walker, and White, Annotated Bibliography of Australian Overseas Travel Writing. For example, see Alice Combes, *Diary of a Trip to the South Sea Islands,* Thomas T. Wilton, Lithgow, 1898; Hannah Chewings, *Amongst Tropical Islands*, J.L.Bonython, Adelaide, 1900; Helen Jerome, *The Japan of Today*, NSW Bookstall, Sydney, 1904; Edith Badham, *Trip to Java,* F. Clark, Sydney, 1909; Marnie Bassett, *Letters from New Guinea, 1921*, Hawthorn Press, Melbourne, 1969; Florence Taylor, *A Pot-pourri of Eastern Asia with Comparison and Reflections*, Building Pub. Co., Sydney, 1935.

57 *A Season in India. Letters of Ruby Madden. Experiences of an Australian Girl at The Great Coronation Durbar Delhi: 1903*, Helen Rutledge (ed.), National Trust of Australia, Sydney, 1976. For another example, Ethel Kelly, *Frivolous Peeps at India*, George Robertson, Melbourne, 1911.

58 *A Season in India*, Rutledge (ed.), p. 20.

59 See, for example, Diane Langmore, *Missionary Lives. Papua 1874–1914*, University of Hawaii Press, Honolulu, 1989. For recollections by women working in the mission field, see, for example, Florence Young, *Pearls from the Pacific*, Marshall Bros, London, 1926; Helen Cato, *The House on the Hill*, Book Depot, Melbourne, 1947; Eleanor Rivett, *Memory Plays a Tune: Being Recollections of India 1907–1947*, Eleanor Rivett, Sydney, 1965; and Mackinnon, *The New Women*, for Laura Fowler in India.

60 Chilla Bulbeck, *Australian Women in Papua-New Guinea: Colonial Passages 1920–1960,* CUP, Cambridge, 1992.

61 Adam-Smith, *Australian Women at War*; Jan Bassett, *Guns and Brooches*; Jessie Simons, *While History Passed: The Story of the Australian Nurses who were Prisoners of the Japanese for three and a half years,* Heinemann, Melbourne, 1954.

Postlude

1 Jessica Anderson, *Tirra Lirra by the River*.
2 Jessie Mitchell, letter, 6 September 1934, Jessie Mitchell papers.
3 Marjory Casson, diaries, SASL, PRG28, series 1, December 1949.

Bibliography

For reasons of space, the bibliography is confined to primary material only. References to secondary sources are fully cited in the endnotes.

Unpublished Sources

Carl A.Krober Library Cornell University, Ithaca
Ford Madox Ford, papers.

Centre for the History of the Resistance, Como, Italy
Partisan records.

Historic Houses Trust of NSW
Wentworth, Sarah, papers, typescripts of letters in Mitchell Library ML A868.

Mitchell Library
Anonymous diary of an overseas trip, March–August 1939, ML MSS 5148.
Crowley, Grace, papers, ML MSS 3252.
Deamer, Dulcie, The Golden Decade, ML MSS 3173.
Dowling, Mabel, diary 3 April–7 August 1928, ML MSS 4249.
Falkiner, Una, diaries, ML MSS 423.
Fullerton, Mary, papers, ML MSS 2342.
Gentile, Doris, papers, ML MSS 2897.
Hudson, M., M. Hudson's Trip Through America, England and the Continent, January–October 1881, ML MSS 1948.
Ironside, Adelaide, papers, ML MSS 272/1.
James, Florence, papers, ML MSS 5877.
Lang, John Dunmore, papers, ML Doc. 1873.
Mackenzie, Isabel, papers, ML MSS 2996.
Moore, Eleanor, papers, ML MSS 4170.
Reibey, Mary, journal 1820–1821, ML, MSS 2132.
Sulman, Florence, letters, typescript, ML MSS A1387.

Mosman Municipal Library, NSW
Birtles, Dora, papers.

National Library of Australia
Birtles, Dora, The Cruise of the *Gullmarn*, typescript, MS 8305.
Christesen, Clem, papers, MS 5019.
Couvreur, Jessie, journal 1889-1891, Mfm G24 751.
Cusack, Dymphna, papers, MS 4621.

Garran, Sir Robert, papers, MS 2102.
Gibson, Dorothy and Ralph, papers, MS 7844.
Gilmore, Mary, papers, MS 125.
Lewis, Amy, Paths to Happiness: A Mosaic of Scenes and Portraits, type-
    script, MS 6147.
Loch, Sydney, Autobiography, typescript, MS 2948.
Palmer, Aileen, papers, MS 6759.
Palmer, Nettie and Vance, papers, MS1174.
Rischbieth, Bessie, papers, MS 2004.
Rush, Irene, My Years in Russia, typescript, MS 8316.
Street, Jessie, papers, MS 2683.

National Library of Australia Oral Histories
Crowley, Grace, Hazel de Berg, interview with Grace Crowley, 1966,
    ORAL DeB 173
Cullen, Barbara, Catherine Johnson, interview with Barbara Cullen, 10
    November 1987, NSW Bicentennial Oral History Collection, ORAL
    TRC 2301, INT 128.
Duncan, Catherine, Hazel de Berg, conversations with Catherine
    Duncan, 5 April 1971, ORAL DeB 528.
Hewitt, Hope, Mark Cranfield, interview with Hope Hewitt,
    20 January–23 April 1982, ORAL TRC History Program TRC 1114.
Hollander, Hazel, Ros Bowden, interview with Hazel Hollander, 16
    December 1987, NSW Bicentennial Oral History Collection, ORAL
    TRC 2301.
Proctor, Thea, Hazel de Berg, interview with Thea Proctor, 25 September
    1962, ORAL DeB 26.
Rich, Ruby, Hazel de Berg, conversations with Ruby Rich, ORAL DeB
    836.

State Library of South Australia
Bollen, Christobel, letters, Bagot papers, PRG 278.
Casson, Marjory Rose, diaries, PRG 28, series 1.
Duncan, Annie, Reminiscences, PRG 532.
McCracken, Mattie, Diary of a voyage on a sailing ship from Melbourne
    to India, *c.*1875, Cudmore papers, PRG 189, series 3.

State Library of Victoria
Black, Grace, diary, 1852, MS 8996, 59(a).
Cameron, M., diary kept on a passage to England in ship *Sobraon*, 1878,
    copy, MS 9517, MSB469.
Chomley, Violet, papers, MS 12478, box 3299/8.
Davies, June, journal 1969–1970, uncatalogued.
Gilruth, Margaret, papers, MS 7983.
Grant Bruce, Mary, diaries, MS 9975.
Hayball, Ada Doris, papers, MS 7067.
Haysom, Ida, diaries, MSB 128A

Hughes, Gwen, Balkan Fever, typescript, uncatalogued.
James, Winifred, papers, MS 11624.
Kerr, Edna May, Here, There, Everywhere, typescript, MS 12101, box 2590/4(b).
Le Souef, Mrs A.A.C., Journal of a Voyage to London from Melbourne, nd, copy, MS 9096, MSB 571.
Muhler-Schulte, Muriel, Biography of Hans-Joachim Muhler-Schulte 1908-1945, MS 12419, Box 294/2.
Murray Smith, Jane, letters, H15968.
Pinnock, Dorothy, diaries, MS 11536, box 1762.
Rigall, Louise, Diary of an Italian Tour 1905, MS12257, box 2896.
Traill, Jessie, papers, MS 7975, box 795.
Tripp, Margaret, letters to her mother 6 January–27 April 1873, written during a voyage on board the SS *Belar*, the *Surat* and the *Malta* and subsequently in England and France, MS 11539.

University of Sydney Archives
Mackie, Margaret, letters.
Marks, Gladys, papers.

Papers privately held
Edwards, Lilian, diary
Fitzharding, Maude and Una, letters and postcards.
Gentile, Doris, letters and photographs.
Hopper, Patricia, diary.
Mitchell, Jessie, diaries, papers.
Whiffen, Marjorie, diary.

Newspapers

Australasian
BP Magazine
British–Australasian
Bulletin
Centennial Magazine
Everylady's Journal
Home
Lone Hand
Magazine of the Women's College (University of Sydney)
Newsletter of the Women's College (University of Sydney)
New Idea
Sydney Morning Herald
Undergrowth
Women's Weekly

Newspaper cuttings
Art Gallery of NSW
Ohlfsen, Dora.
Australian Dictionary of Biography
Winifred James.
National Library of Australia
Heagney, Muriel.

Published Sources

Abramovich, Suzanne, *So This is Russia!!*, Friends of the Soviet Union, Sydney, 1930.
Adams, Glenda, *Dancing on Coral*, Viking, New York, 1987.
Adams, Nancy, *Family Fresco*, Cheshire, Melbourne, 1966.
Anderson, Jessica, *The Impersonators*, Macmillan, Melbourne, 1980.
Anderson, Jessica, *Tirra Lirra by the River*, Macmillan, Melbourne, 1978.
Anglo-Australian (Agnes Grant Hay), *After-Glow Memories*, Methuen, London, 1905.
Armstrong, Mrs Richard, 'Our Italian Friend', *Centennial Magazine* 2, March 1890.
Banfield, E.J., *The Torres Strait Route from Queensland to England by the British-Indian Steam Navigation Company's Royal Mail Steamer 'Chyebassa'*, T.Wilmett, Townsville, 1885.
Bedford, Randolph, *Explorations in Civilization*, S. Day, Sydney, 1914.
Bennett, Mrs Alfred (Emily Anne), *Vignettes of Travel*, George Murray & Co., Sydney, 1886.
Birtles, Dora, *North-West by North: A Journal of a Voyage*, Jonathan Cape, London, 1934.
Blake, Audrey, *A Proletarian Life*, Kibble Books, Malmsbury, Vic., 1984.
Bockmann, Vera, *Full Circle: An Australian in Berlin 1930-1946*, Decie Denholm (ed.), Wakefield Press, Netley, SA, 1986.
Bouras, Gillian, *A Foreign Wife*, Penguin, Ringwood, 1990.
Bowen, Stella, *Drawn from Life* (with a new introduction by Julia Loewe), Virago, London, 1984.
Boyd, Martin, *The Cardboard Crown*, Cresset Press, London, 1952.
Boyd, Martin, *Lucinda Brayford*, Cresset Press, London, 1946
Boyd, Martin, *Outbreak of Love*, John Murray, London, 1957.
Boyd, Martin, *The Picnic*, Dent, London, 1937.
Boyd, Martin, *When Blackbirds Sing*, Abelard-Schuman, London, 1962.
Brabin, Daisy, *Filaments Unweft,* Bruce & Davies, Melbourne, 1908.
Brennan, Mary, with Elaine McKenna, *Better Than Dancing: The Wandering Years of a Young Australian*, Greenhouse Publications, Melbourne, 1987.
Brookes, Mabel, *Broken Idols*, Melville & Mullen, Melbourne, 1917.

Brookes, Mabel, *Old Desires,* Australasian Authors' Agency, Melbourne, 1922.

Brookes, Mabel, *On the Knees of the Gods*, Melville & Mullen, Melbourne, 1918.

Brookes, Mabel, *Memoirs*, Melbourne, Macmillan, 1974.

Brookes, May, *Wild Flowers and Wanderings under the Northern Star and Southern Cross*, Imprimérie Française de l'Edition, Paris, 1925.

Burchill, Elizabeth, *Paths I've Trod*, Spectrum, Melbourne, 1981.

Byles, Marie, *By Cargo Boat and Mountain: The Unconventional Experiences of a Woman on a Tramp Around the World*, Seely, Service & Co., London, 1931.

Byles, Marie, *Journey into Burmese Silence*, Allen & Unwin, London, 1963.

Cambridge, Ada, *In Two Years' Time*, Bentley, London, 1879.

Cambridge, Ada, *The Retrospect*, Stanley Paul, London, 1913.

Carnegie, Ada, *Yesteryear; Memoirs of My Trip Abroad Nearly Sixty Years Ago*, Hawthorn Press, Melbourne, 1966.

Casey, Maie, *Tides and Eddies*, Michael Joseph, London, 1966.

Caterer, Helen, *People, Places and Blankets Galore: Fifty Years of Memorable Encounters*, Helen Caterer, Myrtle Bank, SA, 1990.

Clift, Charmian, *Being Alone with Oneself: Essays 1968–1969*, Nadia Wheatley (ed.), Angus & Robertson, Sydney, 1991.

Clift, Charmian, *Honour's Mimic,* Hutchinson, London, 1964.

Clift, Charmian, *Mermaid Singing* (1956), Angus & Robertson, Sydney, 1992.

Clift, Charmian, *Peel Me a Lotus* (1959), Collins, Sydney, 1988.

Clift, Charmian, *The Sponge Divers*, Collins, London, 1955.

Clift, Charmian, *Trouble in Lotus Land: Essays 1964–1967,* Nadia Wheatley (ed.), Angus & Robertson, Sydney, 1990.

Clift, Charmian, *The World of Charmian Clift*, George Johnston (ed.), Collins, Sydney, 1983.

Coates, Dora Meeson, *George Coates: His Art and His Life,* J.M. Dent and Sons, London, 1937.

Cole, Margaret, *Growing up into Revolution*, Longmans Green, London, 1949.

Colebrook, Joan, *A House of Tall Trees*, Chatto & Windus, London, 1987.

'Colonial', 'Titled Colonials v. Titled Americans', *Contemporary Review*, June 1905.

Conrad, Peter, *Where I Fell to Earth: A Life in Four Places*, Chatto & Windus, London, 1990.

Conway, Jill Ker, *The Road from Coorain*, Alfred Knopf, New York, 1987.

Conway, Jill Ker, *True North: A Memoir*, Alfred Knopf, New York, 1994.

Cooper, Ethel, *Behind the Lines. One Woman's War 1914–18: The Letters of Caroline Ethel Cooper*, Decie Denholm (ed.), Collins, Sydney, 1982.

Costin, Evelyn, *Shadows on the Grass: An Autobiography from 1901 to 1978 with its Adjacent History*, Edgewaters, Apollo Bay, Vic., 1981.

Couvreur, Jessie ('Tasma'), *A Knight of the White Feather: Incidents and Scenes in Melbourne Life*, Heinemann, London, 1895.

Couvreur, Jessie ('Tasma'), *Not Counting the Cost*, Heinemann, London, 1895.

Couvreur, Jessie ('Tasma'), *The Penance of Portia James*, Heinemann, London, 1891.

Cowen, Rose Scott, *Crossing Dry Creeks 1879–1919*, The Wentworth Press, Sydney, 1961.

Crocker, Walter, *Travelling Back: The Memoirs of Sir Walter Crocker*, Macmillan, Melbourne, 1981.

Cusack, Dymphna, *Chinese Women Speak*, Angus & Robertson, Sydney, 1958.

Cusack, Dymphna, *Heatwave in Berlin*, Heinemann, London, 1961.

Cusack, Dymphna, *Holiday Among Russians*, Heinemann, London, 1954.

Cusack, Dymphna, *Illyria Reborn*, Heinemann, London, 1966.

Cusack, Dymphna, 'Italy, the Romantic', *Overland* 7, 1956, pp.13–15.

Dale, Alice Mary, *With Feet of Clay*, George Robertson, Melbourne, 1895.

Davies, Clare, *This is My Life*, C. Davies, Sydney, 1965.

Deane, Shirley, *The Expectant Mariner*, John Murray, London, 1963.

Deane, Shirley, *The Road to Andorra*, John Murray, London, 1960.

Deane, Shirley, *Rocks and Olives: Portrait of an Italian Village*, John Murray, London, 1954.

Deane, Shirley, *Tomorrow is Manāna: An Andalusian Village*, John Murray, London, 1957.

De Garis, Mary, *Clinical Notes and Deductions of a Peripatetic: Being Fads and Fancies of a General Practitioner*, Ballière, Tindall Cox, London, 1926.

Dixon, Elizabeth, *Journal of a Voyage from Sydney to London in the Barque 'Standerings'* (1842), Blackie & Son, London, 1946.

Downe, Phyllis, *Wind on the Heath*, Georgian House, Melbourne, 1946.

Edgeworth David, Mary, *Passages of Time: An Australian Woman 1890–1974*, UQP, St Lucia, 1975.

(Finn, Florence), *Pigmies Among Potentates or Two Australian Girls in Olden Lands*, Renwick, Pride, Nuttall, Melbourne, 1912.

Fitzpatrick, Kathleen, *Solid Bluestone Foundations and Other Memories of a Melbourne Girlhood* (1983), Penguin, Ringwood, 1986.

Fitzpatrick, Kathleen, 'A Cloistered Life', in *The Door Half Open: Sixteen Modern Australian Women Look at Professional Life and Achievement*, Patricia Grimshaw (ed.), Hale & Iremonger, Sydney, 1982, pp. 120–133.

Ford, Ford Madox, *When the Wicked Men*, Horace Liveright, New York, 1931.

Ford, Ford Madox, *The Correspondence of Ford Madox Ford and Stella Bowen*, Sondra J. Stang and Karen Cochran (eds.), Indiana University Press, Bloomington, 1993.

Franklin, Miles, *My Career Goes Bung*, Georgian House, Melbourne, 1946.

Franklin Miles, *My Congenials: Miles Franklin and Friends in Letters*, 2 vols, Jill Roe (ed.), Angus & Robertson, Sydney, 1993.

Freeman, Joan, *A Passion for Physics: The Story of a Woman Physicist*, A. Hilger, Bristol, 1991.

Freeman, Hilda M., *An Australian Girl in Germany: Through Peace to War (January–October 1914)*, Speciality Press, Melbourne, 1916.

Freeman, Hilda M., *Murrumbidgee Memories and Riverina Reminiscences: A Collection of Old Bush History*, B. Niccol, Emu Plains, 1985.

Gaunt, Mary, *A Broken Journey*, T. Werner Laurie, London, 1919.

Gaunt, Mary, *Alone in West Africa*, T. Werner Laurie, London, 1912.

Gaunt, Mary, *A Woman in China*, London, T. Werner Laurie, 1914

Gaunt, Mary, *Kirkham's Find*, Methuen, London, 1894.

Gaunt, Mary, *Reflection – in Jamaica*, Ernest Benn, London, 1932.

Gifford, Margaret, *I Can Hear Horses*, Methuen-Haynes, Sydney, 1982.

Gilmore, Mary, *Letters of Mary Gilmore*, W.H. Wilde and T. Inglis Moore (eds.), MUP, Melbourne, 1980.

Gilruth, Margaret, *Maiden Voyage: The Unusual Experiences of a Girl on Board a Tramp Ship*, Jonathan Cape, London, 1934.

Groen, Geoffrey de (ed.), *Some Other Dream: The Artists, the Art World and the Expatriate*, Hale & Iremonger, Sydney, 1984.

Hall, Elsie, *The Good Die Young: The Autobiography of Elsie Hall*, Constantia Publishers, Capetown, 1969.

Hancock, Keith, *County and Calling,* Faber and Faber, London, 1934.

Hanrahan, Barbara, *Sea-green* (1974), Fontana, Melbourne, 1980.

Hanrahan, Barbara, *Michael and Me and the Sun*, UQP, St Lucia, 1992.

(Harvie, Maude Jessie), *Madge's Trip to Europe and Back*, George Robertson, Melbourne, 1911.

Hayball, Doris, *Sidelights on the Soviet: A Plain, Unvarnished Tale of a Trip to Russia and its Great Theatre Festival*, G. Batchelor, Melbourne, 1939.

Hazzard, Shirley, *The Transit of Venus* (1980), Penguin, Ringwood, 1981.

Hazzard, Shirley, 'The Tuscan in Each of Us', in *An Antipodean Connection: Australian Writers, Artists and Travellers in Tuscany*, Gaetano Prampolini and M.C. Hubert (eds.), Geneva, Slatkine, 1993.

Hazzard, Shirley, 'The Transit of Hazzard. Jan Garrett interviews Shirley Hazzard', *Look and Listen*, November 1984.

Henry, Alice, *Memoirs of Alice Henry,* Nettie Palmer (ed.), Melbourne, 1944.

Hergenhan, Laurie (ed.), *Changing Places: Australian Writers in Europe 1960s–1990s*, UQP, St Lucia, 1994.

Higham, Charles and Wilding, Michael (eds), *Australians Abroad: An Anthology*, Cheshire, Melbourne, 1967.

Holman, Ada, *My Wander Year: Some Jottings in a Year's Travel*, William Brooks & Co., Sydney, 1914.

Hosmer, Harriet, *Letters and Memoirs of Harriet Hosmer*, Cornelia Carr (ed.), John Lane, London, 1913.

Howorth, Allison, *Coo-ee England: A Travel Diary*, Melbourne, George Batchelor, 1937.

Humphries, Barry, *A Nice Night's Entertainment: Sketches and Monologues 1956–1981*, Granada, Sydney, 1981.

'Iota', (Caffyn, Kathleen) *A Comedy of Spasms*, Hutchinson, London, 1895.

James, Winifred, *A Man for Empire*, Chapman & Hall, London, 1930.

James, Winifred, *A Woman in the Wilderness*, Chapman & Hall, London, 1915.

James, Winifred, *Bachelor Betty*, Constable, London, 1907.

James, Winifred, *Gangways and Corridors*, Allan, London, 1936.

James, Winifred, *Letters of a Spinster*, G. Bell & Sons, London, 1911.

James, Winifred, *Letters to My Son,* Hodder & Stoughton, London, 1910.

James, Winifred, *London is My Lute*, Chapman & Hall, London, 1930.

James, Winifred, *The Mulberry Tree*, G.Bell & Sons, London, 1913.

James, Winifred, *Out of the Shadows*, (no imprint), London, 1924.

James, Winifred, *Patricia Baring,* Constable, London, 1908.

Jenner, Dorothy Gordon, *Darlings, I've had a Ball*, Ure Smith, Sydney, 1975.

Karr, Ethel, *The Australian Guest,* Remington, London, 1886.

Kelly, Ethel, *Twelve Milestones*, Brentano's, London, 1929.

(Kent, Eliza), *Abstract of the Journal of a Voyage from New South Wales to England,* Athenaeum, London, 1800

Kent Hughes, Mary, *Matilda Waltzes with the Tommies*, OUP, Melbourne, 1943.

Kent Hughes, Mary, *Matilda Waltzes On*, Heinemannn, Melbourne, 1954.

Kerr, Anne, *Lanterns over Pinchgut,* Macmillan, Melbourne, 1988.

King, Olive, *One Woman at War: Letters of Olive King 1915–1920*, Hazel King (ed.), MUP, Melbourne, 1986,

Kirkcaldie, Sister R.A., *In Grey and Scarlet*, A. McCubbin, Melbourne, 1922.

Knox, Dorothy, *Time Flies: The Memoirs of Dorothy Knox*, Rigby, Adelaide, 1971.

Krippner, Monica, *Beyond Athens: Journeys Through Greece,* Geoffrey Bles, London, 1957.

'Laker, Jane' (Alice Muskett), *Among the Reeds*, Cassell, London, 1933.

Lawrence, Marjorie, *Interrupted Melody: An Autobiography*, Invincible Press, Sydney, 1949.

Lilley, Ena, *A Possum Abroad*, R.S. Hews & Co., Brisbane, 1901.

Little, Cicely, *The Lass with the Delicate Air*, Angus & Robertson, Sydney, 1948.

Lloyd-Taylor, Nancy, *By Still Harder Fate*, George Robertson, Melbourne, 1898.

Loch, Joice Nankivell, *A Fringe of Blue: An Autobiography*, Murray, London, 1968.

Loch, Joice Nankivell and Loch, Sydney, *Ireland in Travail: The Personal Experience of Two Independent Visitors in 1920-21*, Murray, London, 1922.

Loch, Joice Nankivell and Loch, Sydney, *The River of a Hundred Ways: Life in the War-Devastated Areas of Eastern Poland*, George Allen & Unwin, London, 1924,

Lockett, Jeannie, *Judith Grant*, Hutchinson, London, 1892.

Lucas, Robyn and Foster, Clare (eds), *Wilder Shores: Women's Travel Stories of Australia and Beyond,* UQP, St Lucia, 1992.

'M.D.B.', 'A Day at Colombo', *Australian Nurses' Journal*, 15 March 1909.

Macarthur, Emmeline, *My Dear Miss Macarthur: The Recollections of Emmeline Maria Macarthur*, ed. Jane de Falbe, Kenthurst, NSW, Kangaroo Press, 1988.

McCure, John Bunyan, *Life in England and Australia: Reminiscences of Travels and Voyages over One Hundred Thousand Miles or Forty Years in the Wilderness*, London, Robert Banks, 1876.

Mack, Louise, *A Woman's Experience in the Great War*, Fisher Unwin, London, 1915.

Mack, Louise, *An Australian Girl in London*, Fisher Unwin, London, 1902.

Mack, Louise, *Children of the Sun,* Melrose, London, 1904.

Mack, Louise, *Girls Together*, Angus & Robertson, Sydney, 1898.

Mackellar, Dorothea, *I Love A Sunburnt Country: The Diaries of Dorothea Mackellar*, Jyoti Brunsdon (ed.), Angus & Robertson, Sydney, 1990.

(McNeil, Eugenie), *A Bunyip Close Behind Me and Ladies Didn't: The Recollections of Eugénie Delarue McNeil,* retold by her daughter, Eugenie Crawford, Penguin, Ringwood, 1989.

Macqueen, Mary, 'Living Line', in *The Door Half Open: Sixteen Modern Australian Women Look at Professional Life and Achievement*, Patricia Grimshaw (ed.), Hale & Iremonger, Sydney, 1982, pp. 78–91.

Maguire, Frances, *Bright Morning: The Story of an Australian Family Before 1914*, Rigby, Adelaide, 1975.

Manners-Sutton, D., *Black God*, Longmans Green, London, 1934.

Manners-Sutton, D., *Last Secret*, Longmans Green, London, 1939.

Marlowe, Mary, *Kangaroos in Kingsland: Being the Adventures of Four Australian Girls in England*, Simpkin Marshall, London, 1918.

Marlowe, Mary, *That Fragile Hour: An Autobiography*, Lionel Hudson (ed.), Angus & Robertson, Sydney, 1990.

Martin, Catherine, *An Australian Girl*, Betley, London, 1890.

Martin, Catherine, *The Old Roof-Tree: Letters of Ishbel to her Half-Brother Mark Latimer*, Longmans Green, London, 1906.

Martin, Mrs Patchett (ed.), *Coo-ee: Tales of Australian Life by Australian Ladies*, R.E.King, London, 1891.

Matters, Mrs Leonard W., *Australasians Who Count in London and Who Counts in Western Australia*, Truscott, London, 1913.

Matters, Muriel, 'My Impressions as an Agitator for Social Reform', in Mrs Leonard W. Matters, *Australasians Who Count in London and Who Counts in Western Australia*, Truscott, London, 1913, pp.161-164.

Melba, Nellie, *Melodies and Memories,* Nelson, Melbourne, 1980.

Millear, Millicent, *The Journal of a Wandering Australian*, Melville & Mullen, London, 1902.

Miller, Connie, *Memory Be Green*, Fremantle Arts Centre Press, Fremantle, 1980.

Mitchell, Eliza, *Three Quarters of a Century*, Methuen, London, 1940.

Mitchell, Janet, *Spoils of Opportunity,* Methuen, London, 1938.

Mitchell, Janet, 'Why I am a Catholic', in *This City of Peace: Being the Conversion Stories of 23 Converts to the Catholic Church*, Marjorie Hardy (ed.), Melbourne, 1949, pp.102–3.

Moncrieff, Gladys, *My Life of Song*, Rigby, Adelaide, 1971.

Moore, J.H. (ed.), *Australians in America, 1876-1976,* UQP, St Lucia, 1977.

Moore, Eleanor, *The Quest for Peace as I Have Known it in Australia*, Wilke, Melbourne, 1949.

Moorhouse, Frank, *Grand Days*, Picador, London, 1993.

Morris, Mary (ed.), *Maiden Voyages: Writings of Women Travellers*, New York, Vintage, 1993.

Moyal, Ann, *Breakfast with Beaverbrook: Memoirs of an Independent Woman*, Hale & Iremonger, Sydney, 1995.

Murdoch, Nina, *Seventh Heaven*, Angus & Robertson, Sydney, 1930.

Murdoch, Nina, *She Travelled Alone in Spain*, Harrap, London, 1935.

Nettleton, Alice, *Two Eyes and a Passport*, John Andrew, Sydney, 1956.

Nève, Edward de, *Barred*, trans. Jean Rhys, Desmond Harmsworth, London, 1932.

Neville, Jill, *Fall-Girl*, Weidenfeld & Nicolson, London, 1966.

Nolan, Cynthia, *A Bride for St Thomas*, Constable, London, 1970.

O'Donnell, The Reverend D. (Wesleyan Minister), *Vignettes from a Tourist's Notebook*, Carey & Page, Adelaide, 1886.

(Ogilvie, Edward), *Diary of Travels in Three Quarters of the Globe by an Australian Settler,* 2 vols, Saunders & Otley, London, 1856.

Osmond, Sophie, *An Australian Wooing: A Story of Trade, a Gold Mine and a Ghost*, Garden City Press, Letchworth, 1879.

Parker, Margaret, *Ida Cameron,* Oliphant, Anderson & Ferrier, London, 1893.

Pearce, Angelina, *A Memento of Our Trip to Europe,* Adelaide, nd.

Phelan, Nancy, *The Swift Foot of Time: An Australian in England 1939–45*, Melbourne, Quartet Books, 1983.

Praed, Rosa, *A Summer Wreath*, John Long, London, 1909.

Praed, Rosa, *An Australian Heroine*, Chapman & Hall, London, 1880.

Praed, Rosa, *Christina Chard. A Novel*, Chatto & Windus, London, 1894.

Praed, Rosa, *The Ghost,* Everett, London, 1903.

Praed, Rosa, *Mrs Tregaskiss. A Novel of Anglo-Australian Life*, Chatto &
    Windus, London, 1896.
Preston, Margaret, 'From Eggs to Electrolux', *Art in Australia*, 1927.
Prichard, Katharine Susannah, *Child of the Hurricane: An Autobiography*,
    Angus & Robertson, Sydney, 1963.
Prichard, Katharine Susannah, *The Real Russia*, Modern Publishers,
    Sydney, 1934.
Rhys, Jean, *Quartet*, Harper & Row, New York, 1957.
Richardson, Henry Handel, *Myself When Young (An Unfinished
    Autobiography)*, Heinemann, London, 1948.
Rischbieth, Bessie, *March of Australian Women: A Record of Fifty Years'
    Struggle for Equal Citizenship*, Paterson Brokensha, Perth, 1964.
Robinson, Catherine, *The Green Paradise: The Story of a Woman's Journey
    in the Amazon and the Argentine,* Arthur Barron, London, 1936.
Roland, Betty, *Caviar for Breakfast*, Collins, Sydney, 1989.
Rolfe, Patricia, *No Love Lost,* Macmillan, London, 1965.
Rosman, Alice Grant, *Miss Bryde of England*, Andrew Melrose, London,
    1915.
Rosman, Alice Grant, *The Sixth Journey*, Mills & Boon, London, 1931.
Sandes, Flora, *Autobiography of a Woman Soldier: A Brief Record of
    Adventure with the Serbian Army*, Witherby, London, 1927.
Shaw, Mary Turner, 'Education of a Squatter's Daughter', in *The Door Half
    Open: Sixteen Modern Australian Women Look at Professional Life and
    Achievement*, Patricia Grimshaw (ed.), Hale & Iremonger, Sydney,
    1982, pp.278-303.
Shelley, Bertha, *The Evolution of Eve*, Methuen, London, 1913.
Skinner, M.L., *The Fifth Sparrow: An Autobiography,* SUP, Sydney, 1952.
(Spence, Catherine Helen), 'An Australian's Impressions of England',
    Cornhill Magazine XIII, 1866, pp.110–20.
Spence, Catherine Helen, *An Autobiography*, reprinted from the *Register*,
    Adelaide, 1910.
Spence, Catherine Helen, *Mr Hogarth's Will* (1865), Penguin, Ringwood,
    1988.
Sprengnether, Madelon and Truesdale, C.W. (eds), *The House on Via
    Gombito: Writing by North American Women Abroad*, New Rivers Press,
    Minneapolis, 1991.
Sprent, Mabel, *Love's Apprenticeship*, London, Methuen, 1913.
Stawell, Mary, *My Recollections,* R. Clay & Sons, London, 1911.
Stead, Christina, *A Web of Friendship: Selected Letters (1928–1973)
    Christina Stead*, R.G. Geering (ed.), Angus & Robertson, Sydney,
    1992.
Stead, Christina, *For Love Alone* (1945), Angus & Robertson, Sydney,
    1990.
Stegar, Winifred, *Always Bells*, Angus & Robertson, Sydney, 1969.
Stewart, Nellie, *My Life's Story*, John Sands, Sydney, 1923.
Stirling, Amie Livingstone, *Memories of an Australian Childhood 1880-
    1900*, Schwarz Publishing, Melbourne, 1980.

Street, Jessie, *Truth or Repose*, Australian Book Society, Sydney, 1966.

Thomas, Margaret, *A Painter's Pastime*, Greening, London, 1908

Thomas, Margaret, *A Scamper Through Spain and Tangier*, Hutchinson, London, 1892.

Thomas, Margaret, *Hero of the Workshop and a Somerset Worthy: Charles Summers, Sculptor,* Hamilton, Adams, London, 1879.

Thomas, Margaret, *Denmark: Past and Present*, Anthony Treherne & Co, London, 1902.

Thomas, Margaret, 'Paris Art Schools and Australian Students', *Literary Opinion*, August 1891.

Thomas, Margaret, *Two Years in Palestine and Syria*, John C. Nimmo, London, 1900.

Thompson, Annie, *The Narrow Margin: A Novel*, Sisley's, London, 1907.

Thompson, Patricia, *Accidental Chords*, Penguin, Ringwood, 1988.

Toy, Barbara, *Columbus Was Right! Rover Around the World*, John Murray, London, 1958.

Travers, P.L., *Moscow Excursion*, Reynal & Hitchcock, New York, 1934.

Turner, Ethel, *Ports and Happy Havens*, Hodder & Stoughton, London, 1912.

Wake, Nancy, *The Autobiography of the Woman the Gestapo Called the White Mouse*, Sun Books, Melbourne, 1986.

Weigall, A.S.H., *My Little World: Reminiscences*, Angus & Robertson, Sydney, 1934.

White, Patrick, *The Aunt's Story*, Eyre & Spottiswoode, London, 1958.

'Anna Wickham', *The Writings of Anna Wickham*, R.D. Smith (ed.), Virago, London, 1984.

Wilson, Anne, *Alice Lauder: A Sketch*, Osgood, London, 1893.

Wilson, Anne, *Two Summers*, Harper, London, 1900.

Woman's Christian Temperance Union of Australasia, *Minutes of the Second Triennial Convention*, Brisbane, 1894.

Woman's Christian Temperance Movement of Australasia, *Minutes of Third Triennial Convention*, Brisbane, 1897.

Wood, Essie, *Yachting Days and Yachting Ways*, Walter Scott, London, 1892.

Index